D0126359

THE BOOK CLUB
COOKBOOK

*Recipes and Food for Thought
from Your Book Club's
Favorite Books and Authors*

Judy Gelman *and*
Vicki Levy Krupp

The recipes in this book are to be followed exactly as written. The publisher and authors are not responsible for specific health or allergy needs that may require medical supervision. The publisher and authors are not responsible for any adverse reactions to the recipes in this book.

Most Tarcher/Penguin books are available at special quantity discounts for bulk purchase for sales promotions, premiums, fund-raising, and educational needs. Special books or book excerpts also can be created to fit specific needs. For details, write Penguin Group (USA) Inc. Special Markets, 375 Hudson Street, New York, NY 10014.

Jeremy P. Tarcher/Penguin
a member of
Penguin Group (USA) Inc.
375 Hudson Street
New York, NY 10014
www.penguin.com

Copyright © 2004 by Judy Gelman and Vicki Levy Krupp
All rights reserved. This book, or parts thereof, may not
be reproduced in any form without permission.
Published simultaneously in Canada

Library of Congress Cataloging-in-Publication Data

Gelman, Judy.
The book club cookbook : recipes and food from your book club's favorite
books and authors / Judy Gelman and Vicki Levy Krupp.
p. cm.
Includes index.
ISBN 1-58542-322-X
1. Cookery.   2. Cookery in literature.   3. Food in literature.
I. Krupp, Vicki Levy, date.   II. Title.
TX714.G446   2004   2004045978
641.5—dc22

Printed in the United States of America
3   5   7   9   10   8   6   4   2

This book is printed on acid-free paper. ∞

BOOK DESIGN BY AMANDA DEWEY

For my mother, Doris Gelman,
who inspired my love of literature.

....

And in memory of my father, George Gelman,
who savored good food and good books.

....

In memory of my mother, Barbara Montag Levy,
whose kitchen was always brimming with love.

....

Some books are to be tasted, others to be swallowed, and some few to be chewed and digested. . . .

—FRANCIS BACON

Contents

Introduction

This book was conceived in a local bagel shop. We are both passionate, voracious readers, and we both love preparing and tasting exotic foods. Our shelves overflow with novels, memoirs, biographies, and, of course, cookbooks. And we both belong to book clubs—several of them. To us, pairing books and food was a natural marriage, and we wanted to create a book that united our passions, for ourselves and to share with others. And so, we began by hauling huge stacks of books to our favorite lunch spot (much to the bemusement of the customers and staff). It was here that *The Book Club Cookbook* was born.

We knew we wanted to match books with foods highlighted in literature, but which books would we feature? Where would we get recipes? Should we include appetizers? Entrées? Dinners? To help us answer some of these questions, we started contacting book clubs around the country, asking about favorite books and types of food served at meetings. We quickly found ourselves enrolled in a crash course on the dazzling array of book clubs that meet in living rooms, bookstores, churches, temples, office buildings, classrooms, and restaurants from Maine to Hawaii. There's no doubt about it: Book clubs are a phenomenon sweeping across America.

We found book clubs for men, for women, for environmentalists, for former Peace Corps volunteers, and even for former Enron employees. We spoke with members of African-American book clubs, clubs that read the works of a single author, and clubs that stick to the classics. We found book clubs for couples, parents and children, and publishing executives, clubs that specialize in mysteries, classics, prize-winning books, or books with an American western woman protagonist. Some of the people we spoke with are in new book clubs; others have been meeting for decades. Some come together as a group of old friends, but often people are meeting and making new friends through book groups.

Again and again in our conversations we heard about the powerful bonds among book club members. Besides offering an outlet for talking about ideas, book clubs become sources of strength and support in the face of illness or other personal tragedy. They become a place to celebrate a new baby, a marriage, a promotion, or a graduation. And for many, they simply represent a refuge from the demands of work and home, a place to catch one's breath, a sanctuary from the everyday. Most of all, a word we heard repeatedly was "fun"; many people find their book club experience to be one of the most enjoyable aspects of their lives. And many book clubs, we found, had already discovered the joys of using food to enhance and enliven their meetings.

The book clubs we contacted—and their ideas—became the heart and soul of our book. From hundreds of surveys and interviews with a diverse group of book club members across the country, we identified one hundred titles that stimulated intense discussion, provoked debate, or repeatedly stood out as favorites. The books featured in *The Book Club Cookbook* include contemporary novels, classics, memoirs, and nonfiction, and reflect the recommendations of the ethnically and geographically diverse book clubs we polled. We did not choose books for their obvious gastronomic references. While this might have simplified the process of choosing recipes, we felt strongly that the best starting point for a good book club discussion—even where food is involved—is a provocative, highly recommended book.

The inspiration for our recipes came first and foremost from the pages of those books. Oftentimes a particular dish plays a pivotal role in the narrative or appears in a crucial scene of the book. In Bernice McFadden's *Sugar*, a sweet potato pie brings together two unlikely friends. A group of hostages—and their captors—peel and slice eggplant in Ann Patchett's *Bel Canto*. The protagonist of Jonathan Lethem's *Motherless Brooklyn* obsesses over sandwiches, describing them in detail throughout the novel.

At other times food works more subtly, to set a novel in its time and place or to convey details of the characters' environment, class differences, or the social norms of the period. In *Reading Lolita in Tehran*, Azar Nafisi nurtures her students with books—and with ever-present cream puffs. The ambrosia in Harper Lee's *To Kill a Mockingbird* suggests the American South of the 1930s. In Willa Cather's *My Ántonia*, spiced plum *kolaches* evoke the warmth of a Bohemian farm kitchen. In Amy Tan's *The Bonesetter's Daughter*, a fictional character visits a real San Francisco restaurant, so we visited, too—and gathered some recipes. Many of the recipes we include give form and flavor to the characters, the culture, and the scenes in the books we have chosen.

Our book clubs, too, were bursting with food ideas. From coast to coast we discovered book clubs pairing food and literature with creativity and spirit. In Miami, members of the Sistah Girl Reading Club bring specially prepared dishes to every meeting, dishes that reflect that month's reading selection. In New Prague, Minnesota, the Book Bags, seven creative women, use food, as well as costumes, props, and activities, to bring their chosen books to life. In Los Angeles, Pages and Plates, a book club of Asian professionals, dines each month at a restaurant that reflects the ethnic motif of the books they read. And each month in Park Forest, Illinois, the Cultures Club tastes a new dessert chosen on the basis of the culture and setting of their reading selection. These groups—and many others—fed us an unending supply of recipes and food ideas.

To our delight, we found that many of the authors of the books we selected were enthusiastic about our idea. They, too, generously contributed family recipes and food ideas. In short statements or essays, they give voice to the meaning of food in their work, their culture, or in their lives growing up, explain why they included food in a particular scene of their book, or reveal what they were thinking while writing a particular scene. Their contributions enrich our understanding of these books and the importance of food to their creation.

Thus, the book you hold in your hands is really the result of a unique collaboration of readers and writers, eaters and cooks. The key ingredients came from many places. We simply put them together in what we hope will be an inspiration to lovers of books and lovers of good food.

How to Use This Book

Whether you're looking to start a book club, choose your book club's next reading selection, find a recipe to pair with a book, or gather fresh food ideas, *The Book Club Cookbook* can help. Though *The Book Club Cookbook* was written with book clubs in mind, you don't need to be part of a book club to find inspiration here.

For each of the one hundred reading selections we include a brief synopsis of the book, a discussion of foods that play a role in the book, one or two recipes based on those foods, and a profile of a book club that recommends the book.

Our one hundred book club profiles are filled with myriad ideas for starting a book club, running meetings, organizing extracurricular activities (such as anniversary celebrations and holiday events), and generally creating a book club with camaraderie and character. Any book club member, new or experienced, will get enjoyment and inspiration from the wisdom of our vastly diverse collection of clubs.

Choosing your book club's next selection is infinitely easier with *The Book Club Cookbook*. Our list of titles includes popular bestsellers as well as gems that even the most voracious reader may not have discovered. We provide concise book summaries and, more important, an endorsement from a book club that has read and discussed the book. After all, the best way to choose a book is to talk to someone who has already read it!

In the "More Food for Thought" sections, you will find a variety of ideas from book clubs across the country for pairing foods with the selected titles. Their ideas range from a single dish to an entire meal, from takeout food to dinner at a restaurant to a catered menu. Take these ideas alone or use them to stimulate your book club's culinary creativity.

Even if your book club chews on nothing but ideas, don't despair. In our book club profiles, we feature everything from book groups among whom cheese and crackers is the norm to groups who enjoy an elaborate dinner spread. For these groups, and everything in between, *The Book Club Cookbook* offers food for thought. Even if you never prepare our recipes, our discussions of food, contributions from authors, and book club profiles will help keep your group interested and engaged.

Our culinary-literary odyssey took us, by telephone, coast to coast and around the world. Through a variety of book clubs, we discovered—and devoured—new books. We thought about, created, and sampled good food. Just as it has for us, we hope *The Book Club Cookbook* inspires you to reach new literary and culinary heights.

Bon appétit, and good reading.

The Age of Innocence

Edith Wharton

....

1920

(available in paperback from Penguin, 1996)

Edith Wharton became the first woman to win a Pulitzer Prize when, in 1921, she received the award for *The Age of Innocence*, her novel of New York's inbred high society of the 1870s, its hierarchy, and the rules that govern it.

Newland Archer, a young lawyer, plans his marriage to "docile" May Welland. It is to be the union of two important families of the New York elite.

Newland's life is forever changed when May's cousin, Countess Ellen Olenska, arrives from Europe. Recently separated from her husband under mysterious circumstances, the Countess defies the conventions of the day by seeking a divorce—a scandal in a society "that dreads scandal more than disease."

As Newland advises Ellen on her legal request for a divorce, he falls in love with her. Passionate, intelligent, artistic, and independent, Ellen represents a radical departure from the sterile, conventional culture surrounding Newland, and he is awakened to the oppressive pretensions and cruelty of his world. Although he marries May, Ellen becomes his mistress and his "sanctuary." She is the antithesis of the conventional May, who has been molded by the rule-bound society. As their mutual affection becomes obvious, Newland must choose between his empty marriage to May and a life of passion with Ellen. But it is the society around him that will ultimately determine his fate.

ROMAN PUNCH

Wharton's portrayal of New York society in *The Age of Innocence* is rich with descriptions of food, decorations, lavish dinners, and etiquette.

Roman punch is served at two dinners in *The Age of Innocence*: one to welcome Countess Olenska, the other in honor of her departure. A frozen slush of lemon juice, sugar, rum, and often champagne, Roman punch was popular at elegant New York parties in the nineteenth century.

Typically served after the heavy roasts, the Roman punch "prepared the palate for the canvasback ducks or other game," writes Mary Elizabeth Sherwood in *Manners and Social Usages* (Harper and Brothers, 1887). When Countess Olenska arrives in New York, her grandmother, Mrs. Manson Mingott, invites their "little inner group of people" to "a formal dinner (that is, three extra footmen, two dishes for each course, and a Roman punch in the middle)." The invited guests demonstrate their low opinion of the Countess by refusing Mrs. Mingott's invitation to the elegant affair.

And when May and Newland Archer give their first big dinner party in honor of the Countess's departure for Europe, Roman punch plays a signficant role. Writes Wharton:

But a big dinner, with a hired chef and two borrowed footmen, with Roman punch, roses from Henderson's, and menus on gilt-edged cards, was a different affair, and not to be lightly undertaken. As Mrs. Archer remarked, the Roman punch made all the difference; not in itself but by its manifold implications—since it signified either canvas-backs or terrapin, two soups, a hot and a cold sweet, full décolletage with short sleeves, and guests of a proportionate importance.

NOTE: You can use store-bought lemonade to make the Roman punch, but we recommend our homemade version. Because of its alcohol content, the punch will not freeze solid, but will remain slightly slushy.

6 cups lemonade (see below)	*1 cup rum*
Juice of 2 oranges (about ½ cup)	*1 cup chilled champagne*

In a pitcher, stir together the lemonade, orange juice, and rum. Stir in the champagne. Place in freezer until partially frozen. Stir until smooth, then allow to freeze throughout, for at least eight hours or overnight. Stir well again and serve in sherbet glasses or punch cups.

Yield: 6 to 8 servings

LEMONADE

6 cups water

1 cup sugar

*1 cup plus 2 tablespoons freshly squeezed
lemon juice (about 7 lemons)*

Combine 1 cup of water with the sugar in a small saucepan. Bring to a boil, stirring frequently. Reduce heat immediately and simmer 5 minutes, again stirring frequently. Remove from heat and allow to cool.

In a pitcher, stir together the lemon juice and sugar syrup. Add the remaining water. Refrigerate.

BOOK CLUB PROFILE

"Talk about" is a Cajun idiom—and the name of Nancy Colby's Lafayette, Louisiana, book club. "We Cajuns often describe something we like by using the phrase 'talk about good,' so our club is named 'Talk About' a good book," says Colby.

Colby, a former high school English teacher and college instructor, created Talk About when she noticed many of her students' parents saying they would like to reread the classics. Choosing both classic and modern novels, Talk About explores distinct genres such as Southern and British literature, humor, tragedy, history, and novels by and about women.

According to Colby, the twenty men and women in Talk About want the skills that will enable them to deepen their enjoyment of novels. "I give them the tools to enhance their understanding of character, plot, setting, and theme," says Colby, who charges a small fee to cover the expenses of hosting book club meetings in her home. "It's not as expensive or time-consuming as a college course, and I give them a lot of information to increase their reading enjoyment."

Colby enhances and enlivens book discussions with costumes, music, poetry, plays, field trips, and food. Lafayette, Louisiana, is the principal community in Acadiana—a region referred to as Cajun country—and the group takes advantage of local opportunities to explore Cajun cultural and culinary traditions connected with their reading selections. Talk About took in a stage version of *A Lesson Before Dying* (see p. 235) at the University of Louisiana after reading Lafayette author Ernest Gaines's novel set in Acadiana. For Lalita Tademy's *Cane River* (see p. 58), Colby led Talk About on a tour of Louisiana's Laura Plantation followed by dinner at a Cajun restaurant, where they enjoyed classic Cajun dishes—chicken and sausage gumbo, crayfish étouffée and rice, potato salad (see p. 187), banana pudding, and strong coffee.

Among their favorite reading selections: E. L. Doctorow's classic novel about New York in the early 1900s, *Ragtime,* Gabriel García Márquez's *Love in the Time of Cholera* (see p. 245), and Edith Wharton's *The Age of Innocence.*

"*The Age of Innocence* prompted discussion of New York aristocrats trapped in the strict behavioral codes of their segment of society," says Colby. "What does it mean to have young passionate love suppressed by societal conventions and a strict moral code?" asks Colby. "At first, the newly married Newland is prevented from following his heart when he is attracted to another woman. But later in life, when he has an opportunity to renew this young love affair, he has to decide whether to follow his heart or his moral code. At the end of our discussion, our group had mixed emotions. We felt sadness for the loss of young love but admiration for the fruits of adhering to one's morality."

Talk About thought that Wharton's novel gave an interesting and detailed picture of Victorian New York aristocracy, and showed that the challenges for humankind are universal. "We all try to guide our peers to lead a moral life and sacrifice strong feelings and temptations for others. In *The Age of Innocence,* however, the motivations of the ruling members of Newland's society were not always admirable: They wanted to control Newland's affection for Ellen for selfish reasons," says Colby.

More Food for Thought

Lisa Ryers's San Francisco book club reads only Pulitzer Prize–winning novels. Ryers formed the club as part of her personal pilgrimage to read the entire Pulitzer Prize list. The novels inspire participants to bring food and wine creations based on the novel's setting. "The meal is a platform for creativity," says Ryers. "Otherwise you end up going to your old standbys." For their discussion of *The Age of Innocence*, the group prepared a New York–style meal, including roasted chestnuts, Manhattan clam chowder, cheesecake (see pp. 144 and 271) and Apple Jonathan, a Pennsylvania Dutch dessert made in a cast-iron skillet. "In *The Age of Innocence* the saying 'keeping up with the Joneses' is mentioned. I think we just tried to keep up with ourselves!" says Ryers.

Ahab's Wife:
or, The Star-Gazer

Sena Jeter Naslund

WILLIAM MORROW, *1999*

(available in paperback from Perennial, 2000)

AHAB'S WIFE, Sena Jeter Naslund's feminist reinterpretation of Herman Melville's classic, *Moby-Dick*, centers on the famous Captain Ahab's wife, to whom Melville makes but brief reference in his novel. Naslund chronicles the life and spiritual journey of Una Spenser against the backdrop of nineteenth-century America.

Una's story is part romance, part adventure, and part family drama. At age twelve, she escapes from her tyrannical father in Kentucky and goes to live with relatives in a New England lighthouse. The sea and the ocean adventure stories of two visiting New Bedford sailors, Giles Bonebright and Kit Sparrow, enrapture Una. Freethinking, bold, and independent, Una leaves her aunt and uncle's home at sixteen, disguises herself as a cabin boy, and joins Giles and Kit for a whaling expedition.

Captain Ahab and the crew of the *Pequot* rescue Una and Kit after a harrowing shipwreck. The two marry, but the marriage doesn't survive Kit's descent into madness, a consequence of his ordeal at sea.

Una and Ahab meet again on Nantucket, fall in love, and marry. Theirs is a happy marriage despite Ahab's extended absences as a whaleboat captain. Una raises their child, explores religion, and befriends leading intellectuals of the day, including the feminist Margaret Fuller, the astronomer Maria Mitchell, and the abolitionist Frederick Douglass. Through illness, loss, and catastrophe, including the tragic end of her husband's epic struggle with the great white whale, Una perseveres.

JAN KESHEN'S SEAFOOD CHOWDER

S pinning a tale is sometimes like stirring a chowder. Steam and mist will rise up, different particles are whiffed from the broth," writes Naslund in a chapter of *Ahab's Wife* called "Chowder Swirls." Chowder was ever-present in nineteenth-century New England, and *Ahab's Wife* is suffused with descriptions of rich, creamy chowders. When Una meets Kit at her aunt and uncle's home in New Bedford, "the odor of fish chowder laced with onion and celery filled the room."

Chowder greets Kit and Una when they first come ashore in Nantucket after surviving the shipwreck. Mr. Hussey, proprietor of the Try Pots Tavern, famous for its chowders, beckons them to come back to the tavern so Mrs. Hussey can "feed you chowder till it flows from your ears." Soon Kit and Una are sitting down to "thick-sided, heat-holding bowls of thick creamy chowder."

The chowder in *Ahab's Wife* even seems to have healing powers: "When Ahab came home still bleeding, his soul raging, it was the Husseys' chowder fortified with sweet butter, for which he had the best tolerance," says Una. When Una is sick, Mrs. Hussey brings her bowls of chowder. Later, when Una works in the tavern, she says that "merely dishing up and delivering the chowder kept me on the trot."

Chowders had their origins as a seamen's dish, but eventually "came ashore to mean both the stew and the event at which it was served," explains Mark Zanger in *The American History Cookbook* (Greenwood Press, 2003). Chowders gained in popularity and, in coastal homes throughout New England, became the centerpiece of dinner, according to Jasper White, author of *50 Chowders: One Pot Meals—Clam, Corn and Beyond* (Simon & Schuster, 2000). Chowder picnics were common on New England beaches in the nineteenth century, with chowder-filled kettles hung over open fires. With freshly caught fish, chowder-making was "part of the entertainment," writes White.

Chowder as we know it today has evolved over the centuries. According to White, the earliest American recipes for chowders included fish and shipboard supplies, such as onion, pork, biscuits (hardtack), and spices, layered as in a casserole. Ingredients such as milk, cream, butter, and potatoes did not appear in chowders until the mid-1800s in northern New England.

Jan Keshen of Tallahassee, Florida, treated her book club, the LunaChics Literary Guild, to this seafood chowder when they discussed *Ahab's Wife*. "I was inspired by the small chowder house in Nantucket where Una was living," says Keshen, who developed her own recipe after reading many fish and seafood chowder recipes in cookbooks, magazines, and on the Internet. Keshen's version of the creamy soup—filled with fish, clams, shrimp, and scallops—is truly a fisherman's delight. Keshen suggests serving it with a green salad and crusty French bread.

NOTE: For a for a thicker chowder, mash a few of the potatoes with a potato masher before adding the fish.

6 strips bacon (may substitute turkey bacon)

2 large onions, diced

4 stalks celery, chopped

2 bay leaves

1½ pounds Yukon gold potatoes, diced

1½ cups fish, seafood, or chicken stock

1 8-ounce bottle clam juice

½ cup white wine

8 sprigs fresh thyme, or ½ teaspoon dried

1 teaspoon kosher salt

Freshly ground black pepper

½ pound firm, white-fleshed fish, cut into small cubes

¾ pound bay or sea scallops

¾ pound shrimp, peeled and deveined

2 cups whole milk, or half-and-half

4 cups fresh corn (may substitute frozen kernels, defrosted)

1 10-ounce can minced or whole baby clams, with juice

¼ cup chopped parsley

1. In a large Dutch oven, sauté the bacon (use a little olive oil for turkey bacon) until crisp. Drain on paper towels. Chop or crumble the bacon and set aside.

2. Add the onions, celery, and bay leaves to remaining fat and sauté until soft, about 7 minutes. Add the potatoes, stock, clam juice, wine, and enough water to cover. Simmer uncovered about 10 minutes or until the potatoes are just cooked. Remove the bay leaves.

3. Add the thyme, salt, and pepper, and adjust seasonings to taste. Add the fish, scallops, and shrimp and cook 3–5 minutes, until just done. Add the milk, corn, clams, and parsley. Heat through. Serve topped with bacon pieces as garnish.

Yield: 8 to 10 servings

BOOK CLUB PROFILE

The Our Book Group Kicks Your Book Group's Butt Book Club (that's really their name) of Missoula, Montana, consists of married couples and singles with a variety of professional interests, and includes two teachers, a professor, a librarian, a public defender, a fire department official, a nonprofit administrator, and others.

Club member Mark Sherouse is executive director of the Montana Committee for the Humanities and the Montana Center for the Book and has strong opinions when it comes to choosing readings. But Sherouse says he looks forward to the variety of readings selected by the meeting hosts. "The book group has been great for those of us who have narrower reading interests," Sherouse says. "Over the past several years I've read scores of books I would not otherwise have looked at, and I have benefited greatly from the discussions in our group as well as from some wonderful books."

Sherouse's group began discussing literature over soup, assorted munchies, and drinks, but later began serving dinners—usually a one-pot meal such as chili or stew.

The club has invited local authors whose works the group has read to meet with them, including David James Duncan, author of *The Brothers K,* a novel about baseball, politics, and religion, and Fred Haefele, author of the memoir *Rebuilding the Indian.* "Writers are everywhere," Sherouse says, "and Missoula has more than its share, including quite a number who are delighted to come to book group meetings to discuss their work."

Sherouse says better books lead to better discussions. Barbara Kingsolver's *The Poison-wood Bible* (see p. 353), Arundhati Roy's *The God of Small Things* (see p. 157), Yann Martel's *Life of Pi* (see p. 240), and, in particular, Sena Jeter Naslund's *Ahab's Wife* provoked some of the group's more interesting discussions. "We gave *Ahab's Wife* a ten, and we give very few of these scores," says Sherouse.

The group enjoyed Naslund's concept of revising a classic novel and telling it from a woman's point of view. "Her feminist response to Herman Melville's *Moby-Dick* was spectacular," says Sherouse. "Most of the so-called classics were written by men, about men. *Ahab's Wife* turns the tables, and Naslund does it brilliantly, capturing the nineteenth-century style, but making it intelligible and interesting to a twenty-first-century reader. The credible voice, the panoramic historical sweep, the social issues addressed, the moments of drama, the many points of contact with Melville's fictional world, all make *Ahab's Wife* a superb revisionary novel."

Their enjoyment of *Ahab's Wife* inspired members of the group to read, or reread, *Moby-Dick.* "I suppose that's the ultimate compliment to Naslund. But we came to the conclusion that her book was better," says Sherouse.

More Food for Thought

Julia Shanks of Interactive Cuisine in Cambridge, Massachusetts, creates menus to match literary selections for book clubs in the Boston area. *Ahab's Wife* inspired two book club menus.

"Nantucket and New Bedford are famous for their scallops," says Shanks, "and I also incorporated food reflecting the book's southern setting, as Una was raised in and returns to Kentucky." Fried chicken, for instance, is served aboard the whaling ship *Sussex* in the novel, and Shanks pairs it with coleslaw, a traditional accompaniment. To both recipes she added flavors from the apple pie mentioned in *Ahab's Wife*—apples and cinnamon. Una savors her mother's Kentucky jam cake, made with spices and jam, and topped with caramel frosting, at home in Kentucky. In Nantucket, her cousin Frannie delights her by baking the cake from the recipe Una had given her. Here is the first of Shanks's menus:

Grilled Bacon–Wrapped Bay Scallops
Cinnamon Fried Chicken and Curried Coleslaw with Apples and Raisins
Kentucky Jam Cake

Shanks's second menu features the more traditional New England dishes that Una's friend Judge serves when he invites Una, the astronomer Maria Mitchell, and Mitchell's father to dinner. For dessert Shanks chose apple pie, which Frannie bakes for Una at the end of *Ahab's Wife*.

Baked Scrod Stuffed with Bread Crumbs and Scallops
Mashed Potatoes and Buttered Peas
Apple Pie with Vanilla Ice Cream

The Amazing Adventures of Kavalier & Clay

Michael Chabon

RANDOM HOUSE, 2000

(available in paperback from Picador, 2001)

IN OCTOBER 1939, Josef Kavalier escaped with his life. Trained in his native Czechoslovakia in the use of picks and tiny torque wrenches—the tools of the escapist—Joe, as he is called, smuggles himself out of the country as the Nazis sweep in. Joe escapes concealed in a coffin he shares with a giant clay statue, the Golem, which was revered and protected by the Jews of Prague for centuries.

Joe first takes refuge in his aunt and uncle's apartment in Brooklyn, New York, sharing a bed with his cousin, Sammy, a boy who "dreams of flight and transformation and escape." The cousins quickly discover their shared fascination for escape artists—especially Harry Houdini—and a love of comic books. Within a few years, they have created The Escapist, The Monitor, Luna Moth, and other superheroes, whose adventures find their way into almost every American boy's bedroom.

Not just a rags-to-riches story, *The Amazing Adventures of Kavalier & Clay* captures New York City in the 1930s and 1940s: the horror and isolation of its Jewish immigrants as they watch events unfold overseas; the sleaziness, exploitation, and excitement of an emerging comic book industry; and Americans' urge to escape from the realities of World War II while clinging to a belief in a better future.

The foods served in Michael Chabon's novel reflect the diverse cultures of 1940s New York, a city teeming with immigrants, artists, and bohemians. Joe's girlfriend, Rosa Saks, cooks "strange recipes that her father had acquired a taste for in his travels: *tagine, mole,* something green and slippery that she called *sleek.*" Sammy's mother, Ethel, serves Sammy and his friend Tracy Bacon traditional Eastern European food—flanken (braised short ribs of beef), challah, and, for dessert, babka.

Cocoa-Cinnamon Babka

Babka, or baba, is a breadlike cake sweetened with various fillings, including cinnamon and sugar, fruit, or chocolate. *Baba* means "grandmother," or "old woman," in Ukrainian, where the rich bread was originally baked in vertical pans to resemble a standing woman. *Babka*, a diminutive form of the word, is now more commonly used because modern loaves are smaller and more delicate than the originals.

Although the recipe may have originated in the Ukraine, western Russia and Poland are more often considered the homeland of babka. Russians and Poles enjoyed babka and other festive cakes and breads at Easter. Polish and Russian Jews brought the recipe to New York, where it became associated with Lower East Side Jewish life.

Danny Seti of Bagel's Best in Needham, Massachusetts, has a background in Jewish baking and guided us in selecting babka recipes.

Our recipe is adapted from *The Hadassah Jewish Holiday Cookbook* (Hugh Lauter Levin Associates, Inc., 2002), a collection of recipes contributed by Hadassah members throughout the country. Dedicated to strengthening the unity of the Jewish people through volunteer activities in America and Israel, Hadassah is the largest volunteer organization and the largest women's organization in America. Jeannette Greenwood of New York's Shelanu Hadassah chapter is credited for this moist and elegant-looking Cocoa-Cinnamon Babka.

Jews who keep kosher (that is, observe Jewish dietary laws) are required to keep milk and meat products separate. Pareve foods are dairy-free and thus can accompany either type of meal. If you use nondairy creamer and pareve margarine, the babka can follow either a meat or a milk dinner in a kosher home. If you prefer, you can substitute milk and butter. These loaves freeze well.

NOTE: To scald milk: Heat milk in heavy-bottomed pan over low heat. Stir occasionally, bringing milk just below the boiling point. When bubbles begin to form around edges, remove from heat.

For the dough

4½ teaspoons (2 packets) active dry yeast
½ teaspoon plus ½ cup sugar
¼ cup warm water
1 cup nondairy creamer

½ cup (1 stick) unsalted margarine, softened
1 teaspoon salt
3 eggs, lightly beaten
5–5½ cups all-purpose flour

For the filling and topping

1 cup sugar

1 cup finely chopped walnuts

½ cup raisins

2 tablespoons unsweetened cocoa powder

1 tablespoon ground cinnamon

6 tablespoons unsalted margarine, melted

1 egg white, lightly beaten

1. To make the dough: Sprinkle yeast and ½ teaspoon sugar into warm water (105°–115° F.). Stir and set aside for 10 minutes, or until frothy. Grease and flour three 9x5-inch loaf pans.

2. Heat nondairy creamer to scalding and pour into large mixing bowl. Add margarine and stir to melt. Cool for 5 minutes. Add ½ cup sugar, salt, yeast mixture, and eggs. Gradually add enough flour to form a soft dough. Knead on floured surface 10 minutes, until shiny and elastic. Place in a greased bowl, turning to coat entire surface. Cover with a damp cloth and let rise in a warm place until doubled in size, about 1½ hours.

3. To make the filling and topping: In a small bowl, combine the sugar, nuts, raisins, cocoa powder, and cinnamon.

4. Divide dough in to 6 parts. Working with one part at a time, roll out on a lightly floured surface, forming a rectangle 8 inches wide and ⅛ inch thick. Brush some melted margarine over the dough. Sprinkle with 4–6 tablespoons nut mixture to cover three-quarters of the dough. Roll it up, tuck in the ends, and place the dough in a prepared loaf pan, seam side down. Repeat with a second part of dough and nut mixture, and tuck in alongside first roll.

5. Brush tops with egg white and sprinkle with about 2 tablespoons of nut mixture. Repeat for remaining dough. Cover lightly with a damp cloth and let rise until doubled in size, 1–1½ hours. Preheat oven to 350°F.

6. Bake babka 40–45 minutes, until golden. Cool in pan for 10 minutes, then transfer to a wire rack. Serve warm.

Yield: 3 loaves, 18 to 24 servings

BOOK CLUB PROFILE

"If you enjoy the best in wine and literature and the best people—this is a group for you," says the brochure for the Dubbya Dubbya Club (DDC), which came together during the 2000 presidential election primaries in Chicago. "'Dubbya' was in the air," says the founder,

Dante A. Bacani, "though the two Ws in our name stand for 'words' and 'wine,' and our book club is not politically affiliated. "

In creating the DDC, Bacani aimed to combine two of his passions: wine tasting and literature. "No meeting is complete without bottles being uncorked. I like the excuse to have some wine," says Bacani. A self-employed web designer and computer consultant, Bacani founded the DDC with a friend. Members tend to be single men and women in their late twenties to early forties. Until recently, they met monthly at a variety of wine bars around Chicago, but found a permanent meeting spot in the private, quieter "wine cellar" at Soprano's, a Chicago restaurant with a "particularly good wine list" and pizza and pasta. Occasionally they gather at a different venue, such as Lincoln Park, for a picnic.

At first, Bacani chose twentieth-century fiction he had always wanted to read for the Dubbya reading list. "I was an English major in college, but I never got around to books like *To Kill a Mockingbird,*" he says. Now, he and the co-moderator, Felicia Libbin, poll members. Books receiving the most votes are chosen. The following year's list is announced at the DDC's annual Christmas party.

To keep attendance high, the DDC balances its list of reading selections by length, alternating each month for longer (more than 250 pages) and shorter (less than 250 pages) selections. "It seemed more people would show up for shorter readings, yet others are very voracious readers," observes Bacani. For fun, the DDC's 2001 list featured books that had highly regarded film adaptations, and the group screened movies following the discussions, including Joseph Conrad's *Heart of Darkness* and Anthony Burgess's *A Clockwork Orange*.

The Amazing Adventures of Kavalier & Clay was one of the group's longer selections and a unanimous favorite. The male members of the group, in particular, related to the book's superhero fantasies. "I really connected to the two main characters, Sammy and Joe," says Bacani, "because when I was a kid, I used to draw comics and imagine myself as Superman or Batman. There was something very cathartic about imagining that I had the powers and skills that those characters had."

All group members appreciated Chabon's superior command of the English language (Bacani can't recall a book that sent him "scurrying to the dictionary" as often as this one) and his ability to transport readers to a time and place. Libbin helped the group visualize the book's setting by gathering web images of the 1939 World's Fair and early 1940s New York City street scenes. But according to Bacani, just by reading the book, "you really felt like you were there."

More Food for Thought

The Epicureaders book club of San Francisco prepared an all-American summer barbecue when they discussed *The Amazing Adventures of Kavalier & Clay*. Members contributed Cobb salad and lime-pineapple Jell-O salad, "both American and old-fashioned," says member Lena Shelton. For dessert they enjoyed a red velvet cake with seafoam frosting, which "was mentioned in the book and is reminiscent of mid-twentieth-century America."

Angela's Ashes

Frank McCourt

SCRIBNER, *1996*

(available in paperback from Scribner, 1999)

T HE MATERIAL and intellectual deprivations of Irish slum life in the 1930s and 1940s are re-counted in heart-wrenching detail in this memoir of an impoverished childhood in Limerick, Ireland, which earned Frank McCourt a Pulitzer Prize in 1997. The title is a tribute to McCourt's long-suffering mother, Angela, who would smoke her Woodbines by the fire while waiting in vain for her husband to come home with his pay. McCourt manages to find the absurd in his tragic past, making his story of deprivation ultimately an uplifting one.

Born in Depression-era Brooklyn to recent Irish immigrants, Frank McCourt is the son of a well-meaning but alcoholic father who had a habit of drinking his pay. Malachy McCourt often regaled his eldest son with stories of Cuchulain, a great hero of Ireland, tales that resonated with McCourt throughout his young childhood. McCourt revered his father, but Malachy constantly disappointed. Chronically unemployed, he often came home drunk in the dead of night, rousing McCourt and his four siblings from bed with loud song and making them swear to die for Ireland.

Malachy's employment woes and the sudden death of their youngest child drove the family back to Ireland. Here, in the slums of Limerick, McCourt paints a powerful portrait of a family living on the edge of disaster. Malachy continued to have difficulty holding a job, and his drinking binges persisted as Angela sought handouts from the charitable Saint Vincent de Paul Society to feed and clothe her children. The stench of the nearby lavatory, shared by every family on the street, constantly filled their apartment. At one point, for lack of money to buy coal, the family fueled their stove with wood pulled from the walls of their apartment; at another, McCourt walked to school with rubber-tire patches flapping from his shoes, shamed and disgraced.

McCourt's account resonates with boyish mischief and Catholic guilt, with curiosity and sexual awakening, and always with humor. He recounts his First Communion, when he vomited the Lord's body in his grandmother's backyard, and she dragged him to confession to ask the priest the proper way to clean it up. Simmering below the surface of McCourt's humor, though, is his growing desire to escape slum life for something better.

During World War II, Malachy moved to England in search of work and was barely heard from again. Angela and her children soldiered on, sometimes on the dole and sometimes begging. At fourteen, feeling he had at last reached manhood, McCourt quit school and landed the first in a series of jobs that would eventually earn him passage back to America.

During his childhood years, deprivation and relentless hunger prompted McCourt to focus on the elusive object of his desire. Seeing food—but not having it—was a constant torment. Mr. O'Neill, his fourth-class teacher, pared apples slowly in front of the class, dangling the peel tauntingly as a prize for correct answers. When Fintan Slattery, a classmate, invited McCourt and another impoverished peer to his house, the boys spied a sandwich and a glass of milk on the kitchen table. To McCourt, the milk looked "creamy and cool and delicious and the sandwich bread is almost as white." Although Fintan sliced his sandwich into quarters, then eighths, and then sixteenths, he never offered them a bite. It was a cruel act, a form of torture.

Scenes involving fantasies of food abound in *Angela's Ashes.* When his father brought home his wages on Fridays, McCourt would drift off to sleep with thoughts of the next day's delights: eggs, fried tomatoes, fried bread, tea with sugar and milk, dinner of mashed potatoes, peas, ham, "and a trifle Mam makes, layers of fruit and warm delicious custard on a cake soaked in sherry." After Malachy moved to England in search of work, McCourt fantasized about the egg he would enjoy when his father's telegraph money order arrived: "Tap it around the top, gently crack the shell, lift with a spoon, a dab of butter down into the yolk, salt, take my time, a dip of the spoon, scoop, scoop, more salt, more butter, into the mouth, oh, God above, if heaven has a taste it must be an egg with butter and salt . . ."

Somehow, McCourt's humor helped him endure the indignities of a childhood filled with want. In a February 1997 interview, he recalled sitting around the dinner table with his brothers: "We laughed at diets! We heard Americans did that! Seemed ridiculous. We'd sit at dinner, still hungry, as always, and say, 'I don't want any more'—as if we had enough. Just saying that sent us into stitches."

KATHERINE THOMERSON'S IRISH BROWN SODA BREAD

Bread is a staple of even the poorest Irish families. Throughout *Angela's Ashes*, bread appears in countless situations: mashed with milk and sugar to make "bread and goody" for Mc-Court's twin baby brothers; slathered with jam for a Christmas treat; secreted in Uncle Pat's pocket, so he wouldn't have to share; stolen from the doorsteps of the rich. A Limerick neighbor, Nora Malloy, begs for flour after her husband spends his wages on drink, and then bakes bread obsessively, fearful that her children will starve.

According to Malachi McCormick, in *Irish Country Cooking* (HarperCollins, 1988), "Everybody agrees that soda bread is the most famous Irish bread, but there is no such agreement on how it should be made." Some recipes include raisins plumped up in whiskey or water, others add sour cream or soured eggnog to the buttermilk. Whatever its ingredients, Irish soda bread brings to mind Frank McCourt's question: "After the egg, is there anything in the world lovelier than fresh warm bread and a mug of sweet golden tea?"

Katherine Thomerson, owner of the Frugal Frigate Book Store in Redlands, California, contributed her family recipe for Irish Brown Soda Bread, which she baked for the store's A Room of Her Own book club. Thomerson's recipe for this brown, crusty bread was passed down from her great-grandmother and great-great-grandfather, an Irish Baptist circuit preacher from Galway. She suggests serving the bread with butter and grape or peach jam.

3 cups all-purpose flour
2 cups whole-wheat flour
1 tablespoon baking powder
2 teaspoons baking soda

4 teaspoons brown sugar (use more for sweeter bread), mixed with 1 tablespoon water
2¼ cups buttermilk

1. Adjust oven rack to center position and preheat to 325°F. Place both flours, the baking powder, baking soda, and brown sugar in a large bowl and mix very well. Add the buttermilk and stir until a soft dough is formed. Knead the dough in the bowl, then empty onto a wood board or counter and knead a bit longer. If the dough seems wet, use extra whole-wheat flour. Knead until dough comes together.

2. Divide the dough into two portions and shape each into a round loaf. Press down just to flatten a bit. Place the loaves on an ungreased baking sheet. Sprinkle some additional flour on top of each loaf. Using a sharp carving knife, make a cross on the top of each. Allow to rest for 10 minutes, covered with a cloth, then bake for 40 minutes or until the loaves are golden brown and done to taste. Allow to cool, then serve with butter and jam.

Yield: 2 loaves

BOOK CLUB PROFILE

The Portola Hills Book Group, formed by a group of neighbors in the eponymous California town, incorporates culinary creativity and fun into every book club discussion. "We think having food, drink, or something related to the book enhances the book club experience," says Lynne Sales, a self-described "professional volunteer" who cofounded the book club in 1998. "It adds a sensual element."

The thirteen members—women of different faiths: Protestant, Catholic, and Jewish— read mainly current fiction, although historical fiction, classics, memoirs, nonfiction, and award winners also grace the group's reading list. Favorite titles include Wallace Stegner's *Angle of Repose* (see p. 22), T. C. Boyle's *The Tortilla Curtain* (see p. 447), Anita Diamant's *The Red Tent* (see p. 374), and Sena Jeter Naslund's *Ahab's Wife* (see p. 6).

The group's creative enhancements are as varied as the books they read. After reading Laura Hillenbrand's *Seabiscuit* (see p. 391), members invited their husbands to join them for a day of Thoroughbred racing at the Del Mar Racetrack, thirty miles south of Portola Hills, where the famed Thoroughbred actually raced. Sometimes the group attends movie versions of the books they read, as they have for Frank McCourt's *Angela's Ashes* and Rebecca Wells's *Divine Secrets of the Ya-Ya Sisterhood*, about the friendship and exploits of four Louisiana women.

Perhaps most memorable have been the meals prepared to accompany certain books. The group ate lamb kabobs from a local Persian restaurant when they discussed Andre Dubus III's *House of Sand and Fog* (see p. 197) and Anita Diamant's *The Red Tent.* For Sue Monk Kidd's *The Secret Life of Bees* (see p. 398), the group shared fried chicken (see p. 189), cheese straws (see p. 328), and salad, and drank peach sangria. And sushi and sake were on the menu for the club's discussion of Arthur Golden's *Memoirs of a Geisha* (see p. 255). Food figures into holiday time, too, when the group celebrates with a "high tea"—including scones with lemon curd, bite-size pastries, tea sandwiches (see p. 211), champagne, and an assortment of teas—at a fancy hotel.

Of the many books the group has read and discussed, the one that touched the members most profoundly was *Angela's Ashes*. "The book was depressing but so well written," says Sales. "Frank McCourt has a unique voice." Sales added that the group had a particularly good discussion because one member, Eileen McGervey, felt a strong personal connection to McCourt's story.

McGervey's husband, Francis, or Frank, as he is called, is one of a group of two thousand or so people born in Ireland to unwed mothers between 1949 and 1972 and quietly shipped to America for adoption. During these years, babies born in Ireland to women out of wedlock would be housed in "orphanages" run by nuns, where the mothers would visit, nursing and caring for their babies for up to two years. The nuns would then pressure the young mothers to sign over custody of their children. The mothers often did not realize that their babies would be adopted abroad. Many people found this arrangement useful for the Catholic Church of Ireland—ridding it of embarrassment—and for the children, who were to be raised in relative affluence.

Frank McGervey was adopted at the age of two by an Irish-American family. Like so many other Irish adoptees of this era, he hoped to locate his biological mother, although there is no central depository of records to consult. One of Frank McGervey's adoptive uncles traveled to Ireland in 1998 and found a biological aunt still living in the town where Frank was born. She pointed him to London, where she knew that five of Frank's biological siblings were living. Frank traveled to England and was reunited with his biological family.

Frank McGervey's story of his beginnings in Ireland touched the group deeply and helped them better appreciate Frank McCourt's memoir. "My husband's story helped confirm the authenticity of McCourt's experiences to the group," says McGervey. "The way in which religion drove Frank McCourt's family touched a chord. Even though they endured hardships, they still had faith. My husband's family, too, felt that as long as they went to church on Sunday, everything else would be taken care of." McGervey added that her husband's story of poverty and moral censure helped give context to McCourt's account. "When the group understood better the world McCourt was living in, some of the decisions people made, like spending their last dollar on cigarettes, made more sense," says McGervey.

For her group's discussion of *Angela's Ashes*, Eileen McGervey served tea and Irish soda bread. McGervey's Irish soda bread recipe came from her mother-in-law, as did the cream-colored teapot covered with Irish shamrocks used to serve the tea. "My mother- and father-in-law are very Irish, and they were intent on adopting an Irish child," explains McGervey. "Ever since I met my husband, at age fifteen, he warned me not to tell his parents that I don't have a drop of Irish blood in me!"

More Food for Thought

Mary Breen's Boston-area book club enjoyed an Irish feast of vegetarian shepherd's pie, boxty (Irish potato and onion pancakes), green salad, and Irish soda bread for their discussion of *Angela's Ashes*. "I'd like to say we had Guinness, too," says Breen, "but our group never drinks!" They topped the meal off with a berry trifle that member Erika Gardiner brought in spite of its English, rather than Irish, roots.

At their meeting, Breen's group listened to a recording of an interview with Frank McCourt. "Between reading the book, hearing the author's voice, and eating the Irish food, this was a meeting that involved all our senses," says Breen.

The Movie Stars Book Club of Portland, Oregon, enjoyed baked potatoes with all the fixin's—butter, sour cream, cheese, chives, broccoli, chili, and salsa—for their discussion of *Angela's Ashes*. "The fact that *Angela's Ashes* was set in Ireland during a poverty-stricken time in the life of Frank McCourt made me think of the great potato famine," says Sandi Hildreth, who hosted the meeting. "Potatoes seemed like a thematically appropriate food."

Angle of Repose

Wallace Stegner

DOUBLEDAY, *1971*

(available in paperback from Penguin, 1992)

LYMAN WARD, the narrator of *Angle of Repose*, Wallace Stegner's 1972 Pulitzer Prize–winning novel, is a historian and man of letters who suffers from a degenerative bone disease and is confined to a wheelchair. Committed to a degree of self-sufficiency, Lyman lives alone in Zodiac Cottage in Grass Valley, California, once the home of his parents and grandparents, attended only by a caretaker.

In 1970, Lyman reconstructs the story of the marriage of his beloved grandmother, Susan Burling, a Quaker from a modest New York abolitionist background, to Oliver Ward, a handsome, ambitious young engineer with grand ideas. Oliver Ward's career as a mining engineer, surveyor, and irrigation and canal planner takes the young couple to the West of the post–Civil War era—not the mythic West of cowboys and Indians, but the West of the settlers who tamed new landscapes "of raw beauty" and transformed them into a version of eastern civilization and culture. Susan's letters to her lifelong friend Augusta Drake are the primary source Lyman uses to tell his grandparents' story.

An artist and illustrator, Susan is both gentle and genteel, qualities that complement Oliver's more robust response to the challenges of frontier life. Their complementary qualities unite them at times and divide them at others. Susan comes to appreciate the nature of Oliver's creativity, and Oliver in turn encourages her blossoming career as an illustrator.

Stegner, known for his love of the West and his ability to describe its grand landscapes, also captures moments of intimacy in this novel about lost hopes and the capacity to recover and grow.

During Oliver and Susan's travels to California, Colorado, and Idaho, they encounter many different terrains, lifestyles, and people. But, when they travel to Michoacán in Mexico, where Oliver will inspect an old mine, Susan falls in love with the place, mesmerized by the culture and unusual surroundings. She describes to her grandson Lyman how she would have loved to stay there: "I had been married five years and lived most of that time in mining camps. Mexico was my Paris and my Rome."

A letter from Susan to Augusta describes how the exotic foods in the Michoacán marketplace captivate her. She writes of turkeys, beans, onions, tortillas, *pulque* (a fermented beverage derived from agave plants), and "mysterious sweet and coarse sugar like cracked corn. . . . Such a colorful jumble, such a hum of life."

MEXICAN CHOCOLATE TORTE

L ena Shelton selected this Mexican Chocolate Torte recipe from *Gourmet* magazine (March 1993) for her San Francisco, California, book club, the Epicureaders, when they held their dinner discussion of *Angle of Repose*. Shelton says she chose the torte because Mexico was so beloved by Susan. "The torte features cinnamon and almonds, two popular ingredients in Mexican baking, which add spice and depth to the intensely chocolate cake," says Shelton.

Mexican chocolate is a combination of chocolate, cinnamon, and almonds, and this dessert highlights these delicious flavors.

For the torte

1 cup (about 5 ounces) whole almonds (with skins)

⅓ cup firmly packed light brown sugar

1 tablespoon ground cinnamon

¾ teaspoon salt

5 ounces good-quality bittersweet chocolate, chopped

5 eggs, separated

1 teaspoon vanilla extract

⅓ cup granulated sugar

For the glaze

4 ounces fine-quality bittersweet chocolate, chopped

2 tablespoons unsalted butter

2 tablespoons heavy cream

1 tablespoon light corn syrup

For the icing

⅓ cup confectioners' sugar

1½ teaspoons milk

1. Preheat oven to 350°F, with rack in center position.

2. To make the torte: Spread the almonds in a single layer in a shallow baking pan and toast, tossing every 3–4 minutes, until the nut meat is a light golden brown, about 10–15 minutes in all. Remove from oven and allow to cool completely.

3. Lower oven temperature to 325°F. Butter an 8½-inch springform pan and line the bottom with a round of parchment paper. Butter the paper and dust the pan with flour, knocking out the excess.

4. In a food processor, blend together the almonds, brown sugar, cinnamon, and salt until the almonds are finely ground. Add the chocolate and blend until finely ground. Add the egg yolks and vanilla and blend until combined well (the mixture will be very thick). Transfer to a bowl and set aside.

5. Place the egg whites and a pinch of salt in a mixing bowl and beat with an electric mixer until soft peaks form. Gradually beat in the granulated sugar until the meringue just holds stiff peaks.

6. Fold about ⅓ of the meringue into the chocolate mixture, then fold in the remaining meringue gently but thoroughly. Pour the batter into the pan, smooth the top, and bake 45–55 minutes, or until a toothpick inserted in the center comes out clean. Cool on a rack for 5 minutes, then run a thin knife around the edge and remove the sides of the pan. Invert the torte onto the rack, discarding the parchment paper, and allow to cool.

7. To make the glaze: In a metal bowl set over barely simmering water, combine the chocolate, butter, cream, and corn syrup. Stir until smooth, and let the glaze cool until it is just lukewarm.

8. Turn the torte right side up on the rack with something underneath to catch the drips, and pour glaze over top, smoothing with a spatula and letting the excess drip down the sides.

9. To make the icing: Whisk together the confectioners' sugar and 1 teaspoon of the milk in a small mixing bowl. Add just enough of the remaining milk, drop by drop, to form a thick icing.

10. Transfer the icing to a small pastry bag fitted with a ⅛-inch plain tip and pipe it decoratively onto the torte. Transfer the torte to a serving plate and let stand for 2 hours, or until glaze is set.

Yield: 8 to 12 servings

Each month the Epicureaders—five women from San Francisco's Bay Area with great enthusiasm for food and literature—delve into their reading and are inspired to new culinary heights. "We all love to cook, and food had to be an integral part of the reading group," says Lena Shelton, an analyst for the University of California's California Digital Library.

The Epicureaders create meals from foods mentioned in their reading selections, but also seek out unusual, inventive themes for their literary feasts. "Dinner themes are where we really shine," says Shelton. For Jack London's *Sea Wolf,* a tale of survival following a rescue from a ferryboat accident, each member contributed a salad to a Fantasy Cruise Salad Bar. For A. S. Byatt's short stories, *The Djinn in the Nightingale's Eye,* in which the title story revolves around a woman's relationship with a genie, they prepared The Dervish's Delight Turkish Dinner, with *doner kabob* (lamb kabobs), *piyaz* (white bean salad), and *patates bastisi* (potato casserole). The theme was Springtime Food with Flowers for one of their poetry interludes, and they dined on dishes with flowers: curried fried zucchini blossoms, goat cheese scalloped potatoes with chive blossoms, and lavender creme-caramel tart.

Two weeks prior to each meeting, the host announces the dinner theme. The host provides the main course and members provide other courses and beverages to match the dinner, posting recipes on the club's website (www.epicureaders.com) to coordinate contributions. Their multicourse meals are so bountiful that Epicureader Margo Kieser, a music librarian at the San Francisco Symphony, gave each member a gift of personalized Tupperware for the leftovers.

"We try not to consciously choose our books based on potential dinner themes, but food can be the deciding factor when choosing between finalists," admits Shelton. "If a book has an explicit dinner theme we have not done in the past, this increases its chances of being selected."

Occasionally the group opts to eat out. For their Beatniks theme, the Epicureaders read Jack Kerouac's *On the Road* as well as Beat poetry by Allen Ginsberg and Lawrence Ferlinghetti, and then took a Beatnik tour of San Francisco's historic North Beach, heart of the West Coast Beat movement of the 1950s and 1960s. Their first stop was Vesuvio's, a hangout for the Beats at the time, for Jack Kerouac drinks, combinations of rum, tequila, orange and cranberry juices, and lime, followed by a visit next door to the City Lights bookstore, founded by Ferlinghetti.

Lena Shelton founded the Epicureaders in 2000 to create an intellectual forum for discussion of literature as well as to provide a regular time to meet with friends. Members include writers, a musician, and a dancer. "Our members always manage to come up with inspired ideas for reading choices, dinners, and ways to keep the group fresh," says Shelton.

The Epicureaders have established a reading calendar. They begin each year with a meeting to reflect on the past year and plan for the next. One such meeting resulted in a decision to read works by Nobel Prize–winners. Each February, the Epicureaders read a work by an African-American author for Black History Month; in April (National Poetry Month) and December they have poetry interludes, and every July they take a break for a movie night. Among their favorite titles are Leonora Carrington's novel *The Hearing Trumpet,* the adventures of a ninety-two-year-old woman whose family sends her to a retirement home; Jhumpa Lahiri's *Interpreter of Maladies;* and Wallace Stegner's *Angle of Repose,* which they chose as part of an experiment to read a longer book over two months.

"*Angle of Repose* takes place during America's westward movement, a period of history that is not very well chronicled, especially in literature," says member Stacey Pelinka. "As a California-based reading group, we are interested in California history and the California locations described in the book are meaningful to us."

The Epicureaders explored how the difficulties of narrator Lyman Ward's grandparents paralleled those in his own life: understanding his wife's infidelity, his own difficulties understanding his children, and his dreams of success.

"*Angle of Repose* has weighty subject matter, surprises in the plot that keep the lengthy narrative fresh, and dual perspectives, modern and historical, that parallel one another," says Kieser. "The past always influences the present."

More Food for Thought

The Epicureaders chose a California dinner theme for their *Angle of Repose* menu. "We stopped short of re-creating meals from California's earlier days, in which the book is set," says Lena Shelton, "and chose contemporary recipes with characteristic California ingredients such as avocados, goat cheese, wild mushrooms, and Dungeness crab."

Their menu included *vin de cerise*, a sweet drink made with cherries, wine, and sugar; wild mushrooms on croutons; chilled cucumber-avocado soup and dilled carrot soup; seafood pasta salad with lemon-dill dressing; spicy brown rice with eggplant and tomatoes; asparagus with hazelnuts and hazelnut oil vinaigrette; and goat cheese scalloped potatoes with chive blossoms—all followed by lemon pie, strawberry sorbet with rosemary, and Mexican Chocolate Torte for dessert.

Anna Karenina

Leo Tolstoy

....

1886

(available in paperback from Penguin, 2002)

L EO TOLSTOY'S celebrated novel *Anna Karenina* is set against the backdrop of czarist Russia. Through an intricate plot and in numerous settings, Tolstoy reveals the spectrum of nineteenth-century Russian politics and political philosophy and its many layers of social class from peasantry to aristocracy and nobility.

Marriage and family are powerful themes in this complex novel, wherein characters experience intensely the joys, hopes, betrayals, and disappointments of love.

Anna Karenina—wife of the cold, officious Karenin, a wealthy bureaucrat—is trapped in an unhappy marriage. Anna's brother, Stepan Oblonsky, has an outwardly conventional marriage to Dolly Scherbatsky, but Stepan's infidelity and extravagant tastes create unhappiness. Konstantin Levin, an idealistic nobleman and friend of Stepan's, is enamored of Dolly's sister Kitty. Although Kitty loses the attentions of the charming Count Vronsky, a military officer, to the beautiful Anna, she responds to Levin's pureness of heart and falls in love and marries him.

Central to the story is Anna's affair with Vronsky—at first discreet, but later public—which exposes Anna to the severe censure of her husband and St. Petersburg society, and leads to her separation from her beloved son and, ultimately, to tragedy. The reader inevitably is led to judge Anna, who is portrayed as both immoral woman and victim.

WILD MUSHROOMS ON TOAST

M ushrooms, a Russian passion, appear frequently in the detailed descriptions of family life and social events in *Anna Karenina*. Salted mushrooms are served as an hors d'oeuvre when Levin dines with Stepan at his club. In a scene in the country, the Oblonsky family delights together in the recreational gathering of mushrooms. A conversation about mushrooms manages to derail a marriage proposal by Levin's brother, Koznyshev, to Kitty's friend Varenka. Levin's sense of community with the peasants and his land is heightened when he observes the simple scene of a peasant picking a choice mushroom and setting it aside for his wife.

For centuries mushrooms have been a Russian culinary staple, and the country's pine and birch forests are rich with wild mushrooms that Russians delight in gathering. Wild mushrooms such as morels and chanterelles are marinated, dried, salted, baked, and simmered in soups.

Our recipe for mushroom toasts, a wonderful accompaniment to *Anna Karenina*, is adapted from *Please to the Table: The Russian Cookbook* by Anya Von Bremzen and John Welchman (Workman, 1990).

2 ounces dried porcini mushrooms
¼–½ pound fresh wild mushrooms (e.g.,
    shiitake, chanterelle, morel), gently cleaned
    with a damp cloth
4 tablespoons butter
1 small onion, finely chopped
1½ teaspoons all-purpose flour
3 tablespoons sour cream

2 cloves garlic, minced
Pinch of paprika
Salt and pepper
3 tablespoons extra-virgin olive oil
1 baguette, thinly sliced
3 tablespoons grated Parmesan cheese
3 tablespoons chopped fresh parsley

1. Preheat oven to 350°F.
2. Place the dried porcini mushrooms in a small saucepan with 2 cups of water. Simmer until soft, about 40 minutes. Remove mushrooms from pan with a fork or slotted spoon and pat dry on paper towels. Pour the cooking liquid through a cheesecloth-lined strainer and set aside.
3. Finely chop both the porcini and fresh mushrooms. Melt butter in a medium skillet. Add mushrooms and onion and sauté over medium heat for 15 minutes, stirring frequently. Sprinkle the flour over the mixture and cook for 1 minute, stirring constantly. Stir in ⅓ cup of the reserved porcini cooking liquid and simmer for 2 more minutes. Stir in sour cream and simmer for 5 minutes, stirring frequently. Add garlic and season to taste with paprika, salt, and pepper. Simmer for 2 minutes. Adjust seasonings.
4. Heat 1½ tablespoons olive oil in a large skillet. Lightly fry bread slices on both sides, adding more olive oil to the pan as needed. Arrange toast in a single layer in a baking dish. Top each piece with some of the mushroom mixture and sprinkle with Parmesan cheese. Bake for 10 minutes. Remove from oven and sprinkle each toast with parsley. Serve immediately.

Yield: 6 servings

"When I die and go to heaven, there will be a book club that meets every day," says Dennis Minsky, a high school science teacher, who speaks with great affection for his book club of eighteen years, the Englewood, New Jersey–based Reading Society. "There is a passion that our members bring to discussions. These are people who believe in the written word and rejoice in the sharing of it."

The Reading Society was born in 1982 when three English teachers at the private Dwight-Englewood School in Englewood discovered that they all loved the work of the poet Rainer Maria Rilke. Hoping to illuminate their reading of Rilke's work, the three teachers met for weekly readings and discussions, and found they had finally begun to grasp Rilke's ten *Duino Elegies.* The shared reading was so beneficial that they chose to continue with Joseph Conrad's classic novel *Lord Jim.* They invited fellow teachers to join them and a group of thirteen has continued to meet monthly at the home of Frimi Sagan, one of the original members of the group and a teacher of literature.

The Reading Society is primarily interested in classic texts because, as Sagan says, "they promise challenges and rewards."

"The classics offer complicated ideas put forth in a very demanding way," adds Sagan, "and if you read them, they will stretch your imagination. We relish being together in the presence of great writers and great texts."

Discussion is typically initiated with a strong opinion or a favorite passage. "Nobody is responsible for leading the discussion," says Sagan. "It just flows and there is an assumption that everyone is worth listening to."

Minsky enjoys sitting back and observing the interchanges among his old friends. "There is an absolute rhythm to these discussions, a give-and-take based on years of knowledge," says Minsky. "Some of these differences of opinion resurface, such as the feud over whether the characters in Jane Austen's work have anything to complain about relative to their counterparts in Tolstoy and Dostoyevsky."

The Reading Society takes a break from its often-animated discussion for refreshments. Sagan always serves fruit and elegant pastries, and, if one comes to mind, a thematic dessert. When they read Thomas Mann's *The Magic Mountain,* set in an Alpine sanatorium, Sagan served a cake with whipped-cream peaks. "Someone finally made the connection and said, 'Oh my, it's the mountain!'" says Sagan.

For Marcel Proust's autobiographical novel, *Remembrance of Things Past,* Sagan served madeleines—scallop-shaped cookies. "In the novel, Marcel, the narrator, dips his madeleine into his cup of herbal tea, and the taste of the cookie enables him to recall his childhood," Sagan says.

Sagan is passionate about Leo Tolstoy's *Anna Karenina,* calling it one of the great nineteenth-century novels. She recalls that she bristled when the group's discussion began with a member expressing annoyance at the predictability of the book's theme of adultery. "*Anna Karenina* is not boring," says Sagan. "Tolstoy offers an intense characterization of Anna, the wife of a government official in St. Petersburg, and her desire and despair. This is not just a novel about a woman having an affair. Anna has an extraordinary range of gifts. She is vital, imaginative, beautiful, and kindhearted. But she is consumed by Vronsky, a wealthy and handsome army officer, and can't function without this relationship."

The novel's two pivotal characters, Anna and Levin, provided considerable fodder for the group's examination. "Anna's crude, vulgar, sexual love for Vronsky is contrasted with Levin's sacred love for Kitty," says Sagan. "Levin struggles with the meaning of his life. He tries desperately to be a good person. Anna's struggle is circular. She is consumed by her passion for Vronsky, and can't think about society, religion, or family as Levin can. Her inability to change is catastrophic."

The group discussed society's condemnation of Anna's adulterous behavior. Countess Vronsky, Vronsky's mother, has a reputation for sexual liaisons, but unlike Anna, who flaunts her affair with Vronsky in public, the Countess plays by society's rules. "Anna has lived quietly, but suddenly has intense feelings, and seeks sexual and emotional fulfillment," says Sagan. "Yet, marriage and family are Anna's only options."

The group explored the limited options authors had for dealing with adulterous women toward the end of the nineteenth century. "Authors frequently got rid of adulterous women," Sagan adds. "It wasn't until the twentieth century that writers could stop sacrificing them. There's no doubt the story would have ended differently if written later."

The Reading Society also appreciated Tolstoy's artistry. "We all admired the beautiful prose, such as Levin's first glimpse of Kitty at the skating rink, or Vronsky's first glance of Anna at the train station," says Minsky.

The group agreed that Tolstoy's narrative writing is exhilarating. "His writing is so alive," says Sagan. "You are drawn in immediately. As an example, take the scene where Kitty meets Levin. Levin has his skates on, and goes dashing down steps to the rink, yet he doesn't fall—he jumps down and lands brilliantly on the ice. Tolstoy makes you want to do all of those things yourself."

"*Anna Karenina* is a major work of art and nothing less," says Minsky. "Anyone who considers himself a reader must surely live with it at least once a decade."

More Food for Thought

The Maine Humanities Council's Winter Weekends focus on a classic work and combine lectures by academic specialists, small group discussions, film versions of the book, and excellent food. Proceeds from the events fund the Council's programs for troubled teenagers. More than one hundred participants, from high school students to retirees, met to explore and discuss *Anna Karenina* for the council's 2003 "Weekend in Old Russia," held at Bowdoin College in Brunswick, Maine.

During the weekend, Ronald LeBlanc, professor of Russian and Humanities at the University of New Hampshire, explored the complex relationship between food and sexual desire in a presentation to the group. "He explored the notion of how emotional and gastronomic appetites were linked in the novel," says Charles Calhoun, codirector of the Winter Weekends program.

The Friday night menu for Dinner à la Russe, prepared by the Bowdoin College Dining Service, was written in the French of "*vieux St.-Pétersbourg.*" "French was the language normally spoken by most of the characters in *Anna Karenina*," says Calhoun. The lavish buffet dinner featured many traditional Russian foods mentioned in the novel, beets, cucumbers, mushrooms, salmon, and kasha (buckwheat groats), and included *champignons à la grecque* (mushrooms cooked with lemon, olive oil, and spices), *salade de betteraves* (beet salad), *potage bortsch* (borsch soup, see p. 492), and *boeuf à la mode de M. le comte Stroganoff*, or beef Stroganoff, an authentic Russian dish with origins in St. Petersburg.

"What lingered after the event, after so much listening and talking, is a conclusion that might seem obvious," says Calhoun. "Tolstoy is a genius with few peers."

Atonement

Ian McEwan

NAN A. TALESE, 2002

(available in paperback from Anchor, 2003)

WITH A GIFT for manipulation, a wild imagination, but an incomplete understanding of the adult world around her, a thirteen-year-old English girl, Briony Tallis, sets in motion a tragic series of events that leaves her older sister's lover, Robbie Turner, wrongly accused of an unspeakable crime. Briony's search for atonement spans six decades as she seeks, in her own unique way, to repair the damage she has done to the lives of her sister, Cecilia, and Robbie. Through the London blitz and the blood-soaked fields of northern France, Briony seeks to rewrite the history she has created, and to right the wrongs of decades past.

In one memorable scene before the war, the extended Tallis family and several guests take their seats at the family table on a day so hot no one has an appetite . . . not for food or, because of a shocking event known only to some at the table, for conversation either. This leaves Robbie Turner, one of the leading characters, to wonder whether it is his imagination or "malign intent" on the part of Betty, the household cook, "that made the adults' portions appear twice the size of the children's." Imagination and intent, malign and otherwise, are recurring themes throughout *Atonement.*

MARY KATE DILLON'S
BREAD-AND-BUTTER PUDDING

At the conclusion of a languid meal featuring roast beef and potatoes, Betty serves a traditional English bread-and-butter pudding.

Bill Pryor and his wife, Debbie, prepared this recipe, which they got from their friend Mary Kate

Dillon, to serve to Real Men, Real Books, a men's book club in the Boston suburbs, when they discussed *Atonement*. "The pudding was hearty and delicious," says Pryor. "The men inhaled it."

Bread-and-butter pudding, a British dessert dating back centuries, is a simple comfort food that has made a comeback in the last decade, appearing on menus at some of England's tonier restaurants. Puddings are a staple of British cuisine, considered "a sensible and economical bundle of food values for the relatively well-off," says Daniel Pool, author of *What Jane Austen Ate and Charles Dickens Knew* (Simon & Schuster, 1993). If you like rich desserts as an accompaniment to rich discussion, we recommend this version of the English classic.

½ cup light brown sugar

2 teaspoons ground cinnamon

¼ teaspoon ground nutmeg

½ cup (1 stick) unsalted butter, softened

12 slices white sandwich bread

1 cup raisins (dried cranberries or sultanas
   may be substituted)

4 cups half-and-half

4 eggs

4 egg yolks

2 teaspoons vanilla extract

Sweetened Whipped Cream (optional,
   see p. 424)

1. Preheat oven to 350°F.
2. In a small bowl, mix the brown sugar, cinnamon, and nutmeg. Set aside.
3. Spread butter on one side of each piece of bread and slice in half diagonally. Overlap bread triangles in a baking dish, buttered sides up, with cut edges facing the same direction. Sprinkle with the brown-sugar mixture and top with raisins.
4. In a small bowl, mix the half-and-half, eggs, egg yolks, and vanilla with a whisk. Pour the mixture over the bread and raisins in baking dish. Press edges of bread down and set aside for 15 minutes to let bread absorb the liquid.
5. Place the baking dish inside a larger pan and fill the outer pan halfway with water. Bake 30–40 minutes, or until top is golden brown and a knife inserted in the center comes out clean. Serve warm, topped with Sweetened Whipped Cream if desired.

Yield: 8 to 10 servings

"In *Atonement,* Ian McEwan seems to be saying something about writing, and about the writer's imagination," says novelist Bill Littlefield of the Real Men, Real Books book group of Needham, Massachusetts. "McEwan's exploring the way a writer uses what happens in his or her life as material for creating another reality, in this case a reality in which atonement is possible, whereas the unmanageable real world might not have allowed it," adds Littlefield, who hosts National Public Radio's *Only a Game.*

Atonement won universal praise from the members of the Real Men, Real Books book group because of its "you are there" depictions of the English retreat across northern France, scenes of profound sensuality, a deep exploration of the power of imagination to shape events, and an unexpected twist that challenges the reader to reevaluate everything that has gone before.

"*Atonement* was more than just a good read; it was an extraordinary experience," says Bill Pryor, a publishing company executive.

"There were unexpected insights in our discussion," says Tom Anderson, a corporate communications executive. "We noted the exact point—an obscene word in a love letter that was supposed to remain private—where the book turned from something interesting to something compelling, and the choices of structure and language that made this work so effectively. Linking the domestic tragedy with the war provoked analysis of the abstract issues of evil, ego, and the downside of creating the world in one's own image. The heroics of a man caught in someone else's drama was also something I hadn't thought about before."

Stan Hitron, the chair of the English Department at Middlesex Community College, outside Boston, founded Real Men, Real Books. "I saw how much my wife had enjoyed her book group over ten years," says Hitron. "I love literature; it's a part of my professional life, but I don't often get to discuss it with my colleagues. I thought it would be intellectually and emotionally invigorating to discuss it with a bunch of intelligent guys, and so it has been. It's nice to talk about something other than sports, politics, real estate, or home improvement." Among the group's reading selections have been *White Teeth,* Zadie Smith's multicultural novel set in London, and *The Quiet American,* Graham Greene's novel about Vietnam.

Tom Anderson was the first in the group to connect food and books. When the group met at Anderson's home to discuss T. C. Boyle's *Drop City,* a novel about a California commune that relocates to Alaska, Anderson served Moosehead beer and Klondike bars, inspiring member Tad Staley to prepare vegetarian Indian food for *White Teeth* and Pryor to serve English ale and cheeses along with bread-and-butter pudding for *Atonement*.

More Food for Thought

Sue Gray prepared an English high tea for her Seattle-based Wuthering Bites book club's discussion of *Atonement*. "The menu for *Atonement* was fun," says Gray. "I love the little sandwiches that go with high tea." Gray served a variety of finger sandwiches, including cucumber and chicken salad, as well as cranberry chutney and cream cheese on crackers, along with a Pimm's Cup, a drink that she heard was Prince Charles's favorite, made with Pimm's liqueur and club soda, and garnished with lemon. "High tea has changed over the years to include anything from the most elegant of pastries to the simplest of sandwiches. It's a wonderful tradition and a great way to break up the day and share a bit of conversation, good food, and a spot of revitalizing tea," added Gray.

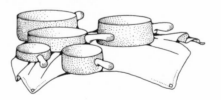

Balzac and the Little Chinese Seamstress

Dai Sijie

KNOPF, 2001

(availble in paperback from Anchor, 2002)

*B*ALZAC AND THE *LITTLE CHINESE SEAMSTRESS* is set in Communist China in 1971, when Mao's Cultural Revolution was sweeping the country, closing universities, banning Western literature, and sending young urban intellectuals to the countryside for "reeducation." When their parents are named "enemies of the people," two teenage boys—the unnamed narrator and his best friend, Luo—are sent from the city of Chengdu to the poorest village on a remote mountain, known as Phoenix in the Sky. Their reeducation means backbreaking labor carrying buckets of excrement up and down the mountain's winding roads to fertilize the fields and hauling coal from the mines.

Despite the harsh setting, the novel's tone is lighthearted and comical, chronicling the boys' adventures as they charm, outwit, and entertain the villagers. The spirited pals discover a way to obtain Chinese translations of forbidden Western classics, including Honoré de Balzac's novel *Ursule Mirouet,* from Four-Eyes, a fellow exile in a nearby village. The narrator cherishes Balzac's story and discovers "awakening desire, passion, impulsive action, love, all the subjects that had, until then, been hidden."

The daughter of a tailor from the next village, the "Little Seamstress," enchants the boys, and a love triangle forms among the three. The boys hatch a plan to steal Four-Eyes's cache of books to feed their souls and to begin their own reeducation program: transforming the illiterate peasant seamstress into a worldly, sophisticated woman.

When the boys become known for their storytelling abilities, the village headman dispatches them to watch movies in a neighboring town, so they can entertain villagers with oral presentations of the film upon their return. Their trips provide a respite from hard labor, and even the tiny village of Jong Ying, where they go to see movies, is one step closer to the city life—including the culinary pleasures—they have left behind. "Believe me, even the smell of beef and onions savoured of sophistication," says the narrator, of the scents that greet the boys in Jong Ying. The boys feel like "criminals huddling conspiratorially around the oil lamp" during meals of ingredients purloined with their friend Four Eyes—meals "delicious with aromas that plunged the three of us, famished, to frenzy of anticipation."

SPICY PORK WITH ORANGE HOISIN SAUCE
IN WONTON CUPS

Thematic food helps us focus on the time period and culture of the book we're reading and draws us into discussion," says Ellen Masterson of her Westborough, Massachusetts, book club. Masterson says choosing food to accompany *Balzac and the Little Chinese Seamstress* was difficult because the characters didn't eat "high off the hog."

Masterson opted for a general Chinese theme. Along with shrimp and mango with green curry paste and store-bought fortune cookies, she served her "sure hit" Spicy Pork with Orange Hoisin Sauce in Wonton Cups, a recipe adapted from *Bon Appétit* (January 2001). "These pork wontons are delicious and easy to prepare using premade wonton wrappers and muffin pans to shape the wontons," says Masterson. "I have been asked for the recipe many times."

For the sauce

2 scallions, minced

½ teaspoon grated orange peel

½ cup hoisin sauce

3 tablespoons frozen orange juice, thawed

1 tablespoon Chinese chile-garlic sauce
   (see Purchasing Information, p. 499)

Salt and pepper to taste

For the filling

1¼ pounds ground pork

3 scallions, chopped

4 cloves garlic, minced

1½ tablespoons minced fresh ginger

½ teaspoon grated orange peel

2 tablespoons hoisin sauce

1 tablespoon soy sauce

1 tablespoon sesame oil

1 teaspoon salt

1 egg yolk

60 square wonton wrappers

Vegetable oil for brushing wontons

1. Adjust oven rack to lowest position. Preheat oven to 475°F.

2. To make the sauce: Mix all the sauce ingredients in a small bowl. Season to taste with salt and pepper. Sauce may be made ahead of time and refrigerated up to 2 days.

3. To make the filling: Place all the filling ingredients in a mixing bowl and use your hands to combine well.

4. Using a 2¾-inch-round biscuit or cookie cutter, cut each wonton wrapper into a round and arrange on waxed paper.

5. Brush one side of each wrapper with vegetable oil. Press rounds, oiled side down, into the cups of a mini-muffin tin. Add a heaping teaspoon of filling to each cup. Bake, in batches, until wonton wrappers are brown and crisp, 10–15 minutes. Transfer to a serving platter and top with sauce. (Wontons may be made ahead of time. Cool, remove from muffin cups, and refrigerate, covered, up to 1 day. Reheat on a baking sheet in a hot oven until warmed through, then top with sauce.)

Yield: About 60 wontons

BOOK CLUB PROFILE

"It was serendipitous that we lunched in a library," says Kathleen Phillips of the genesis of the Lovely Ladies Book Club of Bryan–College Station, Texas, in 1997. Women from St. Andrew's Episcopal Church were invited for lunch at Kathy Culver's home and found themselves surrounded by books. "We learned we all shared a passion for reading," says Phillips, "and when Mary Lou Laubach mentioned that she wished she were in a book club, the Lovely Ladies formed on the spot."

"Our motto is 'absolutely totally temporary and completely changeable,'" says Phillips, a journalist and news coordinator for the Texas A&M University System Agriculture Program. "Our carefully selected annual reading list is always subject to change."

The members—career women and volunteer workers alike—range in age from forty-eight to seventy-seven and enjoy diversity in their reading: Old and new, fiction and nonfiction, mysteries and classics are all on the reading list.

"We love decorations, accessories, and foods to complement our reading," says Phillips. "But more importantly, we love to laugh." The Lovely Ladies enjoy vacationing together and traveled to Savannah, Georgia, after reading *Midnight in the Garden of Good and Evil,* John Berendt's wickedly funny look at life in Savannah. "We've helped each other celebrate and mourn the events of our lives and have become very close," says Phillips. "The Lovely Ladies have some lovely meals to go with our books," adds Phillips. "Meals are the comfort part of the evening. Bonding over food has made us genuine friends."

Meals often complement the books they discuss. Lovely Lady Dianne Stropp created a memorable Kentucky Derby dinner for their discussion of Laura Hillenbrand's *Seabiscuit* (see p. 391), including icy mint juleps (see p. 172), southern fried chicken, cheese grits, and a Kentucky Derby pie, a classic dessert with pecans, chocolate chips, and bourbon. Stropp's table was set with Kentucky Derby tickets, a jockey cap for each Lovely Lady, and roses, a nod to the wreath that adorns the Derby winner.

For their discussion of David McCullough's *John Adams,* Phillips served deviled crab cakes and baked beans in tribute to Adams's New England roots.

For a change of pace, the Lovely Ladies recently agreed to skip literature for a month and review cookbooks. Each member prepared a dish from her favorite cookbook. "We didn't assign any courses, but there was an amazing array of wonderful food and not one of us brought a dessert," says Alma Pruessner, who brought Guinness beef stew and colcannon, an Irish dish of mashed potatoes and cabbage, from a cookbook she had purchased in England. The dinner also included roasted pork tenderloin with dried-cranberry stuffing, spinach loaf, and chilled cucumber soup.

The cultural repression under Mao was the focus of the Lovely Ladies' discussion about *Balzac and the Little Chinese Seamstress.* For a group of women who "devour" books, the forced absence of books in the novel was especially poignant.

"We considered what we would do without our books, and what lengths we would go to to have something to read," says Phillips. "We often come to our book club meetings with sacks of books we have read to share with other members. What treasures they would be for someone who's been told they cannot have them."

There is a scene in *Balzac and the Little Chinese Seamstress* where the protagonists burn books. "Luo, one of the boys, intended the books to revolutionize the seamstress culturally and turn her into a proper wife for the sophisticated man he was sure to become," says Susan Parker of the Lovely Ladies. "The books fulfilled their mission, but in a way Luo never intended."

Members compared their own youths to the lives of the boys in the novel. "I was going through the typical American teenage dramas at the same time these boys were hauling sewage day in and day out," says Dianne Stropp. "And yet, they found humor and continued to grow under adverse conditions. The boys demonstrated the resiliency of the young human soul through their refusal to let their present conditions become their identities."

"Many of the Lovely Ladies wanted to read another work of Dai Sijie—and Balzac!" says Phillips.

More Food for Thought

When they discussed Dai Sijie's *Balzac and the Little Chinese Seamstress*, hostess Kathleen Dyke greeted members of the Lovely Ladies with instructions to remove their shoes—as is customary in China—and handed each a pair of hot pink socks. "We pitter-pattered to the living room to begin our talk, with wontons, appetizers, and wine," says Kathleen Phillips.

Dyke used the book's "seamstress" theme as inspiration for her decorations. She wove a tape measure around miniature spools of thread and miniature parasols, the colorful umbrellas traditionally used by Chinese women to shield themselves from the sun. Travel sewing kits were given as party favors. Her dinner featured orange chicken with apricots and currants, and green tea and orange soufflé (a cold dessert garnished with mandarin orange slices and gingersnaps).

Bee Season

Myla Goldberg

DOUBLEDAY, 2000

(available in paperback from Anchor, 2001)

*B*EE SEASON is the painful tale of a father, mother, and two children, each searching for meaning and acceptance as their family unravels.

The family's descent into chaos is precipitated by nine-year-old Eliza Naumann's discovery of a hidden talent, an aptitude for spelling. Eliza is an indifferent student, placed by her teachers in a class for slow learners. Unexpectedly, she wins the school and district spelling bees, and for the first time, teachers and classmates pay attention to her. More important, Eliza's father, Saul, looks anew at the child he thought had little promise.

Saul, a rabbinical scholar and cantor at the local synagogue, had pinned his vicarious academic dreams on his son, Aaron, an overachiever who seemed destined for the rabbinate. When Eliza's talent for spelling reveals itself, Saul shifts his attention from Aaron to Eliza. He encourages her to explore the teachings of the ancient Kabbalah scholar Abulafia, preparing her to receive *shefa*, or God-knowledge. Eliza's single-minded focus on the discipline borders on the desperate; she hopes her spelling can hold her family together.

While busy with Eliza, Saul fails to notice that his withdrawal from Aaron has left his son angry and hurt. Aaron turns to the Hare Krishnas for the meaning and acceptance that elude him at home. Eliza's mother, Miriam, a brilliant lawyer who fails to connect with her husband and children, finds herself descending deeper into the dark abyss of mental illness.

As each character in *Bee Season* searches for personal and spiritual fulfillment, the family spirals into sad and lonely chaos.

Aaron's choices about food mark the first visible sign that he is breaking away from his family to join another. As a Hare Krishna initiate, Aaron must become a vegetarian. While his sister and parents grab pieces of barbecued chicken at a family dinner, Aaron piles his plate with macaroni and cheese, announcing to all that he is a vegetarian because "it just made sense." However, "he wishes he could describe the delicious meals he's had at the temple, the intensity of the flavors making a convincing case for the food being suffused with Krishna's spirit."

The smells and flavors of foods prepared at the temple seem to draw Aaron deeper into a feeling of acceptance, of being "home." The first breakfast at a weekend temple retreat disappoints Aaron—he feels homesick for Frosted Flakes with bananas, and remembers the way his father magically sliced a banana within its peel with a needle and thread. But later, watching his mentor, Chali, cook *prasadam*, a food whose preparation and consumption is considered integral to devotional service to Krishna, Aaron is drawn toward the temple and away from his father: "Aaron closes his eyes to better appreciate the smell, a mix of spices that has never graced his father's pots, a scent full of promise."

The final act of culinary alienation comes when Aaron makes a vegetarian meal for Saul and Eliza. Since religious guidelines forbid Aaron to prepare *prasadam* outside of his own shrine, he cooks other vegetarian foods—chickpeas in ghee, zucchini and rice—as substitutions. His cooking produces crunchy chickpeas that are barely edible. When Saul asks Aaron if he sampled them while cooking, Aaron explodes: "You're not supposed to taste them. Okay? There are rules. You don't know anything so how am I supposed to talk to you? Don't eat it if you don't like it. Go back to your meat. I'm going to eat in my room." He carries his plate of burned rice and limp zucchini upstairs. The rift between father and son grows ever wider.

CHOCOLATE CHIP
SHORTBREAD COOKIES

In their early years, Eliza and Aaron spent their Friday evenings attending services at Temple Beth Amicha. As is the custom in many American synagogues, worshippers filter into a community hall after services for an *oneg*—a light meal—and conversation.

Temple Beth Amicha's *oneg* features watered-down juice and dry cookies, "chalky shortbreads that crumble into little pieces unless the whole thing is ingested at once." In spite of the food's questionable quality, the event has magical appeal for Aaron and Eliza, who practice strategic placement in order to snag a prime wafer cookie, or, on a birthday, a piece of cake with a flower on it.

We have included a recipe for a much-improved shortbread cookie, slightly crumbly and full of chocolate chips. We suggest strategic placement by the cookie plate to get one before they disappear.

1 cup (2 sticks) butter

½ cup granulated sugar

2 teaspoons vanilla extract

2 eggs

2 cups sifted all-purpose flour

2 cups old-fashioned rolled oats

6 to 12 ounces mini semi-sweet chocolate morsels, to taste

½ cup confectioners' sugar

1. Preheat oven to 325°F.
2. Cream the butter and granulated sugar. Add the vanilla and eggs and mix until combined. Stir in the flour, oats, and chocolate chips and mix well. Chill the dough for easier handling.
3. Roll a teaspoon of dough in your hands and shape into a crescent about 3 inches from tip to tip. Place on an ungreased cookie sheet. Repeat, placing cookies 1 inch apart, until the sheet is full, then bake for 15–20 minutes until just slightly browned.
4. Put confectioners' sugar in a bowl and roll crescents in sugar while they're still warm.

Yield: About 50 cookies

BOOK CLUB PROFILE

Three men and eleven "opinionated females who vociferously defend their positions" make up the Borders Books and Music Best Sellers Book Club of Waipahu, Hawaii. The group has been described as a United Nations of book lovers, with members of Hawaiian, Chinese, Spanish, Irish, French, Polish, Lithuanian, Greek, Portuguese, and Scandinavian descent. Members meet monthly at Borders Books and Music to discuss current bestsellers and "advance publication" books provided by the store. "That's how we discovered Andre Dubus III's *House of Sand and Fog* (see p. 197) even before Oprah announced it as her choice," says member Lillian M. Jeskey-Lubag.

Group members include a social worker, a systems analyst, and military wives, but no one integrates book club ideas into their professional lives like the public school teachers who belong to the group. Using ideas from book club discussions, the teachers promote student dialogue and launch classroom projects. "I'm immensely proud of the teachers in our group," says Jeskey-Lubag, a social worker. "The seeding of ideas is a top priority for them."

Bryan Chun, vice principal at Kaimuki Middle School in Honolulu, saw an opportunity to promote discussion among his faculty when the group read *Bee Season,* a book they particularly enjoyed. Chun introduced *Bee Season* to the faculty, encouraging dialogue around issues the book raises. Subsequently, students, teachers, and several members of the Best Sellers group attended a conference at the University of Hawaii, where author Myla Goldberg discussed the writing process. The students were particularly intrigued and peppered her with questions.

In their discussion, the Best Sellers focused on the harsh treatment that Eliza experienced at the hands of her father. "We felt that the rigors he put her through were tantamount to child abuse," Jeskey-Lubag says. They also speculated about the inspiration for Goldberg's book. Their question was answered when Goldberg explained that a television documentary about children in spelling bees inspired the writing of *Bee Season*.

More Food for Thought

Boston-Area Returned Peace Corps Volunteer book group members Bill Varnell and Mary Knasas brought alphabet cookies from Trader Joe's for her group's discussion of *Bee Season*. "I thought our group of articulate people would have a serious discussion of the book," says member Elizabeth Lang, "but we can also be wildly funny. We spelled out a few words, and then ate our words. But I think it was the *potential* of spelling out words that drew us in and fit so well with the book."

Bel Canto

Ann Patchett

HARPERCOLLINS, 2001

(available in paperback from Perennial, 2002)

A NN PATCHETT's *Bel Canto*, inspired by a true event, opens in an unnamed South American country where the vice president hosts international dignitaries and officials at a birthday party honoring a visiting Japanese businessman, Mr. Hosokawa. A lavish dinner is served: white asparagus in hollandaise, turbot with crispy onions, and pork chops in a cranberry demiglaze.

Mr. Hosakawa's idol, Roxane Coss, the gifted and beautiful lyric soprano, has just finished performing, when the room is plunged into darkness. Terrorists invade the mansion to kidnap the country's president, who, it turns out, is not at the party. Determined to fulfill their mission, the confused, ragtag terrorists take the group of partygoers hostage. They release all the women, except Roxane Coss, whose voice captivates them.

As weeks pass, Roxane's magical singing, the only common language of the hostages and their captors, mesmerizes the group and bridges the barriers between them. Tensions lessen, and for the group of fifty-eight living inside the vice president's mansion, the boundaries between hostage and captor are blurred. As chess games are played, politics discussed, and music performed, friendships are forged and love blooms. For Mr. Hosokawa, who has the opportunity to become acquainted with his idol, Roxane Coss, the world inside the compound is blissful.

The hostages' memories of the fine meal that began their odyssey quickly vanish. The first meals sent in after they are taken captive consist of soda and unappetizing sandwiches.

When the hostages' regular food supplies—casseroles and prepared sandwiches—are replaced by raw vegetables and chickens, Vice President Ruben Iglesias views the unprepared foods as a sign of waning public interest in their ordeal. Iglesias, who "did not know marjoram from thyme" recruits the French diplomat, Simon Thibault, the only hostage with culinary savoir faire, to transform the raw ingredients into dinner. When Thibault realizes the terrorists hold all the kitchen knives, he directs them in chopping vegetables, teaching them how to mince garlic and slice peppers. The camaraderie is momentarily shattered when the diplomat takes the knife to show Ishmael, his young captor, how to peel, seed, and chop an eggplant. Seeing Thibault hold the knife, Beatriz, another terrorist in the kitchen, becomes agitated. The diplomat, with his hands up, proposes a compromise so dinner may be prepared in the proper manner: "Everyone can stand away from me and I can show Ishmael how to peel an eggplant. You keep your gun right on me and if it looks like I'm about to do something funny you may shoot me."

Eggplant Caponata

Ann Patchett liked the idea of pairing an eggplant appetizer recipe with a discussion of *Bel Canto*. She explained to us why she chose to write about eggplant in her novel's pivotal kitchen scene:

I chose the eggplant for the kitchen scene in *Bel Canto* because I think that eggplants are such misunderstood vegetables. If you have a bunch of people trying to cook who don't speak the same language, some of whom have guns, some of whom are in love, it creates an air of confusion that is best represented by the eggplant. It is, after all, a singularly beautiful vegetable, but also impenetrable. It's horrible raw and difficult to know how to cook. It's something that really needs to be mixed with something else in order to work, and how it looks on the outside and how it is on the inside are completely different things. The eggplant makes a fine metaphor, and a fine appetizer.

To help demystify the enigmatic and misunderstood eggplant we mixed ours with onions and peppers—ingredients mentioned in *Bel Canto*'s kitchen scene—to create this delicious caponata, a Sicilian sweet and sour eggplant appetizer. Caponata can be served with crackers or crostini (little toasts) as an appetizer, or served as part of an antipasto or sandwich filling.

4 ripe tomatoes, or 6 ripe Roma tomatoes

3 tablespoons extra-virgin olive oil

2 pounds small eggplant, peeled, seeded, and cut into ¼-inch dice

1 large red bell pepper, seeded and cut into ¼-inch dice

1 large yellow bell pepper, seeded and cut into ¼-inch dice

3 medium onions, chopped

2 cups good-quality pitted green olives, halved

½ cup red wine vinegar

¼ cup water

2 tablespoons sugar	2 tablespoons pine nuts
½ teaspoon salt	2 tablespoons capers
½ teaspoon dried oregano	Salt and freshly ground black pepper to taste

1. Blanch the tomatoes in boiling water for 1 minute, then remove and rinse under cold running water. Peel, seed, and chop tomatoes. Set aside.

2. Heat the oil in a large, heavy skillet. Add the eggplant and sauté, stirring constantly, until soft (15–25 minutes on low). Eggplant may be sautéed in two batches if necessary. Add the peppers, tomatoes, onions, and olives. Cook 10 more minutes, stirring frequently. Remove from the heat.

3. Make a dressing by combining the vinegar, water, sugar, and salt in a bowl. Add to the vegetable mixture along with the oregano and stir well.

4. Toast the pine nuts in a hot skillet until fragrant and lightly browned. Stir the pine nuts and capers into the caponata, mixing well. Season to taste with salt and black pepper.

5. Cover the caponata and allow to cool, then refrigerate at least 6 hours. Serve at room temperature, accompanied by toasted baguette slices.

Yield: 12 to 16 appetizer servings

 BOOK CLUB PROFILE

Guests of the Milwaukee School of Engineering's Great Books Dinner and Discussion Series often find their thoughts and their discussion drifting beyond the book. Tantalizing smells of the multicourse meal being prepared for them waft into the parlor of the MSOE Alumni Partnership Center, where the group congregates for opening comments, drinks, and music.

"You could smell the garlic from the escargots the moment you walked in, and it was heavenly," says Judy Steininger, discussion leader of the meeting to discuss Dan Brown's *The Da Vinci Code* (see p. 85).

Steininger is an emerita professor of American and Third World Literature in MSOE's General Studies Department, which founded the dinner-discussion series in 1996. The monthly meetings have become a unique literary and gourmet experience for guests. The school's alumni center, a turn-of-the-century building with dark wood, high ceilings, and stained glass, is the perfect location.

"It's a breathtaking venue for our meetings," says Steininger. "It's like walking into Bavaria. When we saw this elegant dining facility, we knew we had to serve dinner."

After meeting in the parlor, the group moves to a dining room, where a four-course gourmet meal, inspired by the reading selection, is served with white linen, china, crystal, and flowers. "This is meant to be an elegant dining experience," says Steininger. After dinner, the group returns to the parlor for their book discussion.

The dinner and discussion series sells out quickly, and most guests are not directly affiliated with the school. The series has many regular members but attracts those drawn to a particular reading selection, as well as members of local book clubs from throughout southeastern Wisconsin.

Steininger and four professors from MSOE's Humanities Department take turns leading discussions, choosing a variety of contemporary and classic works for the series. The discussion leaders collaborate with the MSOE catering staff, which creates the dinner menus. "The chefs have been unfailingly creative," says Steininger, "and they always wow us with the dessert."

The lavish dinners have always been connected to the books' themes and have evolved to include food specifically mentioned in the selected novels. Some discussion leaders invent clever names for dishes, and the chefs have fun with the recipe titles, such as "neurotic Caesar salad," served with Jonathan Franzen's *The Corrections,* a novel about a dysfunctional family.

"Many guests are surprised an engineering school sponsors this literary experience," says Dr. David Kent, a discussion leader who is an associate professor and department chair of General Studies at MSOE. "We work hard to reinforce the value of the humanities." Kent facilitates several discussions each year and tries to choose a variety of literature, including Fyodor Dostoyevsky's *The Brothers Karamazov,* Joseph Heller's *Catch-22,* and a recent favorite, Ann Patchett's *Bel Canto.*

Kent hails from Nashville, Tennessee, Patchett's hometown, and was interested in reading her work. "I loved the book. Her writing style is authentic, and the story is gripping," says Kent. "But there is another reason I picked *Bel Canto*: my mother recommended it. She constantly updates me on up-and-coming southern writers. And who can say no to their mom?"

Before dinner, Kent explains why he chose the book and solicits general reactions. "This lets me 'take the temperature' of the group so when we come back together after dinner, I have an idea of points to focus on during our discussion. Many people wanted to discuss the message the book seems to send about the power of music in our lives, as well as the importance of being empathic." To spark discussion, Kent often asks the group to name a character in the novel with whom they would like to have dinner. For most of the group, it was Roxane Coss, the lyric soprano.

The group enjoyed exploring the role of humor in Patchett's novel, such as the fastidious but endearing mannerisms of Ruben Iglesias, the vice president of the unidentified country. "The group thought it amusing that President Masuda could not attend the dinner in the opening scene because he had to watch his favorite soap opera," says Kent.

The group also discussed the extent to which opera appreciation contributed to an understanding of the novel. "Some members asked how realistic it was that Roxane Coss could have such a mesmerizing effect on the audience," says Kent. "But others were opera aficionados and it was easy for them to imagine. Opera singers have the ability to enchant. As someone who has recently fallen in love with opera, I can attest to that."

More Food for Thought

"As the hostage situation drags on in *Bel Canto*, Vice President Iglesias is concerned because the food brought in is increasingly less well prepared, with little attention to detail," says David Kent. Kent says there was no such concern about the meal served at the Milwaukee School of Engineering's Great Books Dinner and Discussion that evening. In fact, the novel inspired MSOE chef Terri Tollefsrud to create a menu including bacon-wrapped water chestnuts, medallions of pork tenderloin, garlic smashed potatoes, green beans almondine, spinach salad with strawberries and mandarin oranges, and for dessert, *xangos*, a Mexican cheesecake. "Several guests said it was one the best meals they had ever eaten," says Kent.

More Food for Thought

"We didn't know in which South American country *Bel Canto* was set," says Suzanne Brust of her St. Paul, Minnesota, book club, "but we had an exchange student from Brazil living with us, so I made a Brazilian seafood stew."

The stew, from *Steve Raichlen's Healthy Latin Cooking: 200 Sizzling Recipes* (Rodale, 1998), was a huge success with the four married couples that discuss literature in their homes after church on Sunday afternoons. "It was really different from our usual fare, but everyone loved it," says Brust. "It was the perfect complement to the discussion of one of our favorite books."

The Bonesetter's Daughter

Amy Tan

....

G. P. PUTNAM'S SONS, 2001

(available in paperback from Ballantine, 2002)

IN CONTEMPORARY San Francisco, Luling, an elderly Chinese widow, struggles with dementia and remains haunted by the notion that a curse from the past still plagues her family.

Her American-born daughter, Ruth, a ghostwriter of self-help books, is distanced from her Chinese heritage and knows little of her mother's past. Ruth faces her own challenges: her dissatisfaction with her harried lifestyle; her relationship with Art, her Caucasian partner, and his two daughters; her career—in addition to her tense relationship with her mother.

Her mother's declining memory and unpredictable behavior alarm Ruth. Caring for the ailing Luling, she discovers her mother's diaries, written in Chinese ideograms, and has them translated. Luling has documented the "things I must not forget"—the story of her childhood in a remote mountain village known as Immortal Heart in the 1930s. Luling's diaries reveal a tragic history she has never been able to communicate to her daughter about the life of her own mother, the daughter of a famous bonesetter, a Chinese doctor who mends bones, and Luling's beloved caregiver, Precious Auntie. Reading of her mother's struggles, Ruth comes to understand Luling's fears and superstitions.

In *The Bonesetter's Daughter*, Amy Tan interweaves Luling's childhood story with that of Luling and Ruth in modern San Francisco, exploring the bond and conflict between mothers and daughters and the often difficult dynamic between first-generation Americans and their immigrant parents.

In Tan's novel, the contrast and conflict between American and Chinese cultures is underscored by the characters' culinary preferences. Ruth's American partner, Art, won't eat the prawns in shells she loves, while the pickled turnips Ruth craves repulse Art's daughters.

This divergence is highlighted during a family gathering Ruth hosts during the Full Moon Festival, a Chinese holiday when family reunites to watch the full moon and eat moon cakes. Ruth has carefully planned this "Chinese Thanksgiving" reunion for Luling and Ruth's Auntie Gal, and for Art, his daughters, his parents, and surprise guests: Art's ex-wife and her family.

The Fountain Court restaurant is packed for the Full Moon Festival. Ruth has selected the Fountain Court "because it was one of the few restaurants where her mother had not questioned the preparation of the dishes, the attitude of the waiters or the cleanliness of the bowls." Ruth knows that no matter what transpires, they will have a delicious meal.

Dinner starts off with some of Luling's favorites, such as jellyfish—dishes the non-Chinese guests find unappealing—which, to Luling's consternation, results in teasing from the children. Ruth becomes tense as things begin to unravel. But, just in time, new dishes arrive, including eggplant sautéed with fresh basil leaves and a lion's head clay pot of meatballs and rice vermicelli. Luling notes that even the Caucasians are enjoying these foods.

San Francisco's Fountain Court is a real restaurant frequented by Amy Tan, and it is often jammed for the Full Moon Festival, says owner Doreen Chin. "With both parents working these days, many people tend to eat out for the holidays," she adds. "They have moon cakes and go home to enjoy the moon."

FOUNTAIN COURT EGGPLANT SAUTÉED WITH FRESH BASIL

The dishes Tan describes in the family reunion dinner scene are on the restaurant's menu. Chef Terry Chin demonstrated preparation of the Eggplant Sautéed with Fresh Basil and the Lion's Head Clay Pot of Meatballs and Rice Vermicelli, two Fountain Court favorites, for *The Book Club Cookbook*. Courtesy of the Chins, you can bring the fabulous flavors of the Fountain Court to your discussion of the *The Bonesetter's Daughter*.

NOTE: The eggplant can be prepared with less oil, but hot deep-frying will retain the lovely purple color. The bean sauce in this recipe is a brown bean sauce made from fermented soybeans, available in Asian groceries (see Purchasing Information, p. 499), and is different from black bean sauce, which has a much sharper flavor.

¾ pound Chinese eggplant (2 to 3 eggplants)
Vegetable oil for deep-frying, plus 2
   tablespoons for stir-frying
1 teaspoon minced garlic

1 teaspoon minced ginger
½ tablespoon brown bean sauce (see note
   above)
¾ cup water

1 tablespoon soy sauce	1 teaspoon cornstarch dissolved in
1½ tablespoons sugar	a little water
½ cup fresh basil leaves, packed	1 teaspoon sesame oil

1. Wash the eggplant; cut off and discard ends. Cut crosswise into thirds, and then quarter each piece lengthwise into wedges.

2. Heat the oil in a wok or deep fryer to 400° F. Add the eggplant and fry for about 1 minute, until the white part starts to brown. Drain eggplant on paper towels.

3. In a wok, heat the 2 tablespoons vegetable oil on high heat. Add the garlic and ginger, and stir-fry just until aromatic. Add the bean sauce and stir briefly. Add the water, soy sauce, and sugar, and stir to combine. Add fried eggplant and basil, and cook about 1 minute, stirring constantly.

4. Add enough cornstarch dissolved in water to thicken the sauce slightly. Stir in the sesame oil. Serve with steamed rice.

Yield: 4 appetizer servings

FOUNTAIN COURT
LION'S HEAD CLAY POT OF MEATBALLS
AND RICE VERMICELLI

Terry Chin recommends using a fatty cut of pork, such as the leg, for the meatballs and slicing and chopping it yourself. Ground pork can be substituted, but the fatty pork produces moist, tender, more flavorful meatballs. You can pan-fry the meatballs instead of deep-frying, but use as much oil as possible and turn the meatballs gently so they don't lose their shape. Although any soup tureen will suffice, the dish is traditionally served in a clay pot to preserve heat.

For the meatballs

1½ pounds fatty pork	2 tablespoons soy sauce
½ tablespoon cornstarch	1 tablespoon sugar
⅓ cup water	½ teaspoon salt

1 teaspoon sesame oil

⅛ teaspoon ground white pepper

¾ teaspoon minced fresh ginger

1 tablespoon Chinese rice wine or sake

Vegetable oil (cottonseed or safflower)
   for deep-frying

For the soup

8–10 cups water

2 tablespoons oil (cottonseed or safflower)

1 teaspoon sugar

⅔ cup soy sauce

1 pound Napa cabbage, cut in 1 x 2-inch pieces

4 dried black Chinese mushrooms, soaked
   in hot water to reconstitute, drained

¼ pound bean-thread rice noodles (saifun),
   soaked in warm water for 20 minutes and
   drained (see Purchasing Information, p. 499)

1. To make the meatballs: Slice pork as thinly as possible, then cut the slices into very thin strips. Mince the strips into tiny pieces.

2. Dissolve the cornstarch in the water. Place pork, soy sauce, sugar, salt, sesame oil, white pepper, ginger, rice wine, and cornstarch mixture in a large bowl. Mix together with your hands until ingredients are completely blended. Pack the mixture down tightly using your palms. Cover and refrigerate 40 minutes.

3. Form the meat mixture into 4 large balls, and place them on an oiled plate to keep them from sticking. Heat 4–5 inches of oil, enough to cover the meatballs, to 400°F in a pot or deep fryer. When oil is hot, add meatballs and fry for 1 minute (if using a smaller pot for frying, fry the meatballs in batches). Remove meatballs and set aside.

4. When the water is hot, add the oil, sugar, soy sauce, cabbage, mushrooms, and a single layer of the meatballs on top. Cover the pot and simmer over high heat for 10–15 minutes. Add noodles, and simmer an additional 15 minutes until meatballs are cooked through and cabbage is very tender. Serve in bowls, giving each person 1 meatball and 1 mushroom.

Yield: 4 servings

Frieda Ling, a reference librarian at the Glendale Public Library in Arizona, formed the Sino-American Book Discussion Group in 2003 to appreciate works of notable Chinese authors. "I believe literature enhances intercultural understanding and helps bridge cultures," says Ling. The group has nine members—seven Caucasian and two Chinese. Ling says she would like to attract more Chinese members, but the area does not have a large Chinese population.

Ling was motivated to begin the group in part from her experience teaching children's literature from a multicultural perspective at York University in Toronto, Canada. "That experience allowed me to witness firsthand how literature can impact human relationships by showing us how unique and different, and yet the same we all are," says Ling. "It allows us to better appreciate our own heritage as well as that of others."

Ling has introduced culinary activities to her book club, such as treating the group to a Chinese meal of shrimp, fish, and other delicacies as prepared in Amy Tan's *The Joy Luck Club* and Mei Ng's *Eating Chinese Food Naked*. She serves foods associated with traditional Chinese festivities—sweet lotus seeds for the Lunar Year; *zongzi,* a special meat-and-rice dumpling for the Dragon Boat Festival; and moon cakes, a traditional sweet cake with mashed lotus and egg-yolk fillings, for the Mid-Autumn Festival.

Ling's group reads fiction and nonfiction by Chinese authors published in English or in English translation, and the group plans to expand the list to include Asian authors as well as non-Asian authors writing about Asia. Ling provides comprehensive background information about the author, history, time period, and geography and culture for each reading selection, and members take turns reviewing the plot of the story. For Nien Cheng's memoir, *Life and Death in Shanghai,* Ling shared details of the history and impact of the Cultural Revolution, the subject of the book, and provided a photo display of Old Shanghai. For Patricia-Mei Natasha's *Bound Feet and Western Dress,* a book about the first wife of Zhu Chi-Mo, a modern Chinese poet, Ling explained the now-outlawed customs of bound feet and arranged marriages. Whenever available, Ling reads both the English and Chinese versions of the reading selection and compares them for the group.

Ling chose Amy Tan's *The Bonesetter's Daughter* to kick off her new book discussion program. "Amy Tan was an ideal first author," says Ling. "She is a popular Chinese-American author known for her intriguing plots, lively characterizations, and universal themes."

Ling says her group discusses both the uniqueness and universality of each title they read, and although there are many themes common to all of Tan's stories, "the author never fails to offer a twist that gives the familiar a sense of freshness."

Tan's abundance of universal themes—family secrets, cultural clashes, the immigrant experience, the search for identity, intercultural marriage, and caring for the aged—kept the group's conversation lively. "We had a special interest in the intergenerational conflict focused upon the mother-daughter relationship," says Ling.

The exotic backdrop of the drama—an isolated village in postrevolutionary China—sparked the group's interest. "The feudal tradition still had a strong hold on people's mindset and lives," says Ling, "such as ink making and the revered art of calligraphy." The group admired Tan's gift with language. "Tan can be ornately descriptive with the most ordinary of objects," says Ling, "or express the most profound thoughts in a few simple words."

More Food for Thought

Guests of the Milwaukee School of Engineering's Great Books Dinner and Discussion Series enjoyed a Chinese feast when they discussed *The Bonesetter's Daughter*. The menu featured sweet-and-sour meatballs, Peking duck with vegetables, white rice, mandarin oranges on salad greens, and melon balls in coconut, with a fortune cookie for dessert.

"In the book, there was a search for Peking man, so Peking duck seemed an appropriate choice," said Susannah Locke, an MSOE humanities professor who facilitated the discussion.

For her group's discussion of *The Bonesetter's Daughter*, Tandy Seery of the LunaChics Literary Guild in Tallahassee, Florida, served homemade meat and vegetarian eggrolls, vegetable fried rice, and stir-fried tofu with Chinese vegetables. She topped the meal with her own special creation, homemade mango ice cream.

Cane River

Lalita Tademy

WARNER BOOKS, 2002

(available in paperback from Warner, 2002)

WHEN LALITA TADEMY left her job as an executive at a Fortune 500 company to research her family's history, she did not know where her work would lead. After two years of intense genealogical study, Tademy published *Cane River*, an epic novel based on the lives of four generations of her family's women—slave and free.

Tademy's fictionalized account begins in 1834. It is set on a nineteen-mile stretch of Louisiana's Cane River, where a community of Creole plantation owners, slaves, and free blacks coexist. Whites, free blacks, and slaves attend the same Catholic church. Slaves' and plantation owners' children grow up and play together and interracial relationships are tolerated.

This is the world in which Elizabeth, Tademy's great-great-great-great-grandmother, and her daughter Suzette live. Elizabeth toils in the cookhouse of the Louisiana plantation of Françoise and Louis Derbanne. Young Suzette helps her mother, performs chores in the big house, and is a companion for Oreline, the Derbannes' daughter.

Despite the community's outward appearance of harmony, however, slave girls suffer a quiet indignity. As a young girl, Suzette is repeatedly raped by Louis Derbanne's French cousin, Eugène Daurat, and eventually bears him two children. Suzette's daughter, Philomène, meets the same fate as her mother, bearing eight children to a plantation owner she does not love. So begins the long line of increasingly light-skinned progeny, some of whom can eventually pass for white.

Yet, as Tademy's forebears knew well, neither light skin nor emancipation could ensure a stable future for the family. In 1865, the family moves onto land secured for them by Narcisse Fredieu, the father of Philomène's children, where amidst momentary peace and unity they celebrate Sunday family dinners together. But the country's growing postwar resentment toward free blacks—and interracial unions—rears up a generation later, portending the region's long, difficult path toward racial harmony and acceptance.

The Natchitoches region of Louisiana, where the events of *Cane River* unfold, has seen a remarkable commingling of cultures, which is evident in its food. Although Tademy's novel focuses on French planters and African slaves, other Europeans—English, Spanish, German, Italian—arrived throughout the eighteenth century, establishing their own communities. The offspring of intermarriages of these European, African, and Native American groups became known as Creoles.

Not surprisingly, Creole food represents a marriage of many cuisines. "Here in Louisiana, we're the gumbo," says chef and culinary historian John Folse, who has written seven books on Louisiana cooking. "Even within this area, there's a great diversity of recipes. If a Frenchman married an Italian, their gumbo would be different from that of some other cultural pairing. The Spanish word *creola* means 'mixture'—just like Crayola crayons are a mixture of colors. The diversity of Creole food is tremendous."

In the opening pages of *Cane River,* Elizabeth is preparing a meal for Oreline's birthday dinner. It includes tasso jambalaya, a food that beautifully illustrates this diversity. According to Folse, tasso, pork rubbed with spicy seasonings and then smoked, originated with the Spanish. Jambalaya, a mixture of rice, meats, and seafood, emerged from the French, Spanish, and Italian Creole desire to re-create a beloved Mediterranean rice dish, paella. Many Ivory Coast slaves, Folse says, were brought to the colonies for their expertise growing rice and grain. The name of the dish itself—jambalaya—embodies its heritage: *jambon* (French for "pork"), *à la* (French), and *ya-ya* (an African word for "rice").

More important to the women of *Cane River* than the origin of the foods they prepare is the skill and camaraderie of cooking. The family matriarch, Elizabeth, hones her skills in the plantation cookhouse, and Suzette learns at her side. As a free woman, Elizabeth presides over Sunday dinner preparations, offering advice on "coaxing the lumps out of gravy, whipping the butter and sugar together to get the fluffiness for sweet-potato pie, and heating the grease exactly hot enough, the secret to frying the best chicken." In slavery and in freedom, Elizabeth's culinary skills define her.

JOAN AND LALITA'S PEACH COBBLER

When we asked Lalita Tademy about the meaning of food in *Cane River,* she told us that "food is as necessary to a southern family's story as oxygen is to the rest of the world, whether during the heyday of Cane River, Louisiana, in the eighteen hundreds or today."

Cobblers, deep-dish baked fruit desserts covered with a layer of crust or cake, had become commonplace in the South by the 1860s. In *Cane River*, Elizabeth prepares a peach cobbler for Oreline's birthday, adding an extra cup of sugar to "make sure [it] bubbles up nice and sweet."

Culinary historian John Folse sees the peach cobbler as an example of a larger trend: blacks' strong influence on southern culinary traditions, a phenomenon he calls "the black hand in the pot." Although Folse credits several cultures with the peach cobbler—the English, who likely brought the concept to Louisiana; the Spanish, who planted peach trees throughout the Spanish colonies; and the French, who already ate a cobblerlike like *croustade*—southern blacks "grabbed the cobbler concept and probably kept it alive. Even in their own cabins, the black slaves were the cooks of the South. They had a heavy influence in maintaining traditions."

Lalita Tademy's family recipe for peach cobbler emerged from this long culinary tradition. Cobblers are a highly flexible dessert, and over the years their toppings have taken various forms, from thick spoonfuls of biscuit dough to dough rolled and fitted atop the fruit to dough layered with the fruit. The Tademy family recipe, given by Tademy's sister, Joan Tademy Lothery ("the real cook in the family, after my mother, of course," says Tademy), uses a thick crust layered with fruit, a common form for southern cobblers. Lothery told us that her recipe has been passed from mother to daughter.

"Because a good deal of the passing down has been via observation of the cooking process, which has included a pinch of this, a handful of that, or an eyeball of how much liquid to add to get the desired consistency, I have had to approximate measurements for this recipe. I hope this is sufficient, as most good creations lie 'in the touch.'"

And Lothery adds, "Don't forget the ice cream!"

For the crust

3 cups all-purpose flour

2 tablespoons sugar

1 teaspoon baking powder

¼ teaspoon salt

¾ cup (1½ sticks) chilled butter, cut into
  small pieces

½ cup milk mixed with ¼ cup ice water

For the filling

8 cups fresh peaches, peeled, pitted, and sliced,
  or 8 cups frozen peach slices, thawed and
  drained (see Purchasing Information, p. 499)

1 cup sugar

4 teaspoons all-purpose flour

1¼ teaspoons ground cinnamon

8 tablespoons (1 stick) butter, cut into
  small pieces

1. Preheat oven to 400°F. Lightly butter a 9x9-inch baking dish.

2. To make the crust: Sift together the flour, sugar, baking powder, and salt into a large bowl. Cut the butter into the flour mixture using a pastry blender or a fork until it forms a crumbly meal. Add the milk and ice water, and stir with a fork until a pastry ball forms. Knead gently for 4 or 5 turns, and divide dough into two balls, one twice the size of the other.

3. On a lightly floured surface, roll the larger ball of dough into a 9x26-inch rectangle. Roll out the second ball to form a 9x9-inch square. Set aside.

4. To make filling: In a large bowl, toss the peaches gently with the sugar, flour, and cinnamon.

5. Cut the larger pastry into four 6½x9-inch strips. Line each side of baking dish with a strip, allowing the pastry to hang over each side by 4½ inches. Spread half the peach mixture in baking dish. Dot with 4 tablespoons of butter pieces.

6. Lay the smaller square of pastry over top of peaches. Add remaining peach mixture, dot with another 4 tablespoons of butter, and sprinkle with 3 tablespoons of water.

7. Take the side-wall pastry overlap and fold over into center, joining together to cover the top of the cobbler. Be careful not to stretch the dough. Cut several slits in the top crust for steam vents.

8. Bake 25 minutes. Reduce heat to 375°F and bake an additional 25–35 minutes, or until the crust is golden brown and the filling bubbles at the edges. Cool for 15 minutes before serving.

Yield: 8 to 12 servings

BOOK CLUB PROFILE

At South Seattle Community College, half the students consider themselves ethnic minorities— African American, Asian-Pacific American, Chicano/Hispanic/Latino, and Native American. In this multiracial environment, building bridges of communication is essential.

Promoting communication is a key goal of the college's Office of Diversity and Retention. Cessa Heard-Johnson, director of the office, hoped to help the college realize its mission when she established the DRUM (Diverse Readings to Understand Multiculturalism) Book Club in 2001.

"We discuss books that offer insight into diverse cultures," Heard-Johnson says. "We choose books that help people get to know more about a particular ethnic group, whether or not they belong to that group. It is our hope that by reading and discussing these books, we will break down the barriers that divide us."

Heard-Johnson chooses one book each academic quarter. Staff, students, and faculty of the college are invited to attend one of two possible discussion groups. Group size averages about ten, and each group meets three times per quarter: once for an introductory session, and twice to discuss the chosen book.

DRUM Book Club meetings generally attract people of various ethnicities, and women usually outnumber men. The theme of the book often determines who attends meetings. When the group discussed James McBride's *The Color of Water* (see p. 77), about an inter-racial marriage, eight of the twenty participants identified themselves as biracial or multi-racial. Julie Otsuka's *When the Emperor Was Divine*, about a Japanese-American family interned during World War II, drew a largely Asian–Pacific American crowd, although African Americans, Latinos, and Caucasians also participated.

Heard-Johnson selected Lalita Tademy's *Cane River* to coincide with the college's annual Juneteenth festivities. The oldest known celebration of the ending of slavery, Juneteenth dates back to June 19, 1865, two years after Abraham Lincoln's Emancipation Proclamation, when Union soldiers marched into Galveston, Texas, to announce that the war had ended and the slaves were free. The reason for the delay in informing slaves of their freedom still provokes debate. Nonetheless, the freed slaves and their descendants came to regard June 19 as their official day of freedom, and began a tradition of revelry—barbecues, horseback riding, and fishing—that continues to this day.

In keeping with the day's focus on remembrance, in 2003, South Seattle Community College hosted a variety of activities on campus, including an interpretive dance performance of the Middle Passage, the grueling ocean crossing imposed on enslaved Africans, and a talk by a representative of the National Association for the Advancement of Colored People on current views of reparations for slave descendants. Participants also sampled a variety of traditional soul foods—collard greens (see p. 150), hot-water cornbread, peach cobbler, sweet-potato pie (see p. 423), and roasted yams—while learning about the importance of these foods during slavery.

The DRUM Book Club's discussion of *Cane River* in the month following Juneteenth complemented the celebration beautifully. "We wanted people to know more about slavery, and *Cane River* put a personal face on the institution," says Heard-Johnson. "We came to know these women so well. We all felt like we could relate to these women, regardless of race."

The diverse group of students, staff members, and faculty that gathered to discuss the book included eight African Americans, four Caucasians, three Asian Americans, two Latinos, and two Native Americans—all women. They immediately found common ground in their shared gender. "As women, group members spoke about how they had been socialized to nurture and to take care of family, just as the women in the book were struggling to take care of family in the best way they could," says Heard-Johnson. "We started talking about what makes a good mother."

Tademy's portrayal of the breaking up of families also resonated with the group. "How do you destroy a people?" asks Heard-Johnson. "You go after the family." All the ethnic groups represented at the meeting seemed to have suffered some trauma related to threats to the family. Says Heard-Johnson, "The Native Americans talked about the Indian Removal Act, when the legislature said the children were to be removed and raised in boarding schools. A Jewish woman spoke of the *Kindertransporte* in Nazi Germany, which removed children from their homes. And the Asian Americans talked about the Japanese internment camps during World War II. Even in modern times, families are broken apart when a husband or a child is removed from a household. Everyone, regardless of race, could relate to this book, and to what was happening to these slave families."

Finally, the group turned to the issue of the changes that the passage of time visits on a family. In *Cane River,* the older generation tried to protect the younger ones from exposure to stories about slavery; the light-skinned matriarch of the last generation portrayed in the book did not want anyone with dark skin coming into her house. "What does that do, to purposely bleach the line?" says Heard-Johnson. "That started a whole conversation about interracial dating, interracial relationships, and passing"—that is, the practice of light-skinned African Americans passing for white.

More Food for Thought

Although members of the DRUM Book Club usually bring bag lunches, group facilitator Cessa Heard-Johnson made an exception for *Cane River*, preparing traditional southern foods—sweet-potato pudding, hot-water cornbread, and macaroni and cheese—for the discussion.

"So much of the book involved families making food and bonding in the kitchen," says Heard-Johnson. "The group talked about how much the heart of family and the heart of home was in the kitchen. Even though, early on, the women were slaves, there was still the expectation that they would be able to take care of their family. They had to know how to cook."

After reading *Cane River*, Talk About, a book club in Lafayette, Louisiana, took a tour of Louisiana's Laura Plantation in Vacherie, followed by dinner at a Cajun restaurant. Talk About members enjoyed classic Cajun dishes—chicken and sausage gumbo, crayfish étouffée and rice, potato salad (see p. 187), banana pudding, and strong coffee. "Walking through the plantation mansion and slave quarters, and strolling through grounds which duplicated *Cane River*'s setting, brought the novel vividly to life for us," says Nancy Colby, Talk About's facilitator. "We felt the presence of the characters."

The Minga Suma Book Club of Los Angeles ate homemade Creole food—seafood gumbo, crawfish étouffée, seafood salad, peach cobbler, and wine—for the group's discussion of *Cane River*. "Every time someone took a bite, we started talking about Creole food," says Shareta Caldwell, cofounder of the group. "We felt the food helped us identify more with the characters of *Cane River*. It set the mood for the meeting."

Chocolat

Joanne Harris

VIKING, *1999*

(available in paperback from Penguin, 2000)

*C*HOCOLAT BEGINS with the arrival of Vianne Rocher, a single mother, and her six-year-old daughter, Anouk, in the tiny old-fashioned French village of Lansquenet-sous-Tannes in the 1950s. In a blatant contradiction to the austere Lenten fast, Vianne opens La Céleste Praline, a shop featuring mouthwatering chocolate confections and luscious hot chocolate drinks.

With the exception of eighty-year-old Armande Voizin, the village's eldest resident, a self-proclaimed witch who quickly befriends Vianne and Anouk, the villagers are not welcoming. The straitlaced, gossipy locals are wary of Vianne. The stern parish priest, Francis Reynaud, quickly takes offense at the chocolaterie's location opposite the village church, finding the shop's indulgences at odds with the modesty and piety he preaches. Reynaud deems "the concentration of sweetness" unwholesome, as he tries to avoid the temptation of gazing at shelves of confections and inhaling "bewildering scents" emanating from across the street.

Vianne, a sorceress's daughter who shares her mother's distrust of the clergy, further affronts Reynaud when she makes it clear that she does not attend church. Despite Reynaud's cautions to the villagers and attempts to curb her "pernicious" influence, Vianne draws many of them into the chocolaterie with her gift for knowing the favorite chocolate of each customer—"like a fortune teller reading palms."

One by one the troubled townsfolk, such as Guillaume Duplessis, concerned about his ailing dog, and the battered wife Joséphine Muscat, are transformed. As they abandon themselves to temptation and find their taste for pleasure in chocolate brazils and double-chocolate truffles that melt in their mouths, their secrets and troubles seem to melt away. Love is reawakened and hidden yearnings unlocked. Reynaud even discovers his parishioners, their appetites for pleasure and happiness aroused, eating chocolates during confession.

When Vianne announces a Grand Festival of Chocolate, to commence Easter Sunday, Reynaud considers this the ultimate insult to the Catholic church and a mockery of everything the holiday stands for. His campaign against the chocolate shop leads to a confrontation between the austere priest and his villagers.

HOT COCOA

Vianne pours steaming mugs of hot chocolate throughout *Chocolat*. On La Céleste Praline's opening day, her pot of *chocolat chaud* sits untouched as she and Anouk wait for customers. They finally help themselves to a cup, Anouk's topped with crème chantilly and chocolate curls and, for Vianne, black chocolate "stronger than espresso." As the villagers warm to her chocolate, Vianne knows just which cocoa will tantalize each patron: for Roux, a river Gypsy, black chocolate laced with Kahlúa; for Joséphine, chocolate espresso with cognac and chocolate chips. As Armande tastes her mocha with a splash of Kahlúa, she comments, "This is better than anything I remember, even from childhood."

The smell of warm chocolate simmering on the stove filled the house all day as Hope Roel prepared for the Literary Society of San Diego's *Chocolat* meeting. "*Chocolat* was a sensuous feast for our literary society," says Roel, who loves to bake with chocolate. Roel whipped up an assortment of treats: chocolate fondue, brownies, and rich, thick hot cocoa made from scratch.

Roel prepared cocoa following a recipe from *The Joy of Cooking*, by Irma S. Rombauer and Marion Rombauer Becker (New American Library, 1964). Roel says she served this classic recipe for cocoa with whipped cream and Kahlúa, a Mexican coffee liqueur, topped with grated chocolate shavings to emulate the coffee bar atmosphere and hot chocolate offerings at La Céleste Praline. We're sure it will warm the souls of your book club when you sit down to discuss *Chocolat*.

NOTE: To scald milk, heat the milk in a heavy-bottomed pan over low heat. Stir occasionally, bringing milk just below the boiling point. When bubbles begin to form around the edge of the pan, remove from heat.

1 cup boiling water
¼ cup unsweetened cocoa powder
2–4 tablespoons sugar
⅛ teaspoon salt

½ teaspoon ground cinnamon
¹⁄₁₆ teaspoon ground cloves and/or ground nutmeg
3 cups scalded milk

1. Fill the bottom of a double boiler half full of of water. Bring to a boil over high heat.
2. Combine the boiling water, cocoa, sugar, and salt in the top of a double boiler. Place top directly over the heat source and stir for 2 minutes over low heat.
3. Add the cinnamon, cloves, and/or nutmeg and place top over the bottom of the double boiler. Add the milk; stir and heat through. Cover the cocoa and keep over hot water for 10 more minutes. Beat with a wire whisk before serving.

Yield: 4 servings

CHOCOLATE FONDUE

When Vianne caters Armande Voizin's birthday party, she prepares Chocolate Fondue for dessert. "Make it on a clear day—cloudy weather dims the gloss on the melted chocolate," says Vianne in the novel. She also recommends dipping cake and fruit in the chocolate mixture.

Hope Roel sliced strawberries, along with bananas, croissants, breads, and other dippables for the fondue. Her recipe, from Natalie Haughton's *365 Great Chocolate Desserts* (HarperCollins, 1996), is simple and delicious, perfect for any weather.

1 pound bittersweet or semisweet chocolate
1 cup heavy cream
2 tablespoons rum

Strawberries, bananas, pineapple, croissant,
or cake, cut into bite-size pieces

In a 2-quart nonmetal bowl, combine the chocolate and heavy cream. Microwave on high power until the chocolate is melted when stirred, 2–2½ minutes. Heat an additional 1–1½ minutes until warm throughout. Stir in the rum. Transfer to fondue pot and keep warm until ready to serve.

Yield: 8 servings

"You name it we have it," says member Diana Girard of her NBA (No Boys Allowed) Reading Circus book club in Miami, whose members are Cuban, Cuban American, Venezuelan, Costa Rican, Jewish, and Anglo-Saxon.

Girard, who is Cuban American, says diversity adds much to their discussions, which usually revolve around contemporary fiction. "Everyone has something to share," says Girard. "When we read Anita Diamant's *The Red Tent* [see p. 374] and Elinor Lipman's *The Inn at Lake Devine,* the Jewish members had a lot more input to the discussion." Similarly, the Cuban members had much to share when the NBA discussed *Blessed by Thunder: Memoir of a Cuban Girlhood* by Flor Fernandez Barrios, and Girard says that their varied political outlooks—some members are quite liberal, while others are conservative—also make for interesting discussions.

Seven of the ten NBA members are attorneys, and the group also includes a judge, a flower boutique owner, and a real estate agent. Girard, a homemaker, mother, and former airport employee, says she was invited to join because the mostly legal group aimed to diversify in order to limit "talking shop."

NBA founder Jacquie Valdespino says she formed the club to fill the postcollege void, missing the times she and friends would "just sit around talking about great authors." She and friend Marcia Soto picked women whom they liked, but did not necessarily know well, to join the NBA. "The club has evolved and grown beyond all my expectations," says Valdespino. "We come together to discuss literature, but our friendship and camaraderie are the highlight of our evenings, as we share trials, tribulations, and joys each month. Going to the book club meetings is like getting a hug."

Diana Girard says the group started preparing meals because many members are amazing cooks. "These women are successful attorneys, but they also cook like Martha Stewart," says Girard. And they enjoy foods that pertain to the books they are reading. For Bapsi Sidhwa's *An American Brat,* about an Indian girl who immigrated to the United States, the menu included samosas (small turnovers), *kuku paka* (a chicken dish made with curry and coconut milk), and Indian tea. Sushi, beef and vegetables, and green tea were served with Arthur Golden's novel *Memoirs of a Geisha* (see p. 255), and brisket, potato latkes, and mandel bread (Jewish biscotti) with *The Inn at Lake Devine,* by Elinor Lipman, a novel about a Jewish girl who is intrigued by a Vermont inn that doesn't allow Jews as guests.

Joanne Harris's *Chocolat* was selected by meeting host Patricia Giralt simply because she loves chocolate, but it became a favorite of the NBA. *Chocolat*'s juxtaposition of good and evil was a major conversation topic. "Vianne Rocher opens a chocolate shop across from a church," says Valdespino, "and this simple act highlights the conflicts between good and evil, between saints and sinners, that run throughout the book. The local priest finds the 'pleasure' of chocolate an act of defiance against the Church, and when Vianne announces her Easter Chocolate Festival, it becomes an all-out war."

NBA members could not understand the priest's maliciousness. "We wondered why a French priest would be concerned about a chocolate shop, in a country filled with chocolate shops," says Valdespino.

Deborah White-Labora, a judge serving in the Domestic Violence Division of the Eleventh Judicial Circuit in Miami-Dade County, offered insight into the character of Joséphine, the battered wife in the novel. Like many victims of domestic violence, Joséphine withstood humiliation that escalated to physical violence. As White-Labora explained, Joséphine found her "safe space" within the chocolate shop, surrounded by inviting confections.

Valdespino says the discussion stimulated their chocolate cravings, and after the discussion, the NBA indulged in a mini–chocolate festival featuring Patricia Giralt's bonbons and French crêpes. "The story is irresistible," says Valdespino. "Much like chocolate, it has many layers and all are delicious."

More Food for Thought

In Waco, Texas, the Black Madonna Book Group members brought family recipes that had been handed down as well as newer chocolate creations for their *Chocolat* feast. Juli Rosenbaum made her secret dark-chocolate cake, a rich dessert made with Kahlúa and topped with chocolate frosting that Rosenbaum says "has evolved over the years at her house. The Black Madonnas also enjoyed coffee ice cream pie made with an Oreo-cookie crust, coffee ice cream, whipped cream with Kahlúa, and hot fudge sauce—this from Julie Burleson, who along with club member Suzy Nettles runs the Mud Pie Cooking School for children in Waco.

More Food for Thought

For her Contemporary Book Discussion Club's *Chocolat* get-together, Carol Goewey of Tempe, Arizona, served Godiva chocolates, chocolate-covered nuts and pretzels, chocolate cookies, and cocoa. She also made chocolate dirt cake from a recipe she uses for her children's birthday parties: fill small plastic dishes with chocolate pudding, top with a few gummy worms, and sprinkle with "dirt"— crumbled Oreo cookies. "I thought it would be fun to serve this cake to my grown-up friends," says Goewey.

The Coldest Winter Ever

Sister Souljah

WASHINGTON SQUARE PRESS, *1999*

(available in paperback from Pocket, 2000)

HIP-HOP ARTIST, writer, and political activist Sister Souljah casts herself as a character in her first novel, a gritty portrayal of the urban drug culture and violence in New York's African-American community. *The Coldest Winter Ever* is a platform for the author's views on a number of issues, including drugs, sex, and community building.

Winter, the wealthy teenage daughter of a powerful Brooklyn drug lord, Ricky Santiaga, is savvy, sexy, street smart, and spoiled. Santiaga gives Winter, her mother, and her three sisters every luxury, and Winter's world of self-indulgence revolves around expensive clothes, the worship of rap stars, partying, and making herself appealing to men. Although Winter takes up with a "sugar daddy"—from whom she obtains money and rides in exchange for sexual favors—and other men, the mysterious Midnight, her father's employee, is the real object of Winter's affection. Midnight, a devotee of Sister Souljah, is quiet, serious and indifferent to Winter's many attempts to seduce him.

When Winter's father moves the family from the Brooklyn projects to a Long Island mansion, separating them from the life they knew, a series of misfortunes ensues. Winter's comfortable life begins to unravel quickly: Her father is arrested, the family's possessions are seized, her sisters are sent to foster homes, and her mother becomes a drug addict.

The story of Winter's survival and decline then unfolds. After a brief stay in a Brooklyn group home for teenagers, a friend brings Winter to a home Sister Souljah established to help troubled youth. Winter is skeptical of Sister Souljah's ability to help, but believes Sister Souljah may lead her to Midnight. But her failure to heed Sister Souljah's message and her continued attraction to a decadent lifestyle present a cautionary tale about poverty, racism, and values in contemporary urban America.

Winter prefers her food on the spicy side: Jamaican beef patties, ginger beer, and drinks with Alizé, a passion fruit–flavored liqueur, are staples of her diet. At one of Souljah's womanhood meetings, Winter scoffs at the vegetables and dips as "rabbit food."

While living at Souljah's, Winter has to feed herself. But Winter invests the last of her food money in an expensive new dress, aiming to be the "baddest bitch in the universe," with her sights set on seducing Souljah's friend, the popular rapper GS, at his birthday party: "I knew if I could hook him, my problems would be over. Life would be all Range Rovers, rugs, chips, cheddar and pleasure."

Stephanie Groves's
Spicy Buffalo Wings

Buffalo wings are a favorite of Winter's. She orders Buffalo wings from room service during a hotel-room party, and Buffalo wings are among the finger foods served at the rapper GS's birthday party, which Winter attends.

Distinguished by a spicy pepper sauce and accompanied by blue-cheese dressing and celery sticks, Buffalo wings have their roots in Buffalo, New York. Buffalo's Anchor Bar claims to have originated the recipe. Anchor Bar history has it that chef and owner Teressa Bellissimo deep-fried chicken wings, coating them with a spicy sauce. "The wings were an instant hit and it didn't take long for people to flock to the bar to experience this new eating sensation," writes Ivano Tuscani, the restaurant's executive chef, on the Anchor Bar website. "From that point on, Buffalo wings became a regular part of the menu at the Anchor Bar."

In *Third Helpings* (Penguin, 1984), a collection of culinary essays, Calvin Trillin explains that he "did not truly appreciate the difficulties historians face" until he attempted to chronicle the history of Buffalo wings. While acknowledging the Anchor Bar's claim to inventing the wing, Trillin writes that the distinctive wings are thought to be rooted in Buffalo's African-American culture, originating at John Young's Buffalo restaurant, Wings n' Things, in the mid-1960s.

Either way, the Buffalo phenomenon has gone nationwide. Tasty, inexpensive, and easy to make, chicken wings took flight from the Northeast to bars, restaurants, and fast-food chains across the country, making a permanent mark on American culinary culture by the 1980s.

Stephanie Groves, cofounder of two chapters of the Go On Girl! Book Club in Indianapolis, Indiana, contributed this recipe for Spicy Buffalo Wings. "Although I'm not a big fan of blue cheese, I never serve my hot wings without it," says Groves. This is a version her book club loves, and it is sure to spice up your group's discussion of *The Coldest Winter Ever.*

NOTE: These wings may be made ahead of time: Follow instructions through to coating wings with butter sauce, then cover the baking dish and refrigerate until ready to eat. Reheat in oven as indicated.

We offer two blue-cheese sauces for your Buffalo wings. The first is a more "gourmet" dressing, the second a traditional Buffalo wings dipping sauce with a very strong blue-cheese flavor.

2 pounds chicken wings (about 24)

1 tablespoon seasoned salt

1 tablespoon garlic powder

1½ teaspoons lemon pepper

1½ quarts or more vegetable oil for deep-frying

4 tablespoons butter, melted

4 teaspoons hot sauce (such as Tabasco)

1 teaspoon white vinegar

Blue-Cheese Dressing or Blue-Cheese Dipping Sauce (see below)

Crudités for dipping, such as celery sticks and carrots

1. Preheat the oven to 350°F.
2. Cut off tips of chicken wings at top joint and discard tips. Cut each of the remaining wings into two pieces. Rinse the wings and dry well with paper towels. Sprinkle wings all over with seasoned salt, garlic powder, and lemon pepper.
3. Heat the oil in a deep fryer or pot to 375°F. If not using a fryer with a built-in temperature gauge, it is helpful to clip a high-temperature thermometer, such as a candy thermometer, to the side of the pot to regulate the heat. Add the chicken wings, a few at a time. Try to keep the temperature between 350° and 375°F while frying. Deep-fry for 6–10 minutes or until crisp and golden brown. Remove the wings and drain on brown paper or paper towels. Continue until all wings have been fried.
4. Stir together the butter, hot sauce, and vinegar (adjust the amount of hot sauce for your guests). Place one-third of the wings in a large bowl and pour some of the sauce over them. Toss to coat well. Transfer wings to a baking dish. Repeat the process with the remaining wings. Heat in oven about 20 minutes before serving.
5. Serve with crudités and Blue-Cheese Dressing or Blue-Cheese Dipping Sauce.

Yield: 6 to 8 servings

BLUE-CHEESE DRESSING

3 eggs	*1 teaspoon Worcestershire sauce*
¼ cup chopped onions	*½ teaspoon salt*
¼ cup chopped celery	*½ teaspoon white pepper*
½ teaspoon minced garlic	*⅛ teaspoon cayenne pepper*
1 tablespoon fresh lemon juice	*2 cups olive oil*
1 tablespoon apple cider vinegar	*1 cup (4 ounces) crumbled blue cheese*

Place eggs, onions, celery, garlic, lemon juice, vinegar, Worcestershire, salt, white pepper, and cayenne in a blender or food processor. Blend for 20 seconds, then, with the motor running, add the oil in a thin stream. Continue to blend for 45 seconds to 1 minute after oil is added, or until thick. Place dressing in a bowl and stir the blue cheese in by hand until well mixed. Refrigerate until ready to use.

Yield: About 3 cups

BLUE-CHEESE DIPPING SAUCE

1 cup (4 ounces) blue cheese	*1 tablespoon fresh lemon juice*
½ cup mayonnaise	*1 tablespoon white wine vinegar*
½ cup sour cream	*Several dashes of hot pepper sauce to taste*

Mash the blue cheese in a mixing bowl, leaving some small lumps. Whisk in the mayonnaise and sour cream until blended. Add the lemon juice, vinegar, and pepper sauce and whisk to blend well. Adjust seasonings. Cover and refrigerate until ready to serve.

Yield: 1½ cups

BOOK CLUB PROFILE

According to its mission statement, the Go On Girl! Book Club, Inc. (GOG), aims to increase the reading and appreciation of works by African-American authors and to provide a forum for exchange of ideas and opinions. Through a highly organized structure and clear set of rules, GOG is succeeding: More than thirty chapters have blossomed in ten states, and the organization continues to grow.

The rules governing book selection and group composition set by the national organization ensure unity among its chapters. Membership in each chapter is capped at twelve, although there is no limit to the number of chapters in each state. At its annual conference, the national GOG organization establishes the reading list for the year. Although the committee chooses books from several genres—including fantasy–science fiction, historical fiction, mystery-suspense, classics, and international—all books are authored or coauthored by African Americans.

In addition to six books from the national list, the eleven women of Indiana 5, a GOG chapter formed in Indianapolis in 2003, read several titles of their own choosing. "Sometimes we have a hard time getting the books selected by National, or the group has decided as a whole that we don't like that month's selection," explains Tracy Smith-Grady, an accounts payable clerk and cofounder of Indiana 5. The group gravitates toward fiction and biography, and some of their favorites include Lalita Tademy's *Cane River* (see p. 58); Antwone Fisher's *Finding Fish,* an autobiography portraying a childhood spent in foster care; and *Church Folk,* a novel about a young clergyman in the 1960s, by Andrea Bowen.

In keeping with the four other Indiana chapters, Indiana 5 members assume roles within their group: facilitator, secretary, treasurer, and chaplain (who says a prayer before meetings and grace before eating), and epistoler (who maintains a scrapbook of the group's history). Upon joining, members pay a $200 initiation fee and $20 yearly dues, money that helps fund the annual national conference.

The women of Indiana 5 fully immerse themselves in their chosen books through food, dress, and imagination. Occasionally the group meets at a local restaurant, but usually they meet at a member's home and prepare a thematic meal. "We like to match food with books, because it gives us an opportunity to go inside the books. It takes us back to that era," says Smith-Grady. "It's fun to get as engrossed in the book as you can."

Smith-Grady hosted the meeting for Valerie Boyd's *Zora Neale Hurston: Wrapped in Rainbows,* a biography of the Florida-born author, and her menu was derived from foods in the book: chicken, green beans, and fried peach and apple pies. Accounting clerk and cofounder of Indiana 5 Stephanie Groves made the pies by wrapping peaches and apples in pie dough and then deep-frying them. "They were delicious!" recalls Smith-Grady.

One of the group's favorite books, Sister Souljah's *The Coldest Winter Ever,* inspired lively conversation about the characters and their motives. "Everyone in the group gave this book five stars," says Groves. "We discussed the book at our meeting, and then again when we met with two other book clubs for drinks several weeks later. We could see ourselves getting caught up by a fine, slick brother, being naïve, and thinking we could handle all the drama."

More Food for Thought

The Cultures Club at the Park Forest Public Library in Park Forest, Illinois, serving Park Forest and Olympia Fields, explores world cultures through literature. Members research the culture featured in the literature, and Leslie Simms, the group's facilitator, displays related materials. One of the group's best discussions was about *The Coldest Winter Ever*, which they read for its insight into the hip-hop subculture. "Some of our members were unfamiliar with the culture depicted in *The Coldest Winter Ever*, while others with more experience used the discussion as an opportunity to share personal knowledge," says Simms.

Each month, the Cultures Club enjoys a dessert reflecting the culture of the month. "Since the foods mentioned in the novel were standard American junk food, I served pop and chocolate chip cookies," says Simms.

The Color of Water: A Black Man's Tribute to His White Mother

James McBride

RIVERHEAD BOOKS, *1996*

(available in paperback from Riverhead Books, 1997)

JOURNALIST JAMES McBRIDE'S memoir of childhood is both a tribute to a resourceful and mysterious mother and a meditation on race and identity.

McBride was one of twelve black children raised in a Brooklyn housing project. His mother looked different from the other mothers in the neighborhood, and different from her own children. She put all twelve through college, and many through graduate school, yet her children never knew her maiden name, where she came from, or why she seemed to have no parents or siblings of her own. It took McBride fourteen years to solve the mystery, finally convincing his reluctant mother to tell her story, "more as a favor to me than out of any desire to revisit her past," writes McBride.

The Color of Water is the remarkable story of both McBride's mother and the author's struggle to understand himself, his family, his origins, and his place in society. The mystery of McBride's mother is so improbable and so surprising that readers may find it hard to believe this is a memoir and not a work of inventive fiction.

McBride interweaves the story of his mother's life with his own, and both have memories related to peanuts and peanut butter. Food was scarce in the McBride household, where the twelve siblings were constantly hungry, scavenging for food in the kitchen, swiping food from one another, and creating secret stashes. McBride recalls how the normally friendly siblings became enemies over food. When his mother brought peanut butter home from a local benevolent agency, the huge jars became the focus of intense competition. "We'd gather around the cans, open them, and spoon up the peanut butter like soup, giggling as our mouths stuck closed with the gooey stuff," writes McBride.

His mother, Ruth McBride Jordan, recalls her childhood in Suffolk, Virginia, headquarters of Planters Peanuts: "I still remember the smell of the South. It smelled like azaleas. And leaves. And peanuts. Peanuts everywhere."

DOTTIE'S FAMOUS
PEANUT BUTTER PIE

For *The Book Club Cookbook*, Susan Danner, who hosts many book club meetings at Danner's Books and Coffeeshop in Muncie, Indiana, shared her recipe for Peanut Butter Pie. In 1964 Danner was visiting her grandparents in Fort Pierce, Florida, and enjoyed a wonderful peanut butter pie at Simenson's restaurant. Danner asked the owners for the recipe, and they graciously obliged. Danner brought the recipe back to Muncie, where her parents were part owners of the Westbrook Country Club. Her mother, Dottie, began baking and serving the peanut butter pie in the clubhouse restaurant—and it was a huge success: "My parents sold the country club about twenty years ago, but people still ask about the pie," says Danner.

In 1995, Danner relocated her Muncie bookstore to a new building with space for a coffee shop. Along with coffee and sandwiches, Danner put her mother's famous peanut butter pie on the menu. "People who had not been in our store came just to get a slice of pie and reminisce about their days at the country club," says Danner. "Eventually, the demand for pie became too great, and we had to set aside a special day, Wednesday, for peanut butter pie and take reservations for pieces. No one dared to come in and get just one piece. Some customers even put in standing orders."

In case you can't get to Danner's to enjoy a good book with a slice of Dottie's Famous Peanut Butter Pie—described on their menu as "smooth, rich, vanilla cream pudding in a flaky pie crust with a special peanut butter mixture in between, topped with a fluffy meringue"—the recipe follows. Danner says the pie is just heavenly . . . and rich. It's the pie for a real sweet tooth. As the Danner's Coffeeshop menu says, "Life is short, why not have dessert first?"

For the pie crust
½ recipe Basic Pie Crust, p. 112

For the bottom filling
1 cup confectioners' sugar
½ cup creamy peanut butter

For the pudding filling

2 cups milk

2 tablespoons butter

⅔ cup granulated sugar

¼ cup cornstarch

2 egg yolks

¼ teaspoon vanilla extract

For the meringue

2 egg whites

Dash of cream of tartar

⅓ cup granulated sugar

1. To prebake the pie crust: Prick crust with fork all over and bake at 425°F for 8–10 minutes, until lightly browned. Remove from oven and allow to cool.

2. Lower oven temperature to 350°F.

3. To make the bottom filling: Mix the sugar and peanut butter until crumbly. Spread three-fourths of the mixture evenly across the bottom of the baked pie shell (the remainder will be used as a topping).

4. To make the pudding filling: Heat the milk and butter in a heavy-bottomed saucepan over low heat, stirring occasionally. When the milk is just steaming and small bubbles appear around the edges, remove from heat.

5. In a large saucepan, mix the sugar and cornstarch. Add the egg yolks and mix well. Gradually add the scalded milk and butter, stirring until smooth after each addition. Simmer, stirring until pudding is thick. Stir in vanilla and remove from heat.

6. To make the meringue: Using an electric mixer, beat the egg whites until frothy. Add the cream of tartar and continue beating until stiff peaks form. Gradually add the sugar, beating on low speed until completely dissolved.

7. To assemble: Pour hot pudding filling into pie shell. Spread meringue over the top and seal edges. Sprinkle remaining peanut butter mixture over meringue. Bake in oven until top is golden, 10–15 minutes. Serve warm or at room temperature.

Yield: 1 9-inch pie, 6 to 8 servings

BOOK CLUB PROFILE

When Susan Anderson moved to Tempe, Arizona, from Washington, D.C., in 1983, one of her first goals was to organize a book club. "I had been in a book group since 1962, and already missed it," says Anderson, who went door to door, inviting new neighbors to join. Neighbors asked friends, and the fourteen women of the Contemporary Book Discussion Club continue to meet one Wednesday morning each month in their homes in suburban Phoenix. "The book club keeps our minds active and allows us to recharge our batteries each month," says Anderson. "We're a diverse group that has lived from coast to coast and in foreign countries. We bring a wealth of life experiences and we all believe we should learn something new every day."

They have coffee, tea, and light refreshments during the morning meetings, and go out to lunch afterward, often to restaurants reflecting the books' themes. They had Chinese food for Jung Chang's *Wild Swans: Three Daughters of China* (see p. 486) and Mexican food for Gabriel García Márquez's *One Hundred Years of Solitude*. Occasionally, the host will provide refreshments to complement the reading selection, such as Carol Goewey's chocolate feast—chocolate cake, pie, and candy—when they discussed Joanne Harris's *Chocolat* (see p. 65).

Each May, the group has a separate meeting to plan the annual reading calendar. Anderson says this keeps them from having to take time from regular meetings to discuss what to read next, and it allows the participants to have the books in advance. Each member submits several books she would like to read or thinks would make for lively discussions. They choose primarily contemporary fiction, and diversify the list with a biography or memoir, a mystery, books about travel, politics, and self-help, and a book set in Arizona or by an Arizona author.

Among more than two hundred titles the group has discussed, Anderson names Barbara Ehrenreich's *Nickel and Dimed* (see p. 300) and James McBride's *The Color of Water* as favorites.

Anderson says *The Color of Water* had enormous appeal. It was well written, easy to read, and contemporary. "We were intrigued by the story of a Jewish woman marrying a black man and moving to a small southern town," says Anderson, "especially at a time when discrimination was so prevalent." She adds that McBride's memoir exposed them to a mixed marriage, not only of race but also of religion, but it didn't preach. The group was fascinated by how McBride's mother worked the New York City public school system to help advance her children's education. "Her determination for her children to have a good education and the positive attitude she maintained were inspiring," says Anderson. "All mothers want the best for their children, but don't go about it and succeed in this way. She had drive to succeed and she did."

The group discussed the difficulties of raising a big family. "Given their financial limitations, this was just remarkable," says Anderson. "The thought of maintaining a household for such a large family is mind-boggling."

Corelli's Mandolin

Louis de Bernières

PANTHEON, *1994*

(available in paperback from Vintage, 1995)

H
E LET HIS RIFLE RUST, and even lost it once or twice, but he won battles armed with nothing but a mandolin." So a soldier describes his commander, Captain Antonio Corelli, upon entering his service in the spring of 1941. Corelli and his battalion of Italian soldiers have been ordered to occupy the small Greek island of Cephalonia, but Corelli is more interested in music than battle.

Corelli takes up residence in the home of Dr. Iannis and his willful daughter, Pelagia. Although Dr. Iannis and Pelagia take every opportunity to make the Italian intruders feel unwelcome, the charming, likeable Corelli is hard to resist. A love story narrated in many different voices—including the egomaniacal voice of Italian leader Benito Mussolini, Il Duce—*Corelli's Mandolin* spans more than fifty years, beginning with the invasion of Cephalonia, and explores the after-effects of the war.

At the outset, Pelagia and her father resent Corelli's intrusion into their home. Food serves as a convenient tool of resistance. Pelagia often sets a plate of food in front of Corelli with such force that it spills. When it does, Pelagia takes a cloth and "smear[s] the soup or the stew in a wide circle about his tunic, all the time apologizing cynically for the terrible mess." Eventually, Pelagia notices that Corelli waits until after she has "slopped the food onto the table" to pull in his chair.

SPANAKOPITA

A
s acts of resistance, Dr. Iannis harasses and humiliates Corelli when he can, and practically forces Corelli and his men to dine on various Greek appetizers, or *mezedakia*. The doctor has already insisted that Corelli sleep in Pelagia's bed to undermine his sense of honor and chivalry, relegating her to the kitchen floor, to the captain's horror. Then Dr. Iannis imposes the snacks upon Corelli and Carlo, his bombardier. "It is our tradition," Dr. Iannis says to Corelli, "to

be hospitable even to those who do not merit it." Corelli and Carlo warily eat the appetizers, which included fried baby squid, stuffed grape leaves (*dolmades*), and tiny spinach pies (*spanakopita*).

We offer a recipe for *spanakopita* below. When you taste these triangular treats, we think you'll agree that resistance is futile.

> NOTE: Phyllo (or filo) dough is the ultrathin pastry used in much Greek cooking. It can be found at specialty stores, and frozen phyllo is available at most supermarkets. To defrost, leave the box in the refrigerator overnight. Phyllo generally comes in 1-pound boxes containing 24–30 sheets.

Phyllo dough dries out very quickly, so it is important to have a pastry brush and a bowl of melted butter handy. Keep your stack of phyllo dough covered with plastic wrap or a damp dish towel, removing one sheet at a time. Brush the sheet well with butter, working from the edges in. Try to work quickly before it dries out.

It is crucial to remove *all* liquid from the spinach. Wet spinach will ruin the *spanakopita*.

2 10-ounce packages frozen chopped spinach	*8 eggs*
1 bunch (6 to 8) scallions	*1 8-ounce package cream cheese, at room*
1½ cups (3 sticks) butter	*temperature*
8 ounces feta cheese, crumbled	*Salt and pepper*
12 ounces small-curd cottage cheese (1½ cups)	*1 pound phyllo dough*

1. Preheat oven to 350°F.
2. Thaw the spinach and drain in a colander. Taking a handful of spinach at a time, squeeze out all moisture. Roll spinach in a clean dish towel and wring dry. Place in a large bowl.
3. Chop the green and white parts of scallions separately. Melt 2 tablespoons of butter in a small frying pan and sauté the scallion whites until soft, about 5 minutes. Remove from heat and stir in scallion greens. Add to the spinach, along with the feta and cottage cheese.
4. In a separate bowl, using an electric mixer at medium speed, beat the eggs briefly. Add the cream cheese and continue to beat until smooth. Add to the spinach mixture.
5. Stir in 3 tablespoons melted butter. Add salt and pepper to taste (be careful with the salt— feta cheeses vary in their saltiness).
6. Prepare a clean work surface. Keep a bowl of melted butter handy at all times. Cut the phyllo lengthwise into 3 equal strips, about 3 inches wide. While making the *spanakopita*, always keep the phyllo covered with plastic wrap or a damp dish cloth to prevent drying.

7. Remove one strip of phyllo, place on work surface, and brush well with butter, using a pastry brush. Place a teaspoon of filling near the bottom of the strip and fold one corner up to meet the opposite edge, making a triangle. Continue to fold the triangle edge over edge like a flag to the end of the strip. Place seam side down on a sheet of aluminum foil. Repeat this process with remaining phyllo strips. Nestle finished *spanakopitas* together in squares. As you fill a sheet of foil, brush the tops of the *spanakopitas* with butter and cover with another sheet of foil. *Spanakopitas* may be prepared ahead of time and refrigerated or frozen until ready to cook.

8. Place *spanakopitas* on an ungreased baking sheet and bake 20–25 minutes, until puffy and golden. Serve warm.

Yield: About 5 dozen

BOOK CLUB PROFILE

"*Corelli's Mandolin* ranks as one of the best book club books I've ever read," says Natalie Kemmitt, a professional book club discussion leader. A former literature teacher from England, Kemmitt joined book clubs when she came to the United States in 1994. She quickly became disillusioned with their lack of "book-talk," and started her own book club at a local library. That was the beginning. Kemmitt now leads book clubs all over Indiana, runs workshops for librarians, consults to communities doing community-wide book discussions, and produces a quarterly newsletter, *Fiction & Friends* (contact Kemmitt at nkemmitt@earthlink.net for subscription information), that spreads her enthusiasm for reading across the country.

Kemmitt's creative enhancement of book club meetings is one reason for her success as a leader. "If I'm being paid to make everyone's experience of a book as interesting, lively, and fun as possible, I not only do extensive research and run a very tight and literary discussion, but I aim to put smiles on faces," says Kemmitt. Helped by enthusiastic librarians, Kemmitt uses a dazzling array of warm-up games, quizzes with prizes, music, art, and food to motivate book club members and stimulate discussion. She played opera for a book group discussion of *Bel Canto* by Ann Patchett (see p. 46), showed a slide show of the Yorkshire countryside for Charlotte Brontë's *Jane Eyre* (see p. 210), and distributed copies of Vermeer masterpieces from a children's coloring book for a discussion of *Girl with a Pearl Earring* by Tracy Chevalier (see p. 153).

Inspired and assisted by librarians, Kemmitt sometimes incorporates thematic food into her meetings. She distributed tiny bars of Mexican chocolate for a discussion of *Like Water for Chocolate* by Laura Esquivel and supplied Dutch cheese as a snack for a discussion of *Girl with a Pearl Earring.* Kemmitt finds this creativity contagious. "The more I provide, the more group members are encouraged to bring in interesting artifacts, do research, or bake their own goodies," she says.

To choose books, Kemmitt asks pointed questions: Do the characters, situations, and settings hold our interest? Are there at least five themes worthy of discussion? Has the book won any literary awards? For *Corelli's Mandolin,* the answers were all yes. The group that chose this book, Critical Mass, meets at the Carmel-Clay Public Library in Hamilton County, an affluent area north of Indianapolis, Indiana. The club's roster of twenty-four members, mostly women, ranges in age from thirties to eighties, and includes two mother-daughter pairings. "This is a cultured area, with independent movies, operas, and plays," says Kemmitt. "People in Critical Mass don't want to read easy books. They expect a good literary discussion."

They got it with the Commonwealth Writers Prize–winning book, *Corelli's Mandolin.* Club members marveled at the book's character development. "From the rambling, insane voice at the beginning of the book, to Mandras [Pelagia's first love] and his Greek myth–like travels, to Corelli himself, all these characters came alive for us," says Kemmitt. "We really cared what happened to them. De Bernières wove such a vivid tale that group members got very upset about what was happening, as if they were physically there," according to Kemmitt, who attributes this effect to masterful writing. "The ability of this man to write incredible tragedy, but still make you laugh out loud, is a wonderful gift," says Kemmitt.

More Food for Thought

Bob Morrill, a librarian at the East Regional Library in Knightsdale, North Carolina, is a gourmet chef, and one of his specialties is Greek food. He treated the Regional Readers, a book club of twenty-five women who meet at the library, to some delicious Greek appetizers when they read *Corelli's Mandolin:* dolmades (stuffed grape leaves), assorted marinated olives, and *spanakopita.* The festive meal was topped off with a dessert of baklava, a Greek pastry. "Tasting the food at the same time lent a good flavor to the discussion," said Janet Morley, the Regional Readers facilitator.

The Da Vinci Code

Dan Brown

....

DOUBLEDAY, 2003

J ACQUES SAUNIÈRE, well-respected curator of the Louvre in Paris, lives a furtive second life. As a leader of a secret European society, the Priory of Sion, Saunière carries with him knowledge that only three others share, and all three have been murdered in the last twenty-four hours by fundamentalist adherents of Opus Dei, a devout Catholic group. When Saunière is shot in the stomach in the Louvre's Grand Gallery by an assassin making his fourth and presumably final stop, Saunière has only minutes to devise a way to perform his last, perhaps most important, act: He must transmit his secrets to the one person he can trust, his estranged granddaughter, Sophie, a professional cryptographer.

So begins *The Da Vinci Code*, Dan Brown's masterfully intricate murder mystery. As the French police attempt to answer the questions surrounding Saunière's murder, they find themselves racing to decipher the codes and clues simultaneously being unraveled by Saunière's granddaughter and the prime suspect, Robert Langdon, a Harvard professor of religious symbology who happens to be in Paris at the time. To reveal meaning in Saunière's clues, the police—and the reader—must learn about the Priory of Sion, the once-close relationship between Saunière and his granddaughter, and the storied historical iconography of the divine feminine. Almost every fact is indispensable to unmasking Saunière's secrets.

Throughout the book, the power of symbols transcends even the fast-moving plot. Pagan and religious symbols fill *The Da Vinci Code*, linking the reader to the past, to dogmas, to revolutionary ideas, and to deeper secrets. Symbols incorporated into art—Leonardo da Vinci's paintings, for example—and architecture serve as effective ways for artists to communicate to one another and to generations to come.

No symbol is more important to unraveling the mystery of Saunière's death than the rose, which is found in numerous key places. "Rather than lock each other out," Saunière tells Sophie as a child, "we can each hang a rose—*la fleur des secrets*—on our door when we need privacy. This way we learn to respect and trust each other. Hanging a rose is an ancient Roman custom."

As Langdon explains to Sophie, the rose has also symbolized the Holy Grail. "The Rose was a symbol that spoke of the Grail on many levels—secrecy, womanhood, and guidance—the feminine chalice and guiding star that led to secret truth," Langdon explains.

Still later, another symbologist drawn into the mystery describes the rose as "the premier symbol of female sexuality," representing "the five stations of female life—birth, menstruation, mother-hood, menopause, and death."

JULI ROSENBAUM'S
ROSEMARY SPAGHETTI

The plot of *The Da Vinci Code* moves so quickly that the characters have no time for food. But the innumerable symbols used in the book offer opportunities for creativity in the kitchen, extending the story's symbolism to the palate.

Rosemary is one ingredient that evokes the symbols in *The Da Vinci Code*. Called "the holy herb" by Christians in Spain, rosemary is revered as the bush that sheltered Mary Magdalene in her flight to Egypt. Rosemary symbolically weds icons of the rose and of Mary, an incarnation of the divine feminine, both of which are integral to *The Da Vinci Code*.

Juli Rosenbaum prepared an Italian feast with rosemary spaghetti, lasagna, garlic bread, fruit, wine, and cream-cheese cake for the Black Madonna Book Group's discussion of *The Da Vinci Code* in Waco, Texas. "Although there is no mention of rosemary in *The Da Vinci Code*, Mary Magdalene and the symbol of the rose are very important in the novel," says Rosenbaum, who concocted rosemary spaghetti years ago when she planted an herb garden. "I wanted to use everything from my garden I could, and my family likes spicy, robust food. One herb led to another, and the recipe evolved over the years."

For a vegetarian version of rosemary spaghetti, Rosenbaum suggests replacing the meat with chopped vegetables such as zucchini, yellow squash, bell peppers, and carrots.

NOTE: This sauce may be made a day ahead of time and reheated before serving—Rosenbaum says it will taste even better!

3 tablespoons olive oil

1 pound extralean ground beef

1 large sweet onion, chopped

1 28-ounce can diced tomatoes

1 15-ounce can tomato sauce

1 6-ounce can tomato paste

1 tablespoon chili powder

1 teaspoon sugar

½ teaspoon salt

½ teaspoon dried marjoram

¼ teaspoon hot sauce, such as Tabasco

3 bay leaves

½ pound fresh mushrooms, sliced

5 cloves garlic, minced

2 teaspoons finely chopped fresh oregano

2 tablespoons finely chopped fresh rosemary

2 tablespoons finely chopped fresh basil

1 pound dried thin spaghetti (or 1½ pounds fresh pasta)

1. Heat 2 tablespoons of the olive oil in a large skillet. Sauté the beef and onion together until meat is crumbly and onion is softened. Add the next 14 ingredients and simmer, covered, 1 hour, stirring occasionally. Adjust seasonings and simmer another hour, uncovered.

2. Cook the pasta according to package directions. Toss in a large bowl with 1 tablespoon olive oil and top with sauce.

Yield: About 6 servings

For more on Rosemary Spaghetti, see p. 146.

JOHN HORNBURG'S
DEATH BY CHOCOLATE

Chef John Hornburg engineered a supreme Death by Chocolate for the *Da Vinci Code* dinner sponsored by the Milwaukee School of Engineering's Great Books Dinner and Discussion Series.

"The Death by Chocolate cake was, appropriately, a dessert to die for," says Judy Steininger, who led the discussion of *The Da Vinci Code* in Milwaukee. "Never underestimate the power of a dessert."

For the cake

8 ounces dark chocolate

⅝ cup (1¼ sticks) butter

4 eggs

1 cup sugar

¼ cup all-purpose flour

¼ cup unsweetened cocoa powder

2 teaspoons baking powder

1 teaspoon vanilla extract

¼ cup sour cream

For the frosting

⅔ cup heavy cream

9 ounces dark chocolate, chopped

1. Preheat oven to 350°F. Butter a 9-inch-square baking pan, dust with flour, and tap out excess.

2. To make the cake: In the top of a double boiler or in a small saucepan set in boiling water, melt the chocolate and butter together. Set aside.

3. With an electric mixer, beat together the eggs and sugar. Mix in the flour, cocoa powder, baking powder, and vanilla. Gently fold in the melted butter and chocolate, and the sour cream.

4. Pour the batter into the prepared pan. Bake 50 minutes, or until a toothpick inserted in the center comes out clean. Allow to cool.

5. To make the frosting: Heat the cream in a small saucepan. Add the chocolate and stir until the chocolate is completely melted and the mixture is smooth.

6. Remove the cooled cake from the pan. Pour frosting over cake and spread to even out. Serve at room temperature.

Yield: 9 servings

BOOK CLUB PROFILE

"Bring your open book, some open wine, and an open mind," reads the invitation to the Black Madonna Book Group meeting. "The name Black Madonna expresses the freedom women experience to be strong, beautiful, and successful, and their wisdom in acknowledging the sacred aspects of everyday living," says Juli Rosenbaum, the founder of the Waco, Texas, book group.

The name Black Madonna is derived from two books: Rebecca Wells's *Divine Secrets of the Ya-Ya Sisterhood* and Sue Monk Kidd's *The Secret Life of Bees* (see p. 398). "In each of these books the Black Madonna represents the feminine face of the divine, which serves as a beautiful and natural counterpart to the more typical masculine divinity of our culture. The Black Madonna has traditionally represented women who have broken out of some form of bondage," adds Rosenbaum.

A lecturer in business writing at Baylor University, Rosenbaum invites thirty women, including other Baylor professors, stay-at-home moms, ministers, teachers, and psychotherapists, to discuss fiction at her home each month. "Waco can be a hard place to break in and make new friends," says Rosenbaum. "Friendship circles in Waco tend to be long-established and strictly family- or couple-oriented. I knew so many interesting, intelligent women, but they didn't know each other. The Black Madonnas are very eclectic and open to new ideas."

Rosenbaum chooses novels that embrace different cultures, lifestyles, and religions; most are about women who struggle to overcome difficulties, such as Anita Diamant's *The Red Tent* (see p. 374), and Billie Letts's *Where the Heart Is* (see p. 482). "Waco is in the buckle of the Bible Belt, and religion is an important part of people's lives here," says Rosenbaum. "A natural consequence of an environment with a strong religious identity is a fear of nontraditional religious settings. That's why I thought it was important for our book group to promote tolerance. Anything goes, as long as it promotes tolerance and women's strength."

The Black Madonnas always serve meals that relate to the books they read. Feasting together fosters a relaxed, intimate atmosphere. Members contribute dishes without being asked, but Rosenbaum hosts and prepares each book club meal as "a gift to my community."

"This is a time to eat, bond, make new friends, and have a fairly thorough discussion about the book," says Rosenbaum. "We linger to discuss our lives, and the food is one more thing that helps us bond."

When they read Laura Esquivel's *Like Water for Chocolate* and Joanne Harris's *Chocolat* (see p. 65), members prepared chocolate desserts from family recipes. They brought the original recipes and photographs of the mothers and grandmothers who had handed them down. "It was a celebration of women who had played an important part in our lives and those of our matrilineal ancestors," says Rosenbaum.

Dan Brown's *The Da Vinci Code* fit well into the Black Madonnas' reading list. "It tied in beautifully with our theme because this is a book about the divine feminine, which, in this novel, is represented by Mary Magdalene," says Rosenbaum.

The group used the questions on Dan Brown's website to guide their conversation, along with quotations from Mary Starbird's *The Woman with the Alabaster Jar,* a book offering indirect proof of Jesus' marriage to Mary Magdalene, which made an excellent companion to *The Da Vinci Code.* "Starbird explains and documents many of the historical issues Dan Brown introduces in his thriller," says Rosenbaum. To help visualize *The Da Vinci Code*'s references to art history, Rosenbaum shared books on Da Vinci's paintings, the architectural history of the Louvre, and color photographs of Da Vinci's *The Last Supper, Madonna of the Rocks,* and the *Mona Lisa,* as well as the controversial architectural wonder at the Louvre, Pei's Pyramid. "The photographs were extremely helpful to illustrate portions of *The Da Vinci Code,*" says Rosenbaum.

More Food for Thought

Chef John Hornburg brought mystery and French themes to his menu for *The Da Vinci Code* dinner at the Milwaukee School of Engineering's Great Books Dinner and Discussion. He presented the menu in the form of clues, which the delighted guests needed to decipher:

Appetizer: In a race, I would lose to this fast-paced book.
Salad: What French chef created me?
Entrée: "Suprême de volaille Françoise." I am served at the Hotel Ritz, Paris.
Dessert: A terrible way to go unless you live in Pennsylvania!

So what did Chef Hornburg serve for dinner? Escargots for an appetizer, followed by salade niçoise, chicken breasts with tied asparagus spears and mini double baked potatoes, and, for dessert, Death by Chocolate.

Daughter of Fortune

Isabel Allende

....

HARPERCOLLINS, *1999*

(available in paperback from HaperTorch, 2001)

S ET IN VALPARAISO, Chile, in the early 1800s, *Daughter of Fortune* is the story of Eliza Som-mers, an orphan raised by spinster Miss Rose, her brother Jeremy, and Mama Fresia, the Indian housekeeper and nanny. When Eliza falls in love with Joaquín Andieta, a clerk who works for Jeremy, her appalled caretakers make plans to ship Eliza off to England. Instead, she stows aboard a ship to follow her lover to California, where he has gone, hoping to make his fortune panning for gold. The story takes Eliza and her traveling companion, Chinese doctor Tao Chi'en, through a region swept by gold fever and dotted with brothels. Her adventures, and the end of her search, bring Eliza to a realization about what she truly seeks.

Eliza grows up in Chile but lives "in exile" in America for much of *Daughter of Fortune*. The tastes and smells of food and the art of cooking link Eliza to Chile. Early on, we learn that Eliza "had a rare culinary gift: at seven, without turning a hair, she could skin a beef tongue, dress a hen, make twenty empanadas without drawing a breath." Although Miss Rose considers Eliza's culinary interest a waste of time, Eliza is not deterred. By fourteen, Eliza's cooking skills have surpassed those of Miss Rose and Mama Fresia: "She could spend entire days grinding spices and nuts for tortes or maize for Chilean cakes, dressing turtledoves for pickling and chopping fruit for preserves."

SPICED TURKEY EMPANADAS

I t is no surprise, then, that Eliza puts the skills honed in childhood to work in her adopted country. When she and Tao Chi'en move to Sacramento in pursuit of Joaquín Andieta, Eliza sets up an empanada business. Her cooking reminds panhandlers of family dinners far away, just as the empanadas bring Eliza closer to the only home she has ever known. Allende understands

Chileans' vast devotion to their homeland and its foods. In her memoir, *My Invented Country* (Perennial, 2003), Allende writes, "If Marco Polo had descended on our coast after thirty years of adventuring through Asia, the first thing he would have been told is that our empanadas are much more delicious than anything in the cuisine of the Celestial Empire."

Empanadas are small meat pies that can be made with a variety of meats and spices. When beef becomes scarce in Sacramento, Eliza experiments with other meats, such as venison, hare, wild geese, turtle, salmon, and even bear. We are partial to spiced turkey and give you our own filling recipe below. The dough recipe comes from Richard Visconte, Isabel Allende's friend and caterer, who has prepared empanadas with this flaky crust for parties at Allende's home overlooking San Francisco Bay. The recipe appeared in *Coastal Living* magazine (November/December 2003).

Serve with a salad of baby greens, fresh ripe tomatoes, and your favorite vinaigrette.

For the filling
2 tablespoons canola oil
1 tablespoon butter
¾ cup finely chopped onions
¾ cup diced red bell pepper
3 teaspoons minced garlic
¾ pound lean ground turkey or chicken
¼ cup chicken broth
¾ teaspoon salt
½ teaspoon ground cinnamon
¼ teaspoon cayenne pepper
¼ teaspoon ground cumin
3 tablespoons raisins
10 pimento-stuffed green olives, sliced
1 medium tomato, diced

For the dough
5 cups all-purpose flour
1⅔ cups vegetable shortening, softened
2 teaspoons salt
⅔ to ¾ cup ice water
1 egg yolk, beaten with a little water

3 hard-cooked eggs, peeled and chopped

1. Preheat the oven to 450°F. Line a baking sheet with foil.
2. To make the filling: Heat the oil and butter in a large skillet over medium heat. Add the onions and bell pepper and sauté 2 minutes. Add the garlic and continue to cook until onion is soft. Add the turkey and sauté until cooked through. Stir in the broth, salt, cinnamon, cayenne, cumin, raisins, olives, and tomato. Cook a few more minutes until most of the liquid is absorbed, but the filling is still moist.

3. To make the dough: Combine the flour, shortening, and salt, using a fork or pastry blender until mixture is crumbly. (Mixture should have small lumps.) Sprinkle ⅔ cup ice water, 1 tablespoon at a time, evenly over the surface; stir with a fork until dry ingredients are moistened. Add a little more water if necessary.

4. Shape the dough into a ball, then roll it out to ⅛-inch thickness on a lightly floured surface. Using a cutter or the top of a glass, cut the dough into 4-inch circles.

5. Place 1–2 tablespoons of filling in the center of each dough circle. Add 2 pieces of chopped egg on top of the filling. Moisten the edges of the dough with water. Fold the dough over the filling, and pinch to seal.

6. Brush each empanada with egg yolk wash. Transfer to a baking sheet. Bake for 18 minutes or until golden. Serve hot.

Yield: 2 dozen

BOOK CLUB PROFILE

Although plans for a multi-million-dollar museum in Boulder, Colorado, celebrating the lives and accomplishments of American western women got scrapped in 1999, the book discussion group attached to the project, Women of the West Book Club, endured. Club members have been meeting at the Boulder Public Library every month since 1997, discussing books by or about western women. Anyone is welcome to attend Women of the West Book Club meetings, which are publicized in community newsletters. Usually, the core group of six is joined by three or four others.

The core members of the club, all educated women in midlife and beyond, reflect Colorado's rich melting pot community of longtime residents and new arrivals. At eighty-three, Laura King is the group's oldest member, the author of two books, and a sixty-year resident of Colorado. "It's immeasurable what she brings to the group," says fellow member Jeannie Patton. "She's the voice of experience, the bearer of history." Jill Ertl, a practicing Buddhist, has family roots in Colorado that reach back seven generations. At the other end of the spectrum, school librarian Betsy Pink moved west just three years ago, fulfilling a lifelong dream. Together these women, like their book list, personify the state's diversity and rugged history.

Because they have strict criteria for choosing a book—it must be written by a western woman or the protagonist must be a woman of the West (by "West" they mean west of the one hundredth meridian, a common demarcation line running roughly from the middle of

North Dakota through the middle of Texas to distinguish the western U.S. from the eastern U.S.)—the group often reads less mainstream works. Past favorites include Molly Glass's *The Jump-Off Creek,* a portrait of pioneer life in the 1890s; Kathleen Norris's *Dakota: A Spiritual Geography,* the author's recollections and observations of life on the High Plains; and Allende's *Daughter of Fortune.*

The Women of the West Book Club ranks *Daughter of Fortune* among their top five books. The variety of places and people that the main character encounters on her travels speaks to the West's cultural and geographic diversity. "The broad sweep of history and the protagonist's experiences were delightfully rich," says Patton. "Following her adventures gave us plenty of opportunity to explore aspects of western history."

The Devil Wears Prada

Lauren Weisberger

DOUBLEDAY, 2003

L AUREN WEISBERGER, a former assistant to *Vogue* editor Anna Wintour, made her literary debut with this wry, comic novel about a recent Brown graduate, Andrea Sachs, who is determined to write for *The New Yorker* before her five-year college reunion. Andrea is lucky; she lands the job "a million girls would die for" as the assistant to Miranda Priestly, the successful, driven editor of *Runway*, a leading New York fashion magazine.

Andrea, whose "clothes, hair and attitude are all wrong," hails from suburban Connecticut. She is a fish out of water in *Runway*'s slick fashion-magazine culture of "tall and impossibly thin" fashionistas. But she makes a yearlong commitment to the perpetually dissatisfied Priestly, knowing her boss's recommendation will help her land her dream job. But the year will prove to be a long one.

Andrea's Ivy League education hasn't prepared her for her new tasks—picking up Miranda's dry cleaning, wrapping her gifts, hiring nannies, tracking down advance copies of *Harry Potter* for her daughters, delivering hot lattes, and trying to decipher the vague instructions Miranda shouts over her cell phone, a device that ensures that Andrea "was always only seven digits away from Miranda."

Andrea's "fetching, sending, hunting, and gathering" ultimately takes its toll. She sacrifices her relationships with her boyfriend, her best friend, and her family on the altar of her career. She is miserable. Ultimately, Andrea must decide if the job that could be the pivotal stepping stone in her career is worth the price she is paying.

Food plays a significant role in Andrea's unhappy existence at *Runway*. Her workday mornings are spent fetching multiple breakfasts, so a hot meal will await Miranda upon her unpredictable arrival. Though her world is filled with models starving themselves to remain thin, Miranda somehow maintains her trim figure despite regular breakfasts of bacon, sausage, and cheese-filled pastries.

Andrea also makes repeated trips to Starbucks so Miranda can have a piping hot latte, no matter what time she arrives at her desk. She gets a modicum of revenge by distributing caramel macchiatos and mocha Frappuccinos to New York's homeless population—all on *Runway*'s tab—as she shuttles back and forth between her office and Starbucks.

Andrea's first foray into the famed glass-and-granite *Runway* cafeteria reveals many gourmet specials—most untouched. Most of *Runway*'s weight-conscious employees head for the salad bar, which Andrea describes as "the size of an airport landing strip and accessible from four different directions." Andrea becomes the sole patron at the "lone soup station," the menu slashed to a single soup per day by *Runway* executives because of the chef's refusal to concoct lowfat soups for the chronic dieters that make up Runway's workforce. When Andrea selects a bowl of New England clam chowder, she meets the stares of "tall, willowy *Runway* blondes" and the questions of the cafeteria cashier, who asks, "Do you have any idea how many calories are in that?"

Sun-Dried Tomato and Goat Cheese Pizza

Among the many items that go untouched in the *Runway* cafeteria is the "sundried tomato and goat cheese pizza special (which resided on a small table banished to the sidelines that everyone referred to as 'Carb Corner')." Like Andrea, we would probably pass on the salad bar and the sushi table and head straight to Carb Corner. Our version of Sun-Dried Tomato and Goat Cheese Pizza may not have you sashaying down a New York City runway, but it is guaranteed to satisfy even a robust hunger.

Keep the goat cheese cold until ready to top the pizza, and it will crumble much more easily.

For the pizza dough
2¼ teaspoons (1 packet) active dry yeast
2 teaspoons sugar
1 cup warm water
3 cups all-purpose flour
1 teaspoon salt
¼ cup grated Parmesan cheese
2 tablespoons extra-virgin olive oil

Cornmeal and flour (for rolling out the dough)

Toppings
3 cloves garlic, minced
½ teaspoon salt
4 teaspoons minced fresh oregano or marjoram
½ cup extra-virgin olive oil
1 large onion, thinly sliced
1½ cups oil-packed sun-dried tomatoes, slivered
1 pound creamy goat cheese
Salt and freshly ground black pepper

1. To make the pizza dough: Dissolve the yeast and 1 teaspoon of the sugar in $\frac{1}{2}$ cup warm water. Set aside until the yeast is foamy, about 5 minutes.

2. Place the flour, salt, Parmesan, and remaining teaspoon sugar in the bowl of a food processor and pulse together until well blended. With the motor running, add the yeast mixture and olive oil. Very slowly pour in additional warm water, if needed, just until the dough forms a single ball that holds together (even a little too much water will produce dough that is too sticky). The dough should hold together when handled, but still be a bit sticky.

   To mix the dough by hand, combine flour, salt, Parmesan, and remaining teaspoon sugar in a large bowl. Make a well in the center and pour in the yeast mixture and warm water, as needed, until the dough holds together. Gradually mix, working out from the center. Add remaining water as needed.

   Transfer the dough to a floured work surface and knead vigorously until smooth and stretchy, about 5 to 7 minutes.

3. Transfer the dough to a large oiled bowl and cover with a dampened kitchen towel. Allow to rise in a warm place for 1 hour. Punch the dough down and allow it to sit an additional 15 minutes.

4. To make the pizza: Place a pizza stone or baking sheet in the oven and preheat to 500°F.

5. In a small bowl, gently mash together the minced garlic and salt. Add 2 teaspoons of the oregano or marjoram and stir in olive oil. Set aside.

6. Divide the dough into 4 equal parts and shape each into a disk. Place a disk of dough on a work surface that has been generously sprinkled with cornmeal. Dust a rolling pin with flour and roll the dough out into an 8- to 9-inch circle. Using your fingers, stretch the dough farther until it is very thin but not in danger of tearing. Pinch around the edge to produce a raised rim.

7. With an oven mitt or thick potholder, remove the pizza stone or baking pan from the oven and place on a heatproof surface. Sprinkle the stone with cornmeal and lay the prepared crust on top (either lift it gently or use a floured pizza paddle).

8. Brush the dough with the garlic mixture. Spread one-fourth of the onions over the top, cover with one-fourth of the sun-dried tomatoes, and dot with one-fourth of the goat cheese. Sprinkle with remaining teaspoon of oregano or marjoram and season to taste with salt and pepper. Bake 5–7 minutes, until crust is golden and crisp and cheese is melted. Repeat process for remaining pizzas.

Yield: 4 9-inch pizzas, serves 12 as an appetizer

Since June 2003, a group of young magazine staffers have been meeting every other month over burgers and beer at Chumley's, an old speakeasy and a famous Greenwich Village literary establishment, to discuss magazine-related books. Chandra Czape, deputy articles editor for *Ladies' Home Journal,* is founder and president of Ed2010, a national networking organization for aspiring editors who hope to reach their ideal jobs by the year 2010.

The Ed2010 New York chapter's book club comprises primarily junior-level staffers from magazines such as *People, Glamour, O: The Oprah Magazine, Time,* and *Sports Illustrated for Kids.* "We like to keep it as low-key as possible so people are not intimidated about talking about the book or coming to meet with strangers," says Czape. "We want newcomers to feel comfortable and relax over a beer."

Although Czape's book group reads only fiction and nonfiction related in some way to the magazine publishing industry, there are, she says, a remarkably large number of choices. Selections have included *Nothing to Fall Back On,* a memoir by women's magazine editor Betsy Carter; *Bright Lights, Big City* by Jay McInerney, about a young editor who works for a high-powered New York magazine; and *Shutterbabe: Adventures in Love and War,* by Deborah Copaken Kogan, a wartime photojournalist's memoir. "*The Devil Wears Prada* was the talk of the magazine industry in 2003," says Czape.

"*The Devil Wears Prada* was the group's best-attended meeting and provoked our liveliest discussion," says Czape, "even though it was not universally liked by group members." Because most group members are, like the protagonist, young female magazine editors, there was a lot of discussion about Andrea's complaints about her boss being small-minded and pretentious. "Though in truth," says Czape, compared to her villainous boss, Andrea "was just as pretentious, as evidenced by her obsession with designer labels and her keen ability to talk down to everyone from the building doorman to the limo driver."

The Devil in the White City: Murder, Magic, and Madness at the Fair That Changed America

Erik Larson

CROWN, 2003

(available in paperback from Vintage, 2004)

I n 1890, Chicago was named the site of the 1893 World's Fair. Although Chicagoans rejoiced, many around the country met the news with derision and outright contempt. Some, especially many in New York, privately hoped Chicago would fail. New York had campaigned hard to win the fair, and many of its cultural and political leaders thought Chicago unworthy and perhaps unable to stage an event, so important to the nation, that would surpass the spectacularly successful Paris Exposition Universelle of 1878.

Chicago threw its civic pride into the preparation for the fair. As officials coordinating construction efforts encountered one seemingly insurmountable obstacle after another, including fire, mud, inclement weather, and labor shortages, completing the fairgrounds became a race against time.

The hero of what was officially known as the World's Columbian Exposition was a brilliant and single-minded architect, Daniel Hudson Burnham, who was responsible for converting Jackson Park, a muddy lakeside tract, into the dazzling fairgrounds that came to be known as the White City. The world's first Ferris wheel soared 264 feet into the sky, attracting thousands of riders daily. Foreigners and exotic creatures from around the world populated the pavilions of the thirteen-block Avenue of Nations.

With its enormous whitewashed pavilions illuminated at night in a fanciful landscape created by the legendary Frederick Law Olmsted, the White City was both the realization of a vision and a magnificent creation.

On the fair's periphery, however, a darker, more sinister vision was being realized, this one by a dashing and charming young physician, Henry H. Holmes. Just west of the fairgrounds, Holmes built the World's Fair Hotel to attract visitors expected for the Columbian Exposition. But Holmes, a brilliant and articulate sociopath, had built no ordinary hotel. His hotel contained a dissection table, a gas chamber, and a crematorium that could reach temperatures of 3,000 degrees. In this private torture chamber, many hotel guests, including vulnerable young women taken with the young doctor's charms, met their end.

Erik Larson's *The Devil in the White City* juxtaposes these stories of light and darkness and creation and destruction in a nonfiction narrative that is alternately uplifting and deeply disturbing, inspiring and haunting.

After Chicago was chosen to host the World's Fair, it began a process of self-improvement to show the world that Chicago was a world-class city. When Ward McAllister, general servant to Mrs. William Astor, doyenne of New York high society, suggested in a column to the *New York Post* that Chicagoans improve their cuisine by hiring more French chefs, residents of "the second city" collectively cringed. Ward's advice was derided in the Chicago press, but it nevertheless struck a nerve among Chicagoans, who feared that their cuisine might cast them as second-class.

As he set about preparing for the World's Fair, Burnham acutely felt his city's insecurity. Not surprisingly, in January 1891, when trying to lure five nationally known architects to the project, Burnham hosted a dinner of fine French cuisine. The menu, including oysters, consommé of green turtle, filet mignon, and kirsch sorbet, was clearly intended to signal to the architects that Chicago was a city of sophistication and class, fully capable of hosting a grand World's Fair. In March 1893, Burnham himself was fêted with French food—pâté, striped bass with hollandaise sauce, veal cutlets, petits-fours—in honor of his accomplishments. French food represented the pinnacle of fine dining in late-nineteenth-century Chicago, and some in the city were eager to embrace it.

Once under way, the fair introduced Americans to new foods, both foreign and American. Visitors to the fair sampled "ostrich" omelets (made from chicken eggs) or stopped by the Java Lunch Room for pure Java coffee. New food products, including Aunt Jemima's pancake mix, Juicy Fruit gum, Cracker Jack, and Shredded Wheat, were introduced to the public for the first time at the fair. For decoration, a Venus de Milo sculpted out of chocolate and a 22,000-pound cheese, on display at the Wisconsin Pavilion, graced the fairgrounds. And the official menu of the Midway ball, bringing senior officers of the fair and exotic foreigners together, included jerked buffalo, boiled camel humps, monkey stew, and fricassee of reindeer. Foods novel and exotic awaited visitors to the White City.

When we asked Erik Larson about foods important to *The Devil in the White City*, he pointed to the foods that sustained him while he was writing the book.

When I travel, I try to create little rituals in what I suppose is an effort to replicate the comforting routines of home. I select one or two restaurants, and haunt them. I go for dinner fairly early, circa 5:30, to avoid crowds. In Chicago, I chose Shaw's, a restaurant I'd first encountered while on a magazine assignment in the late 1980s. This time around my dinners at Shaw's were shamelessly repetitive: a Wild Turkey Manhattan, one dozen fresh oysters (a different variety each night), and a bowl of lobster bisque, with a plate of bread to soak up every last drop—of the bisque, that is. It made a perfect meal. Not too heavy for steamy summer evenings, but plenty warm for frigid January nights.

SHAW'S CRAB HOUSE LOBSTER BISQUE

Located at 21 East Hubbard Street in River North, just north of downtown Chicago, Shaw's Crab House and Blue Crab Lounge specializes in fresh seafood, including crab, lobster, shrimp, and a half dozen varieties of fresh oysters. Shaw's Crab House is a dressy restaurant, but Erik Larson frequented the more casual, exposed-brick bar, the Blue Crab Lounge.

Chef William Eudy generously contributed the restaurant's recipe for luscious lobster bisque. Eudy's recipe makes enough for upward of one hundred people, so we reduced it to serve a book club–sized group of 8–10.

Don't forget the crusty bread to soak up the last drops, as Larson suggests.

NOTE: Lobster base is a thick, concentrated paste that gives the bisque a full-bodied flavor. Shaw's uses a lobster base made by J. L. Minor, which is available to home cooks. You can order it (see Purchasing Information, p. 499) or simply substitute salt to taste as the recipe indicates.

Call local fish stores to ask for lobster bodies and shrimp shells.

For the lobster stock

2 pounds lobster bodies

1 pound shrimp shells

1 medium yellow onion, roughly chopped

1–2 stalks celery, roughly chopped

1–2 stalks fennel, roughly chopped

2–3 sprigs Italian parsley

1 sprig fresh thyme

1–2 bay leaves

1/8 teaspoon black peppercorns

4 tablespoons tomato paste

For the lobster bisque base

1 cup (2 sticks) unsalted butter

2 carrots, diced

4 stalks celery, diced

2 small yellow onions, chopped

3 cloves garlic, peeled and minced

1¼ teaspoons dried tarragon

¾ teaspoon whole fennel seed

½ teaspoon ground black pepper

½ teaspoon cayenne pepper

¾ teaspoon dried thyme

¾ teaspoon dried oregano

¾ teaspoon dried basil

1¾ cups all-purpose flour

1 cup tomato paste

2½ tablespoons lobster base, or salt to taste

2½ tablespoons brandy

Salt and pepper

2 cups heavy cream

1. To make the lobster stock: Rinse the lobster bodies and shells in cold water. Place in a large pot with cold water to cover.

2. Add the remaining ingredients. Bring to a boil, then reduce heat and simmer, covered, for 3 hours. Skim off any film from the surface while cooking.

3. Remove from heat. Skim off any fat from the surface and strain, discarding solids. You should have about 4 quarts of stock. (If you have more, reserve the extra for another use.) Set aside.

4. To make the lobster bisque base: Melt the butter in a large pot or Dutch oven over medium-high heat. Add the carrots, celery, onions, and garlic and stir. Add the tarragon, fennel seed, black and cayenne peppers, thyme, oregano, and basil. Sauté at medium-low heat until vegetables are soft (approximately 30 minutes).

5. Add the flour, stirring to incorporate with the butter, and cook for approximately 4 minutes.

6. Add the lobster stock, tomato paste, and lobster base. Combine thoroughly with a whisk. Bring to a boil and allow to reduce by one-fourth.

7. Purée using a hand blender, blender, or food processor. Strain.

8. Add the brandy and season to taste with salt and pepper.

9. In a large pot, combine 4 quarts of the lobster bisque base with the heavy cream. (If the quantity of base is more or less than 4 quarts, adjust the amount of cream accordingly.) Bring to a boil. Remove from heat and serve warm.

Yield: 8 to 10 servings

SHAW'S CRAB HOUSE WILD TURKEY MANHATTAN

Erik Larson claims that the "charismatic bartender" at Shaw's Blue Crab Lounge added a lot to his enjoyment of this drink. But even without the bartender, we think you'll savor this taste of the Windy City.

2 ounces (¼ cup) Wild Turkey whiskey   *1 maraschino cherry*
Splash sweet vermouth

In a cocktail shaker filled with ice, shake the Wild Turkey and vermouth. Strain into a cocktail or martini glass. Garnish with a cherry. This drink can also be stirred without ice and served on the rocks.

Yield: 1 drink

BOOK CLUB PROFILE

Every year, thirty thousand children from the Dallas–Fort Worth area visit Old City Park: The Historical Village of Dallas to peruse its historic collections and enjoy its interactive exhibits. Old City Park strives to preserve structures and artifacts related to the history of Dallas and North Central Texas between the years 1840 and 1910 and interpret these materials for the public through educational programming.

With a successful children's program in place, the museum turned its attention to adults. "We wanted to attract more adults to our exhibits, especially the many young, upwardly mobile singles moving into the Dallas area," says Bethany Schirmer, program manager at Old City Park. As part of her effort to bring more adults to the site, Schirmer launched a book club in 2003. Every other month, five to ten men and women gather over box lunches to discuss books related to Texas history in the latter decades of the 1800s.

As she charts the book club's course, Schirmer focuses on the mission of the museum. Schirmer often brings artifacts from the museum's collection to discussions. She bases her selection of books, which are reviewed by a staff member for historical accuracy and appropriate focus, on particular sections of, or exhibits at, the museum.

For example, the museum is located near Dallas's original Jewish neighborhood. Old City Park boasts one of only two Jewish living history projects in the country, where an interpreter re-creates the daily life of a middle-class Jewish family living in Dallas in the year

1901. The house is kept kosher (that is, consistent with Jewish dietary laws) and the Jewish holidays are celebrated throughout the year, just as a traditional Jewish family did in the early twentieth century. This exhibit inspired Schirmer's choice of Rose Biderman's history, *They Came to Stay: The Story of the Jews of Dallas, 1870–1997.* The author, a local resident, thrilled book club members by attending the meeting.

When Schirmer chose Erik Larson's *The Devil in the White City: Murder, Magic, and Madness at the Fair That Changed America,* she departed slightly from the usual book selection criteria. "We fudged on this book because it's not set in Texas," says Schirmer. "But it falls within our time period, and we know that many people from Texas would have traveled to Chicago to see the World's Fair. Trains had come to Dallas in the 1870s. By the 1890s, a trip to Chicago would have been a comfortable ride and a good day's adventure."

The group was intrigued with Larson's depiction of Chicago during this period. "We talked about the atmosphere of the city that would allow a killer to get away with so much," says Schirmer. "So many people at the time thought Holmes's forward manner was appealing, that this was the way city folks must act."

Members were also struck by Americans' varying perceptions of the giant Ferris wheel erected for the fair. Visitors to the World's Fair criticized the wheel as looking flimsy and "airy," and worried that it might come crashing down. After studying photos of the 1893 structure, though, Schirmer's book club thought that, by today's standards, it looked "chunky."

Schirmer shared other photographs and artifacts with the group, including a picture book depicting the world in 1893 that included a section on the World's Fair, and photos that appeared to be taken from the top of the Ferris wheel. Most disturbing to the group were photos of two children, the serial killer's last victims, which the museum's collections manager found on the Internet. "To see children that you have heard and read so much about was haunting," says Schirmer.

More Food for Thought

Chef Julia Shanks of Interactive Cuisine in Cambridge, Massachusetts, creates unique dinner parties in her clients' homes, providing cooking demonstrations for hosts and their guests while preparing a gourmet three-course dinner. She also creates thematically appropriate menus for book clubs in the Boston area.

She found great culinary inspiration in the French menus reprinted in *The Devil in the White City*.

We asked Shanks to translate some of the dishes featured on the French menus in Larson's book and provide appropriate substitutions for the modern American home cook. The menus in the book involved many courses of small dishes, but Shanks recommends instead serving a large buffet, with each book club member bringing a dish.

The first menu, served to the architects who were considering joining head architect Daniel Hudson Burnham's team, utilizes seasonal spring produce: shad, asparagus, artichokes, and cucumbers. "Now you can find these ingredients year-round," says Shanks, "but in the late 1800s they would need to be in season."

Recipes for many of the French dishes mentioned in *The Devil in the White City* can be found in *Larousse Gastronomique* (Clarkson Potter, 2001), a classic French food encyclopedia. For those who prefer simpler adaptations, here are Shanks's suggestions:

Consommé of green turtle: Serve chicken broth with vegetables and chicken.

Broiled shad à la maréchal (breaded, fried shad): Substitute arctic char or mackerel, as shad is typically available only in the spring.

Potatoes à la duchesse (mashed potatoes enriched with egg yolks, piped into rosettes and baked): Serve mashed potatoes.

Filet mignon à la Rossini (filet of beef topped with a slab of foie gras and a slice of truffle): As foie gras and truffles are specialty items (and expensive), Shanks suggests serving beef tenderloin stuffed with pâté, roasted and drizzled with truffle oil or porcini oil.

Fonds d'artichaut farcis (stuffed artichoke hearts): Stuff artichoke hearts with herbed bread crumbs, crab salad, or another stuffing of your choice.

Sorbet au kirsch (cherry sorbet), used to cleanse the palate between courses: You may substitute a lemon or grapefruit sorbet.

Woodcock on toast: Serve a simple chicken liver pâté, or a more elegant duck pâté, from a gourmet grocer, on toast points.

Asparagus sala: Serve cold steamed asparagus.

Disgrace

J. M. Coetzee

RANDOM HOUSE (UK), 2003

(available in paperback from Penguin, 2003)

Professor David Lurie, the central character in Nobel laureate J. M. Coetzee's *Disgrace*, winner of the 1999 Booker Prize, is a middle-aged, twice divorced academic at a Cape Town, South Africa, college. Lurie leads a comfortable, contented, if uninspired, life. When his manipulative seduction of a young student leads to his dismissal from the college, and social disgrace, he lands on the doorstep of his daughter, Lucy, who is living a hardscrabble life on a small landholding in the country, where she farms and operates a small animal refuge.

At first, Lurie seems to regain his emotional balance in the country. He helps care for the animals, brings produce to a nearby market, and thinks about embarking on a scholarly work about Byron. But when Lucy and David are victimized in a brutal attack at the hands of two black neighbors, David becomes determined, against Lucy's wishes, to seek justice. The attack brings to the fore all the fault lines in their relationship and in postapartheid South Africa as well, where the balance of power between white and black is rapidly changing.

Coetzee's protagonist, David Lurie, has a sophisticated palate. David's idea of a simple dinner is anchovies on tagliatelle with a mushroom sauce, a dish he prepares for Melanie, the student he seduces. After visiting with his daughter, Lucy, on her farm, David makes an impromptu visit to Melanie's parents, who invite him to dinner. The dinner, "chicken in a bubbling tomato stew that gives off aromas of ginger and cumin, rice, an array of salads and pickles," is the "kind of food he most missed, living with Lucy." But there is one dish David enjoys at Lucy's: sweet potatoes.

Sweet Potatoes

Meals at Lucy's are usually simple affairs: bread, soup, and, sometimes, a sweet-potato dish that David especially enjoys. Usually David doesn't care for sweet potatoes, but "Lucy does something with lemon peel and butter and allspice that makes them palatable, more than palatable."

Beth Preiss recommended *Disgrace* to her Vegetarian Society of Washington, D.C., book club, after hearing Coetzee, who is vegetarian, read from the book at an animal rights conference. "What happens to people and animals in the book is disturbing, and we see the connection between the two," says Preiss.

We thought a vegetarian recipe for sweet potatoes would be appropriate to pair with *Disgrace*.

6 large sweet potatoes, peeled and cut into 2-inch cubes

2 tablespoons vegetable oil

1 cup brown sugar, packed

4 tablespoons butter

1 tablespoon freshly grated lemon peel

3 tablespoons lemon juice

½ teaspoon ground allspice

1. Preheat oven to 375°F. Place the cubed potatoes in a roasting pan. Drizzle with oil and toss to coat the pieces evenly. Bake until almost done, about 30 minutes.
2. While the potatoes are roasting, heat the brown sugar, butter, lemon peel, lemon juice, and allspice in a small saucepan until the butter is melted and the sugar is completely dissolved. Remove potatoes from oven and toss with the butter-sugar mixture. Return to the oven and continue cooking for 10 minutes, until the potatoes are cooked through.

Yield: 6 to 8 servings

BOOK CLUB PROFILE

"We all suffer from food snobbery to some extent, so it's important that our members can cook well, or at least order well," says Sarah Wortman of her Chicago-area book club. Her club's meetings are the perfect place to combine members' enthusiasm for cooking and literature, and the host often matches their brunch, lunch, or dinner menu to the monthly literary theme. "The friendly culinary competition started early on," says member Lisa von

Drehle. "One member's husband is a very ambitious cook, and he threw down the gauntlet by creating a theme meal to reflect and complement the reading selection."

Wortman, whose husband is Iraqi, prepared *fatoosh* (a bread salad), red lentil soup with *kubba* (ground meat and spices encased in bulgur), Middle Eastern sweets such as *kunafa* (a pastry filled with sweet cheese or pistachios) and baklava, Arabic coffee, and tea with cardamom when they discussed Adhaf Soueif's novel of Egypt, *The Map of Love.*

Rose Parisi invited the group to her lake house in Lakeside, Michigan, when they discussed Barbara Kingsolver's novel about a naturalist, *Prodigal Summer.* In keeping with the book's theme of living off the land, she served lamb and hummus, grilled vegetable salad, and classic homemade apple pie.

Each of the seven members of Wortman's book group works in an arts-related field—interior design, arts administration, museum administration, and video production—and each member brings a different professional, personal, and political viewpoint to the group.

The group reads many award-winning novels, as well as nonfiction about culture, politics, or the environment—books that challenge traditional ideas or tackle difficult subjects. "Our book club operates as a rotating dictatorship, not a democracy," says von Drehle. "Rose chooses interesting ethnic titles, I like the classics, and Janet selects earthy Americana. And Sarah likes more exotic books, and can back them up with Middle Eastern cooking to die for."

For von Drehle, membership in the club has introduced her to topics she might not have explored, such as mistreatment of Native Americans, from reading Dee Brown's *Bury My Heart at Wounded Knee,* or the lives of early American settlers, from reading Wallace Stegner's *Angle of Repose* (see p. 22).

"The books everyone likes often lead to the lamest discussions," says von Drehle. It is the difficult or disliked books that lead to very meaty discussions. J. M. Coetzee's *Disgrace* was an anomaly—a book everyone admired, but one that spawned a lively, invigorating discussion. "*Disgrace* was poetic in the simplicity of the writing but visceral in subject matter," says von Drehle. Wortman agrees: "*Disgrace* was a rich, dense novel, and it tackled many complex issues, including race, class, sexuality, sexual harassment, the academic establishment, and the transition from apartheid to an integrated society and government in South Africa."

The group was especially interested in Coetzee's treatment of sexual harassment. "We wondered whether or not the student, Melanie, would have brought sexual harassment charges against her instructor, Professor Lurie, had it not been for pressure from her boyfriend and father," says Wortman. "Why Professor Lurie chose to respond defiantly to charges of sexual harassment prompted a lot of lively discussion."

The group was also interested in the challenges Lucy, David's daughter, faced as she tried to maintain her farm. "She's alone on a farm and lives under the supposed protection of her closest neighbors, among whose circle lived her attackers," says Wortman. "The complexities of the situation in South Africa, the difficulties of assimilating a new set of values and cultural codes, and the ways people play out their history in a newly reconstructed present were all part of Lucy's life and our discussion."

More Food for Thought

For their discussion of *Disgrace*, Lisa von Drehle prepared a Serbian meal for her Chicago book club. Her husband is a Serb, and she had been learning about his native cuisine. "The idea was to serve cuisine from a tough, embattled part of the world," she says. "These are two parts of the world that have been torn apart by civil war and strife." Her menu included grilled *čevapčiči* (a Serbian sausage), *shopska* (salad with tomatoes, cucumbers, and feta), and what she calls "the Serbian national starch," bread.

The Dive from Clausen's Pier

Ann Packer

KNOPF, 2002

(available in paperback from Vintage, 2003)

For recent college graduate Carrie Bell, the protagonist of Ann Packer's first novel, *The Dive from Clausen's Pier*, life in her hometown of Madison, Wisconsin, is stifling. Carrie's passion for her fiancé, Mike, is waning and she is tiring of their group of friends. She feels stuck in time and place. But when a tragic accident leaves Mike a quadriplegic, Carrie is forced to make a painful choice between Mike and her own desire for independence. Pressured to care for him, Carrie flees Madison for New York City. There, she takes a recent acquaintance, Kilroy, as her lover, enrolls in fashion design classes, and begins a new life. Yet Carrie is plagued by guilt. "How much do we owe the people we love?" she asks as she tries to reconcile her past and future.

SOUR CHERRY PIE

Just after Mike's accident, the sight of a basket of cherries at the farmers' market in Madison stops Carrie "in her tracks" and summons memories of summers when she and Mike devoured sour cherry pies with their friends:

> Mike loved cherry pie, but it was Rooster who had a thing about it—the pinnacle of pie, he always said. Sour cherries had a short season, but at least once a summer a vanload from Michigan showed up at the Farmer's Market, and I bought enough for a couple of pies. A small group of us would skip dinner that night and gather for dessert on my second-story porch instead, sweet vanilla ice cream turning the cooked cherries the exact pink of bubble gum. "Perfect," Rooster would sigh, and for a while the only sound would be of forks scraping plates.

The vivid imagery of making a cherry pie remains with Carrie. She recalls a time when Mike's friend, Rooster, asked her to make three or four pies. When Rooster and Mike arrived at her house, "I was still pitting—slicing open cherry after cherry and pulling the stone out with the tip of my finger, my hands crimson."

Ann Packer described for us how she discovered sour cherries and sour cherry pie when she lived in Madison, Wisconsin. Packer's description of Carrie's cherry pitting and pie baking mirrors her own experience. Says Packer:

I had never understood cherry pie. What was the appeal of the overly sweet, gelatinous filling? Other fruit pies delighted me: I baked peach pies, blueberry, raspberry, mixed berry, but based on what I'd tasted—and seen—in the occasional diner, never did I try to bake a cherry pie. Then one summer I found myself living in Madison, Wisconsin, and at the wonderful farmers' market there I discovered a fruit stand advertising Michigan sour cherries.

A native Californian, I'd never seen these small red orbs before, but the line to buy them was long and I was curious, so I bought a quart or so, took them home, and sliced out each pit by hand. The juice stained everything, but the fruit was tart and delicious. Into a crust they went, and soon I was a convert: cherry pie in any other form was second tier at best, but sour cherry pie, made from cherries grown in Michigan, where, I suppose, the extremes of climate supply just what these cherries need to grow: now that is good pie. The memory remained even after I'd left the Midwest, and the pie made its way into my first novel.

NOTE: Sour cherries, also called tart cherries, grown in large quantities in Michigan as well as other North American states, are harvested in July and can usually be found at farmers' markets. Since the season for fresh sour cherries is so short, most cooks will need to find canned or jarred sour cherries for this recipe. *Cook's Illustrated* magazine recommends baking with jarred morello cherries when fresh sour cherries are not available. (See Purchasing Information, p. 499.)

If using fresh cherries, pit the fruit with a cherry pitter or a small, sharp knife.

1 Basic Pie Crust (see below)

4 cups fresh sour cherries, pitted, or
*   2 24-ounce jars morello cherries, drained*
*   (see note above)*

½ cup granulated sugar
½ cup brown sugar
¼ cup all-purpose flour

1 teaspoon ground cinnamon (optional)

1 tablespoon lemon juice

1 teaspoon vanilla extract

½ teaspoon almond extract

1 tablespoon butter, cut into pieces

1. Preheat oven to 425°F. Make Basic Pie Crust, following steps 1 and 2. Refrigerate dough while preparing filling.
2. In a large bowl, combine the cherries, sugars, flour, cinnamon, lemon juice, and vanilla and almond extracts. Stir to mix well.
3. Roll out one disc of chilled dough and line a 9-inch pie plate. Fill the pastry shell with cherry mixture and dot with butter.
4. Roll top crust, cover pie with top crust, and trim and flute edges. Pierce several times with a fork to make steam vents. Cover loosely with aluminum foil.
5. Bake 25 minutes. Reduce heat to 350°F and bake an additional 15 minutes. Remove foil and bake until crust is lightly browned, about 15 minutes. Cool on a wire rack. Serve with vanilla ice cream.

Yield: 1 9-inch pie; 6 to 8 servings

BASIC PIE CRUST

3 cups sifted all-purpose flour

2 tablespoons sugar

¼ teaspoon salt

1 cup vegetable shortening

12–16 tablespoons ice water

1. Combine the flour, sugar, and salt in a medium bowl. Cut in the shortening using a pastry cutter or a fork until a pea-sized coarse meal forms. Sprinkle with ice water while mixing gently with a fork, until the mixture forms a dough. The dough should not be wet but should form a ball when pressed together. A little more water may be added if needed.
2. Form the dough into two flat discs. Cover with plastic wrap and refrigerate for at least 30 minutes or until ready to use.
3. Lightly flour a rolling surface (you will need a surface at least 15 inches square). With a lightly floured rolling pin, roll a ball of dough out into a circle, working outward from the center. The crust should be about ⅛ inch thick and 14 inches in diameter. Lift the dough from the rolling surface and place in a 9-inch pie plate. Gently press crust flat against the bottom and

sides. Trim off excess. Roll top crust, lay over filling, trim off excess, and crimp edge to finish (or use for a second single-crust pie).

Yield: Pastry for 2 9-inch pie crusts, or 1 double-crust pie

BOOK CLUB PROFILE

Northwest Passages meets in members' Seattle-area homes one Friday evening a month. "We're all at the age where none of us craves fettuccine Alfredo anymore," jokes member Susan Beaty. The hostess prepares a big salad and each member brings an appetizer, dessert, or wine. "We've always had good food at meetings but started preparing food to complement the book; it helps us identify with the book's theme, and it just makes it more fun," says Beaty.

Among their theme meals: a seafood spread for Annie Proulx's novel about fishermen in Newfoundland, *The Shipping News;* Middle Eastern food for Andre Dubus III's *House of Sand and Fog* (see p. 197); and a southern buffet for Sue Monk Kidd's *The Secret Life of Bees* (see p. 398). Beaty's sister, Nancy Hurley, started the group in 2000 so friends could meet at a regular time and talk about something other than kids, carpools, and jobs. The members, all female, have a variety of professional backgrounds; they are schoolteachers, sales representatives, and medical professionals.

Ann Packer's *The Dive from Clausen's Pier* "inspired much speculation about our own lives," says Beaty. "How might we feel if we were twenty-three and facing Carrie's quandary, and what would we have done? Some members felt that as difficult a choice as it would be, they would have gone to New York. But some felt an obligation to Mike. He lost his ability to walk, his independence, and his best friend and lover. It seemed as if it was all due to the accident, though unknowingly he had lost Carrie before the accident," says Beaty. "We thought that when Carrie did go back to Wisconsin, she was motivated by her guilt and her need to have resolution to what their relationship had been and what it would be in the future," she adds.

More Food for Thought

The SeaDogs book club is named for the Computer Science and Artificial Intelligence Laboratory (CSAIL) at the Massachusetts Institute of Technology in Cambridge, Massachusetts, where members conduct artificial intelligence research. The doctoral candidates in computer science prepared upscale New York–style finger foods for their discussion of *The Dive from Clausen's Pier*.

SeaDogs members sipped champagne cosmopolitans while they nibbled on caramelized onion, apple, and brie tartlets, artichokes with saffron garlic aioli, yellow pepper pork loin, spinach and cheese tortellini with pesto, and bacon-wrapped soy-ginger water chestnuts, with key lime parfait for dessert. "New York food wasn't necessarily the most obvious selection, although much of the book takes place in Manhattan," says Jaime Teevan, a SeaDog member. "Casseroles and sour cherry pie might have made more sense, but dinner sure was good."

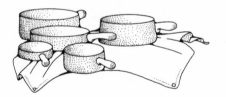

Douglass' Women

Jewell Parker Rhodes

....

ATRIA, 2002

(available in paperback from Washington Square Press, 2003)

I N *DOUGLASS' WOMEN*, Jewell Parker Rhodes imagines a romantic triangle involving the African-American abolitionist Frederick Douglass, his African-American wife, and his white mistress. This work of historical fiction is told through the alternating narratives of the two women who knew and loved him best: his wife, Anna, a southern housekeeper and a freed woman of color, who facilitates Douglass's escape to freedom from slavery, and Ottilie Assing, his wealthy German half-Jewish mistress, who serves as his translator during travels abroad.

Anna's is a portrait of wife as victim. Douglass marries her out of loyalty and a sense of obligation, and leaves her for extended periods while he travels in Europe promoting his cause—and avoiding the slave catchers back home. Douglass takes for granted Anna's hard work cleaning, cooking, gardening, and raising his five children, and has an affair with Ottilie aboard ship and in Europe, which then continues under Anna's roof. Yet Anna and "Freddy" share tender and passionate domestic moments, and he is an adoring father.

Ottilie has money, social experience, and a network of friends who can support the abolitionist movement. She also has a knowledge of languages, which is a great help to Douglass in Europe. Ottilie's life with Douglass is in many ways the opposite of Anna's: She is lovely, whereas Anna is plain; she is educated, whereas Anna cannot read. Ottilie yearns for a child by Douglass, whereas Anna becomes pregnant easily and often.

Through the accounts of Anna and Ottilie, Rhodes gives us a humane portrait of Douglass—who rose from slavery to become adviser to President Lincoln and was known and acclaimed on two continents as a leader of the abolitionist movement—as he struggles with the cultural contradictions of his time and the tangled, tumultuous love relationships of his personal life.

Jewell Parker Rhodes shared these thoughts on the importance of food in the life of Anna Douglass.

Food, for Anna Douglass, always meant love. Tending the garden, making preserves, baking biscuits, stewing greens, and braising meat were all examples of her womanly skills and beauty.

In my novel, *Douglass' Women*, Anna rejects reading and writing when she discovers that her husband, the great abolitionist Frederick Douglass, is ashamed of her. Anna believed in literacy and encouraged her children to be well educated, but in my fictional world, she refuses to read until her husband learns to value her domestic skills. Feeding the body is akin to feeding the spirit, and many times, Anna fed Frederick so that he could carry on his freedom fighting. She fed her children too, making small banquets infused with all the care, love, and kindness in her heart.

Cooking is a celebration of self. It is a gift to one's family and community. It is a talent that ensures survival.

Anna, newly fallen in love with the slave Frederick, packs him a dinner. Chicken and biscuits. Banana pie. The pie is rich, exotic, sweetened with bananas from the tropics. It is no ordinary berry, pumpkin, or apple pie. Banana pie, with its crisp crust and melt-in-the-mouth filling, conjures dreams of sensuality. Banana pie is Anna's way of saying, "Oh, see what my womanly hands can do. See the depth of passion in my heart."

BANANA CREAM PIE

In *Douglass' Women*, Anna notes that Baltimore Harbor in 1841 was the port of entry for a variety of goods, including sugarcane from Haiti and bananas.

Early American cream pies were butter cakes with cream or cooked-custard fillings, according to Beatrice Ojakangas, author of *Great Old-Fashioned American Desserts* (Dutton, 1987). "In the late 1800s, cream pie with a baked pastry crust began to be popular," writes Ojakangas. "Bananas were imported from the West Indies and were incorporated into the cream pie."

Stephanie Koura of Seattle's Wuthering Bites Book Club enjoys this version of Banana Cream Pie, from *The Best Recipe*, by the editors of *Cook's Illustrated* magazine (Boston Common Press, 1999). Koura calls it the perfect comfort food for a potluck. "It's both special and homey," she says, "and rich and light at the same time." Top with Sweetened Whipped Cream (see p. 424).

For the graham cracker crust

1¼ cups all-purpose flour

½ teaspoon salt

1 tablespoon sugar

4 tablespoons unsalted butter, cut into
¼-inch pieces and chilled

3 tablespoons vegetable shortening, chilled

4–5 tablespoons ice water

½ cup graham-cracker crumbs

Flour for dusting

For the cream filling

½ cup plus 2 tablespoons sugar

¼ cup cornstarch

⅛ teaspoon salt

5 large egg yolks, lightly beaten

2 cups milk

½ cup evaporated milk

½ vanilla bean, split lengthwise

2 tablespoons unsalted butter

1–2 teaspoons brandy

2 bananas, peeled and sliced

1. To make the crust: In a food processor, pulse together the flour, salt, and sugar. Scatter the butter over the flour, tossing to coat with flour, and cut butter into flour with 5 1-second pulses. Add the shortening and continue cutting in until flour is pale yellow and resembles coarse cornmeal. Turn mixture into a medium bowl.

2. Sprinkle 4 tablespoons of ice water over the mixture. With the blade of a rubber spatula, mix the water in with a folding motion. Press down on the mixture with the broad side of the spatula until the dough sticks together (add up to 1 more tablespoon of ice water if needed). Shape the dough into a ball, squeezing 2 or 3 times with your hands until it's cohesive, then flatten it into a 4-inch-wide disk. Dust lightly with flour, wrap in plastic, and refrigerate at least 30 minutes, or up to 2 days, before rolling.

3. Remove the dough from the refrigerator and let stand at room temperature to soften slightly. Sprinkle a couple of tablespoons of graham-cracker crumbs on work surface. Roll out the dough into a 12-inch disk about ⅛-inch thick, sprinkling both the top and the bottom of the pie crust with the remaining graham-cracker crumbs as you roll. Fold the dough into quarters, then place the dough point in the center of a 9-inch pie pan. Unfold dough.

4. Working around the pan, press the dough carefully into the pan by gently lifting dough edges with one hand while pressing around the pan bottom with the other hand. Trim edge to ½ inch beyond the lip of the pan. Tuck this rim of dough underneath itself so that the folded edge is about ¼ inch beyond the lip. Flute dough in your own fashion. Refrigerate the shell for 40 minutes and then freeze for 20 minutes.

5. Adjust oven rack to middle position and preheat to 375°F. Remove shell from freezer. Press a doubled 12-inch square of aluminum foil inside the pie shell. Evenly distribute about 1 cup of ceramic or metal pie weights over the foil. Bake, leaving foil and weights in place, until dough dries out, about 17 minutes. Carefully remove foil and weights. Continue baking

until crust is a deep golden brown, about 15 more minutes. Transfer to a wire rack to cool completely.

6. To make the cream filling: Whisk together the sugar, cornstarch, and salt in a medium saucepan. Add the egg yolks, then immediately but gradually whisk in the milk and evaporated milk. Drop in the vanilla bean. Cook 8–10 minutes over medium heat, stirring frequently at first, then constantly as mixture starts to thicken and begins to simmer. After the mixture comes to a simmer, continue to cook, stirring constantly, for 1 minute longer. Remove pan from heat. Whisk in the butter and brandy. Remove vanilla bean, scrape out seeds, and whisk them back into the filling.

7. Pour the filling into a shallow pan. Put plastic wrap directly over filling surface to prevent a skin from forming; allow to cool about 20–30 minutes, but filling should still be warm. Pour ½ of warm filling into prepared pie shell. Top with the banana slices, then cover with remaining pie filling. Cover with plastic wrap and refrigerate until completely chilled, about 3 more hours.

8. To make the whipped-cream topping: Beat the cream and sugar with an electric mixer until soft peaks form; add the vanilla. Continue to beat to barely stiff peaks. Spread over filling and refrigerate until ready to serve.

Yield: 1 (9-inch) pie, 6 to 8 servings

BOOK CLUB PROFILE

As a coed book club devoted to African-American literature, the Soulfull Readers offer something unique to the Atlanta, Georgia, area. "Our group is currently one of the few African-American book clubs in Atlanta that welcomes both men and women," says Trenee Seward, who founded the group in 2001, soon after graduating from college with a degree in English. "We think a mixed group makes discussions more well-rounded," says Seward. "Having men in attendance helps the ladies of the group steer clear of male bashing. And most of the male members are former English majors themselves, so when discussion questions run short, they always step right up to the plate and start asking the questions that force us to see new things."

Others agree that a coed format works well. The club's mailing list includes close to two hundred names, although meetings generally attract about twenty-five people. The group— usually composed largely of twentysomething and thirtysomething women, with a handful of men—gathers monthly "to discuss classic and contemporary African-American fiction (and occasionally nonfiction) and enjoy a good meal at a local Atlanta restaurant. Needless to say, we are a group of book lovers who enjoy thought-provoking, in-depth discussions about African-American literature," reads the Soulfull Readers website.

The club tackles books from many genres, including mystery, historical fiction, and classic and contemporary fiction. Favorites include Maxine Clair's *October Suite* (see p. 316), Sister Souljah's *The Coldest Winter Ever* (see p. 71), and Michael Baisden's *God's Gift to Women*, about the consequences of casual sex with a stranger.

Food adds a festive element to Soulfull Readers meetings. Each month, the group meets at a different local restaurant for a meal and book discussion. "Going out to a different restaurant every month gives us all a chance to get out and socialize," says Seward. "And good food puts new members at ease, so they start feeling comfortable in a group of strange people." Restaurants, all in the greater Atlanta area, are chosen for their location and the quality of their food.

Occasionally the Soulfull Readers gather in a more intimate setting, as they did for their discussion of one of the group's favorites, Jewell Parker Rhodes's *Douglass' Women*. Over pizza in a group member's office, the dozen or so women and men compared their reactions to the book's not-so-complimentary revelations about a much-beloved historical figure. "The major discussion we got into is how we expect some of our black leaders to lead perfect lives, to basically not be human. Reading *Douglass' Women* really caught us off guard and made us think," says Seward. "Although Rhodes's story was fictional, we had the sense that many of the things going on in this novel actually did take place."

Members tried to identify with the female characters in the book, with limited success. "We all agreed that we would never have acted the way Douglass's wife, Anna, did," says Seward. "But then we reminded ourselves that the characters lived in a different time, and expectations were different."

Seward says the group also shared a laugh over how Douglass's mistress stayed around all that time, hoping that he'd finally marry her or that she'd bear his children. Neither ever happened. "What a life wasted," says Seward.

The Emperor of Ocean Park

Stephen L. Carter

KNOPF, 2002

(available in paperback from Vintage, 2003)

*T*HE *EMPEROR OF OCEAN PARK* combines mystery with a peek at East Coast black intellectual society. Set in a fictional New England college town and on Martha's Vineyard, *The Emperor of Ocean Park* is the story of Talcott Garland, a law professor whose father—"the Judge"—dies under mysterious circumstances. Talcott sets out to unravel the mystery of the death of his father, a prominent conservative whose earlier Supreme Court nomination had withered under the attack of political opponents. Talcott is following a trail, but he also is being followed: FBI agents, an underworld boss, and a seductive spy, Maxine, badger him for information. His search for the truth puts pressure on his already-crumbling marriage. Talcott seeks spiritual guidance from a compassionate minister who helps him find serenity in some, but by no means all, aspects of his restless life.

CRAB CAKES WITH SPICY REMOULADE

I n his will, the Judge has left Talcott his upper-crust Martha's Vineyard home, the setting for many of the book's climactic scenes. In one of these scenes, Talcott is driving on the island when Maxine, in hot pursuit, smashes into him. The two end up discussing business at a local restaurant that touts its crab cakes as the best, a claim common among island eateries. The crab cakes turn out to be "delicious, for the chef has managed to keep them flaky and light without leaving them with the fishy taste that is a sure sign of undercooking. The sauce is peppy but unintrusive." We have cooked up our own version of typical New England crab cakes, along with a peppy sauce, below.

NOTE: You may substitute saltines, ground in a food processor, for the cracker meal.

2 teaspoons Old Bay seasoning

2 eggs

2 tablespoons minced shallot

¼ cup chopped fresh parsley

4 tablespoons mayonnaise

2 tablespoons Worcestershire sauce

2 teaspoons Dijon-style mustard

⅔ cup cracker meal

2 pounds cooked lump crab meat, picked over

4 tablespoons vegetable oil

All-purpose flour for dusting

Spicy Remoulade (see below)

1. Whisk together the Old Bay seasoning, eggs, shallot, parsley, mayonnaise, Worcestershire sauce, and mustard. Stir in cracker meal, then gently mix in crab meat. Shape into patties about 3 inches across, place on waxed paper, and refrigerate 1 hour.

2. Heat half the oil in a large frying pan over medium-high heat. Dust the crab cakes with flour and sauté in batches, a few minutes on each side, until golden brown. Add oil to the pan as needed. Serve warm with Spicy Remoulade.

Yield: 15–20 cakes (serves 8 to 10 as an appetizer)

SPICY REMOULADE

1 cup mayonnaise

4 tablespoons minced cornichons

2 tablespoons minced red onion

2 tablespoons capers, chopped

2 tablespoons finely chopped red bell pepper

2 tablespoons finely chopped yellow bell pepper

2 teaspoons minced garlic

2 tablespoons fresh lemon juice

Salt and black pepper

Cayenne pepper

Tabasco sauce

Combine the mayonnaise, cornichons, onion, capers, red and yellow peppers, garlic, and lemon juice in a bowl. Add salt, black pepper, cayenne, and Tabasco sauce to taste. Mix thoroughly and refrigerate.

Yield: 2 cups

Occasionally, a book club changes peoples' lives. The Book Lovers Club of Ann Arbor, Michigan, is one of them. Formed in 1997 by librarians Margaret Wolfe and Sonia Matthews of the Washtenaw County Library for the Blind and Physically Disabled, members of the Book Lovers Club are almost all visually impaired. For each of their six yearly meetings, they listen to three audio books and then meet at the library to discuss the selections.

A meeting of the Book Lovers Club is much more than a book discussion; it is a way for people, isolated and sometimes lonely, to communicate and connect with others. While the group boasts a diverse membership—African Americans, Asians, Caucasians; liberals, conservatives; men, women; young and old—the members' disabilities and their love of books unite them. "Most have become disabled as a result of aging," says Wolfe, "and this makes them feel particularly isolated. It's the disability that separates them from others in the Ann Arbor community." The book club combats this isolation, a fact proved by its burgeoning membership. In six years, it has grown from five or six members to more than thirty. "This group has brought people together," says Matthews. "The trust and friendship between members has grown over the years as a result of coming every other month. People who are isolated because of a disability coming together, offering opinions, making friends—this is something that is meaningful to our lives."

And nothing brings people together like food. Wolfe and Matthews are as effusive about food as they are about their book club's mission. "We have the best food in town!" they boast, which usually includes desserts, savory snacks, coffee, and beverages. The leaders believe food has helped create a comfortable social environment that encourages open sharing. They always provide large quantities of food ("If you have just a little, people won't eat it!") and freely replenish portions. "This makes people feel more comfortable, which means they're more likely to be vulnerable, more likely to share," says Matthews. "People often come an hour early just to get food and sit and talk to each other," she reports. "People take doggie bags home, people talk about the food, share the food, and linger over the food. It's a crucial part of our meetings."

The Book Lovers Club read and adored *The Emperor of Ocean Park*. They found a wealth of topics for discussion, including race, religion, marriage, politics, and family relationships. The upper-class African-American society featured in the book fascinated members of all races, and African-American group members spoke of the reality that lighter-skinned blacks "pass" more easily, even in African-American circles. Group discussion fixed on the character of the Christian minister, too. While some members appreciated his advice to Talcott to look beyond his own anger and view his situation more broadly, others felt that as a character, the minister was overblown. "It was like being a witness to an event," says member Morry Nathan, who is legally blind. "Everyone has a different story as to what they saw. There were twenty different opinions. This was a particularly lively discussion!"

The group's open discussion of race and religion—difficult, controversial topics for any group—prompted Wolfe to comment on how far her book club has come. "A couple of years ago, we couldn't have had this discussion," she says. "But the group has coalesced. Members are not afraid of saying things that people might be critical of, or of letting their vulnerabilities come out."

More Food for Thought

Talcott and his young son would have enjoyed "vanilla malts or strawberry cones" at Mad Martha's, a signature island ice cream shop, had it been open. Instead, they travel to a local candy shop, Murdick's, for cranberry fudge. When the Book Lovers Club group leader Sonia Matthews visited Martha's Vineyard, the island setting of *The Emperor of Ocean Park*, she discovered lemon sorbet with cranberry topping—and decided to serve it to her book group back in Michigan.

The game of chess, Talcott's hobby and a key to solving the mystery of the Judge's death, inspired the Bookenders Book Club of Lee's Summit, Missouri. For their *Emperor of Ocean Park* meeting, they served chess pie, a dessert dating to colonial times and still popular in the South today, made with a simple filling of eggs, butter, sugar, and lemon juice, and Pepperidge Farm Chessmen butter cookies.

More Food for Thought

The Novel Women, readers from several of Massachusetts' North Shore communities, held their *Emperor of Ocean Park* book club meeting at the Manchester Bath and Tennis Club overlooking the beach, where they served wine and hors d'oeuvres that the chic partygoers described in the mystery might enjoy: cheddar cheese thumbprint biscuits with pepper jelly, a salmon ring, cherry tomatoes stuffed with crabmeat and chicken salad, skewers of cheddar cheese with candied ginger, shrimp cocktail, petite Italian pastries, and a fruit bowl with kirsch.

Empire Falls

Richard Russo

KNOPF, 2001

(available in paperback from Vintage, 2002)

RICHARD RUSSO's Pulitzer Prize—winning novel is a portrait of a depressed small New England mill town whose fate has been in the hands of a powerful and wealthy family for nearly a century.

The Whitings own the mills and the real estate, and employ the majority of residents in the imaginary town of Empire Falls, Maine. Their sale of the textile businesses to multinational corporations abroad has a devastating economic impact on the town. The abandoned factories are a constant reminder of the town's economic decline, yet residents continue to believe "that Empire Falls would be restored to its old economic viability."

For the last fifteen years, forty-year-old Miles Roby has managed the Empire Grill, the town diner. As a teenager he worked at the restaurant under the thumb of Francine Whiting, the town's conniving matriarch, who has assured Miles that he will inherit the Empire Grill upon her death.

Miles left college, returning to Empire Falls to care for his ailing mother, and never left. His mother's dream was for Miles to have a life beyond Empire Falls, the same wish Miles has for his teenage daughter, Tick. In the midst of a divorce, and burdened by an irresponsible father and a brother recovering from alcoholism, Miles bears the weight of the world on his shoulders. To salvage the future for himself and his daughter, Miles must overcome the inertia that has anchored him to Empire Falls.

Miles's brother David helps him run the Grill and dreams of upgrading the diner's greasy-spoon fare to increase business. David convinces Miles to open the Empire Grill weekend nights for dinner to serve "good, cheap ethnic food" to attract a new clientele: college students and professors from nearby Fairhaven, who would consider the diner's "worn out cigarette-burned countertop and wobbly booths 'honest' or 'retro.'"

Although Miles is skeptical, David's culinary initiative succeeds. The college crowd makes the seven-mile trip for international nights. Chinese night features Twice-Cooked Noodles with

Scallops in Hoisin Sauce—a radical departure from the typical fried haddock and mashed-potato specials.

SHRIMP FLAUTAS

Miles arrives at the Grill one Friday night to find the parking lot full and a waiting list for tables. It is Mexican night, and David has concocted shrimp flautas as the featured special. "Who knew Dexter County would go for *flautas*?" Miles asks Charlene, the longtime waitress at the Empire Grill.

A flauta is a tortilla rolled around a filling, and fried until crisp. Our Shrimp Flautas, certainly not your typical diner fare, are a tribute to David's Down East ingenuity. Try topping the flautas with Green Chile Salsa (p. 449).

NOTE: Wear plastic or rubber gloves while handling the chiles to protect your skin from the oil in them. Avoid direct contact with your eyes, and wash your hands thoroughly after handling.

16 7- to 8-inch-diameter flour tortillas

3 cloves garlic, minced

4 tablespoons butter

3 jalapeño chiles, stems and seeds removed,
   cut in ⅛-inch slivers

1 pound medium-size shrimp,
   shelled and deveined

Salt

¾ cup shredded Monterey Jack cheese
   (preferably high-quality)

2 tablespoons olive oil

2 cups salsa

1 cup sour cream

1. Slice a strip about 1½ inches wide from opposite sides of each tortilla. The idea is to have an oblong measuring about 4x7 inches. Cover the tortillas to keep them moist.

2. Place the minced garlic in a small bowl and combine with 1 tablespoon of water. Set aside.

3. Melt 1 tablespoon of butter in a large saucepan. Add the jalapeño chiles and sauté 1 minute, until they begin to soften. Add the garlic with its water and stir. Add another tablespoon of butter and the shrimp. Sauté, turning frequently, until the shrimp are pink, about 2 minutes. Add salt to taste. Do not overcook. After the mixture has cooled a bit, chop the shrimp very coarsely.

4. Heat a nonstick or cast-iron skillet over medium-high heat. Place a small bowl of water beside your work area. Briefly heat a tortilla on each side in the skillet to soften it. Working on

a flat surface, spread about 2 tablespoons of the shrimp mixture and 1 tablespoon of cheese along one long edge of the tortilla. Roll tightly into a long, thin shape. Before closing, dip a finger in the water and wet the edge of the tortilla—this will help hold it together. Repeat with remaining tortilllas.

5. Heat the remaining 2 tablespoons of butter and the olive oil in a frying pan and fry the flautas, in batches, 1–2 minutes, until golden-brown and crispy on all sides. Drain well on brown paper or paper towels.

6. Serve each flauta garnished with a dollop of salsa and sour cream.

Yield: 16 flautas

BOOK CLUB PROFILE

The four men and four women of the Madisonville Community College Book Discussion Group are faculty members at the Kentucky college, "but there are no lectures during the meetings," says Marcella Davis, an instructor of developmental writing, who founded the group in 1999.

Davis employs a method she calls "shared inquiry" to encourage a free flow of ideas during meetings. "This brings everyone into the conversation rather than having a member responsible for 'teaching' the book to the others," says Davis. "One member asks a question and the discussion takes off from there," she adds.

Reading selections are chosen from many categories and based on recommendations from group members. During the summer, members read books of their own choosing, and, when they meet back at school in August, members create a reading list for the year. The monthly meetings take place over potluck breakfast on Friday mornings. The menu has become a tradition—each member regularly contributes his or her selected food: a breakfast casserole, sweet rolls, orange juice, grapes, sometimes even gravy and biscuits.

The group's favorite book of 2003 was Richard Russo's *Empire Falls*. "We all agreed Russo deserved the Pulitzer Prize for this book," says Davis. "Russo unfolded the plot so gradually that the reader doesn't realize that vengeance covers entire lifetimes until the end."

The group spent a lot of time pondering the character of Miles Roby, the book's protagonist, his unfulfilled dreams, and how he had become reconciled to his life and its disappointments. "We also explored the symbolism in the novel. For example, the black cat was the epitome of evil and is washed away in the floodwaters of self-awareness in the closing scene," says Davis.

More Food for Thought

Katherine Thomerson, owner of the Frugal Frigate bookstore in Redlands, California, served diner fare—miniature hamburgers from Trader Joe's, along with potato chips, wine, and cider—when her store's A Room of Her Own Reading Group discussed *Empire Falls*. "The diner-style food put us in the mood for discussion," says Thomerson, "and it was just fun."

Endurance: Shackleton's Incredible Voyage

Alfred Lansing

ORION PUBLISHING CO., 2000

(available in paperback from Carroll & Graf, 1999)

*E*NDURANCE: SHACKLETON'S INCREDIBLE VOYAGE is a thrilling chronicle of the heroic survival of a small group of explorers during a failed attempt to cross Antarctica in 1914 and 1915.

By the early 1900s, the British explorer Sir Ernest Shackleton had already attempted to reach the South Pole twice. After the Norwegian explorer Roald Amundsen became the first person to reach the South Pole in 1912 (beating the British explorer Robert F. Scott by weeks), Shackleton decided it was time to restore honor to his country—and bring fame and wealth to himself—by crossing the Antarctic on foot.

In August 1914, Shackleton's ship, the *Endurance*, sailed from England, carrying twenty-seven men and sixty-nine sledge dogs. Fifteen months later, immobilized in the ice of the Weddell Sea (southeast of the southern tip of South America, south of the Antarctic Circle), the *Endurance* succumbed to the enormous pressure of the frozen sea, leaving its crew stranded on an island of ice six feet thick and 346 miles from tiny Paulet Island, where they hoped to find stores of food. With nothing but the sled dogs, several crates of food, three small boats, and his wits, Shackleton had to lead his men back to civilization.

In 1959, after scouring journals and photographs from the adventure, journalist Alfred Lansing wrote what has become the definitive account of Shackleton's voyage. In *Endurance*, Lansing paints a portrait of leadership, as Shackleton and his men manage to feed themselves from the spare offerings of the arctic landscape; shelter themselves against severe weather with snow, mud, and rock; and prepare a small boat to make a daring open ocean run across some of the world's most unforgiving seas.

A crew member later called Shackleton "the greatest leader that ever came on God's earth, bar none."

OATMEAL BISCUITS

Food and nutrition played a large role in the success or failure of the British and Norwegian explorers of the early decades of the twentieth century. Scurvy, caused by a lack of vitamin C, plagued sailors in large numbers. Fresh food was known to cure the illness. Unbeknownst to Shackleton's crew, the seal and penguin meat they found contained enough vitamin C to prevent scurvy. If, however, Charles J. Green, the ship's cook, followed the British custom of overcooking the meat to kill the fishy taste, he also would have destroyed the vitamin C.

Similar to crackers, biscuits were usually a staple of explorers' diets. Small and crisp, biscuits packed easily and rarely got stale. Their ingredients varied. Shackleton's crew probably ate the British version, made with white flour and sodium bicarbonate. Norwegian explorers such as Amundsen enjoyed more nutritious biscuits made with oatmeal and yeast, which provided essential B vitamins. Amundsen described his oatmeal biscuits in his account of his 1912 expedition, *The South Pole, Volume 1:*

> The biscuits were a present from a well-known Norwegian factory, and did all honour to their origin. They were specially baked for us, and were made of oatmeal with the addition of dried milk and a little sugar; they were extremely nourishing and pleasant to the taste. Thanks to efficient packing, they kept fresh and crisp all the time. These biscuits formed a great part of our daily diet, and undoubtedly contributed in no small degree to the successful result.

We include below a recipe for a sweet Norwegian-style biscuit. Containing oatmeal and buttermilk, as well as our own addition of sweet dried fruit, these biscuits are best served warm, straight from the oven, accompanied by honey, butter, or jam.

1 cup all-purpose flour
1 tablespoon sugar
1 tablespoon baking powder
½ teaspoon ground cinnamon
¼ teaspoon salt
⅛ teaspoon ground ginger
4 tablespoons cold butter, cut into pieces
1 cup old-fashioned rolled oats

⅓ cup mixed dried fruit (any combination of golden raisins, cherries, cranberries, and blueberries)
⅓ cup buttermilk
1 egg
2 tablespoons honey
Coarse sugar for topping (see Purchasing Information, p. 499)

1. Preheat oven to 425°F. Combine the flour, sugar, baking powder, cinnamon, salt, and ginger in a mixing bowl. Cut the butter in using a pastry knife or a fork, until mixture resembles coarse meal. With a fork, stir in the oats and dried fruit.

2. In a separate bowl, beat together the buttermilk, egg, and honey. Add to the flour mixture and stir with a fork until a soft dough forms.

3. Drop the dough by spoonfuls onto a cookie sheet lined with parchment. Press down lightly on the tops of the biscuits and sprinkle generously with coarse sugar. Bake until lightly browned, about 10 minutes.

Yield: 14 to 16 biscuits

For more on oatmeal biscuits, see p. 243.

BOOK CLUB PROFILE

The Last Thursday Book Club of Albuquerque, New Mexico, is made up of twelve self-described "mildly mature males"—retired military and present and former employees of Sandia National Laboratories and the University of New Mexico—who love to read. Inspired, albeit gradually, by their wives' book club, which had been meeting since 1977, the husbands formed the Last Thursday Book Club in 1993. Today, two couples are still represented in both groups.

With their professional backgrounds, the men's penchant for numbers should come as no surprise. They have rated more than one hundred books using a numerical system that carries out to the third decimal place (you can view their ratings at http://mike.blackledge.com/LTBC_ordered_ballot.htm). They're not just techies, though. The rhymes of Keith Gilbert, the group's poet laureate, can also be found on the website, where he has posted irreverent reviews of books.

Last Thursday tends to read historical nonfiction, books by southwestern authors (such as Tony Hillerman, Rudolfo Anaya, and Cormac McCarthy) or with southwestern themes, and books from the Modern Library's top one hundred list of novels. For their tenth anniversary, Last Thursday tackled *Ulysses* by James Joyce. Most members didn't finish it, and some hated it—but it made for provocative discussion. Charter member Tom Genoni, whose unblemished attendance record over the club's ten-year history is known as "The Streak," says the club has "introduced me to many classics and great authors I probably should have read a long time ago."

Food at the Last Thursday Book Club meetings is simple: snacks, dessert, soft drinks, beer, and wine. The host serves dessert only after the book votes are cast, "wherein the tradition is that those voting down the host's selection receive the smallest portions," according to longtime member Mike Blackledge, a manager for Software Quality at Sandia National Labs.

The group read and admired *Endurance: Shackleton's Incredible Voyage,* which ranks third on Last Thursday's all-time list. Members talked about the almost unbelievable series of events during the voyage, as well as Shackleton's extraordinary leadership. "We were struck by how much Shackleton and his men were able to accomplish, how they managed to save every last member of the crew," Genoni says. "I don't think Alfred Lansing received enough recognition for his wonderful narrative." Blackledge agreed, characterizing the tale as an illustration of "true leadership, perseverance, and the successes of the indomitable spirit of man" and a "thrilling reading experience."

More Food for Thought

To accompany his book club's discussion of *Endurance*, Don Benoist of the Last Thursday Book Club served strawberry shortcake with fresh strawberries and thick whipped cream. According to member Mike Blackledge, the rich dessert offered both a visual reminder of the Antarctic landscape and a luxurious contrast to the thin fare that Shackleton's men were able to glean from that harsh environment. "We would have prepared more authentic fare," says Blackledge, "but Lansing never told us how to cook blubber or squeeze hoosh from a seal."

Fair and Tender Ladies

Lee Smith

G. P. PUTNAM'S SONS, *1988*

(available in paperback from Ballantine, 1989)

I WANT TO BE A WRITTER, it is what I love the bestest in this world," writes young Ivy Rowe. Ivy's misspellings bespeak a lack of education that never dampens her spirit.

Born in a small cabin in backwoods Virginia, Ivy tells her life story in *Fair and Tender Ladies* through letters written over almost a century. Ivy's letters reveal her personal determination, imagination, and strength as she encounters obstacles, and the poverty and hardships of life in Appalachia.

Lee Smith comes naturally by her knowledge of Appalachian life and its rhythmic speech. She was born and raised in Grundy, Virginia, a small coal-mining town in the Blue Ridge Mountains. As a girl, Smith developed an ear for storytelling by listening to shoppers through a peephole in the ceiling of her father's dime store. Since then, Smith's many novels have revealed her love of Appalachia—an area she calls "the most beautiful, the most interesting place in the world"—and her empathy for Appalachian people and their culture.

The foods described in *Fair and Tender Ladies* convey the dependence of Appalachian people on the earth. "We grow cabbages and sweet taters and white taters both and shucky beans and we have got some apple trees too," writes Ivy of her childhood home. "We raise what we need."

LEE SMITH'S PIMENTO CHEESE

A traditional southern food, pimento cheese is held sacred by southerners, in spite of being largely unknown outside the South. Pimento is the sweet, thick-fleshed, aromatic red pepper used to stuff olives. When diced and combined with grated cheddar cheese, cayenne pepper, and mayonnaise, the resulting cheese spread is delicious on sandwiches and crackers, stuffed into celery stalks or tomatoes, or used as a topping on burgers.

Many southern writers have recalled with fondness and nostalgia the pimento cheese sandwiches of their youth. Lee Smith remembers that she and other "town kids whose parents owned the stores and didn't go down into the mines" brought pimento cheese sandwiches to school, while the poor kids from "the hollers" brought cornbread and buttermilk in Mason jars. Among the poor of Appalachia featured in *Fair and Tender Ladies* and other Smith novels, pimento cheese was a sign of relative affluence.

In October 2003, as part of its mission to preserve and celebrate the diverse cultures of the American South, the Mississippi-based Southern Foodways Alliance (SFA) held a conference on the foods of Appalachia at the University of Mississippi at Oxford. Lee Smith was a featured speaker. The featured food? Pimento cheese. More than three hundred people from around the country had submitted favorite pimento cheese recipes—and stories—for the 2003 Pimento Cheese Invitational, and the winners were announced at the conference.

"Pimento cheese matters because it's a food that spans race and class," says John T. Edge, director of SFA. "It transcends its base ingredients and becomes something grander. Whether in a paper sack lunch or on a white tablecloth, the merits of pimento cheese are equally recognizable." According to Edge, the SFA is as interested in the provenance of food as in the recipes themselves. "We celebrate births and mourn deaths by way of platters of pimento cheese sandwiches. It's a cultural artifact as well as a comestible."

We offer two versions of this versatile and beloved spread. The first is Lee Smith's family recipe.

NOTE: Durkee Famous Sauce, a commercially prepared mayonnaise and mustard sauce, is a staple in southern cupboards (see Purchasing Information, p. 499). Combined with the garlic and cayenne, it lends a deep, rich flavor to the pimento cheese of Smith's childhood.

½ cup mayonnaise

¼ cup Durkee Famous Sauce (see note above)

1½ teaspoons Dijon mustard

1 4-ounce jar chopped pimentos, drained

2 cloves garlic, minced

¼ teaspoon cayenne pepper

1 pound sharp cheddar cheese, grated

Combine the mayonnaise, Durkee Famous Sauce, mustard, pimentos, garlic, and cayenne in a large bowl and stir to mix well. Add the cheese and mix until blended. Refrigerate overnight. Serve as a stuffing for celery stalks or with crackers or slices of French bread.

Yield: 3 cups

Patsy Hopkins's Pimento Cheese

Patsy Hopkins, a book club member from Savannah, Georgia, makes a creamy pimento cheese that gets its zing from high-quality cheddar and pimentos—with a little sugar. Hopkins recommends serving her family recipe on Ritz crackers, but it's also delicious stuffed in celery.

10 ounces mild white cheddar cheese, grated (preferably high-quality)

6 tablespoons mayonnaise

¼ teaspoon sugar

1 tablespoon chopped pimentos

Mix all the ingredients together well and refrigerate. Serve chilled.

Yield: 1½ cups

Apple Stack-Cake

When Ivy and her friends receive "a hunk of apple stack-cake apiece" from a friend's mother, Ivy proclaims, "It was the bestest thing I have put in my mouth so far." An impressive cake, sometimes eight layers high and spread with dried apple filling, the apple stack-cake has its roots in southern Appalachia. Legend has it that early mountain settlers used apple stack-cakes in lieu of fancy wedding cakes. Neighbors would bring individual layers to the bride's family, who would spread the filling on each layer, thus building a wedding cake. The more popular the family, the taller the cake.

Lee Smith remembers apple stack-cake from her own childhood. "I especially associate it with funerals—and feel guilty for enjoying it so much, given the circumstances," she tells us.

You can find a classic apple stack-cake recipe in Ronni Lundy's *Butter Beans to Blackberries: Recipes from the Southern Garden* (North Point Press, 2003).

"We named ourselves Fair and Tender Ladies because Fair and Tender Ladies was the first book our group read when we started meeting in 1997," says Nancy Jacob. "But it doesn't necessarily describe us or the women in the book." Jacob is a bankruptcy attorney in Cincinnati and one of several founders of the group, which now goes by the initials FTL.

"Ivy was not a flower child," Jacob says of *Fair and Tender Ladies*'s protagonist. "It was nice for our group to start with a book about strong women. The story is told through a series of Ivy's letters, and it's fascinating how her correspondence chronicles her life." Jacob offers readers this tip: "Ivy's grammar improves as she matures, but it helps to read the book out loud to understand what she's saying."

"We are a homogeneous group," says Jacob, "so we try for diversity in our reading selections." The members of FTL choose books by authors they have never read and vary the subject matter. They usually read fiction for their monthly meetings, but FTL diversifies the list by choosing a classic, a biography, a collection of short stories, and a book by an African-American author or with an African-American theme, and a book with a Jewish theme each year.

A high point for the book club was when A'Lelia Bundles, author and descendent of Madam C. J. Walker, America's first African-American woman millionaire, discussed her book *On Her Own Ground: The Life and Times of Madam C. J. Walker* with the group via telephone. The group has also invited local residents who can enhance their understanding of the reading selection, including an English professor to discuss Michael Cunningham's *The Hours* (see p. 192) and the daughter of Holocaust survivors to discuss Elie Wiesel's *Night,* about a young boy's experiences in the Nazi death camps.

Usually the group munches on a selection of appetizers or desserts during meetings. For their discussion of *Night,* group members ate Jewish foods like rugelach, small cookies with a variety of fillings, and kugel, baked pudding with potatoes or noodles, both recipes from *In Memory's Kitchen: A Legacy from the Women of Terezín* (Jason Aronson, 1996).

A Fine Balance

Rohinton Mistry

....

KNOPF, *1997*

(available in paperback from Vintage, 2001)

S ET IN INDIA in the mid-1970s, Rohinton Mistry's novel unfolds in an unnamed seaside city ruled by chaos and corruption during a period of political and social upheaval. Prime Minister Indira Gandhi has defied a court order calling for her resignation and declared a state of emergency. Thousands opposing the government are imprisoned and brutal social policies, such as a forced sterilization campaign, are put in place. Mistry illustrates the tragic impact of the political chaos and inhuman living conditions on the lives of four central characters, as well as a host of minor ones.

Two itinerant Hindu tailors, Ishvar Darji and his seventeen-year-old nephew, Omprakash, have fled to the city to escape cruel caste violence in their native village, but Ishvar remains devoted to the task of finding a wife for his nephew. Maneck Kohlah arrives in the city to attend college, uprooted from his beloved Himalayan village, where his parents run a failing general store.

Widowed early when her husband, Rustom, was the victim of a bicycle accident, Dina Dalal now lives independently, eking out a living as a tailor. Dina hires the homeless Omprakash and Ishvar to help her in her tailoring business, but appears indifferent to their hardships and at first refuses to invite them to take shelter or meals at her apartment. Maneck, the son of Dina's college friend, rents a room in her apartment when his living situation at a student hostel becomes unbearable. As these four souls struggle to survive in a heartless and cruel society, their suspicions and distrust of one another slowly abate and friendships develop—alliances critical to surviving the wretched circumstances in which they find themselves.

Omprakash and Ishvar often depend on the kindness of homeless friends for food when they first arrive in the city. When the tailors begin working with Dina, they take their meals—usually buns and tea, or whatever their wages will allow—at the Vishram Vegetarian Hotel, a run-down, greasy but lively restaurant. When Maneck arrives in the city, he quickly gives up on the "ghastly" meals at the college and frequents the city's food stalls for sandwiches or samosas, taking comfort in the familiarity of watching food being prepared.

Ultimately, food unites the four. The tailors eat out while working for Dina, although Ishvar suspects she longs for company. When Ishvar and Omprakash propose to reduce food expenses and cooking responsibilities by eating with Maneck and Dina, she warms to the idea. Food preparation and communal dining quickly create a convivial mood and a family-like atmosphere. Dina notes the change: "From the saddest, dingiest room in the flat, the kitchen was transformed into a bright place of mirth and energy," and the "bleakest hour" becomes her "happiest."

Over the weeks Omprakash and Ishvar expand their culinary contributions from breads, such as chapatis and puris, to *aloo masala* (spicy potatoes) and *shak-bhaji* (a spinach dish). Dina wonders whether "something uncontrollable had been started here, with all this cooking together and eating together. Too much intimacy."

The Taal Restaurant's Chicken Biryani (Basmati Rice with Chicken)

Biryani, a delicacy of northern Indian cuisine, features basmati rice—a long-grained rice with a fine texture—combined with spices and lamb or chicken. The dish is served at Dina and Rustom's wedding in Mistry's novel, and the couple celebrates their first wedding anniversary with a meal of chicken biryani. At the end of the novel, Maneck has mutton biryani at the Grand Hotel and returns to the newly expanded, prosperous Vishram Vegetarian Hotel, where biryani is one of the offerings.

The Second Wednesday Dinner Book Club, a gourmet book club based in Fullerton, California, discussed *A Fine Balance* over an Indian meal at the Taal Restaurant in Fullerton. The Taal's owner, Balbir Ghotra, shared his recipe for chicken biryani, a dish the book club enjoyed thoroughly.

NOTE: Garam masala is a mixture of toasted spices. There are many variations, but most feature cumin, cardamom, cinnamon, cloves, and black peppercorns. You will find several different preparations of garam masala at most Indian groceries. (See Purchasing Information, p. 499.) You can also make your own fairly simply, and doing so results in a very fresh and fragrant spice mix.

Red chili powder has a different flavor than the dark chili powder commonly found in grocery stores. It can be found in most Indian groceries (see Purchasing Information, p. 499).

For the chicken

2 tablespoons corn oil

2 large onions, chopped

1 tablespoon minced fresh ginger

2 teaspoons minced garlic (about 4 cloves)

2 large tomatoes, seeded and diced, or
   2 15-ounce cans diced tomatoes, drained

2 teaspoons garam masala (see note above)

2 teaspoons ground coriander

2 teaspoons ground cumin

2 teaspoons red chili powder (see note above)
   (use up to 2 additional teaspoons for a
   spicier dish)

½ tablespoon salt

1½ pounds skinned, boned chicken breast,
   cut into 1-inch cubes

For the rice

3½ cups water

2 teaspoons cumin seed

4 bay leaves

½ teaspoon salt

1 teaspoon corn oil

2 cups uncooked basmati rice

For the garnish

¼ cup golden raisins

¼ cup cilantro leaves, coarsely chopped

¼ cup fresh mint leaves, coarsely chopped

1. To make the chicken: Heat the oil in a large skillet. Sauté the onions until they begin to soften. Add the ginger, garlic, and tomatoes and cook for 2 minutes. Stir in the garam masala, coriander, cumin, chili powder, and salt. Add chicken pieces and cook until done but still tender, 15–20 minutes, stirring occasionally.

2. To make the rice: Bring the water to a boil in a saucepan. Add the cumin, bay leaves, salt, and corn oil. Stir in the rice. Cover and steam over low heat until done, 15–20 minutes.

3. Combine the chicken and rice in a large serving bowl. Garnish with raisins, cilantro, and mint. Serve hot.

Yield: 6 to 8 servings

Garam Masala

1 3-inch stick cinnamon, broken up

2 tablespoons cumin seed

2 tablespoons cardamom seed

1 tablespoon coriander seed

  (see Purchasing Information, p. 499)

1 tablespoon black peppercorns

1 teaspoon whole cloves

1 teaspoon fennel seed

1 teaspoon caraway seed

½ teaspoon freshly grated nutmeg

1. Combine the cinnamon, cumin, cardamom, coriander, peppercorns, cloves, fennel, and caraway in a skillet over medium-high heat. Toast the spices, shaking and stirring constantly, until they darken by a few shades and are very fragrant, about 5 minutes. Do not burn. Remove from heat and transfer to a dish immediately.

2. Grind to a fine powder in a spice mill. Stir in nutmeg.

3. Store garam masala in a sealed airtight container. It will keep fresh and potent for up to 3 months.

Yield: About 6 tablespoons

BOOK CLUB PROFILE

"Book groups are one of the few places you can have an in-depth discussion about ideas," says Dalene Bradford, a charter member of the twenty-five-year-old Rockhill Book Club in Kansas City, Missouri. "People who are supposedly discussing ideas on TV basically yell at each other and in many social venues people often shy away from a serious discussion. We pick books that put ideas in front of you."

The eighteen members of the Rockhill Book Club—women in their fifties, sixties, and seventies—thrive on the exploration of ideas. In its early years, the group limited discussion to short stories, generally analyzing three to five stories per meeting. "That way, you can really get your arms around them," says Bradford. Group members still refer to stories they read in the 1980s such as "The Yellow Wall-Paper" by Charlotte Perkins Gilman and "I Stand Here Ironing" by Tillie Olsen, both from the collection *Women & Fiction: Short Stories by and About Women,* edited by Susan Cahill (New American Library, 1975). "Reading great literature that sticks with you and becomes part of your collective consciousness is a wonderful experience," says Bradford.

After exhausting many of the available short-story collections, the group began to include novels and nonfiction in its reading list. To find books that challenge them, members speak to friends and other book clubs and pore over book reviews. "We work hard to find literature that operates on multiple levels, contains controversy or has room for interpretation, provides different points of view, or invites literary analysis," says Bradford. Their long list of favorites includes Charles Johnson's *Middle Passage*, about a newly freed slave in 1830 New Orleans who accidentally boards a slave ship bound for Africa. Arundhati Roy's *The God of Small Things* (see p. 157), Wallace Stegner's *Angle of Repose* (see p. 22), Zora Neale Hurston's *Their Eyes Were Watching God* (see p. 427), and Rohinton Mistry's *A Fine Balance*.

Rockhill members were particularly taken with the exotic location and universal themes of Mistry's book. "*A Fine Balance* represented one of our favorite types of books," says Bradford, "one that opens up a new world to us but points out our commonalities with others. The themes were universal, getting along in the world despite our differences, but the setting, India, was new to us and gave us ample opportunity for discussion about a country so different from ours." The group was reminded of issues in Indian history, class structure and partition, and discussed India's diversity and current political tensions. The group considered a universal question—what does it take to get along?—as it explored Dina Dalal's evolving relationship with the two men she hired for her business and ended up taking into her apartment.

Sometimes an idea or theme discussed in a meeting has inspired the book club, or individual club members, to delve deeper.

The group's discussion of Truman Capote's "Handcarved Coffins," found in his collection *Music for Chameleons*, inspired one member to launch an exhaustive investigation into the story's veracity. Member Mary Beth Gordon, a freelance writer, recommended the account of a series of bizarre murders in the Midwest to the group, believing the story to be true. When some group members disagreed, Gordon set out to prove them wrong. She made at least fifty phone calls, including one to a Kansas detective who had befriended Capote and another to the Nebraska state office of the FBI; corresponded with the late George Plimpton, a writer and a friend of Capote's; and made an exhaustive search of Capote's notes and interviews in the microfilm collection at the New York Public Library. She presented her findings—the story appears to be fictional—in a written report to a fascinated audience. "Talk about books taking you places you've never been before," says Bradford. "What fun!"

Food figures into the Rockhill Book Club's special occasions. After reading *Mrs. Dalloway* by Virginia Woolf and *The Hours* by Michael Cunningham (see p. 192), the group enjoyed the movie version of *The Hours* with spouses and friends, and a meal out afterward. And Rockhill Book Club members celebrated their twentieth anniversary over dinner at a favorite local establishment, the Rockhill Tennis Club. They called on the longest-participating members to tell stories of the book group's beginnings, argued over a few divergent memories, and shared funny and memorable episodes from meetings.

More Food for Thought

When the Second Wednesday Dinner Book Club discussed *A Fine Balance*, their Indian dinner at the Taal Restaurant in Fullerton, California, included tandoori chicken, *bengan bartha* (a spiced eggplant dish), potatoes and cauliflower, garlic naan (bread), and chicken biryani. "Enjoying the spices and flavors of Indian cuisine greatly enhanced our discussion," says club member Judy Bart Kancigor, "although the opulent ambience of Taal could not be more different from the meager surroundings in which these foods were cooked in this beautifully written book."

Galileo's Daughter: A Historical Memoir of Science, Faith, and Love

Dava Sobel

WALKER & COMPANY, *1999*

(available in paperback from Penguin, 2000)

I N A LETTER to a friend after her death, the mathematician and astronomer Galileo Galilei described his eldest daughter as "a woman of exquisite mind, singular goodness, and most tenderly attached to me." These words sum up the warmth and closeness between Galileo and his daughter portrayed in the pages of Dava Sobel's compassionate depiction of the work and family life of the seventeenth-century Italian scientist.

Sobel recounts the story of Galileo's life in a text peppered with the letters of Suor Maria Celeste, written to her father from behind the walls of the Convent of San Matteo in Arcetri, Italy. Originally named Virginia and cloistered at the age of thirteen, Suor Maria Celeste's adopted name reflects her early interest in her father's work studying the heavens. At age twenty-three, Suor Maria Celeste begins a faithful correspondence with her father that spans her lifetime. Her letters reflect her life as a Poor Clare nun, living under a vow of poverty; supporting her father by preparing foods, sewing and bleaching his collars, and reviewing his work; and aspiring to better her own living conditions. Galileo responds generously to his daughter, never denying her requests for money or other donations and supporting the convent with gifts and occasional repairs to convent equipment, like its clock. The affections of father and daughter are clearly mutual.

Sobel integrates her research into the personal dimension of Galileo's life with the more commonly told stories of Galileo's career, his adoption and expansion of the Polish astronomer Nicolaus Copernicus's theories of a sun-centered universe; his persecution by the Catholic Church in Rome, which forbade any interpretation of Scripture that departed from the Holy Father's declared belief that the sun moved about the earth; and his trial for and conviction of heinous crimes and heresy.

Through the story of Galileo's revolutionary work and the personal letters of his daughter,

Galileo's Daughter gives readers a multidimensional picture of one of history's greatest thinkers, and a picture of the political and religious forces that controlled life in seventeenth-century Italy.

Food helps bridge the physical gap between the cloistered Suor Maria Celeste and her peripatetic father. The relationship between Suor Maria Celeste and Galileo takes place at a distance, for the rules of her order forbid Suor Maria Celeste from leaving the grounds of the convent. It is during Galileo's brief visits to the convent that he brings the raw materials that Suor Maria Celeste will make into gifts to nurture her father: fabric for sewing into collars, vials and containers to hold the plague preventatives that she creates in the apothecary, and citrus fruits for candy. Galileo has a weakness for candied citrons. He regularly brings Suor Maria Celeste fresh citrons or lemons from his garden, which she returns to him quickly, "candied to his liking." Suor Maria Celeste wants to please her father and expresses her fear that the fruit he brings lacks the freshness necessary for her candies to reach perfection.

Suor Maria Celeste also uses food to try to ease her father's financial burden when her brother, Vincenzio, marries. Although she is not free to attend the wedding feast, she offers to bake a platter of pastries, listing in a letter the more expensive items—white sugar, almonds, and fine confectioners' sugar—that she hopes her father will provide. "After this, Sire, you will be able to see if you want me to cook other sweet things for you, such as savories and the like; because I firmly believe you would spend less this way than buying them already prepared in the grocer's shop."

Galileo reciprocates Suor Maria Celeste's kindnesses, bringing her gifts of his own: money, a warm quilt, and food, "including meats, sweets, and even a special spinach dish he cooked himself especially for her."

LEMONY RICOTTA–
GOAT CHEESE CAKE

When we asked Dava Sobel about food in *Galileo's Daughter*, she pointed us to the College of Saint Catherine in St. Paul, Minnesota, where she spoke in 2002. In honor of Sobel's visit, Julie Miller Jones, professor of nutrition and director of the Center for Women, Science, and Technology, served a Renaissance feast for the faculty book club discussion of *Galileo's Daughter*. One of the menu items, goat cheese cake, inspired the development of our own Renaissance recipe.

Our recipe combines citrus, Galileo's favorite flavor, with cheese, a staple of the Renaissance diet. "Cheese was an important ingredient in seventeenth-century Italy because of the lack of re-frigeration," Jones told us. "It was salted and stored in cool caves to maintain freshness. It was a great way for people to keep milk without refrigeration."

Although cheesecake recipes are now ubiquitous in the United States, the idea of baking cheese into cheesecake dates to the ancient Romans and has been adopted throughout the world. Our recipe couples ricotta cheese, commonly found in Italian cheesecake recipes, with goat cheese and lemon peel for a tangy tart that is out of this world. But watch your own heavenly body—this is one rich dessert.

This cake freezes beautifully. In fact, the longer it sets, the better, so try to make it at least a full day before serving.

1½ cups graham-cracker crumbs

6 tablespoons butter, melted

2 cups sugar

Grated peel of 4 lemons

15 ounces whole-milk ricotta cheese

7 ounces creamy goat cheese

1 8-ounce package cream cheese, softened

½ cup fresh lemon juice

8 large eggs

Fresh raspberries or lemon slices for garnish

(optional)

1. Preheat oven to 350°F. Butter the bottom and sides of a 9-inch springform pan.
2. In a bowl, stir the graham-cracker crumbs and melted butter with a fork until blended. Put crumbs in buttered pan and press firmly with fingers to cover the bottom. Bake for 8 to 10 minutes. Cool on a wire rack.
3. Reduce oven temperature to 325°F. In a food processor, blend the sugar and lemon peel, pulsing until peel is finely ground and sugar takes on a lemony color; put aside.
4. Using an electric mixer on high speed, beat together the ricotta, goat, and cream cheeses un-til light and fluffy. Reduce speed to medium. Add the sugar mixture and the lemon juice and beat until smooth. Add the eggs one at a time, beating well after each addition.
5. Boil a kettle of water. Wrap the outside (not the top) of the springform pan with heavy-duty aluminum foil and place it in a roasting pan. Pour the cake filling into the springform pan on top of the crust. Place roasting pan in oven and carefully pour boiling water into roasting pan (water should go about halfway up the sides of the springform pan). Bake 1½ hours, or until the center is set but still slightly jiggly.
6. Cool the cake in its water bath for 15 minutes, then remove from bath, take off foil, and cool

on a wire rack. Refrigerate, loosely covered, for at least 8 hours. When ready to serve, run a knife around the edge and remove the sides of the pan. Place on a serving dish. Serve garnished with lemon slices or fresh raspberries if desired.

Yield: 12 to 16 servings

ROSEMARY SPAGHETTI

Suor Maria Celeste concocted healing elixirs in the convent apothecary to protect her father from illness. When the bubonic plague reached Florence in 1629, Suor Maria Celeste sent Galileo a paste of dried figs, nuts, rue, and salt, held together by honey.

One of the herbs grown in the convent garden and at the time considered to have great medicinal properties was rosemary. Rosemary was thought to fortify the brain and memory and reduce nausea. Galileo would send "gifts of food, and [supply] his homegrown citrus fruits, wine, and rosemary leaves for the kitchen and apothecary at San Matteo."

Consider serving Juli Rosenbaum's Rosemary Spaghetti (p. 86) at your *Galileo's Daughter* book club discussion.

BOOK CLUB PROFILE

"The shades of night were falling ere the interested members bade their charming hostess goodbye and each member felt that the afternoon had been profitably spent." So end the December 5, 1899, minutes of the Wednesday Club of Fort Smith, Arkansas, one of the country's oldest and most tradition-rich book clubs.

Formed in 1879 by several young women whose mothers belonged to a book club of their own called the Fortnightly Club, the new book club became known as the Fortnightly Juniors. The twenty-five charter members hoped to form a permanent literary society with the stated aim of "mutual improvement of its members by the study of literature in its various branches and for social pleasure." The group initially began meeting every other Wednesday and, within a few years, changed their name to the Wednesday Club, feeling they had outgrown the term "junior."

In 1897, Wednesday Club members paid dues of fifty cents a year. Most of the money was spent on "civic betterment," a goal added to the group's constitution in 1903. In those early years, the group's work focused on cleaning up and beautifying the alleys of Fort Smith.

Early meetings bore little resemblance to most modern book club gatherings. Rather than requiring all members to buy and discuss the same book—impractical and expensive in the days of limited press runs—groups of three to six women would study a topic and present findings to the club. Early on, groups were assigned to various periods of French literature, art, and architecture, followed by Italian art, sculpture, and architecture. According to the minutes, the group studied its first novel, Nathaniel Hawthorne's *The Scarlet Letter,* in 1899.

The modern-day Wednesday Club honors many of the hallowed traditions of its founders. The group maintains a roster of twenty-five women, as set in the original bylaws, and new members join by invitation only. The group's colors are green and white, and their official flower is the carnation. In keeping with custom, the women—most college-educated, between thirty and eighty-five years old, and all with a keen interest in serious literature and self-improvement—address each other formally, using "Missus" or "Miss." The group follows the practice, established sometime in the 1930s or 1940s, of reading only works of nonfiction.

"I guess fiction was too flighty for them," speculates Mrs. Rose Bethell, a member of the Wednesday Club for the past fifty-five years. As the club's elder statesman, although not its eldest member, Mrs. Bethell is an informal historian and guardian of the club's minutes, which span 106 years. She has watched the club's customs and practices evolve over the years, even as its fundamental goals and traditions remain intact.

Food is one example of how the group has changed over the years. "The club used to serve 'refreshments and tea,'" says Mrs. Bethell, "but during the 1920s and 1930s, and then again after World War II, hostesses started serving an elegant tea, something that would be called high tea." During these years, the hostess might serve chicken salad, finger sandwiches, desserts, mints, cakes, coffee, and tea, all with an "elaborate presentation." When the group meeting time changed to 1 P.M., hostesses switched back to serving dessert, coffee, and tea. "We do not do the kinds of formal serving we used to, although there is still white linen on the table, linen napkins, and family silver," says Mrs. Bethell. "Nowadays we might have dessert, nuts, and mints, and often the desserts are catered. People today do not do as much baking at home as they used to."

After enjoying dessert and coffee, the group holds a short business meeting, followed by a lecture-style presentation of the book and a short group discussion. The club's enjoyment of biography and history is evident in past favorites: William Manchester's *A World Lit Only by Fire: The Medieval Mind and the Renaissance,* Katharine Graham's *Personal History* (see

p. 344), Stephen Ambrose's *Undaunted Courage* (see p. 462), and Dava Sobel's *Galileo's Daughter*.

The Wednesday Club loved the way Dava Sobel's book painted a vivid portrait of a distant time and place. "We felt it was interesting to see what was going on in the scientific world, and the way the Catholic Church controlled lives so completely during this time," says Mrs. Bethell. "We had a general discussion about life in Italy during the seventeenth century."

Galileo's relationship with his daughters also interested the group. Mrs. Bethell, who presented the book to the group, felt that the two girls received poor treatment at the hands of their father. "He was not really interested in them for a long while," she says. "As they grew older, he became more attached to them, but for a long time he was busy with his own life and had little interest in the girls."

More Food for Thought

Julie Miller Jones prepared a Renaissance feast in honor of Dava Sobel's 2002 visit to the College of Saint Catherine in St. Paul, Minnesota. Interested faculty, staff, and students discussed *Galileo's Daughter* while enjoying goat cheese cake (made with feta cheese, honey, wine, and pistachios), honey-roasted almonds, traveler's balls (made with wheat, dates, and nuts), a *torta* of herbs, and a chickpea tart. The recipes came from *The Medieval Kitchen: Recipes from France and Italy* (University of Chicago Press, 2000) and A Boke of Gode Cookery (www.godecookery. com/godeboke/godeboke.htm), both of which have authentic medieval recipes adapted for the modern kitchen.

Jones teaches courses on intercultural food patterns and food history, and was familiar with foods of seventeenth-century Italy. She chose recipes with ingredients—including cheese, honey, nuts, and herbs—that played important roles in the Renaissance diet.

Getting Mother's Body

Suzan-Lori Parks

RANDOM HOUSE, 2003

Billy Beede is dirt-poor and pregnant. She sleeps on a pallet under the cash register of her aunt and uncle's gas station in tiny Lincoln, Texas, dreaming of marriage. But when Billy gets word that her mother's gravesite in Arizona will be plowed up for a supermarket, she decides to head west. Legend has it that Billy's mother, Willa Mae, was buried six years earlier with her jewels. Billy and her aunt and uncle set off to claim their rightful share of the riches, and to bring Willa Mae's body back home.

Events of this unusual road trip are narrated from constantly shifting viewpoints, bringing out a host of interesting characters. There is Laz, who worships Billy with an unrequited love; Aunt June, who hopes to use her part of the fortune to buy a prosthetic limb; and Uncle Roosevelt, a onetime minister who has lost his calling. And then there is Dill, Willa Mae's former lover and the only one who was present at her burial. As Billy, Aunt June, and Uncle Roosevelt head to Arizona, Dill races there, too, hoping to prevent her own secret from being unearthed along with Willa Mae's body. With wit and a keen ear for dialogue, Suzan-Lori Parks tells the story of a hard-luck family that hopes and strives to "rise above their Beedeism" and improve their lives.

In *Getting Mother's Body* there is little narrative description, and the details of Texas life simply emerge through the words and actions of the book's many colorful characters—including their eating habits. Hearty foods—pork chops smothered in brown onion gravy, macaroni and cheese, grits, chicken wings, steamed cabbage, biscuits, cornbread, chocolate layer cake, pumpkin pie, and cherry pie—are present throughout the novel, evoking the book's rich Texas setting.

RHONDA HANEY'S GREENS

Before they decide to marry, Roosevelt and June sit on the banks of the Brazos River, plates filled with chicken, cornbread, greens, and cake.

Greens of all kinds—kale, collard, turnip, mustard, and spinach—are a staple of southern kitchens. According to the traditional method, greens are boiled for long periods with ham hocks until the meat falls off the bone. The vitamin-rich broth left in the pot after cooking is called pot liquor, which folks customarily sop up with bits of cornbread.

The history of greens dates to pre–Civil War days, when slaves on plantations were often expected to make their meals from leftovers. Slaves would add collards or turnip greens picked from a small garden to the pig's feet or ham hocks discarded by the plantation kitchens. The resulting meal, full of vitamins and fiber, would sustain them. Incidentally, the term "soul food" originated in these concoctions—meals cooked with not much more than the slaves' heart and soul.

When her book club's selections suggest soulful fare, Rhonda Haney of the We Just Wanna Have Fun Book Club in Atlanta, Georgia, serves these greens. "This is my New Orleans recipe from watching my momma—with modifications," says Haney. She suggests white rice, fried chicken or pork chops, and french bread or cornbread as accompaniments.

For the makings of a complete southern meal from our cookbook, pair these greens with spicy chicken wings (p. 72), potato salad (p. 187), and sweet-potato pie (p. 423).

1 1-pound slice of ham cut into large chunks (may substitute smoked turkey sausage)	*1 large onion, chopped*
	4 cloves garlic, chopped
4 pounds collard, mustard, or turnip greens, or any combination	*2 cups water or chicken broth*
	1 teaspoon salt
½ cup (1 stick) margarine or butter	*1 teaspoon black pepper*

1. Place ham chunks (or turkey sausage, if using) in the bottom of a large, heavy soup pot and pan-fry for approximately 15 minutes, turning once during cooking.
2. Wash the greens thoroughly. Cut the stems off at the base of the leaves. For larger leaves with thick stems, use a paring knife to cut the stems out of the leaves. Stack several leaves together, roll them up, and slice into thin strips. Repeat until all greens are sliced. Set greens aside.

3. Add the margarine or butter to the pot with the meat. Add the onion and sauté until it begins to soften. Add the garlic and continue to sauté until fragrant.

4. Add the greens and water or chicken broth to the pot. Season with salt and pepper. Cover and simmer 45–60 minutes or until greens reach desired tenderness, stirring occasionally. Adjust seasonings and serve.

Yield: 8 to 10 servings

BOOK CLUB PROFILE

Since 1997, the Sistah Girl Reading Club in Miami, Florida, has found a way to celebrate reading and eating.

The fourteen African-American members—all women, including nurses, teachers, counselors, and postal workers—attend monthly book club meetings with food in hand, often food related to the book they have just read. When they read Margaret Johnson-Hodge's *Butterscotch Blues,* a novel about a woman's romance with a man from Trinidad, they enjoyed a Caribbean meal of sweet-potato pie (see p. 423), peas and rice, oxtails, turkey wings, and lemon cake. The hostess also served a huge bowl of butterscotch candy. For Carl Weber's novel *Married Men,* group members brought soul foods like cornbread and collard greens, both referenced in the book.

Even when they do not match the food to the book, there is always a big spread with meats, vegetables, salads, desserts, appetizers, and drinks. "Food is very important to our group," says Annette Breedlove, a letter carrier and member since 1997. "It's a way to increase fellowship and to get new recipe ideas."

Women of the Sistah Girl Reading Club also bond outside of meetings during spa days, movie nights, family picnics, and year-end parties. Every other year, they take an African-American literary cruise out of Port Canaveral, Florida. This seven-day adventure brings book lovers together with prominent authors, including Lolita Files, Eric Jerome Dickey, Victoria Murray, Omar Tyree, Patricia Haley, and Yolanda Joe. "Our group was so excited to be socializing with these authors, and sharing meals together," says Breedlove. "We joined the first cruise in 1998 and vowed to continue going every other year after that."

The Sistah Girl Reading Club has also spawned the Sistah Girl Investment Club, for those who want to increase their knowledge of money management and investments. The eleven members who have opted to join meet monthly at their local library and decide how to invest their pool of collected money with the help of an investment adviser.

The Sistah Girl Reading Club reads and discusses all kinds of books, including fiction, romance, and mysteries. They especially enjoy new releases and found *Getting Mother's Body* particularly impressive.

Suzan-Lori Parks's vivid writing and character development struck the group. "Both the desolation and happiness of being black in a small Texas town was brilliantly captured with humor and softness," says paralegal Karen McGee. "We liked the way the author used first person to let each character tell their own story. This book really made us use our imaginations to see what each of these characters looked like."

Members also focused on the relationship between Billy Beede and her mother. "We couldn't get over how the daughter, Billy, never called her mother Mother, and how she had grown up with no motherly love," says Breedlove.

Group members appreciated the controversial nature of the material covered in the book, including a homosexual relationship gone bad, abortion, and adultery. The provocative subject matter and powerful writing had group members clamoring for more from this Pultizer Prize–winning playwright and debut novelist. "It was truly illuminating and different from the books we have read lately," says McGee. "We give her two thumbs up and look forward to reading more of her books."

More Food for Thought

In keeping with its tradition of matching books and food, the Sistah Girl Reading Club served foods mentioned in the book—cornbread, greens, and chicken—for their discussion of *Getting Mother's Body*. "The food was delicious, especially the lemon-pepper chicken, which had a different flavor," says Annette Breedlove. They topped off their meal with a moist coconut cake.

Girl with a Pearl Earring

Tracy Chevalier

DUTTON, 2000

(available in paperback from Penguin, 2003)

I N HER FIRST NOVEL, Tracy Chevalier brings to life the young woman who inspired the seventeenth-century Dutch masterpiece by Vermeer. Set in the small city of Delft in the 1660s, *Girl with a Pearl Earring* is narrated by sixteen-year-old Griet, who is compelled to work as a maid in the Vermeer household to help her struggling family. Vermeer quickly recognizes Griet's artistic talent and has her assist him in his attic studio, where she learns to grind and mix paints. Griet becomes entranced with the master's creative process, and domestic tensions in the household increase when Vermeer's jealous wife, Catharina, and mother-in-law, Maria Thins, become wary of the increasing intimacy between the painter and the servant. As Griet becomes part of Vermeer's work and, eventually, the subject of Vermeer's next painting, scandal and turmoil erupt, threatening to ruin them all.

GRIET'S VEGETABLE SOUP

I n the novel's opening scene, Vermeer and his wife, Catharina, visit Griet's home to arrange for her hire. Vermeer instantly notices Griet's artistic inclinations. Griet is chopping vegetables for soup and Vermeer is drawn to the color pattern she has created. Says Griet: "I always laid vegetables out in a circle, each with its own section like a slice of pie. There were five slices: red cabbage, onions, leeks, carrots and turnips. I had used a knife edge to shape each slice, and placed a carrot disk in the center." Intrigued by the composition, Vermeer studies the circle and asks Griet if the vegetables are laid out in the order in which they will go into the soup. Griet responds:

"No, sir." I hesitated. I could not say why I had laid out the vegetables as I did. I simply set them as I felt they should be, but I was too frightened to say so to a gentleman. "I see you have separated the whites," he said, indicating the turnips and onions. "And then the orange and the purple, they do not sit together. Why is that?" He picked up a shred of cabbage and a piece of carrot and shook them like dice in his hand. I looked at my mother, who nodded slightly. "The colors fight when they are side by side, sir."

With the order of the vegetables now in disarray, Griet, in an observation that foreshadows what is to come, says, "The pie slices I had made so carefully were ruined."

Tracy Chevalier thought vegetable soup would be a perfect accompaniment to a book group discussion of *Girl with a Pearl Earring*, and told us this anecdote about writing the opening scene of her novel.

When I was writing that first scene where Griet is chopping vegetables and Vermeer comes to her house, I needed to see how the color wheel would look, so I chopped up a lot of vegetables and laid them out. Afterwards, I figured I really ought to make a soup with them, so I threw them into a pot with some herbs and boiled them up. The problem was, I was in the early stages of pregnancy and when I looked at the end result—a kind of pink-gray sludge, because of the red cabbage, I suspect—I couldn't touch the stuff. I put the huge pot of it in the fridge, but even the thought of it sitting in there made me feel sick, so I had to throw the whole thing away!

Our version of Griet's vegetable soup features onions, leeks, carrots, and turnips. We took Tracy Chevalier's advice and included the red cabbage only as a garnish. The recipe was adapted from Ruth Van Waerebeek's *Everybody Eats Well in Belgium Cookbook* (Workman, 1996). Chevalier suggests serving the soup with a hearty, rustic brown or rye bread.

NOTE: For a vegetarian version of this soup, replace the bacon with 2 tablespoons olive or canola oil, and add 1 teaspoon each of thyme, dill, basil, and marjoram. To save time, use a food processor to chop leeks and onions.

2 large leeks

8 ounces lean slab bacon, cut into ½-inch dice, or 2 tablespoons olive or canola oil

2 medium onions, finely diced

2 cups finely diced green cabbage

2 cups finely diced peeled carrots

1 cup finely diced peeled turnips

10 cups beef, chicken, or vegetable stock

Salt and freshly ground black pepper

½ cup red cabbage, cut into paper-thin slivers

½ cup fresh parsley, finely minced

1. Rinse the leeks well and soak in cool water for 15 minutes to remove all grit. Halve leeks lengthwise and cut into fine dice.
2. Cook the bacon gently in a Dutch oven or stockpot for 5 minutes. Add the leeks and onion, and cook gently for 5 minutes more, stirring occasionally. Drain off bacon fat.
3. Add the green cabbage, carrots, turnips, and broth. Bring to a boil, cover, and reduce heat. Simmer for 25 minutes or until vegetables are tender. Season to taste with salt and pepper. Garnish individual servings with red cabbage slivers and parsley.

Yield: 10 to 12 servings

BOOK CLUB PROFILE

In the early 1980s, a group of parents from the Grassroots Free School in Tallahassee, Florida, decided to link their futures in shared living. They found acreage to build homes and to provide a permanent site for the school and held meetings to hammer out agreements. Thus their "intentional community" was born. In contrast to the "circumstantial communities" that prevail in most American neighborhoods, the residents of an intentional community decide to live near one another because of friendship or shared values. The twenty-five families own their own land and houses, as well as common land, a community pool, and a playground. "We all know each other and look out for each other," says Lyn Kittle, an early member of the community. "If there is serious illness or a new baby, weeks of dinners are organized. And we expect to be there for each other as we age."

In 1992, community member Jan Keshen invited interested neighbors to form the Luna-Chics Literary Guild, a book club that today includes residents of the intentional community and others from the greater Tallahassee area. The eleven LunaChics—women in their thirties, forties, and fifties—include a high school principal, a teacher, a psychologist, a stained-glass artist, a speech pathologist, a media specialist, an office manager, and a stay-at-home mom.

The LunaChics have been reading fiction and classics together for more than ten years. After each month's meeting, members rate the book on a scale of one to ten. They "confidently recommend" books rated seven or higher, but warn that "you can't discount our mood at the time of rating. We hope these ratings will be of use to others, but don't take them *too* seriously."

Girl with a Pearl Earring earned a nine from the LunaChics, all of whom admired the ingenuity of the subject matter. "The whole idea was a brilliant stroke!" says Kittle. "It was like going inside the painting or having the girl step out of the painting. I had seen this painting many times and had never given any thought to the young woman who inspired it. Chevalier made this girl and Vermeer come alive for me."

When Nina Hatton produced earrings similar to the ones worn in the painting, group members spontaneously decided to dress up a fellow member, some taking turns covering the earring to see how "the picture" changed. "It makes a big difference," says Kittle. "I never thought that such a small detail could be so important in a painting. It made the painting and the life of these people seem very real."

More Food for Thought

The LunaChics regularly serve food at their meetings, often thematically related to the book. For *Girl with a Pearl Earring*, Nina Hatton served Belgian chocolates, Dutch cheeses, and Dutch waffles and coffee with chocolate and whipped cream. The evening's fare was served on Delft china from Holland, collected by Hatton's father when he was working in the Netherlands. To add to the Dutch ambience, Hatton set tulips in Dutch vases and displayed wooden clogs collected from Holland.

The God of Small Things

Arundhati Roy

RANDOM HOUSE, *1997*

(available in paperback from Perennial, 1998)

IN HER PRIZE-WINNING NOVEL, *The God of Small Things*, Arundhati Roy introduces readers to the Kochamma family of Ayemenem, Kerala, India, in 1969. At the center of the story are "two-egg twins," Estha (the brother) and Rahel (the sister). Though physically separate, they are joined at the soul: They know each other's thoughts and dreams, they can taste what the other is eating and sense each other's unseen presence. As their family unravels against a backdrop of political upheaval and traditional social taboos, Roy captures beautifully the twins' childlike perceptions of the adult world and their assumption of responsibility for events beyond their control.

From the beginning, the reader senses that the Kochamma family is fragmenting. Ammu, the twins' beautiful and educated mother, has divorced her alcoholic husband and returned to the family home because she is unable to sustain herself independently. Ammu's ineffectual Rhodes Scholar brother, Chacko, unable to hold a job in England, has moved back home, too, after his wife has asked for a divorce. The twins' grand-aunt, Baby Kochamma, willful and treacherous, is forever enamored of the forbidden Irish monk, Father Mulligan. Ammu and Chacko's mother, Mammachi, who is nearly blind, plays Handel on the violin and runs the family's pickles and preserves factory. Last, but certainly not least in importance to the story, is an untouchable, Velutha, a skilled carpenter, Marxist activist, and handyman to the family business.

The story, which shifts back and forth in time, begins with Rahel's return to Ayemenem twenty-three years after the tragic accidental death of her visiting cousin, Sophie Mol. Rahel has not seen her twin brother, Estha, during those twenty-three years. He is silent and withdrawn, but the twins' unspoken connection to each other is undiminished.

The story quickly shifts to the funeral of Sophie Mol and the events that led to her death. Childhood traumas unknown to or unacknowledged by adults are among the dangerous secrets kept by both children and adults in the story. And the story's tragic conclusion seems to validate the twins' apprehension that everything can change in a single day. Although a profoundly human story, *The God of Small Things* echoes the high drama, surprising twists of plot, and gorgeous imagery of the great mythic Indian legends that Rahel and Estha love.

Rahel and Esta's childish perceptions give *The God of Small Things* its poignancy. In spite of India's rich culinary tradition, however, *The God of Small Things* includes few details about the preparation and consumption of food, probably because these activities have little relevance to a child. When food is mentioned, it often relates to children's concerns: reward and punishment, and the need for consolation and approval.

The familiarity of Mammachi's Paradise Pickles and Preserves business, which shapes the Kochamma family's identity in Ayemenem, offers sanctuary, or at least distraction, to Estha under traumatic circumstances. When the Orangedrink Lemondrink Man sells Estha a drink in the lobby of the movie theater and then molests him, Estha runs through his grandmother's products in his mind—"pickles: mango, green pepper, bitter gourd, garlic, salted lime; squashes: orange, grape, pineapple, mango; jams: banana, mixed fruit, grapefruit marmalade"—until the act of molestation is over.

Soon after this incident, and another one in which his mother rejects him, Estha visits the Paradise Pickles and Preserves factory, positioning himself by a vat of freshly boiled banana jam. This is where Estha can think, a place where "the smell of vinegar and asafetida stung his nostrils, but Estha was used to it, loved it." Estha especially loves the banana jam because Ammu had allowed him the honor of copying Mammachi's banana jam recipe into her new recipe book. In the quiet of the factory, Estha hatches his fateful plan to escape his mother's rejection. As he stirs the jam and it thickens and cools, "the jam-stirring became a boat-rowing" and his plans for escape congeal.

Rahel, too, expresses her need for approval through food. When she lashes out at Ammu with hurtful words, Ammu implies that she loves Rahel a little less. Desperate to regain the full measure of her mother's love, Rahel begs for punishment, suggesting that she might be made to skip dinner. When Ammu resists, Rahel refuses dinner, hoping to exact punishment on herself. Her uncle, Chacko, eats all the chicken and ice cream with chocolate sauce himself, never understanding the reason for Rahel's refusal to eat.

Amber Masud's Aloo Tikki
(Potato Cutlets) with Green Chutney

The Network of South Asian Professionals (NetSAP–DC) book club of Washington, D.C., reads South Asian literature exclusively. The group named *The God of Small Things* as a favorite selection. For their meetings, members often prepare a variety of South Asian dishes, always featuring a vegetable-based dish to accommodate their many vegetarian members.

Member Amber Masud contributed a Pakistani recipe she prepares for the group, *aloo tikki* (potato cutlets). Masud's mother-in-law, Shafqat Masud, taught her to prepare this old family recipe. Masud has added a modern twist to the preparation to save time—she uses a food processor. "Everyone who eats the potato cutlets loves them. They are quite easy to make and come in very handy for parties or lunch."

4–5 medium red potatoes

1 teaspoon red chili powder (see note below)

1 teaspoon salt

1 small yellow onion

1 tablespoon whole coriander seeds (see Purchasing Information, p. 499), or ¾ teaspoon ground coriander

4–5 scallions

2–3 serrano chiles, seeds and membranes removed

¼ bunch cilantro, stems removed

2 eggs

1 cup vegetable oil for frying

NOTE: The potato cutlets may be made ahead. To store, place the cooked cutlets on a tray and freeze for 2 hours. Once frozen, stack the cutlets in freezer bags or wrap and keep frozen until ready to use. Remove from freezer and microwave for 2 minutes before serving. Red chili powder has a different flavor from chili powders commonly found in grocery stores. It can be found in most Indian groceries (see Purchasing Information, p. 499). Wear plastic or rubber gloves while handling the chiles to protect your skin from the oil in them. Avoid direct contact with your eyes, and wash your hands thoroughly after handling.

1. Wash the potatoes (leave skins on), and add to a large pot of boiling water. When the potatoes are tender, remove them from the water, slip the skins off, and place in a flat tray or baking

dish. Mash with a potato masher or fork immediately, while hot. When cool enough to handle, add red chili powder and salt and, using your hands, mix in well.

2. In a food processor, finely chop the onion. Squeeze out and discard the juice, and add the onion to the potato mixture.

3. Add the coriander to the food processor along with the scallions, serranos, and cilantro. Process to a fine consistency and add to the potato mixture. Mix with your hands until all ingredients are well blended. Adjust salt and chili powder to taste. Let stand for 30 minutes.

4. Form potato mixture into round patties about 2½ inches across and ½ inch thick. In a bowl, beat the eggs with a fork. Heat ½ cup of the oil in a large frying pan over medium-high heat. When the oil is very hot, dip a cutlet in egg to coat and place it in the frying pan. Repeat with more cutlets, frying about three at a time, not overcrowding the pan. When browned (about 1 minute), turn the cutlets over and brown the other side. Remove from the heat, place on brown paper or paper towels to drain, and keep warm. After half the cutlets are cooked, discard the used oil, wipe out the pan, and use the remaining ½ cup of oil.

Yield: 15 to 20 2½-inch cutlets

GREEN CHUTNEY

¼ bunch cilantro

A few sprigs of mint

1–2 teaspoons lemon juice

2 cups plain yogurt

Salt

To make the chutney: Place the cilantro and mint in a blender or food processor with lemon juice. Process to a fine paste. Add to yogurt and stir well to blend. Add salt to taste. Serve at room temperature. Makes about 2 cups.

BOOK CLUB PROFILE

"We specifically choose novels that raise provocative questions about relatively recent political history and related themes of identity," says Tammi Coles of her Booker Tea Reading Group of Washington, D.C. The Booker Tea began discussing Booker Prize–winning fiction over Sunday afternoon tea in 1997, and followed each year with books in other award categories, including the PEN/Faulkner Award and the Columbus Foundation's American Book Awards. Now the group seeks out favorably reviewed works with a commitment to demographic, geographic, and thematic diversity. They also balance their reading list by gender, selecting six male and six female writers each year.

Coles, who founded the Booker Tea Reading Group, drew on friends and colleagues in Washington's nonprofit community. Some members are fresh out of college, and others are near retirement, but all are politically involved professionally or as volunteers on social and political issues such as peace and justice, conservation, criminal justice advocacy, reproductive rights, and cultural-diversity training. "Each book we discuss needs to have a political foundation. Our members are interested in diverse perspectives," says Coles.

The Booker Tea Reading Group continues to meet one Sunday afternoon a month, but meetings have evolved into a potluck brunch at members' homes in various Washington, D.C., neighborhoods. Each member brings either a main dish, dessert, fruit, cheese, or bread.

The Booker Tea Reading Group has read many great works by Indian writers, but Arundhati Roy's *The God of Small Things* had particular resonance. "The characters and politics were so well described," says Coles. "We look for novels that expose us to varied political perspectives on recent world history. The way politics affected the characters was so vivid. It was a novel, but it brought us to a clear understanding of India's real political history."

Booker Tea Reading Group member Katherine Sawyer admired Roy's evocative use of language to create striking imagery and the way she skillfully drew characters from very different walks of life, from an eight-year-old child to a middle-aged man. Coles admired how the book's vivid characters "evoked a strong emotional response."

"I can't say enough about how excellent the book is for a group discussion," she adds.

More Food for Thought

Members of the Meeteetse Book Group in Meeteetse, Wyoming, shared home-cooked Indian dishes, including shrimp curry, spicy chicken curry, rice, and flatbread, over discussion of *The God of Small Things*. The group has read several books set in India that have inspired other menu ideas. "Lentil dal [see p. 379] is a nice side dish," suggests Rosemary Lowther, a group member for five years. "And mango ice cream makes a great dessert for an Indian dinner."

The Good Earth

Pearl S. Buck

....

1931

(available in paperback from Pocket Books, 1994)

Pearl S. Buck won the Nobel Prize for Literature for her portrayal of the life of a Chinese peasant with powerful ties to the land in her classic novel, *The Good Earth.*

The story begins in the early part of the twentieth century in rural Anhwei province. Wang Lung, a peasant, marries a hardworking, resourceful slave, O-lan. Together they begin their life full of hope as they work the fields. They prosper from the land they purchase from the area's most powerful family, the House of Hwang, and start a family.

A few years later, the land betrays them as a devastating drought forces the family to flee in search of food and work. Although they find food in markets to the south, they don't have the means to buy it. Wang Lung and his family are reduced to waiting in food lines and begging. Only when Wang Lung and O-lan are swept up in a group of people pillaging a wealthy family's home does Wang Lung steal the gold that buys them their passage back to their farm.

When Wang Lung returns to his land, he slowly rebuilds his fortune, eventually replacing the House of Hwang as the area's wealthiest family. As he struggles to quell unrest in his own growing family—between his wife and concubine, his nephew and uncle, and his daughters-in-law—he turns to the land for reassurance, for it has sustained his family for many years. As Wang Lung is dying, his sons assure him that they will maintain the land, but their furtive glance over his head suggests otherwise.

Americans applauded *The Good Earth* when it was published in 1931. For many, the book marked their introduction to nonstereotypical Chinese characters and to details of daily peasant life in early-twentieth-century China.

The book's elegant descriptions of the preparation of celebratory Chinese foods revealed to many Americans for the first time the wide array of Chinese customs. When O-lan bears a son, Wang Lung buys fifty eggs, red paper to dye them, and red sugar. Red is seen as a sign of good luck. For the Chinese New Year, O-lan kneads pork fat, rice flour, and white sugar into moon cakes, a traditional food made even today for the Mid-Autumn Festival, a Chinese holiday when families come together to view the full moon. O-lan decorates the moon cakes beautifully with haws—probably hawthorns, or thorn apples—and dried green plums.

For peasant women, the ability to prepare such foods conveyed status. O-lan's cooking skills increase her value as a slave and a wife, and are a source of pride to Wang Lung. When she first arrives at his house, O-lan prepares a meal for seven with the pork, beef, and fish that Wang Lung has provided. Although Wang Lung verbally disparages the food, as was the custom, inside he is bursting with pride, "for with what meats she had the woman had combined sugar and vinegar and a little wine and soy sauce and she had skillfully brought forth all the force of the meat itself." When O-lan prepares her moon cakes for the New Year, Wang Lung thinks that "there was no other woman in the village able to do what his had done, to make cakes such as only the rich ate at the feast."

The Good Earth also reveals the diversity of foods available in the different regions of China. In rural Anhwei province, the family lives off the simple fruits of the land, eating cabbage, bean curd, garlic, rice, pork, beef, and fish. In the south, though, the abundant variety of other foods—pork balls, bamboo sprouts, chestnuts stewed with chicken and goose giblets, yellow crabs, eels, red and white radishes, lotus root, and taro—overwhelms Wang Lung, even though he can't afford to buy any of them.

SCALLION-GINGER FRIED RICE

Wang Lung's family arrives in the south close to starvation. He promises his children that they shall have "white rice every day for all of us and you shall eat and you shall eat." His promise comes true, initially as they stand each day in food lines at public kitchens to receive their bowls of free rice, and later when they return to their own land farther north.

The south of China is legendary for rice production. We offer this recipe as a tribute to the grain that was a staple in *The Good Earth*. Rosemary Lowther of Cody, Wyoming, sent us this recipe for Scallion-Ginger Fried Rice from the April 1998 *Gourmet* magazine, which her Meeteetse Book Group enjoyed along with other Chinese dishes. "We loved the fragrance that the ginger gave the rice," Lowther says.

5 cups white rice, cooked and chilled

3 tablespoons chicken broth

1 tablespoon soy sauce

1 ½ teaspoons dark sesame oil

1 ¼ teaspoons salt, or to taste

¼ teaspoon freshly ground black pepper

2 tablespoons corn or safflower oil

3 bunches scallions, finely chopped
(about 3 cups)

3 tablespoons minced fresh ginger

2 ½ cups fresh mung bean sprouts, rinsed
and drained

⅓ cup Chinese rice wine or sake

1. Spread the rice in a shallow baking pan and separate the grains with a fork. Set aside.

2. In a small bowl, combine the chicken broth, soy sauce, sesame oil, salt, and pepper. Set aside.

3. In a large heavy skillet (a nonstick surface is preferable), heat the corn or safflower oil over moderately high heat until hot but not smoking and stir-fry scallions and ginger until fragrant, about 20 seconds. Add the bean sprouts and rice wine, and stir-fry until sprouts begin to soften, about 1 minute. Add the rice and cook, stirring frequently, until heated through, about 2 to 3 minutes. Stir in the broth mixture, tossing to coat evenly. Serve immediately.

Yield: 6 servings

BOOK CLUB PROFILE

According to Debra Miller, who works in the legal department at Microsoft, the diversity of her "Got Wine" Book Club of Issaquah and Redmond, Washington, consists of "several blondes, several brunettes, and several silvers!"

A close-knit and supportive group, Got Wine women are old and new friends who, Miller says, "share life's problems and triumphs," as well as their thoughts about books. Four neighbors in Issaquah, Washington, formed the group in 1999. As their children moved into high school, they met other parents, who swelled the ranks. Members range in age from their twenties to their fifties and hold jobs in a variety of fields—education, computers, plumbing, law enforcement, appraisal, insurance, and project management—bringing a range of experience to group discussions.

True to their name, Got Wine members sip a glass of wine—or two—at every meeting. Dessert also graces the table each month, and sometimes the group shares a potluck meal or eats dinner out.

The host of each month's meeting researches and recommends several books, from which the group picks one. Members choose books from a variety of genres, including current fiction, memoirs, and classics. Some of their favorite titles include Arthur Golden's *Memoirs of a Geisha* (see p. 255), Jung Chang's *Wild Swans: Three Daughters of China* (see p. 486),

Leif Enger's *Peace like a River* (see p. 335), and Harper Lee's *To Kill a Mockingbird* (see p. 444).

Another favorite, Hampton Sides's *Ghost Soldiers: The Epic Account of World War II's Greatest Rescue Mission*, about the rescue of American POWs held by Japanese soldiers in the Philippines, prompted one of the group's most memorable and moving meetings. Upon learning that one of the soldiers named in the book, Robert Prince, lived in the area, a group member invited him to their meeting. "Mr. Prince was part of a company of Rangers charged with the task of marching 513 POWs thirty miles to safety," explains Miller. "Though Mr. Prince was unable to attend our meeting, he mailed copies of handwritten personal notes and photos of his military experience during World War II. The communication was patriotically stirring for every member of our group."

Pearl S. Buck's *The Good Earth* captivated the group with its portrayal of a distant place and time, where daily life differed dramatically from today's. "We enjoyed the book for its depiction of the hard lives of the peasants in China," says Linda Hauta, a senior budget analyst with Puget Sound Energy and a founding member of the group. "It was interesting to see the importance of land, and how owning it proclaimed a person's wealth and status."

The development of the main character, Wang Lung, and his relationship to women also interested the group. "Wang Lung was so certain that land would bring him happiness. But he got off track, trying to accumulate other signs of wealth," says Hauta.

"Wang Lung's wife sacrificed so much for him, but he became involved with other women because that was his right," says Hauta. "We enjoyed seeing Wang Lung's character unfold, and how he comes to figure out what's really important. In the end he realizes how much his first wife had done for him, but by then it's too late."

More Food for Thought

"I'm not particularly good at cooking Chinese food," says Barb Warden of Colorado's Denver Read and Feed book club, about the food she prepared for her group's *Good Earth* meeting, "so I served a marinated teriyaki pork tenderloin that always gets rave reviews." She added stir-fried peppers, cabbage and water chestnuts, and mashed potatoes, "because I like mashed potatoes better than rice." Warden topped the meal with a "dirt" dessert, made by crushing Oreo cookies over chocolate pudding and adding a gummy worm or two. "The dessert was inspired by the fact that the characters in *The Good Earth* were reduced to eating dirt during a famine," says Warden. She served the "dirt" in small clay flowerpots.

The Grapes of Wrath

John Steinbeck

....

1939

(available in paperback from Penguin, 2002)

ONE OF THE GREAT CLASSICS of American literature, *The Grapes of Wrath* is the story of the Joad family's migration from the Oklahoma Dust Bowl of the 1930s to the promised land of California. But California's verdant valleys are a harsh place for migrant workers. The Joads pick fruit for pennies a day, and fight hunger and despondency while trying to maintain their dignity and humanity.

First published in 1939, *The Grapes of Wrath* has been called John Steinbeck's crowning achievement. Steinbeck won the Pulitzer Prize for Fiction for *The Grapes of Wrath* in 1940, the same year that the film version, starring Henry Fonda, was released. In 1962, after publishing twenty-five novels, John Steinbeck was awarded the Nobel Prize for Literature.

Food, and its absence, plays a big part in *The Grapes of Wrath*. The Joads eat salted pork, convenient for travel, and potatoes as they head west, and enjoy a spare but solid meal of meat, bread, and coffee after their first day of picking peaches. But most of the time they are consumed with a relentless hunger. When the family pulls into a truck stop and asks to buy bread, they're told that the diner sells sandwiches, not loaves of bread. "We're hungry," Pa replies. Daughter Rose of Sharon worries that because she has no milk to drink, her gestating baby is suffering. "This here baby ain't gonna be no good. I ought a had milk," she laments. Hunger and the fear of starvation stalk the Joads.

In contrast to their meager rations, an abundance of Salinas Valley produce—lettuce, cauliflower, artichokes, prunes, cherries, plums, nectarines, peaches, pears, and grapes—greets the Joads when they reach California.

The fertile land of the Salinas Valley, comprising more than 640,000 acres, was central to John Steinbeck's life and work. Born and raised in Salinas, Steinbeck set several of his novels—most notably, *The Grapes of Wrath, Of Mice and Men* (1937), and *East of Eden* (1952)—in the Salinas valley, still an agricultural mecca. Today more than $2 billion worth of agricultural products stream out of the valley annually.

One Main Street Café's
Artichoke-Jalapeño Spread
with Tomato Bruschetta Topping

We wanted to take advantage of this rich, varied produce for a *Grapes of Wrath* recipe, so we turned to the National Steinbeck Center in Salinas. Built in 1998 just blocks from John Steinbeck's childhood home, the National Steinbeck Center provides educational experiences related to Steinbeck's work that inspire visitors to learn about human nature, literature, history, agriculture, and the arts.

The One Main Street Café, at the Steinbeck Center, specializes in foods—particularly fresh fruits and vegetables—associated with the Salinas Valley. The café contributed the following recipe for a spicy artichoke spread on rounds of sourdough baguette. With our Tomato Bruschetta Topping, these warm toasts capture a small measure of the valley's rich offering of produce.

NOTE: For a less filling version of this appetizer, place the spread in a shallow casserole dish, warm in a 350°F oven, cover with the tomato topping, and set out with crackers for your guests.

Wear plastic or rubber gloves while handling the chiles to protect skin from the oil in them. Avoid direct contact with eyes, and wash hands thoroughly after handling.

3 jalapeño chiles
1 8-ounce package cream cheese, softened
1 13- to 16-ounce can water-packed quartered artichokes, drained
1 tablespoon minced garlic

¼ cup shredded mozzarella
2 tablespoons freshly grated Parmesan cheese
1 tablespoon heavy cream
Salt and freshly ground black pepper

Sourdough baguette
Tomato Bruschetta Topping (see below)

1. Preheat oven to 400°F.
2. Roast the chiles directly on a gas burner set to medium-low, turning as needed with tongs until the skin is black and blistered on all sides. If no gas burner is available, place the chiles on a broiler pan and broil approximately 4 inches from the heat source, turning as needed with tongs, until the skin is black and blistered on all sides. Remove each chile as it is done and place in a sealed plastic or paper bag. Allow to cool in the bag for 15 minutes. Remove the skin, stems, and seeds, and coarsely chop peppers.
3. Place the chiles, cream cheese, artichokes, garlic, mozzarella, Parmesan, and cream in the bowl of a food processor. Blend to a paste, about 30 seconds (the spread should have a chunky consistency). Add salt and pepper to taste.
4. Top slices of sourdough baguette with the spread and bake until bread is crisp and the top is bubbly. Serve with Tomato Bruschetta Topping (see below).

Yield: About 2 cups, or 8 appetizer servings

Tomato Bruschetta Topping

2 pounds ripe tomatoes

2 tablespoons extra-virgin olive oil

1½ tablespoons good-quality balsamic vinegar

Sugar, to taste

Salt and freshly ground black pepper

Seed and chop tomatoes and place in a bowl. Drizzle with olive oil and vinegar. Add sugar, salt and pepper to taste and combine. Let sit 1 hour before serving.

BOOK CLUB PROFILE

Once a month since 2000, a group of about ten men and women from Lakeville, Minnesota, have gathered at the Dakota County Heritage Library to discuss books. The composition of the group, which varies slightly each month, reflects Lakeville's growing population. One member moved to Lakeville from Alaska; others hail from various small towns throughout Minnesota. Members range in age from thirty to seventy. To choose books, group moderator and librarian Luann Phillipich nominates books in six genres—fiction, memoir/nonfiction, young adult titles, mysteries, classics, and books by local authors—and group members cast paper ballots for one book in each category.

World events and the personal experiences of group members find their way into the Heritage Library Reading Group's discussions. One of their best dialogues came on the heels of the September 11 attacks on the World Trade Center and the Pentagon.

The group read and discussed *The Grapes of Wrath* and found that some of the book's central themes resonated strongly in the wake of the attacks. "We talked about outsiders," says Phillipich. "The migrant workers in *The Grapes of Wrath* are viewed as outsiders. And after 9/11, Americans became so uncomfortable with 'the other,' with people who are different." The group discussed how the gulf between the haves and the have-nots, vividly portrayed in Steinbeck's 1939 novel, still exists. "It surprised us that things still seemed relevant when the book was written so long ago," says Phillipich.

Life experiences also guided the discussion. Older group members recalled their lives during the Depression; those people from small towns or with farming backgrounds identified with the book's setting. "That's what's nice about our age range," says member Joni Lafky. "Our discussions relate to our lives and the wide range of life experiences that we bring to the group."

More Food for Thought

Their proximity to Salinas, the home of John Steinbeck and the setting for many of his novels, has inspired the East County Mother's Club Book Club of Contra Costa County, California, to read several of his works. For their *Grapes of Wrath* meeting, the group watched the film version of the book and enjoyed casual California fare, including taco-style appetizers, grapes, wine, and margaritas.

The Great Gatsby

F. Scott Fitzgerald

....

1925

(available in paperback from Scribner, 1995)

ONE OF THE MOST intensively analyzed and widely read works of American literature, F. Scott Fitzgerald's *The Great Gatsby*, set during Prohibition, remains a staple for students, adult readers, and book clubs alike.

Fitzgerald's piercing social critique of the decadent life of the American upper class of the 1920s, and those with class aspirations, is told through the tangled lives of Tom and Daisy Buchanan; Daisy's cousin, Nick Carraway, who moves next door to the Buchanans; and the mysterious Gatsby, whose life is consumed with the attainment of wealth and position.

Gatsby's social ambitions are driven by fantasy, including his wish to be reunited with Daisy, with whom he was infatuated in their distant past, before World War I separated them. While Gatsby served overseas, Daisy married wealthy, arrogant Tom Buchanan. When Gatsby purchases an estate across the Long Island Sound from the Buchanans, the relationship between Daisy and Gatsby is renewed, leading to tragic consequences.

The Great Gatsby is about lives carelessly led, lives where the ease and decadence of wealth breed a disregard for the consequences of one's actions.

F. Scott Fitzgerald's protagonist, Jay Gatsby, is a bootlegger, his fortune built on the illegal sale of alcohol. Alcohol consumption is widespread in *The Great Gatsby*, from Gatsby's lavish parties to more informal gatherings. Wine, champagne, ales, and mixed drinks flow liberally in the novel.

When he was stationed at Kentucky's Camp Zachary Taylor during World War I, Fitzgerald frequented the bar at the Seelbach Hotel in Louisville, famous for its mint juleps. The Seelbach Hotel—renamed the Muhlbach in earlier editions of the novel—was immortalized in *The Great Gatsby* as the setting for Daisy and Tom Buchanan's Louisville wedding.

Mint Julep

Fitzgerald's references to mint juleps in *The Great Gatsby* popularized the bourbon and fresh mint cocktail. In the novel's climactic scene, Tom, Daisy, Gatsby, Nick, and Daisy's friend, Jordan, drive to New York City on a hot day and take a suite at the Plaza Hotel to cool off and drink a mint julep. Tom has recently recognized Daisy and Gatsby's romantic involvement, and while waiting for drinks to arrive he confronts Gatsby about his past and his illegal activities. During the confrontation, Daisy begs Tom to open the whiskey so she can make him a mint julep.

An American invention, the mint julep's origin is unknown. Legend has it that a Kentuckian boating on the Mississippi stopped along the banks of the river and picked fresh mint to add to his bourbon-and-water mixture. The drink has become an integral part of Kentucky culture. It is the official drink of the Kentucky Derby and is traditionally served in silver or pewter julep cups.

6 fresh mint leaves

3 ounces (6 tablespoons) bourbon

2 tablespoons Simple Syrup (see below)

3 whole ice cubes

Crushed ice

Soda water

Mint sprig for garnish

1. Bruise mint leaves gently between your fingers and mix with bourbon and Simple Syrup in a glass. Add whole ice cubes and stir. Let stand for several minutes.
2. Strain the mixture into a julep cup or other tall glass filled with crushed ice. Top with soda water and a mint sprig.

Yield: 1 drink

Simple Syrup

1 cup sugar

1 cup water

Bring the water and sugar to a boil in a saucepan. Reduce heat and gently simmer 5 minutes until syrupy, stirring frequently. Cool. Refrigerate until ready to use.

Yield: About 1¼ cups

For more on mint juleps, see p. 329.

After graduating from the University of Michigan, Ann Arbor, Nina Palmer moved to Washington, D.C. Some of her college friends dispersed to New York, Chicago, and Detroit, while others stayed in Ann Arbor. They had been a close-knit group—some had known one another since high school—but now they found themselves apart.

"Suddenly we had all relocated and our lives were chaotic with new jobs," says Palmer, a staff assistant for the economic policy division of the U.S. Chamber of Commerce. "After two months the communication among us had become infrequent."

Around the same time, Palmer's mother sent her a copy of George Orwell's *1984,* which Palmer, like so many of us, had read in high school. "I got so much more out of it the second time," says Palmer. It occurred to her that forming an on-line Classics Book Club with her friends might be a way to keep them better connected. "It's proved to be a great way to stay in touch and continue the learning process together," says Palmer. Several friends and colleagues of members became interested, and they were invited to join as well. As one member described the book club's cyberspace location, "It's a classic book club with a modern twist."

The Classics Book Club members are Asian American, Hispanic, African-American, and Caucasian. They value the dynamic their diverse backgrounds give the group. "In high school and college, discussing issues of race in classic literature didn't often happen," says Palmer. "Now it does. We want to reread many of those books we read years ago, because we have different perspectives." The group also enjoys reading books that explore how racial issues affect our society, by such writers as Richard Wright and James Baldwin.

In 2003, Palmer organized a first annual "offline" meeting of the Classics Book Club in New York City to brainstorm ways to enhance discussions and establish group goals. They created a schedule that has each member taking a turn choosing a book and being responsible for the discussion as well.

Finding a time when the entire group can meet is not an issue for the Classics Book Club. The member who chooses the book creates a reading schedule and leads weekly discussions via e-mail.

"We read about forty pages of the selected book each week," says Palmer. "On Tuesday we submit questions to the group. We meet together on-line Thursday. If you can't get to your computer during the appointed meeting time, you can make comments at your convenience."

F. Scott Fitzgerald's *The Great Gatsby* was the group's first reading selection. Although set in the 1920s, the novel was relevant to their lives. Palmer says group members, all in their early to mid-twenties and relatively new to the working world, were fascinated by the social order portrayed in *The Great Gatsby*. "Fitzgerald provided an excellent portrait of upper-class society and class structure," says Palmer. "Unfortunately, we still live in a society where our job defines who we are, whether you are white collar or blue collar. Nick, the narrator, has an outsider's view of the high-society people he meets, and he sees how materialistic and superficial they are. It's very different from the traditional values he grew up with in the Midwest.

"Many of us feel like observers, too, and we related to Nick," adds Palmer. "We didn't grow up in the cities where we currently live. Nick returns to his native Midwest at the end of the novel, and those of us from Michigan think we will eventually go back, too."

More Food for Thought

In Scranton, Pennsylvania, the Albright Memorial Library selected *The Great Gatsby* for its Scranton Reads program in 2003. The program, designed to engage the entire community in reading and discussing a novel, offers lectures, book discussions, and special events around a selected work.

The library's *Great Gatsby* Kickoff Party in October 2003 attracted five hundred readers from the Scranton community. "We tried to be as authentic as possible," says Fran Garvey, who coordinated the program for the library. Period costumes, a display of antique cars, live flappers, and a jazz group contributed to the Roaring Twenties ambience. At a vintage bar, guests enjoyed martinis, whiskey sours, and Rob Roys, all popular in the 1920s.

Many community groups joined in the festivities by preparing thematic foods. Among the groups participating was BEST, an after-school program for middle-schoolers in Scranton. The students researched foods mentioned in *The Great Gatsby*, as well as foods popular in the 1920s, including New York–style cheesecake (see p. 271 and Purchasing Information, p. 499), tea sandwiches (see p. 211), crudités with Caesar-salad-dressing dip, and sugar cookies.

More Food for Thought

The Boston-Area Returned Peace Corps Volunteer Book Group prepared an elegant buffet for their discussion of *The Great Gatsby*, with oysters on the half shell, chocolate mousse, an assortment of cheeses and crackers, wine, and, of course, champagne. "I passed a seafood store on the way home and thought we had to have oysters," says meeting host Marshall Sikowitz.

Harry Potter and the
Sorcerer's Stone

J. K. Rowling

....

SCHOLASTIC, *1998*

(available in paperback from Scholastic, 1999)

J. K. ROWLING's tale of a boy's magical adventures at the Hogwarts School of Witchcraft and Wizardry took the world by storm. *Harry Potter and the Sorcerer's Stone* is the first in a series that by 2003 had sold almost 200 million copies worldwide and had been translated into fifty-five languages.

Harry Potter and the Sorcerer's Stone introduces Harry on his eleventh birthday, when he receives an invitation to attend Hogwarts. Although his magic-hating uncle tries to stop him, Harry is assisted by Hagrid, the enormous kindhearted Hogwarts groundskeeper. At Hogwarts, Harry learns fundamental spells and charms, and is introduced to quidditch, a fast-moving game played high above the bleachers on lightning-fast airborne broomsticks. He meets Dumbledore, Hogwarts's headmaster; fellow students Ron and Hermione, who become his best friends; and a greasy-haired potions professor, Snape, whom Harry and his friends suspect of plotting to steal the precious Sorcerer's Stone, which ensures its owner's immortality. Harry, Ron, and Hermione are determined to protect the stone, bringing them face-to-face with dark and powerful forces.

Having grown up as a "muggle," or nonmagical person, Harry is constantly surprised by the wizarding world. Food is no exception. On the train to Hogwarts, Harry expects to buy Mars Bars off the food cart, "but the woman didn't have Mars Bars. What she did have were Bertie Bott's Every Flavor Beans, Drooble's Best Blowing Gum, Chocolate Frogs, Pumpkin Pasties, Cauldron Cakes, Licorice Wands, and a number of other strange things Harry had never seen in his life."

The tables of the Great Hall, where Hogwarts students come together to eat, are laden with more typical British fare. At the welcoming feast, Harry is stunned to see plates of food magically materialize—roast beef, roast chicken, pork chops, lamb chops, sausages, bacon, steak, boiled pota-toes, roast potatoes, fries, Yorkshire pudding, peas and carrots. After the meal the plates clean themselves, and luscious desserts—including treacle tarts—appear.

TREACLE TART

Treacle tarts are well known in every English kitchen. Treacle (molasses in America) is the dark, viscous residue left over from the process of refining sugar. Not as sweet as white sugar, but with sweetening properties, treacle has been used in England since the eighteenth century in dishes ranging from treacle gingerbread, said to have been served to Charles II, to oatmeal bis-cuits. By the 1880s, a different method of refining sugar had been invented, which left behind not only the dark molasses, but also a very sweet, light, golden syrup.

Our treacle tart recipe combines Lyle's Golden Syrup with molasses to create a dessert that is pure magic: rich but not too heavy. Although a bit harder to find than dark molasses, the subtle flavor of Lyle's Golden Syrup makes the effort worthwhile.

For the crust

1 cup all-purpose flour

½ teaspoon salt

6 tablespoons butter, cut in small pieces

2 to 3 tablespoons ice water

For the filling

½ cup plus 2 tablespoons golden syrup, such as Lyle's (see Purchasing Information, p. 499)

¼ cup dark molasses

Grated peel of 1 lemon

Juice of one lemon (about 3 tablespoons)

1 cup soft white bread crumbs

1 teaspoon finely grated fresh ginger (optional)

⅔ cup finely chopped almonds (optional)

1. Preheat oven to 375°F.

2. To make the crust: In a pastry blender or a food processor fitted with a mixing blade, com-bine the flour, salt, and butter and process to the consistency of coarse crumbs. Gradually add the ice water until a smooth ball forms. Wrap the dough ball in plastic and refrigerate 30 minutes (dough may be made in advance and refrigerated overnight).

3. Press the dough into a 9-inch pie or tart pan, pressing sides up about 1 inch from the base of pan. Reserve enough dough to make a lattice top if desired (about ¼ of ball). Bake 10 minutes. Allow to cool 15 minutes.

4. To make the filling: Combine all the filling ingredients in a saucepan, and simmer over medium heat until mixture is slightly thinned, stirring occasionally.

5. Pour the mixture into the prebaked pie crust. For a lattice top, crisscross strips of dough on top of the tart. Bake 20–25 minutes, until crust is golden and mixture bubbles. Serve warm with vanilla ice cream.

Yield: 1 9-inch pie, 6 to 8 servings

BOOK CLUB PROFILE

The seven women of the Book Bags of New Prague, Minnesota, seldom miss a monthly meeting. Middle-school teacher Betsy Lasch and her two sisters, also teachers, founded the group in 1999, after convincing friends with whom they were already trading books that a more formal book discussion group would be fun. The group gelled into a dedicated core that has devoured forty-two books in four years, including fiction, nonfiction, poetry, and biography.

A Book Bag meeting celebrates the senses, as the hostess often prepares food, drink, decorations, costumes, and activities related to the book. "Every meeting is an adventure that submerges us into the setting, character, and themes of the book," says Lasch. For *The Bridges of Madison County,* by Robert James Waller, a steamy love story set on an Iowa farm, the hostess set up a toy plastic farm set on the dinner table, prepared a version of Iowa housewife Francesca's stew, and served Hot Sex, a commercially prepared spiced chocolate drink. For their discussion of *Girl in Hyacinth Blue,* by Susan Vreeland, about the influence of a Vermeer painting stolen by Nazis on the lives of eight people, each member received a color copy of a Vermeer painting with a short analysis of the painting, which she in turn presented to the group. And for Jean Shinoda Bolen's *Goddesses in Everywoman: A New Psychology of Women,* an analysis of the powerful internal forces that influence womens' feelings and behavior, members dressed up to represent "the goddesses who dwell within us," according to member Ann Prchals, and wrote poems to explain their choices to the group. Clad in outfits ranging from white togas with garlands of grape leaves to an archer's costume complete with bow and arrow, the group enjoyed Greek food—stuffed grape leaves, beef in phyllo dough, Greek salad, almond cake, and Greek wine—as they discussed the book.

The Book Bags saw opportunity for both fun and serious discussion in *Harry Potter and the Sorcerer's Stone*. The hostess greeted guests at the door, dressed in a black skirt, a wizard's cape, a pointed witch hat, and a magic wand, and served an apple-cinammon-raisin mixture baked in a pumpkin for refreshment, but when the group sat down to talk about the book, discussion focused on efforts by fundamentalists in a nearby community to have the Harry Potter books banned because of their depiction of witchcraft and perceived "dark messages."

More Food for Thought

Jennifer Watson of the Meeteetse Book Group of Meeteetse, Wyoming, enlisted the help of her thirteen-year-old daughter, Amanda, to prepare food and festivities for her Harry Potter book club meeting. Amanda served chocolate frogs that she had made from molds purchased on the Internet (see Purchasing Information, p. 499) and jellybeans, in honor of Bertie Bott's Every Flavor Bean. The soundtrack from the *Harry Potter and the Sorcerer's Stone* movie played in the background as book club members wearing Harry Potter hats ate off plates decorated with images from the movie. "I think by wearing the hats and enjoying the special treats and decorations, we were able to look at the book the way a child would," says member Rosemary Lowther. "We laughed and had a great time, and even in the most serious of groups, sometimes you need to laugh."

Amanda acted as the Sorting Hat, the magical hat that places first-year students into one of the four Hogwarts houses. To her mother's dismay, Amanda placed her in Slytherin House, home to the ruthlessly ambitious, if not downright evil.

More Food for Thought

Linda Gomberg of Seal Beach, California, gave a new twist to some old recipes to create a *Harry Potter* dinner for her Second Wednesday Dinner Club. Her menu included magic mushrooms (portobello mushrooms layered with slices of eggplant, cheese, red onion, and basil leaves), sorcerer's salad, chocolate frogs and "eyes."

"The eyes are cookies that I've been making for over thirty years with my children and grandchildren," says Gomberg. "They're addictive." Formed from balls of margarine–peanut butter dough, the eyes are then dunked into melted chocolate, leaving a bare spot on top—"just like a buckeye," says Gomberg.

Gomberg also scattered brooms around, in case any members felt the urge to play a pickup game of quidditch.

Having Our Say:
The Delany Sisters' First 100 Years

Sarah Louise Delany and A. Elizabeth Delany
with Amy Hill Hearth

KODANSHA INTERNATIONAL, *1993*

(available in paperback from Dell, 1996)

I N T H E I R 1 9 9 3 M E M O I R , the centenarian sisters Sara Louise (Sadie) and Annie Elizabeth (Bessie) Delany chronicle their lives as African Americans throughout the whole of the twentieth century. Daughters of a slave, the Delanys, both over one hundred years old, reflect on faith, racism, education, and careers with warmth and humor and advice about integrity, self-reliance, and discipline. The Delanys earned enough money teaching to leave their native Raleigh, North Carolina, for New York City, where they built successful careers, Bessie as a dentist and Sadie as a high-school teacher. They settled in Harlem, in the midst of the Harlem Renaissance of the 1920s, and were acquainted with some of the leading lights of the African-American community, Booker T. Washington and Paul Robeson among them. Ultimately the Delanys chose careers over men. Lifelong companions, the never-married sisters lived together in a New York suburb until Bessie's death at age 104 in 1995. Sadie passed away in 1999 at the age of 109.

"A big part of self-respect is self-reliance—knowing you can take care of yourself," writes Sadie, describing how she used her cooking skills and ingenuity to land a job as the first African-American home economics teacher in the New York City public school system. Even while teaching, Sadie earned extra money by selling homemade cakes and lollipops to teachers after school. She started a candy business, selling Delany's Delights, hand-dipped chocolate fondants, in shops across Manhattan until the Depression, when candy became a luxury.

The Delany sisters believed that diet and nutrition contributed to their longevity and became increasingly disciplined about their eating habits, eschewing the heavier southern foods of their childhood in favor of fruits and vegetables.

"If you eat a lot of fruit, it will extend your life," advises Sadie. Each morning Bessie and Sadie swallowed a chopped up clove of garlic and a teaspoon of cod liver oil, and they ate seven different vegetables daily. They generally stayed away from liquor, but made an exception for the occasional "Jell-O with wine." They weren't completely fastidious about their diet, however. Sadie warns: "It's important to eat healthy, but you won't live a long time unless you indulge yourself every once in a while!" Entertaining friends and family was the Delanys' true joy. At times they baked four cakes a week for visitors. One of these cakes was always pound cake, a timeless southern classic.

POUND CAKE WITH FRESH
COCONUT FROSTING

Pound cake gets its name from the original recipe, which calls for a pound of butter, a pound of sugar, and a pound of flour.

According to Bessie, family traditions and holiday celebrations were what she cherished most about the past. "Bessie and I were both born in September, and we've always had a joint celebration. We got in the habit of celebrating on Bessie's birthday, September 3—because it was easier for Mama," writes Sadie. Bessie's favorite cake? "A pound cake with fresh coconut icing, served with a Boston cooler—vanilla ice cream in a ginger-ale float. She feels downright sorry for herself if she doesn't have that!"

Ours is a simple recipe for pound cake, rich with buttermilk and topped with fresh coconut frosting in honor of Bessie, a coconut lover. Although their father passed away in 1928, Sadie and Bessie celebrated his memory by preparing his favorite dinner each year on his birthday, February 5. "For dessert we'll have a birthday cake—a pound cake—and ambrosia made with oranges and fresh coconut," writes Bessie. To taste this Delany family tradition, try serving the cake with our Ambrosia (see p. 444).

½ teaspoon baking soda

1 cup buttermilk

3 cups all-purpose flour

⅛ teaspoon salt

½ cup (1 stick) unsalted butter, softened

½ cup vegetable shortening at room temperature

2 cups sugar

4 eggs

2 teaspoons lemon extract

1 teaspoon almond extract

Fresh Coconut Frosting (see below)

Shredded meat of 1 coconut, or ½ cup shredded
  unsweetened coconut (see Purchasing
  Information, p. 499)

1. Preheat oven to 350°F. In a small bowl dissolve the baking soda in the buttermilk. In a separate bowl combine the flour and salt.
2. With an electric mixer, cream together the butter and shortening. Add the sugar gradually, beating well at medium speed. Add the eggs one at a time, beating well after each addition.
3. Alternately add small amounts of the flour and buttermilk mixtures, mixing until just blended after each addition. Repeat this process until all the ingredients have been added, ending with the flour mixture. Stir in the lemon and almond extracts.
4. Pour the batter into a greased and floured 10-inch bundt pan. Bake for 1 hour or until a wooden pick inserted near the center comes out clean. Cool in the pan 10–15 minutes; remove from pan. Serve the cake warm or finish cooling on a wire rack.
5. Spread the frosting on the cake and sprinkle with coconut, lightly pressing the coconut into the frosting.

Yield: 12 servings

FRESH COCONUT FROSTING

1½ cups sugar   *½ teaspoon cream of tartar*

½ cup water   *1 teaspoon vanilla extract*

4 egg whites

Heat the sugar and water in a small saucepan and boil for 2 minutes. Keep hot. Place the egg whites and cream of tartar in a mixing bowl and beat with a mixer on high speed until eggs form stiff peaks, but are not dry. Slowly pour hot sugar syrup into egg whites, beating at high speed. When frosting becomes stiff enough to spread (2–4 minutes), add the vanilla and beat until mixed completely.

Tips for Cracking and Shredding Fresh Coconut

If you have a shredding tool (available at Southeast Asian markets), you may leave the meat in the shell. Otherwise, you need to remove the meat and use a grater. Read these directions all the way through before starting—if you want to remove the meat whole, it is easier to bake the coconut briefly before opening it all the way.

Opening a coconut: Over the sink or a bowl, hold the coconut in one palm with the two ends facing to the side. Rap the center of the coconut sharply with the blunt edge of a cleaver (do *not* use the sharp edge!). Do this several times, rotating the coconut as you hit it. After a few blows, the nut should crack; let the juice run out into a bowl and continue to rap the shell until you can easily pull it into two halves.

Preparing the coconut for shredding: It will be easier to remove the meat for shredding if you bake the coconut briefly before opening it. *Never* put an uncracked coconut in the oven—it can explode, with imaginably horrible consequences for your kitchen.

Preheat oven to 400° F. Crack the shell with the back of a cleaver just until the juice drains out. The coconut should remain whole. Bake for about 15 minutes. Do not leave the coconut in the oven too long, as you do not want to cook the meat. Remove from the oven, and when the coconut is cool enough to handle, crack it open all the way as above. Carve the meat into sections with the tip of a knife, and remove by inserting a knife or clean screwdriver between the shell and the meat. The white meat should have mostly pulled away from the brown skin. Remove any remaining skin with a paring knife. The meat may be shredded easily using a grater.

BOOK CLUB PROFILE

Montevallo, Alabama, is a university town, but the local year-round, permanent population is only about 4,800. Yet the Adelante Book Group—Adelante meaning "progress"—sponsored by the Montevallo Branch of the American Association of University Women (AAUW), has attracted as many as fifty women to its monthly book club meetings. Sandra Lott, an AAUW member, successfully pioneered the Adelante Book Group's outreach effort to involve a diverse cross section of the community.

"We want to bring together readers from a variety of generations and backgrounds to discuss books addressing key concerns of women in our community," says Lott. Each year, the group chooses titles of interest to women from a variety of cultures and historical periods.

Having Our Say: The Delany Sisters' First 100 Years allowed the group to discuss issues of race openly, "something that doesn't happen easily here in a small southern community, where these issues can still be painfully divisive," says Lott. The book also helped dispel racial stereotypes: "The Delanys were relatively privileged African-American women. Yet they struggled to make it in a world where jobs and status were not open to people of all races," says Lott. "They prevailed because they had strength from their family and the power it gave them."

Barbara Belisle, a much loved and respected African-American English teacher, who was the first to integrate the faculty at the local high school, led the Adelante Book Group's discussion of *Having Our Say* and related her memories of growing up in the segregated South. Belisle's memories of her own strong, loving, but sometimes stern family upbringing helped participants to relate the book to people in their own community. "Especially moving," says Lott, "was Barbara's account of her father's repeated and ultimately successful attempts to break down racial barriers by registering to vote.

"This book explored universal themes: families growing up and apart, the ways family shapes our lives, and the quest for individual identity," says Lott. "These issues drew everyone into the discussion, regardless of background. It made us aware of our shared experiences and our common humanity."

A Hope in the Unseen:
An American Odyssey from the
Inner City to the Ivy League

Ron Suskind

TURTLEBACK, *1999*

(available in paperback from Broadway, 1999)

A S AN HONOR STUDENT at Frank W. Ballou Senior High School in southeast Washington, D.C., Cedric Jennings has to watch his back. Scorned as a nerd and isolated by his peers, Cedric tries to avoid attracting too much attention as he strives for academic success, his ticket out of a crime-infested, drug-ridden neighborhood. With the help of dedicated teachers and the unwavering support of his mother, Barbara, along with a fierce determination to succeed and an abiding faith, Cedric earns acceptance to Brown University in Providence, Rhode Island.

Wall Street Journal writer Ron Suskind won a Pulitzer Prize for his two-part feature article about Cedric's experiences at Ballou and the Massachusetts Institute of Technology MITES Program, dedicated to increasing minority representation in the fields of engineering and science. Suskind then followed Cedric to Providence, eventually expanding his article into *A Hope in the Unseen,* an account of Cedric's harrowing high-school days in D.C. and his first year at Brown.

Cedric's adjustment to college is rocky. The manifestations of his inner-city upbringing—his speech patterns and musical tastes—set Cedric apart from his mostly suburban peers. Although his freshman classmates try to accept him, Cedric feels self-conscious and sometimes resentful. Cedric's struggle to overcome the limitations of his past and to succeed in an affluent, predominantly white Ivy League environment tests his faith, while revealing a young man of enormous strength and resilience. His story highlights the burden on inner-city African Americans who must learn to negotiate culturally unfamiliar environments once they gain access to institutions of power and influence.

College socializing revolves around food, so it is no surprise that some of Cedric's moments of greatest discomfort, as he settles into life at Brown, take place at mealtimes. Only two days into his freshman year, Cedric joins fellow freshmen around a large table at the "Ratty," Brown's largest dining hall, eating pork chops with "milky mystery gravy." One student announces his SAT scores, and others follow. Left with no choice, Cedric announces his own score, the lowest at the table: "'I'm not ashamed of it or anything,' he says, not sure what tone he should affect, as others around him go on eating, pretending not to hear."

No scene captures Cedric's alienation from the culture of Brown—and the possibility of finding a way to fit in—better than when his mother and Neddy, his half sister, visit for parents' weekend. Wanting to "do what Brown parents are supposed to do," Barbara insists on eating out. Cedric leads his family to Adesso, a trendy restaurant just off College Hill's main street. With its blond wood and sky-high prices, the family feels awkward at Adesso and starts looking for flaws in the restaurant's smooth veneer to ease their discomfort.

They quickly find an object of scorn in the red molded complimentary appetizer that the waitress delivers to the table: beet flan. After poking fun uncertainly for a while, Barbara urges Cedric to try it. Cedric pronounces it "just like Alpo," to the laughter of his family. The waitress agrees conspiratorially. Barbara seems to settle in after this. "The Jennings clan, she feels, has something to bring to this room, as well."

Cedric Jennings has long since graduated from Brown, having earned advanced degrees in educational psychology and clinical social work (for ongoing updates on Cedric's progress, see www.ronsuskind.com), but he still reminisces about his mother's cooking. Cedric sent us two of his childhood favorites from his home in southeast Washington, D.C.—potato salad and spicy chicken wings—that would be great accompaniments to a discussion of *A Hope in the Unseen*.

Mama's Popular
Trial-and-Error Potato Salad

Potato salad is Barbara Jennings's signature recipe. "My mom used to cook ten or twenty pounds of potato salad for Sunday church dinner," Cedric recalls. "Everyone I know loves her potato salad."

Barbara cooks by "feel," so we have added suggested amounts of herbs and spices. But take the recipe title to heart and adjust seasonings as desired.

5 pounds red-skinned potatoes, well scrubbed

5 hard-cooked eggs, peeled

1 large red or yellow onion, finely chopped

1 large green bell pepper, seeded and finely
chopped

2 medium celery ribs, finely chopped

2 teaspoons celery seed

1½ teaspoons seasoned salt

¼ teaspoon ground black pepper

1 tablespoon dried parsley flakes

½ teaspoon onion powder

¾ teaspoon garlic powder

1 teaspoon crushed red pepper (optional)

⅔ to ¾ cup mayonnaise

3–4 tablespoons yellow mustard

4–5 tablespoons sweet salad cubes (see
Purchasing Information, p. 499; may
substitute sweet pickle relish)

Scant ¼ cup sugar, or to taste

Paprika for sprinkling

1. Place the potatoes in a large pot with enough water to cover. Bring to a boil over high heat. Reduce heat to medium and boil gently until fully cooked (potatoes should be firm, not mushy; pierce with a knife or fork to test). Remove potatoes and rinse in cold water until cool enough to handle.

2. Remove the potato skins. Cut the potatoes into ½-inch dice and place in a large bowl. Chop three of the eggs and add to the potatoes, along with the onion, green pepper, and celery. Season with celery seed, seasoned salt, pepper, parsley flakes, onion and garlic powders, and crushed red pepper to taste.

3. Gently stir in mayonnaise, mustard, and sweet salad cubes, and sugar to taste. Use a large spoon or your hands to do this; you want to thoroughly combine the ingredients, but not smash the potatoes. Adjust seasonings to taste.

4. Slice the remaining eggs in half and arrange on top of the salad. Sprinkle with paprika. Serve immediately, or cover tightly and refrigerate.

Yield: 12 to 14 servings

Mama's Delicious Spicy Fried Party Wings

Cedric used to eagerly anticipate nights when Barbara would cook up her spicy chicken wings. "This was the best! They melt in your mouth," he tells us. "My mom used to get all greasy when she made these, and found cooking them very tedious and bothersome. But it was a real treat for me!"

Adjust the amount of seasonings, especially the cayenne pepper, to your taste.

4 pounds Chicken Wings (about 24)
2 teaspoons seasoned salt
Ground black pepper
2 teaspoons onion powder
1½ teaspoons garlic powder

2–3 teaspoons cayenne pepper
All-purpose flour for coating
½ cup (1 stick) butter-flavored vegetable shortening

1. If the wings are untrimmed, cut them into three sections and discard the tips. Wash and pat dry. Season wings all over with seasoned salt, pepper, onion and garlic powders, and cayenne to taste. Cover and refrigerate overnight.

2. Coat wings with flour, shaking off excess (for spicier wings, mix some cayenne into the flour before coating the chicken).

3. In a large heavy-bottomed skillet, heat about two-thirds of the shortening over medium-high heat. Add wings to the pan (do not crowd the pan—cook in batches, adding more shortening, if necessary). Cook thoroughly, turning once, until golden brown and cooked through, about 15 to 20 minutes. You can ensure that the wings are thoroughly cooked by piercing each with a fork while cooking. Drain on brown paper or paper towels. Serve hot.

Yield: 4 to 6 servings

Opened in 1960, the Marcus Book Store in Oakland, California, is one of the country's oldest African-American bookstores and the monthly meeting spot for the Marcus Book Club.

In exchange for a low annual fee to offset her costs, Marcus Book Store owner Blanche Richardson keeps her doors open late for the after-hours discussion attended by twelve to fifteen African-American women (and sometimes men). Richardson also sets out refreshments, ranging from the usual finger foods—fruit, veggies, meat-and-cheese platter—to pizza, gumbo, or jambalaya.

The Marcus Book Club is affiliated with the United California African-American Book Clubs (UCAAB), an umbrella organization designed to "promote our reading groups and the authors we love to read." Like most of the UCAAB clubs, the Marcus Book Club reads almost exclusively African-American authors, and members demand quality. "We're open to all genres," explains Tira McDonald, a product manager for Visa International and a three-year veteran of the group, "but the writer needs to be very capable and understand the craft of writing. We don't read many relationship books. They have saturated the market, and they don't seem to offer any new insight on the 'boy meets girl' story. So unless they are written by a well-known writer or received excellent reviews, we won't read them."

Walter Mosley, Tananarive Due, Lolita Files, Zora Neale Hurston, and Ralph Ellison are among the group's favorite authors. They particularly enjoy books that speak to the diverse generations of women who attend meetings, such as Melba Pattillo Beals's *Warriors Don't Cry,* about her experiences as one of nine black teenagers who integrated Little Rock's Central High School in 1957. "Some members of our group grew up under Jim Crow," says McDonald, who is in her thirties. "When we read books with themes of racism, they are transported back to that time in their lives. The knowledge and wisdom of these women greatly enriches the group."

Ron Suskind's more contemporary story of a black student attending a predominantly white university, *A Hope in the Unseen,* deeply impressed the women, all of whom gave it a five-star rating. Group members found uplift and inspiration in Cedric Jennings's story. "I found it extremely encouraging that this young man considered education a goal worthy of achievement despite the ridicule of his high-school classmates and oftentimes of the black community at large," says McDonald. "It was nice to see how his faith, and his mother's faith, were instrumental in his success. This book should be required reading for African-

American men in the fourteen-to-eighteen age range. If this story could help one person in this age group, it would have done its job."

Group members marveled at Suskind's objectivity, especially because he is a white man telling a black man's story. "Often, when folks from other ethnicities write about African Americans, it tends to be from a patronizing or paternalistic standpoint," says McDonald. "Suskind was extremely objective and didn't let any misperceptions about African Americans get in the way. He allowed the story of this young man and his life choices to be told."

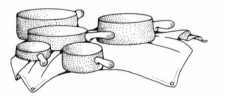

The Hours

Michael Cunningham

FARRAR, STRAUS & GIROUX, *1998*

(available in paperback from Picador, 2002)

In HIS PULITZER PRIZE—winning novel, Michael Cunningham interweaves three parallel stories, each focusing on a single day in the life of a woman. Though each story takes place at a different time in the twentieth century, all are connected by Virginia Woolf's novel, *Mrs. Dalloway*, about a day in the life of Clarissa Dalloway, a London socialite planning a party.

An account of Virginia Woolf's suicide opens *The Hours*. The story then reverts to 1923 in Sussex, as Woolf, longing to be in London, struggles with the writing of *Mrs. Dalloway*.

The second story in *The Hours* is set in the Los Angeles suburbs in 1949. Housewife Laura Brown, who feels trapped in her own life, reads *Mrs. Dalloway*. "Posing" as a wife and mother, she is unable to fulfill the duties expected of her. Laura spends her hours with her young son, preparing the perfect cake for her husband's birthday.

The third story woven into the fabric of *The Hours* is that of Clarissa Vaughn, a book editor in 1990s New York. Like the Mrs. Dalloway of Woolf's novel, Clarissa's day is focused on organizing a party; hers is in honor of her oldest friend, her ex-lover Richard, a poet stricken with AIDS, who has just won a literary prize. Richard playfully nicknames Clarissa "Mrs. Dalloway." Clarissa, dissatisfied with her relationship with her lesbian lover, devotes all of her energies to nurturing Richard.

The three protagonists share many of the same emotions and experiences throughout the novel, and the three stories converge in the novel's final chapter.

In *The Hours*, the state of the characters' emotional and physical health suppresses their appetites. Food often remains untouched or discarded. Virginia Woolf has to feign interest in food as "she reminds herself: food is not sinister."

Laura Brown's hours are consumed with the creation of a perfect birthday cake for her husband. Her goal is to produce a cake "as glossy and resplendent as any photograph in any magazine." To

Laura, the cake she bakes appears "amateurish, handmade," with crumbs caught in the icing and imperfect lettering. "She has produced something cute, when she had hoped . . . to produce something of beauty," writes Cunningham. Laura throws the cake in the trash.

BRITTA'S CRAB CASSEROLE

To Richard, "food doesn't matter much" anymore; to Clarissa Vaughn, "food matters a great deal." Clarissa tries to entice Richard to celebrate his literary prize with his favorite dish, crab casserole. Richard, whose illness has diminished his appetite and left him emaciated, pretends to be interested for Clarissa's benefit. Says Clarissa: "I've made the crab thing. Not that I imagine that's any kind of serious inducement." Richard responds, "Oh, you know how I love the crab thing. It does make a difference, of course it does." In spite of her efforts, Clarissa's crab casserole, along with a table of other food, remains untouched.

At Britta's Café in Irvine, California, chef and owner Britta Pulliam prepares a theme lunch for the book club discussions regularly held at her restaurant. Pulliam replicated the entire array of appetizers Clarissa Vaughn prepared in *The Hours* for her book club's luncheon discussion of the novel, including the crab casserole. After it played to rave reviews at her book club meeting, Pulliam added the crab casserole to her café's lunch menu. "I think I have perfected what Richard would have loved!" says Pulliam.

NOTE: Clarified butter, or ghee, is pure butterfat, made by removing the water from butter. Here is a quick way to clarify butter: Melt 7 tablespoons unsalted butter slowly in a small saucepan. Remove from the heat and allow to cool a bit; the milk solids will sink to the bottom. Skim any foam off the top and discard. Pour off the clear liquid ghee, leaving behind the milk solids.

1 pound cooked lump crab meat, picked over

1 tablespoon olive oil

1 medium red potato, diced

⅓ cup finely chopped white onion

¼ cup chopped red bell pepper

¼ cup chopped fennel

1½ teaspoons minced garlic

1 cup sliced Swiss chard,
stems removed

½ cup baby spinach, stems removed

3 eggs, beaten

½ pound feta cheese, crumbled

3 tablespoons heavy cream

½ cup fresh bread crumbs

½ cup loosely packed cilantro, stems removed

1 tablespoon minced fresh dill

1 tablespoon minced fresh chives

Salt and pepper

4 tablespoons freshly grated Parmesan cheese

12 sheets phyllo dough

⅓ cup (5⅓ tablespoons) clarified butter (see note), melted

1. Preheat oven to 350°F.

2. Thoroughly drain the crab meat, gently squeezing out excess moisture.

3. Heat the oil in a frying pan over medium-high heat. When oil is hot, add the potatoes, onions, peppers, and fennel and sauté until slightly soft, about 2–3 minutes. Add the garlic and sauté briefly. Stir in the chard and spinach and cook until wilted, about 1–2 minutes. Transfer to a mixing bowl and allow to cool completely.

4. Add the eggs, feta cheese, cream, bread crumbs, cilantro, dill, and chives to the cooled vegetable mixture and stir to combine. Gently fold in the crab meat, being careful not to break apart the lumps. Season with salt and pepper to taste.

5. Sprinkle a buttered, 9x12–inch baking dish with 2 tablespoons of Parmesan cheese. Place 1 sheet of phyllo on the bottom of the pan and brush lightly with clarified butter. Lay on 5 more sheets of phyllo, brushing each with butter before adding the next. Sprinkle with remaining Parmesan. Spoon crab mixture evenly over the pastry and top with the remaining phyllo, again buttering each sheet. Score the top with a serrated knife, marking off portion-sized pieces. Bake 30–40 minutes, or until top is golden brown. Cool slightly before serving.

Yield: 8 to 12 servings

BOOK CLUB PROFILE

"We come from a common place," says Lisa Stone of her metro Atlanta, Georgia, book club. "We are eleven Jewish married mothers of young children. Most of us are busy moms or work outside the home, so we choose paperbacks we can read at baseball practices and in carpool lines." Another common thread among book club members is that most women had been members of Stone's Fit for 2 fitness program for pregnant women and new mothers.

The group started matching the food they served to the books they were reading "for fun and to add another dimension to the meeting," says Stone. "This is our girls'-night-out so we want it to be special."

According to Stone, the hostess will offer at least one dish related to the book, such as Greek food with Anne Michaels's story of a Jewish boy in Poland smuggled to Greece during the Holocaust, *Fugitive Pieces;* salsa and chips with T. C. Boyle's *Tortilla Curtain* (see p. 477); and a dessert feast with Joanne Harris's *Chocolat* (see p. 65). When they discussed *Stolen Lives: Twenty Years in a Desert Jail,* the true story of a family imprisoned in Morocco, they dined at a Middle Eastern restaurant. Husbands are invited to an annual couples' night potluck dinner and book discussion. "We choose books that we think men will enjoy reading for this meeting, such as Mitch Albom's *Tuesdays with Morrie,*" says Stone (see p. 457).

In 2002, Stone's book club invited an English teacher and book reviewer for the *Atlanta Journal-Constitution,* Greg Chagnon, to facilitate discussions. "We wanted to move to a more challenging level. I knew we were missing layers and layers of meaning in these books and thought someone with expertise would help us have more in-depth discussions, and help us avoid chitchat," says Stone, who calls Michael Cunningham's *The Hours* "one of the best books ever written."

"Our facilitator came at *The Hours* from a very different perspective. Chagnon asked: 'Why did the author choose this particular format for the book? What does the format of the book tell you about the content of the story?' We discussed the book in terms of the three stories being intertwined and 'the truth' from each character's perspective. Although these women's lives were disparate, and they lived in different eras, the author did an amazing job of weaving their stories together at the end of the book, giving the reader an entirely new 'truth' to ponder." *The Hours* also prompted discussion of the ethical and moral issues of suicide and terminal illness. "We wrestled with the question, 'When is it okay to decide that you've had enough?'" says Stone.

"We talked about Laura Brown's feelings of ambivalence about her role as a wife and mother. Parenting can be so stressful and it can bring you to the end of your rope. We have all been in a place when we wanted to say 'I'm done, I'm finished being a mother,'" says Stone.

More Food for Thought

For their discussion of *The Hours*, the Meeteetse Book Group of Meeteetse, Wyoming, met for a Sunday afternoon English tea. Hostess Catherine Pinegar served a variety of finger sandwiches, including ham-and-cheese and egg salad, as well as scones, English muffins topped with crab meat and cheese, and hot artichoke dip. Pinegar topped off the meal with a rich chocolate truffle cake cut into 2-inch individual servings.

The variety of English teas that accompanied the meal and the fine bone China used for serving created a formal English setting that "put us in the right mindset to discuss the book," according to member Rosemary Lowther. "Tea is intoxicating in itself and a great stimulant, and the formal service provided a much better ambience than paper plates and mugs."

House of Sand and Fog

Andre Dubus III

W. W. NORTON, *1999*

(available in paperback from Vintage, 2000)

IN THIS SUSPENSEFUL NOVEL, Andre Dubus III examines the lives of an unlikely combination of characters who become dangerously entangled in the search for emotional and financial stability in their pursuit of the American dream.

Massoud Amir Behrani, a former officer in the Iranian air force who fled to the United States after the overthrow of the Shah, supports his family through minimum-wage jobs, deceiving them about the true nature of his work. Desperate to keep up appearances, Behrani invests all the money he has in the purchase of a home that was seized for nonpayment of taxes and sold at a government auction, planning to multiply his investment. His plans go awry when it is discovered that the seizure of the home and the eviction of its owner, Kathy Nicolo, resulted from an administrative error.

Nicolo, a recovering alcoholic now living out of her car, protests the sale and becomes increasingly desperate to reclaim her home, which offers the only stability in her life. Lester Burdon, the sheriff who evicted her, becomes romantically involved with Nicolo and is determined to help her seek justice. As the legal quarrel over the house escalates, fueled by mistrust and fragile emotions, the characters are unable to resolve the dispute and avoid the tragedy that ultimately befalls them.

Behrani's wife, Nadi, fills their home with aromas of Persian food and trays of pistachios, sweets, fruit, and tea. Andre Dubus shared with us how food helps him set the scenes in *House of Sand and Fog*.

As a fiction writer, I've come to rely upon the five senses to anchor the reader, and me, in a scene; if you smell freshly cut grass and see leafed-out maples and hear children laughing and splashing in water, then you are probably firmly rooted in a summer somewhere in the Western world. In this way, I found it necessary to describe the food of my Persian characters in my novel, *House of Sand and Fog*. Frankly, it was easier for me to inhabit the role of Colonel Behrani if I could also imagine smelling and tasting what he would: black tea sipped through a sugar cube, saffron and butter over rice and stewed tomatoes, sour yogurt with sweet cucumber.

The senses of smell and taste yield associations, and often while writing, I found myself remembering all the wonderful Persian meals I'd shared with my Iranian friends over the years, sitting on the floor upon a *sofreh*. This sense memory helped me forget the private boundaries of my own life and more readily enter theirs, for I believe food and stories come from the same place—a curious and hungry part of us all that needs our spirits and bodies to be *fed*.

KHOREST BADEMJAN (EGGPLANT AND TOMATO STEW) WITH BEEF

Dubus's good friend Kourosh Zomorodian is Iranian and introduced Dubus to the Persian culture he depicts in *House of Sand and Fog*. "I pretty much immersed myself in the culture, eating the food, listening to the music," says Dubus, who asked Zomorodian to contribute a Persian recipe to *The Book Club Cookbook*. Zomorodian gave us this delicious recipe for *khorest bademjan*, an eggplant-and-tomato stew he has prepared for Dubus on many occasions.

In *House of Sand and Fog*, Nadi prepares *khorest bademjan* for a dinner party in honor of their daughter, their new son-in-law, and his family. When Behrani asks Nadi to prepare the menu for the party, it becomes clear that preserving their cultural identity and customs in their new country is vital. Behrani thinks: "My wife's face became so lighted with happiness, at the modest fashion in which our lives appear to be returning to the old ways."

"Most Iranian dishes include rice, plain or mixed, for a main dish, sometimes served with a stew, such as *khorest bademjan*. Meals are served with yogurt as a garnish, along with radishes and fresh greens such as green onions, basil, parsley, or sliced cucumber. Bread always accompanies the meal," says Zomorodian.

2 pounds small eggplants (Italian or Japanese)
Vegetable oil for frying
2 pounds stew beef, cut in 1-inch cubes
3 medium onions, halved lengthwise and sliced
½ teaspoon ground turmeric

⅛ teaspoon ground cinnamon
Salt and freshly ground black pepper
1 teaspoon sugar
1 tablespoon fresh lime juice
4 teaspoons tomato paste

1. Peel the eggplants and cut lengthwise into ½-inch-thick slices. Salt the slices on both sides, place on a platter or paper towels, and let sit for 20 minutes.

2. Heat 2 tablespoons of oil in a Dutch oven or deep skillet. Add the beef and onions and cook over medium-high heat, stirring frequently, until the meat loses its pink color and the onions soften. Add the turmeric, cinnamon, and 2 cups of water to the meat. Season with salt and pepper, and cook uncovered over medium heat for 45 minutes, stirring occasionally. At the end of this time there should be about 1 cup of liquid remaining; add more water if needed to make a cup. Stir in the sugar, lime juice, and tomato paste.

3. While the meat is cooking, rinse the eggplant slices under cold running water to remove salt. Pat dry with paper towels. Cover the bottom of a large skillet with ¼ inch of oil and place over medium-high heat. When the oil is hot, fry the eggplant in batches, turning once, until golden on both sides. Drain well on paper towels.

4. Lay the eggplant slices over the meat, cover, and cook over low heat for an additional 30 minutes. Serve over hot Persian rice, rice pilaf, or noodles.

Yield: 6 servings

BOOK CLUB PROFILE

Andre Dubus's visit in 2001 to the Thursday Evening Book Group at the Haverhill Public Library in Massachusetts was a crowning moment in the group's three-year history.

The group's members are fifteen professionals who meet monthly to discuss fiction and classics. Unlike many book clubs that meet in libraries, where food is often forbidden, the Thursday Evening Book Group enjoys light refreshments that are often inspired by the book. Sue Bonenfant, financial administrator of the library and group facilitator, made blancmange, a cooked pudding, for the group's discussion of Louisa May Alcott's *Little Women*, and another member treated the group to "decadent scones" when they discussed George Eliot's *Daniel Deronda*.

Bonenfant invited Andre Dubus to join the group for its discussion of *House of Sand and Fog* in celebration of the Thursday Evening Book Group's third anniversary. The club's response to Dubus was overwhelming.

Andre Dubus "treated our group as though we were the first people who'd ever discussed *House of Sand and Fog*," recalls Kathleen Fitts, a charter member of the group. Betsey Copeland characterized the gathering as "warm, funny, interesting, and thought-provoking," while Deborah Dyer says that the meeting with this "perfect guest author" was "something for me to tell my children and grandchildren about."

The group peppered Dubus with questions about his writing process, although Dubus appeared to want feedback on his book as much as he wanted to speak, according to Bonenfant. "We asked him about, the choices he made in writing the book," Bonenfant says, "and our questions made him think about these choices, and look at his work through the reader's eyes."

Bonenfant had chosen *House of Sand and Fog* for her group because she was curious about the work of this author, who grew up in Haverhill and now lives in nearby Newburyport. She found the book dark and compelling. "The plot just rolls out of control, all because of one seemingly benign decision," says Bonenfant. "I put this book on our reading list so I could talk to someone about the decisions the main characters made."

Group members were equally intrigued with Dubus's characters. "The best thing about this book was the way Dubus made the characters come alive on the page," says Fitts. "I found the main characters likable and irritating at the same time. In other words, they seemed very human."

More Food for Thought

When Andre Dubus came to speak to their group about *House of Sand and Fog*, the Thursday Evening Book Group at the Haverhill Public Library welcomed him with Iranian food, music, and decorations. They served Persian fruit salad, *mast-vakhiar* (yogurt-cucumber dip), and hummus. A sign welcomed Dubus in Persian ("*Salomadti*"), while a recording of classical Iranian music played in the background. "Andre seemed very impressed with the Persian salad," says Bonenfant, "and with all the effort we took to create the mood for the meeting."

I Capture the Castle

Dodie Smith

ST. MARTIN'S, *1998*

(available in paperback from St. Martin's, 1999)

Dodie Smith's *I Capture the Castle* was first published in 1948, but has enjoyed a powerful resurgence recently, ever since J. K. Rowling, author of the Harry Potter series, was quoted as saying it was her favorite book. The novel is set in the 1930s and opens in the Mortmain family's decrepit castle in the English countryside. There, teenager Cassandra Mortmain records in her journal the struggles, hopes, and dreams of her eccentric, impoverished family. One day, Cassandra's older sister, Rose, rubs the nose of a castle gargoyle, desperately wishing for a wealthy husband to deliver her from poverty. When the Mortmain's new landlords, the young American brothers Simon and Neil Cotton, appear at the castle, it seems that Rose's wish has been granted and that better days lie ahead for the Mortmain family.

At the center of the novel is a love quadrangle among the Cotton brothers and Mortmain sisters. This romantic square dance is captured in a scene where Cassandra and Rose have lunch with Simon and Neil at a village inn. There, coming of age, Cassandra has her first taste of liquor. "I was going to say lemonade and then a wild idea struck me: could I have a cherry brandy? I've always wanted to taste it."

SINGAPORE SLING

Cherry brandy is *wonderful*," writes Cassandra. Soon the brandy makes everything "more fascinating" and she feels a "haze of content." When Rose asks for a glass of crème de menthe, a drink Cassandra knows her sister doesn't care for, Cassandra suspects that Rose ordered the green drink to complement her red hair.

Weeks later, Cassandra returns to the inn. After a fallout with Rose, she eyes the bottles of crème de menthe and cherry brandy at the bar. "Suddenly I felt the most bitter hatred for Rose's green crème de menthe and a deep affection for my ruby cherry brandy." Cassandra orders a glass of cherry brandy so she can "gloat over there being more gone out of it than out of the crème de menthe bottle. Now everyone will think the cherry brandy's the popular one," she records in her journal.

Cherry brandy, the object of Cassandra's great affection, is featured in our Singapore Sling. Invented at the Raffles Hotel in Singapore in 1915, the Singapore Sling became fashionable worldwide in the 1930s, and was a favorite of the literati, including Ernest Hemingway and Noël Coward.

NOTE: Add more grenadine syrup to taste for a sweeter drink.

4 ounces (½ cup) gin
6 ounces (¾ cup) unsweetened pineapple juice
2 tablespoons cherry brandy
1 tablespoon Cointreau
1 tablespoon Benedictine
1 tablespoon grenadine syrup

1 tablespoon fresh lime juice
2 dashes of Angostura bitters
2 ounces (¼ cup) club soda
Pineapple slices and maraschino cherries for
garnish

Fill a cocktail shaker half full with ice cubes. Add the gin, pineapple juice, cherry brandy, Cointreau, Benedictine, grenadine, lime juice, and bitters. Shake well and strain into 2 ice-filled highball glasses. Float 1 ounce of club soda on each drink and garnish with a slice of pineapple and a cherry on a toothpick.

Yield: 2 drinks

BOOK CLUB PROFILE

The Happy Bookers of Linn, Missouri, delighted in the charm, setting, and romance of *I Capture the Castle*. "A young girl living in poverty in an old English castle, coming of age, and falling in love made for a fun night of discussion, our best ever," says Lisa Klebba, who founded the fifteen-member group in 1993. "We could relate to those young girls, and we tried to remember things you thought about when you were that age," said member Rita Starnes.

The Happy Bookers have enhanced and enlivened their book discussions in many creative ways. Rita Starnes hosts the Happy Bookers end-of-year "pull out all the stops" dinner meeting, according to Klebba. Each member brings a dish, and Starnes creates decorations and party favors to complement the final reading selection. "We believe in having fun and expanding on the book's theme and setting," says Klebba.

More Food for Thought

Following the lead of the characters in *I Capture the Castle* who tried to spruce up the castle by dying curtains and clothing green, Rita Starves of the Happy Bookers sent green invitations for the meeting on this book to her book club members. She placed a mannequin, like Miss Blossom, the dressmaker's dummy Cassandra and Rose talk to in their bedroom, next to the table, and *I Capture the Castle*–themed favors were placed at each setting: perfume bottles wrapped in blue velvet with silver corks like the one Cassandra coveted, and journals, as the story is told through Cassandra's journal entries. To top off the meal, a crème de menthe drink was served, but like Cassandra and Rose, none of the Happy Bookers truly cared for it; they suggested a drink with cherry brandy instead, such as our Singapore Sling.

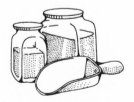

Interpreter of Maladies

Jhumpa Lahiri

HOUGHTON MIFFLIN, *1999*

(available in paperback from Mariner, 1999)

THE CHARACTERS in the nine short stories that make up Pulitzer Prize–winner Jhumpa Lahiri's *Interpreter of Maladies* all have something in common. They are caught betwixt and between two cultures. Living lives without the moorings many of us take for granted, some are new immigrants, some are expatriates, and others are visitors to a homeland they never really knew. Lahiri's characters muddle through universal trials and tribulations, from decaying love to alienation to enduring hope. They are sympathetic individuals.

Cultural assimilation is a major theme in *Interpreter of Maladies,* and food plays a major role throughout the book, principally as a touchstone for the culture left behind. Lahiri infuses her stories with smells and tastes of the Asian foods her characters long for and often re-create in their new surroundings. Food is an important part of their identities, and the rituals around cooking and eating provide a rich backdrop for the stories in *Interpreter of Maladies.*

"When friends dropped by, Shoba would throw together meals that appeared to have taken half a day to prepare," writes Lahiri in "A Temporary Matter," the first of the nine stories. "From things she had frozen and bottled, not cheap things in tins but peppers she had marinated herself with rosemary, and chutneys that she cooked on Sundays, stirring boiling pots of tomatoes and prunes." From shrimp malai, fish cooked with raisins in a yogurt sauce, to chicken with almonds, Lahiri's book is a veritable feast for the senses.

Mrs. Lahiri's Hard-Boiled-Egg Curry in Mustard Sauce

A Bengali immigrant who was schooled in London prior to his arrival in Cambridge, Massachusetts, in 1969 narrates another of Lahiri's stories, "The Third and Final Continent." He has come to establish himself before the arrival of his new bride, Mala, and rents a room in the home of an older woman, Mrs. Croft. When Mala arrives from Calcutta, Mrs. Croft helps ease the awkward transition to the arranged marriage, declaring Mala "a perfect lady." The protagonist recalls this as the moment when "the distance between Mala and me began to lessen."

As "The Third and Final Continent" opens, the protagonist recalls preparing egg curry in the rooming house he shared with other Bengalis in London. He prepares the same dish for Mala as his only gift to welcome her to America.

Jhumpa Lahiri, who is of Indian descent, was born in London, grew up in Rhode Island, and now lives in New York City. Lahiri contributed a recipe created by her mother, Tapati Lahiri, for hard-boiled-egg curry in mustard sauce to *The Book Club Cookbook*, and explained how the dish came to appear in her story.

This is a version of the dish the husband cooks for his wife, Mala, in "The Third and Final Continent," and it is the first meal Mala has in America. The recipe is my mother's invention.

The dish is very much an everyday family dish. I never remember my mother making it for company. (This is why I've never seen it in any Indian restaurant, I gather.) Usually egg curry is what she would make when there was nothing else to cook with, i.e., when supplies were low and a trip to the grocery store was needed. But I always loved eating egg curry and thought of it as a special dish nevertheless, if only because we ate it infrequently. It is also economical, compared to cooking meat or poultry, and I gather that it's often one of those things Bengali bachelors know how to do.

NOTE: You can find mustard oil in most Indian grocery stores (see Purchasing Information, p. 499).

2 tablespoons whole mustard seed
2 tablespoons corn oil
8 hard-cooked eggs, cooled and peeled
1 teaspoon turmeric

Pinch of cayenne pepper
1 teaspoon salt
Mustard oil (optional) (see note above)

1. In a small bowl, soak the mustard seed in a little water to cover, about 20 minutes. Rinse the seeds in fresh water, then blend them with some of the water in a blender until thick, pale, and creamy (this will take a few minutes). Set aside.

2. Heat the oil in a skillet. Add the eggs and fry until reddish brown in color (don't move the eggs around too much, but try to get an even color on all sides). Transfer the eggs to a plate lined with paper towels to absorb the excess oil.

3. Mix the turmeric and cayenne with a bit of water to make a paste. Add this to the remaining oil in the skillet. Return the eggs and cover them generously with the mustard paste.

4. Add salt and simmer, covered, over very low heat until all the oil rises to the top, and the sauce has reduced until it thickly coats the eggs but is not dry-looking. Remove to a serving dish and top the eggs with a drizzle of mustard oil. Serve with white rice.

Yield: 4 servings

MASALA ART'S MANGO LASSI (YOGURT DRINK)

Mango lassi, an Americanized version of India's most popular hot-weather beverage, is common in Indian restaurants. In the United States, it is often flavored and sweetened, but in India it is served plain or salted, rarely sweetened. Either way, it is refreshingly tangy, light, and healthy.

Shikha Kapoor developed this recipe for Masala Art, a restaurant in Needham, Massachusetts, which she owns with her husband, Vinod. For mango pulp and rose water, see Purchasing Information (p. 499).

¾ cup (6 ounces) plain yogurt
1¼ cups cold water
1 cup prepared mango pulp
1 tablespoon sugar

8 ice cubes, crushed (approximately ¾ cup)
1 teaspoon rose water
Crushed pistachios, for garnish

1. In a blender, combine the yogurt, water, and mango pulp and purée until smooth. Add the sugar and crushed ice cubes and blend again.

2. Add the rose water and serve chilled in a tall glass, with pistachios over the top, if desired.

Yield: 6 servings

"We learn about our heritage by reading and discussing books about South Asia or with South Asian themes," says Shalini Passales, coordinator of the Network of South Asian Professionals (NetSAP) Book Club in metropolitan Washington, D.C. NetSAP–DC is a nonprofit organization committed to identifying and celebrating the diversity of South Asians in America through professional development, community service, and public awareness.

NetSAP–DC sponsors an annual South Asian Literary and Theater Festival with author readings, plays, panel discussions, and writing workshops. For members of the book club, the festival is an opportunity to meet many of the authors whose works they have discussed, such as Chitra Banerjee Divakaruni, who wrote *The Unknown Errors of Our Lives* and *Arranged Marriages,* collections of stories set in India and the United States, and William Dalrymple, author of *White Mughals: Love and Betrayal in Eighteenth-Century India,* about a British colonist in Hyderabad who converts to Islam. Any NetSAP member may attend the monthly book club meetings, held in members' homes, and new members join the group each month. "This keeps the discussions fresh and different every time," says Passales.

The diverse group includes Indians, Pakistanis, Bangladeshis, Sri Lankans, and Nepalese. "Many of us are not first-generation Indians," says Passales. " Many of us were born here. We learn another perspective by discussing these works with South Asian book club members who have emigrated to the United States and share their personal experiences."

The group has also read many books about the partition of India and Pakistan, such as Khushwant Singh's novel *Train to Pakistan.* "Those who have lived in India have educated us about their tragic personal experiences, and many lost family members during the Partition," says Passales.

NetSAP book club members enjoy demonstrating their culinary skills through multicultural dinners prepared by the host. Most members prepare a South Asian buffet featuring a variety of vegetable dishes, because many in the group are vegetarians. Samosas; garbanzo bean *chole* (a vegetable dish similar to chili); *biryani* and *pulao,* aromatic rice and vegetable dishes; and *aloo tikki* (potato cutlets, see p. 159), are some NetSAP book club favorites.

The NetSAP book club has discussed more than fifty titles since 1998, including Arundhati Roy's *The God of Small Things* (see p. 157) and Rohinton Mistry's *A Fine Balance* (see p. 137). Jhumpa Lahiri's short story collection, *Interpreter of Maladies,* is a unanimous favorite of the club.

"It takes great talent to develop characters in short stories, but Jhumpa Lahiri takes you right into the characters in each story," says Passales. "Lahiri's prose is less flowery and descriptive than that of some older Indian authors, and her clean, concise writing style appeals to our group members."

Lahiri's title story, about an Indian-American family named Das visiting India with their children, is Passales's personal favorite, and one that provoked an interesting discussion for the group. "Lahiri depicts the crossroads many Indian Americans face," says Passales. "We could relate to the characters returning to India, where some things make sense but others don't. As Americans in India, the characters don't fit because they stand out as foreigners, yet in America, they don't fit in either."

Passales also notes that even Indians who grow up in America have to try to assimilate. "Your parents are Indian. But you're Indian and yet American. You're like a coconut: brown on the outside, white on the inside. You hold on to your Indian culture, your values, and your heritage. Yet if you travel to India, the way you dress, the way you walk, and the way you make eye contact is more American, and people can look at you right away and know you're from abroad, even if you are fluent in the language."

"In the story 'Interpreter of Maladies,' Mrs. Das was able to connect with India on more than a superficial level, even though she didn't feel a sense of belonging when they first arrived," says Passales.

More Food for Thought

The Vegetarian Society of Washington, D.C., promotes vegetarianism through both educational and social activities, and VSDC's book club is one of several social events held each month. Although their book selections often relate to vegetarian themes, the group has read a wide range of fiction and nonfiction over the past twelve years.

The VSDC Book Club discussed *Interpreter of Maladies* over a dinner of South Indian delicacies at the Amma Vegetarian Restaurant in Washington's Georgetown district. They sampled *masala dosas* (pancakes stuffed with potatoes and onions), *alu gobi* (potato and cauliflower curry), and a lentil-and-rice dish. "For appetizers, we chose samosas, fried turnovers filled with vegetables," says Beth Preiss, the club's coordinator. "In one of Lahiri's stories, 'This Blessed House,' samosas were on the menu at the housewarming party that turned into a hilarious hunt for religious 'treasure.'"

Lahiri's beautiful writing and fully realized characters, Indian and American, young and old, female and male, impressed the group. "Lahiri's descriptions of food preparation contributed to the richness of the book," says Preiss. "From the first story, in which a now-troubled couple had marked their recipes with the date they first ate the dishes together, to the last, in which a bowl of cornflakes and milk became one of the most memorable meals in the book, food played a part in crafting her stories."

For their *Interpreter of Maladies* dinner, the Epicureaders of San Francisco created a Fragrant Springtime Indian Feast, a meal that lived up to its title, according to member Lena Shelton.

"I think that one of the predominant qualities of Indian food is the fragrance of the spices," says Shelton, "and this fragrance is also a quality of springtime." For the dinner, the Epicureaders contributed *dal* (lentils), crab curry with basmati rice, *shahi paneer* (a dish made with a soft cheese), curried couscous with roasted vegetables, peach chutney and cilantro yogurt, potato and cabbage rolls, spicy cauliflower, an assortment of Indian breads, and rice pudding with raisins, almonds, and saffron for dessert.

Shelton brought the refreshing Indian drink sweet mango lassi, which she describes as a simple, traditional Indian drink. "The predominant flavor of the lassi is yogurt, so the mango adds a nice touch."

Jane Eyre

Charlotte Brontë

1847

(available in paperback from Penguin, 2003)

Fⁱʳˢᵗ ᴘᴜʙʟɪsʜᴇᴅ ɪɴ 1847, Charlotte Brontë's classic, *Jane Eyre*, is the tale of a resolute, courageous young woman who faces difficult personal challenges. It is also the story of the limitations and conventions imposed on women in Victorian England.

Orphaned at the age of ten, Jane is sent to live with her aunt, Mrs. Reed, in whose home she is cruelly treated by her cousins. Later, at the Lowood School, Jane suffers heartless treatment by the tyrannical headmaster, but knows a loving friendship with the angelic Helen, whose death is a consuming loss. Taking a position as governess to Adele, the daughter of Mr. Rochester, Jane enters a strange household in which Rochester mysteriously comes and goes. While Jane and Rochester come to love each other, a dark secret is concealed from her. Part drama, part romance, and part horror story, *Jane Eyre* raises questions—questions that resonate today—about the struggles a woman of integrity must face in the quest for love and independence.

Jane Eyre's early childhood is marked by deprivation. She is deprived of parenting, love, nurturing—and food. At her Aunt Reed's home, Jane faints with hunger. The withholding of food is also used as a punishment at the Lowood School of her youth. At Lowood, food is "scarcely sufficient to keep alive a delicate invalid." When Jane dines in the gloomy charity school refectory, meals consist of burned porridge—"almost as bad as rotten potatoes"—or dishes with the "aroma of rancid fat."

The villainous Brocklehurst, Lowood's headmaster, is outraged when he learns that a sympathetic teacher, Miss Temple, has indulged the girls with a snack of bread and cheese. This type of pampering is not in keeping with his plan to "render them hardy, patient, self denying." Meanwhile, Jane's cravings lead her to imagine suppers of "hot roast potatoes, white bread and new milk."

Jane's dreams are fulfilled when she leaves Lowood for Thornfield, Rochester's estate, to become the governess. Mrs. Fairfax, the elderly housekeeper, greets Jane with food and warmth. Noticing Jane's cold hands, Mrs. Fairfax invites her to sit by the fire and instructs a servant to "make a little hot negus and cut a sandwich or two" for her. Jane thinks, "A more reassuring introduction for a new governess could scarcely be conceived."

Negus

Negus, a mulled wine made with sugar, nutmeg, and often brandy, was a favorite in Victorian England. Created by Col. Francis Negus in the early eighteenth century, it was popular at balls and social events of the era. Our recipe for negus is the perfect antidote for a chilly night, and a perfect accompaniment to a discussion of Brontë's classic, *Jane Eyre.*

1 cup water
1 cinnamon stick
1 cup port wine
1 cup dry red wine, such as claret, Burgundy,
*   Merlot, or zinfandel*

4 teaspoons brandy
2 tablespoons sugar
1 lemon, sliced into thin rings
Grated or ground nutmeg, to taste (a large
*   pinch works well)*

Heat the water and cinnamon stick in a nonreactive saucepan. Boil gently for a few minutes. Reduce heat and add the remaining ingredients. When heated through, strain into heat-proof serving goblets.

Yield: 4 servings

Walnut Tea Sandwiches

John Montague, the Earl of Sandwich, devoted his life to gambling and would often remain at the gaming table for hours. He is credited with inventing the sandwich in 1762, when he ordered servants to bring him slices of bread, meat, and cheese, and he layered them to prevent his cards from becoming greasy.

We adapted a recipe for tea sandwiches that Cheryl McHugh of Antioch, California, has made for her East County Mother's Club, a recipe she found on whatscookingamerica.net. "Charlotte Brontë drew the reader into the life of Jane Eyre," says McHugh. With bread and cream cheese, you may indulge your book club with these delicate sandwiches, of which Mr. Brocklehurst would never have approved.

NOTE: For these sandwiches, the bread should be thin, but experiment with different varieties. Our testers preferred Pepperidge Farm thinly sliced bread and thought a combination of white and wheat was tasty and appealing. Cover sandwiches loosely with waxed paper, then drape a damp kitchen towel over the waxed paper and refrigerate to prevent them from drying out. Prepare the sandwiches as close to serving time as possible.

12 ounces cream cheese, at room temperature
¾ cup finely chopped toasted walnuts
2 tablespoons finely minced parsley
1 tablespoon finely minced green bell pepper
1 tablespoon finely minced white onion
2 teaspoons fresh lemon juice
⅜ teaspoon freshly grated nutmeg or ⅜ teaspoon ground nutmeg (adjust amount to taste)

Salt and white pepper
24 slices best-quality white bread, preferably thinly sliced
½ cup (1 stick) unsalted butter, at room temperature

1. In a large bowl, combine the cream cheese, walnuts, parsley, and bell pepper. Add the onion, lemon juice, and nutmeg. Stir well. Season to taste with salt and pepper. Refrigerate for 1 hour to allow flavors to blend.

2. Spread one side of each piece of bread lightly with butter. Top the buttered side of 12 of the slices with the cream cheese mixture and cover each with another slice of bread, buttered side down. Carefully cut off the crusts with a sharp knife. Cut each sandwich diagonally into quarters.

Yield: Makes 48 tea sandwiches, 10 to 12 servings

Unlike many book groups, Boulder Great Books of Boulder, Colorado, meets weekly, not monthly. Membership takes a serious commitment. "We ask participants to read the selection twice, so that requires us to keep the weekly choices short," explains Bill Sackett, group leader since 1994. "We usually read short selections from longer texts."

Short selections can be deceiving, though. Members of Boulder Great Books wrestle with timeless questions raised by some of the most difficult texts ever written. The group tries, over time, to read complete works. For example, over a period of two and a half years the group read all of the Platonic dialogues.

Boulder Great Books is one of more than 850 reading groups nationwide associated with the Great Books Foundation. Founded in 1947 by Robert Maynard Hutchins, then president of the University of Chicago, and Mortimer Adler, a philosopher and University of Chicago professor, the Great Books Foundation aims to instill in people "the habits of mind that characterize a self-reliant thinker, reader, and learner" through exploration of great books.

These discussions center on the process of "shared inquiry." A leader guides the process by asking thought-provoking, interpretive questions and following up participants' responses with more questions. Four rules govern Great Books discussions: (1) Only those who have read the selection may take part in discussion; (2) discussion is restricted to the selection that everyone has read; (3) support for opinions should be found within the selection; and (4) leaders may ask, but may not answer, questions.

Since the group started in 1988, members of Boulder Great Books have agreed to adopt some, but not all, of the guidelines suggested by the Great Books Foundation. An eclectic mix of men and women—members range in age from early twenties to eighties and include a psychiatrist, a Shakespearean scholar, a philosopher, a Jesuit college student, and many retired professionals—the group agreed that its leader can both ask and participate in answering questions and that connections can be made with selections the group has previously discussed.

In addition to choosing titles from the Great Books series, including works by Aristotle, Shakespeare, and Chekhov, Boulder Great Books members also read books from a list of fiction and nonfiction titles, compiled by Sackett, that members have expressed an interest in discussing. The group noticed a dearth of female authors in the original Great Books list, so they tackled works by Edith Wharton, Sylvia Plath, Jamaica Kincaid, Charlotte Brontë, and many other women writers. (Incidentally, some of these writers appear in the fiftieth-anniversary series of titles released by the Great Books Foundation in 1997.)

At one point, the group chose a series of books related to South Asia—*The Bhagavad Gita,* R. K. Narayan's *The Man-Eater of Malgudi* and *Mr Sampath—The Printer of Malgudi,* and *A River Sutra* by Gita Mehta (see p. 379)—because one member, Ram Sreerangam, hailed from an area of South India much like Narayan's fictional Malgudi. "Ram contributed so much to those discussions," says Sackett. "He explained Indian concepts to us, like the goals of ascetics. We explored the idea of arranged marriages, and Ram explained to us his choices in life. One thing I like about the group is that we get so much cultural information from our discussions."

Boulder Great Books selected Jean Rhys's 1966 novel, *Wide Sargasso Sea,* from the Great Books Foundation list. Because *Wide Sargasso Sea* is based on the story of *Jane Eyre,* to discuss Rhys's book members would be forced to violate the Great Books rule of not discussing outside books. "It takes away from the discussion when you go to an authority such as a critic, or even to the author," says Sackett. "We try not even to read the introduction to the book, at least not until having read the selection once, so it won't suppress our own ideas about it. And we don't want participants going on about books that nobody else in the group has read. So to be able to discuss the Rhys book, we were almost forced to read and discuss *Jane Eyre* first."

Group members were glad that Rhys's book had led them to *Jane Eyre.* They admired Brontë's literary style and her ability to create a memorable heroine. "The strength of character of Jane Eyre shines throughout the whole book," says Sackett.

The group found that reading both books enriched their literary experience. "Both authors, in different ways, beautifully showed the strength of character of their protagonists," says Sackett. "Reading the books together made us look at the characters in ways we wouldn't have if we'd read just one book or the other."

More Food for Thought

When Alma Pruessner of the Lovely Ladies Book Club in Bryan–College Station, Texas, mentioned a possible menu for her book club's dinner discussion of *Jane Eyre* to her brother-in-law, an English professor, he suggested a bowl of boiled parsnips. "But the Lovely Ladies do have certain requirements for meals, and parsnips is not on the list of favorites," said Pruessner.

Pruessner settled on a spicy meal of Indian chicken curry, using a recipe that she received in 1952 from a British neighbor. Pruessner served the curry over rice with the "side boys"—toasted coconut, golden raisins, toasted almonds, chopped apricots, and homemade pear chutney, along with English beer. The dinner received rave reviews from the Lovely Ladies.

For dessert she made a bread pudding with brandy sauce, from Hermann B. Deutsch's *Brennan's New Orleans Cookbook* (Pelican, 1982, or see our recipe, p. 33). "Bread pudding was a dessert often served in the time of Charlotte Brontë and her character, Jane Eyre," says Pruessner. "It is made with day-old bread, sugar, butter, eggs, and cream—a fairly simple and inexpensive, but delicious, dessert."

The Killer Angels

Michael Shaara

....

McKay, *1974*

(available in paperback from Ballantine, 1987)

I N EXPLAINING his inspiration for *The Killer Angels*, a dramatic novel of the Civil War, Michael Shaara referred to Stephen Crane, author of another Civil War novel, *The Red Badge of Courage*. "Reading the cold history was not enough [for Crane]," wrote Shaara. "He wanted to know what it was like to *be* there, what the weather was like, what men's faces looked like. This book was written for much the same reason."

The Killer Angels re-creates the Battle of Gettysburg from the perspective of the soldiers and their officers. Union and Confederate troops arrived at the battlefield with dreams, fears, longings, and vulnerabilities, details most often left out of history books. As rendered by Shaara, General Robert E. Lee was dignified, respected, and loved by his troops, but beset with worries about his heart condition, advancing age, and his fateful decision to invade Pennsylvania. Lee's right-hand man, James Longstreet, offered key strategic advice while he mourned the deaths of his three children.

A Union colonel, Joshua Chamberlain, his regiment on Little Round Top hopelessly outnumbered and out of ammunition, miraculously repelled the rebel attack. Chamberlain wondered what he would tell his mother—and whether he would feel responsible if something happened to his younger brother, Thomas, a soldier under his command.

The line soldiers' hunger, discomfort, and longing for home, and their loyalty, fear, and humor all emerge in *The Killer Angels.* From an epic event in American history, Shaara has woven a human story focused on people with mortal strengths and failings.

As might be expected during war, the soldiers' rations were simple. At times the men enjoyed fresh meat and chicken, but more often they ate dried beef, bread, coffee, and corn dodgers, elongated baked cornmeal cakes. Deprivation led the soldiers to fantasize about hearty meals. After being wounded in battle, Chamberlain's thoughts drifted to his wife and children: "Owe her a letter. Soon. Kids be playing now. Sitting down to lunch. Eating—cold, cold milk, thick white bread, cheese and cream, ah."

Chamberlain also relied on food to quell the restlessness of the men under his command. Chamberlain's leadership skills were tested when 120 disgruntled Union soldiers who had mutinied from their Maine regiment arrived under armed escort with orders to join Chamberlain's troops. The colonel had to act quickly. Coercing the men to fight might lead to further rebellion; giving in to their demand to be returned home would go against orders. Seeing "hunger and exhaustion and occasional hatred" in the faces of the Maine men, Chamberlain promised them the meat from a butchered steer. After a short meeting to hear their grievances and a moving speech—and a meal of fresh beef—Chamberlain brought the vast majority of the Maine men to his side.

In the summer of 1863, as Confederate and Union troops edged toward their bloody clash in Gettysburg, the cherry trees were laden with ripe fruit. "Cherries are ripening over all Pennsylvania, and the men gorge as they march," wrote Shaara in the foreword to *The Killer Angels*. General Lee was offered flapjacks with "ripe cherries" for breakfast; Confederate Brigadier General Lewis Armistead wondered aloud several times whether he could grow such lovely cherry trees back home in the South.

Despite their popularity, cherries also accounted for one of the soldiers' deadliest afflictions. During the Civil War, disease—measles, smallpox, malaria, and pneumonia—posed a greater threat to soldiers than enemy bullets. Dysentery alone killed more soldiers than wounds suffered in battle. When General Lee asked about Longstreet's health, pointing out that "the Old Soldier's illness is going around," Longstreet replied, "It's the damned cherries . . . too many raw cherries." The Old Soldier's illness was likely dysentery, contracted from eating excessive amounts of fruit, particularly decomposing fruit. Soldiers on their way to Gettysberg undoubtedly ate plenty of the readily available ripe cherries, and they suffered the consequences. The condition was widespread. In *The Killer Angels*, it afflicted not just Longstreet, but also fellow soldiers Garnett and Fremantle, who, after feeling his stomach rumble, thought, "Oh God, not the soldier's disease. Those damned cherries."

Civil War Cherry-Apple Cobbler
with Sweet Vanilla Custard

Fortunately, clean, ripe cherries cooked into this cobbler are unlikely to cause any condition other than delight.

During the early and middle 1800s, cherries were frequently cooked into pies and sometimes into cobblers, deep-dish baked fruit desserts covered with a layer of crust or cake. Cobblers first appeared in Lettice Bryan's *The Kentucky Housewife* in 1839, and since then their toppings have taken many forms, from thick spoonfuls of biscuit dough to dough that is rolled and fitted atop the fruit.

It is said that the term *cobbler* originated in "to cobble up," meaning to put something together roughly, or in a hurry. These easy-to-throw-together desserts were perfectly suited for wartime. In *Civil War Cooking: The Union—Exploring History Through Simple Recipes* (Blue Earth, 2000), Susan Dosier suggests that Civil War soldiers might have baked cherry cobblers after successfully foraging in the countryside for fruits and berries. Although the crusts of these desserts, baked hurriedly in pots over a bed of coals, were often tough, according to Dosier, soldiers still considered cherry cobblers a rare treat.

We have added apples to our cobbler and, true to the era, topped it with sweet vanilla custard. Serve the custard warm as a sauce or let it chill into a pudding consistency. Either way, you'll find this dessert is a cause worth fighting for.

For the filling

1 15.5-ounce can unsweetened cherries,
  drained (see Purchasing Information, p. 499)
5 cups peeled and thinly sliced Cortland
  apples or other cooking apples
½ cup brown sugar
½ cup granulated sugar
⅓ cup all-purpose flour
4 tablespoons black cherry preserves
¼ teaspoon almond extract
Juice of one lemon (about 3 tablespoons)

2 cups Sweet Vanilla Custard (see below)

For the crust

1 cup all-purpose flour
1 tablespoon granulated sugar
1½ teaspoons baking powder
½ teaspoon ground cinnamon
¼ teaspoon salt
3 tablespoons cold butter, cut into small pieces
¼ cup milk
1 egg, beaten
Coarse sugar for sprinkling (see Purchasing
  Information p. 499)

1. Preheat oven to 350°F.

2. To make the filling: In a large bowl, stir together all of the filling ingredients. Set aside.

3. To make the crust: In a medium bowl, combine the flour, sugar, baking powder, cinnamon, and salt with a fork. Using a pastry blender or a fork, cut butter into flour mixture until it resembles a coarse meal.

4. Mix together the milk and half the beaten egg (reserve the remaining egg for brushing the crust). Quickly stir into the flour mixture with a fork, just until a dough forms. Do not overmix. Knead once or twice in the bowl with a small amount of flour to form a ball.

5. Roll out the dough on a lightly floured surface with a floured rolling pin to ¼-inch thickness.

6. To assemble: Pour cherry-apple filling into a greased 2½-quart casserole dish. Cover with the crust and loosely seal the edges. Cut a steam hole in the middle and make several slits in the crust. Mix 3 tablespoons water into the remaining egg and brush over the surface of the crust. Sprinkle with coarse sugar.

7. Bake 55–60 minutes, until the crust is nicely browned and the apples are tender. Serve warm or at room temperature with freshly made Sweet Vanilla Custard (see below). (Vanilla ice cream also goes well with this cobbler.)

Yield: 10 to 12 servings

SWEET VANILLA CUSTARD

⅔ cup sugar

¼ cup all-purpose flour

¼ teaspoon salt

2 cups milk

4 egg yolks

1 teaspoon vanilla extract

1 tablespoon butter

1. In a medium-size heavy-bottomed saucepan, combine the sugar, flour, and salt with a fork. Stir in the milk. Cook over medium heat, stirring with a wire whisk, about 5–7 minutes, until thickened (mixture should coat the edge of the pan). Remove from heat.

2. Beat the egg yolks lightly in a heat-resistant glass measuring cup or bowl. While whisking yolks constantly to prevent curdling, pour in roughly ½ cup of the hot milk mixture. When completely combined, pour the eggs into the saucepan with the remaining milk mixture and whisk to combine. Continue cooking 2 more minutes. Remove from heat and stir in vanilla and butter.

Yield: About 2 cups

For actuary Dawn Epping, joining the twenty-member Dallas Gourmet Book Club has yielded two significant rewards: making new friends and "widening horizons" through books she probably would not have read on her own.

The women of the Dallas Gourmet Book Club range in age from their twenties to their seventies. While some are native Texans, Epping grew up in the Midwest, and many club members hail from across the United States and Canada. The group includes attorneys, paralegals, accountants, and stay-at-home moms. Their reading interests encompass a variety of literary genres, including classic fiction (such as *Silas Marner,* by George Eliot, and *Look Homeward, Angel,* by Thomas Wolfe) and nonfiction (such as Randy Shilts's *And the Band Played On: Politics, People and the AIDS Epidemic* and Anne Fadiman's *The Spirit Catches You and You Fall Down* [see p. 410]).

Epping was also drawn to the club by the opportunity to try new recipes each month with a group of women as committed to good food as good books.

"It's not a cooking competition, but a chance to make and try new dishes," says Epping. The hostess is responsible for serving a light meal, which often features dishes mentioned in the book or from the relevant period. Caribbean drinks and dishes were served for a discussion of *A Trip to the Beach,* by Melinda and Robert Blanchard, about a couple that opens a restaurant on a remote island in the British West Indies. The women dressed in evening wear and dined on elegantly prepared dishes to discuss Katharine Graham's *Personal History* (see p. 344).

"The dinner sets the mood for the book discussion," says Epping, whose husband, Dennis, often researches and helps prepare meals when it is Epping's turn to host. Many of the club's meals have been so memorable that one member collected them in a recipe book that she gave as a holiday gift to club members.

Food aside, it's the warm, open nature of the group that works for Epping. "We tend to share things over books; some sort of personal story will come out," she says.

To foster that spirit of sharing, the club takes an annual retreat to a bed-and-breakfast or lake house within a few hours' drive. "It's a time to get to know one another more personally, which can be difficult with twenty women gathering at shorter monthly meetings," says Katherine Brown, an early member of the club.

Each month a member presents three books, and the group votes to choose the next reading selection. This is how Epping came to read Michael Shaara's *The Killer Angels. The Killer*

Angels was the first title she read with the Dallas Gourmet Book Club, and it was a favorite from among the more than one hundred books the club has read.

"Since I'm not a history buff, the thought of a Civil War book was not enticing, but I loved this book," says Epping. "I was raised in the North, but living in the South I have gotten a different perspective on the war. I appreciated the evenhanded nature of his book, how Shaara covered both sides of the war and offered more than one viewpoint. It was an excellent fictionalization of the soldiers who fought at Gettysburg, including generals Longstreet and Chamberlain. I felt a personal tie to each character."

More Food for Thought

Farrel Hobbs of the Colorado-based Denver Read and Feed book club did some "southern cookin'" for his book club's discussion of *The Killer Angels*. His meal of smoked brisket, cornbread, and black-eyed peas prompted discussion of wartime diets. "We spent quite a bit of time discussing the kinds of rotting, weevily things that Civil War soldiers really ate," says member Barb Warden. "We were grateful to Farrel for sparing us any spark of realism in that regard."

The Kite Runner

Khaled Hosseini

RIVERHEAD BOOKS, 2003

(available in paperback from Berkley, 2004)

*T*HE *KITE RUNNER* is the debut novel of Afghanistan-born Khaled Hosseini, a California physician and son of an Afghani diplomat whose family received political asylum in the United States in 1980.

The novel begins in Hosseini's native country in the 1960s and spans forty years of the country's tragic history. The protagonist and narrator, Amir, is the son of Baba, a wealthy Kabul businessman. Amir's humble, devoted servant and playmate, Hassan, is the son of Baba's servant. Amir and Hassan are both motherless and inseparable. The friends spend idyllic days running kites, a sport at which Hassan excels, and Amir reads stories from the *Shanama*, an ancient national epic about powerful warriors and battles, to the illiterate Hassan.

Amir belongs to the privileged Pashtun ethnic majority. Hassan is a Hazara, an oppressed ethnic minority. During a kite-running competition, local Pashtun bullies victimize Hassan. Amir's failure to defend Hassan leaves him so guilt-ridden that he severs their friendship, changing their lives forever.

When the Russian army invades Afghanistan in 1981, Baba and Amir escape to California. The once influential Baba pumps gas at a service station and dreams of a successful career for his son. Amir becomes a successful novelist and marries Soraya, the daughter of Afghani immigrants. Still, Amir's betrayal of his childhood friend haunts him.

Twenty years later, when Amir returns to his homeland to seek Hassan, he finds Kabul devastated and terrorized by the Taliban, and his journey toward redemption is fraught with danger and trauma.

For *The Book Club Cookbook*, Khaled Hosseini contributed his thoughts on Afghani culinary customs and described the importance of food in his own life and, by extension, the lives of his characters.

There are multiple mentions of Afghan dishes throughout my novel, *The Kite Runner*. In many ways, food plays as important a part in my characters' lives as it did in my own life.

In most Afghan homes, the ritual of eating a meal served as a unifying experience. People connected through the experience of sharing a meal. Typically, families ate together, often in the company of guests and members of the extended family, so it would not be unusual at all for twenty or twenty-five people to sit together for a meal. A large tablecloth, called a *sofrah*, was spread on the floor and everyone sat on mattresses around the room. Two of the household children, usually boys, then made the rounds in the room with an *aftawa*, a carafe of water, a basin and a towel so everyone could wash and dry their hands.

Then the food, often large platters of rice and meat, bread or *naan*, along with bowls of various *qurmas* (*sabzi*, or spinach; *shalgham*, or turnip; *kofta*, or meatballs) was placed on the *sofrah*. Food was not served in individual plates, rather in large platters shared by groups of three or four. The rice and *qurma* was then eaten by hand, and the etiquette was to push the best scrap of meat toward the oldest member of the group.

After water, soap, and towels were passed around again, the *sofrah* was cleared, and tea was served with sweets and dried fruits. I remember this ritual of eating as intensely satisfying and, as I said earlier, as a very pleasant unifying experience, particularly during the month of Ramadan, when everyone was hungry and looked forward to the evening meal. The closeness I felt to my family and relatives during meals is one of the things I remember most fondly about my childhood in Afghanistan.

Britta's Sabzi Challow
(Spinach and Rice) with Lamb

For *The Kite Runner* book club discussion and luncheon held at her Irvine, California, restaurant, Britta's Café, Britta Pulliam prepared *sabzi challow*, a traditional Afghani New Year's Eve dish, made with spinach (*sabzi*), rice (*challow*), and lamb. "In the novel, Soraya prepares *sabzi challow* for a dinner party after she and Amir are married," says Pulliam. "It seemed like a very traditional dish." Pulliam contacted Afghani friends to help her create an authentic *sabzi challow* recipe.

Pulliam first tasted the rice, *challow*, when a friend served it to her for dinner. "At first I thought it was burned," says Pulliam. "It was crispy on the bottom and caramel-colored, but I quickly realized this is the way it should be prepared. Now this is how I always cook my rice. Once you try it, you will always want your rice prepared this way."

Pulliam was happy to share her recipe for *sabzi challow*, and says the dish is also delicious when prepared with beef or chicken.

¼ cup olive oil

8 lamb shanks

3 onions, thinly sliced

1½ teaspoons turmeric

5 cups baby spinach, stems removed (large
  leaves must be chopped)

3 cups cilantro leaves

1 cup Italian parsley, stems removed

16 to 18 scallions, whole, outermost layer and
  tough upper green removed

3 tablespoons minced garlic

3–5 cups beef stock (homemade is preferable)

5 tablespoons fresh lime juice

Salt and pepper to taste

Challow (see below)

1. Preheat oven to 350°F. Heat the oil in a large ovenproof Dutch oven and brown the lamb shanks on all sides. Remove the lamb and set aside. Add the onions to the pot and sauté until soft and lightly browned. Stir in the turmeric. Add the spinach, cilantro, parsley, and scallions. Sauté for 20 minutes, stirring constantly (add more oil if needed). The aroma of the herbs should rise—it is very important for the taste of the stew that this stage be completed. Add the garlic and sauté briefly.

2. Return the lamb to the Dutch oven. Add enough beef stock to barely cover the shanks. Bring to a boil, then cover, transfer to oven, and cook for 2–2½ hours.

3. When the meat is tender, remove from oven. Stir in lime juice and season to taste with salt and pepper. Serve over *challow*.

Yield: 8 servings

CHALLOW

NOTE: For saffron rice, soak 1 teaspoon saffron threads in ¼ cup boiling water for 5 minutes. Remove saffron and discard. Use this water in place of the final ¼ cup water in step 3.

4 cups uncooked basmati rice

1 tablespoon plus 2 teaspoons salt

¼ cup olive oil

1. Rinse and drain the rice three times in tepid water. Place the rice in a large bowl and add 8 cups of water and 1 tablespoon salt. Soak the rice for 2–3 hours.

2. Fill a medium-size pot halfway with water. Add 2 teaspoons of salt and bring to a rapid boil. Drain the rice well and add to the boiling water. Return to a boil and cook for 5 minutes. Test the rice—it should soft on the outside and still firm, but not brittle, inside. Strain the rice and rinse with tepid water. Drain well.

3. Rinse out the pot with water and add the oil. Place over medium-high heat. When oil is hot, add the rice, ¼ cup water, and a pinch of salt. With the handle of a wooden spoon, poke five holes through the rice, one in the center. Cook for 1 or 2 minutes—do not stir. Reduce heat to medium-low, and cover with a lid wrapped in a kitchen towel. Steam the rice for 20 to 30 minutes (do not remove lid to check the rice during this time). The bottom should be crisp.

Yield: 8 servings

BOOK CLUB PROFILE

Britta's Café in Irvine, California, features American cuisine with a European twist. It also offers another kind of twist: The restaurant is home to Britta's Book Club, one of the most popular book clubs in town. "I thought a book club with discussions built around food would be a fun way to combine my two passions: reading and cooking," says owner-chef Britta Pulliam.

"When I read the book club selection, I try to find a memorable, well-described meal," says Pulliam. But she emphasizes that she chooses books for their literary value, not for their culinary potential. "Food is my passion, but the book has to be a good choice for the book club," she adds. "I can create a meal, even if a food is slightly referenced." As an example, Pulliam cites the roasted root vegetables on a bed of polenta she served based on a reference to a vegetable garden in Sheri Reynolds's *A Gracious Plenty,* a novel set in a small southern town.

The menus at Britta's Café change seasonally and feature fresh, local ingredients. Pulliam frequently adds dishes the book club has enjoyed, such as the crab casserole she prepared for the club's discussion of Michael Cunningham's *The Hours* (see p. 192).

Lunch is on the house for members of Britta's Book Club. Pulliam buys the books from the publisher at a discount and resells them at list price to cover her costs. "For the price of the book, we are treated to a delicious meal and a wonderful discussion," says Pat Swan, who has been part of Britta's Book Club since its beginning in 1997. "Britta prepares food with great attention to detail, and this makes it so unique. Her restaurant is a special place. I try to schedule vacations so I won't miss a book club meeting."

Pulliam's book club meetings begin after her regular lunch customers have eaten, so she can relax and join in the book club discussion. When the group is large, she arranges tables on her patio and chooses a leader to ask questions at each table.

Pulliam generally prefers fiction and often selects books by new authors. She takes advantage of her restaurant's proximity to a University of California campus and invites many visiting authors to lead the discussion of their novels, such as Rhoda Huffey, author of *The Hallelujah Side,* a coming-of-age story set in 1950s Iowa.

"Some books ignite the group's passions," says Pulliam, "and *The Kite Runner* was one of those novels." Pulliam chose *The Kite Runner,* hoping the novel would dispel some misperceptions of the Muslim faith. "It was interesting to hear different perspectives on Islam," says Pulliam. "Some members had the idea that all Muslims and Afghanis are radical or members of the Taliban. *The Kite Runner* opened their minds to the idea that many Muslims despise the radical believers."

"Many in our club felt *The Kite Runner* was one of the most interesting books we have read," says Pat Swan. "We often read books *by* women about relationships *among* women. This novel was written by a man and focuses on relationships between men and boys, fathers and sons."

The Kite Runner also shed light on recent world events, providing the group with a realistic picture of contemporary Afghanistan. "It gave us a new understanding of this strife-ridden country," says Swan. "Power was taken away from the people, leaving a very depressed country. It reminds us that we are all vulnerable to a sudden rise in power."

The relationship between Amir and Hassan provoked a strong reaction from the group. "Some felt that Amir was very selfish, and that his acts toward his friend Hassan were unspeakable," says Swan. "We discussed how Amir returned to Afghanistan out of the goodness of his heart, and yet his behavior was still selfish."

More Food for Thought

When Britta's Book Club discussed *The Kite Runner*, Britta Pulliam visited an Iranian market to purchase ingredients for *naan-o-paneer-o-sabzi*. In this Persian appetizer, hunks of *paneer* cheese are topped with walnuts that have been soaked in salty water overnight, and then are centered on a plate surrounded by a variety of fresh herbs, such as watercress, lemon balm, basil, mint, tarragon, and cilantro. The cheese, nuts, and herbs are eaten with *naan*, a flat bread.

Pulliam also grouped pomegranates on each table. "Pomegranates are mentioned often in the novel," says Pulliam, "and the tree in which Amir and Hassan played as children, and which eventually stopped bearing fruit, was a pomegranate tree."

The Cultures Club at the Park Forest Public Library in Park Forest, Illinois, explores world cultures through literature. Members research the culture featured in each month's book selection, and Leslie Simms, the group's facilitator, brings materials about the culture as well as a dessert reflecting the culture of the month.

When they discussed *The Kite Runner*, Simms looked for an almond-and-honey cake recipe, mentioned as a favorite of the protagonist's mother. She located many Mediterranean and Middle Eastern versions of the cake on the Internet, and a baker friend volunteered to bake a Turkish honey-almond cake, selected from www.tamaraskitchen.com.au, for the group. Simms says the cake had a taste reminiscent of gingerbread, even though there was no ginger in the recipe.

Leap of Faith: Memoirs of an Unexpected Life

Queen Noor of Jordan

MIRAMAX, 2003

I N J U N E 1978, a twenty-six-year-old American, Lisa Halaby, married Jordan's King Hussein, a man sixteen years her senior. America was captivated. How had this young Californian, whose father's family originally came from Syria, met the King of Jordan? What would her life be like? How would a member of the first class of women to graduate from Princeton University adjust to life as a queen? Would the Jordanian people accept her?

Twenty-five years later, in *Leap of Faith: Memoirs of an Unexpected Life,* Halaby, who changed her name to Noor Al Hussein ("Light of Hussein") after her marriage, tells her remarkable life story, from an American childhood to the Jordanian throne. The pages of *Leap of Faith* reflect Queen Noor's deep love for her husband and respect for the values that shaped his political goals, her devotion to the people of Jordan and to Islam, and her commitment to advancing the causes of social justice, peace, and economic opportunity.

After studying architecture and urban planning at Princeton, Halaby spent several years working on urban planning projects in Australia and Iran. She then traveled to Jordan to visit and work with her father, Najeeb Halaby, a former airline executive and head of the Federal Aviation Administration, who was in Amman, laying the groundwork for a pan-Arab aviation university. It was on an Amman airport runway that Halaby first met King Hussein, and she continued to have chance meetings with him at the airport in the course of her work for the university. These meetings led to invitations to the royal palace for dinner and movies, and finally to a proposal of marriage.

As King Hussein's fourth wife, Queen Noor immediately became the stepmother of eight children, three of whom were still living at home. (She later had four children of her own.) She embraced Islam wholeheartedly, attracted to its simplicity and emphasis on social justice and tolerance. And she slowly adjusted to the demands of public life, with its scarce private moments.

Although shy by nature, Queen Noor eventually warmed to her role as dignitary. As was frequently required, she participated in state visits and travel as a national emissary, tasks that often involved much pomp and ceremony, but substantive issues continued to engage her. Queen Noor was especially moved by the plight of the 800,000 Palestinian refugees in Jordan, displaced by the creation of the state of Israel. She devotes a good deal of her memoir to describing her perspective on events in the Middle East conflict and her husband's efforts to find a peaceful resolution. After Iraq's invasion of Kuwait in 1990, Queen Noor embarked on a public relations campaign to defend her husband's neutral stance. She also plunged herself into causes inside Jordan, including child welfare reforms, creation of parks and open spaces, preservation of Jordan's architectural heritage, economic development and empowerment for women, and removal of land mines along Jordan's borders.

Just as she embraced other aspects of Jordanian culture, Queen Noor relished the foods of her adopted country. On her first, brief, visit to Jordan in 1976 with her father, she listened intently and asked many questions as dinner conversation veered to politics "over the *mezzah*, an assortment of appetizers including tabbouleh, hummus, and marinated vegetables." Later, when she returned to Jordan for a more extended stay, she met Jordanian friends who welcomed her into their homes. One friend's mother, a good cook, taught the future queen how to prepare her favorite dishes: *bamieh*, or okra; *foul*, or fava beans; and *fasoulieh*, "green beans in tomato sauce, which I would go home and prepare in my little apartment." Her food memories are some of her earliest, most pleasant impressions of a land she would come to love.

After ascending the throne, Queen Noor enjoyed lavish state dinners with leaders from around the world. Still, the foods she savored continued to be Middle Eastern. When she traveled she would bring "emergency supplies" of date brownies and granola bars from Amman. While she was living at Al Nadwa Palace, ordering falafel from a downtown Amman restaurant was a "special treat." When she hosted official *iftars*—evening meals to break the daily fasts during Ramadan— Queen Noor would serve *qamareddin*, "a delicious drink made out of apricot paste that I had loved since childhood."

Perhaps part of the appeal of Middle Eastern food for Queen Noor lay in its health benefits. The vegetable and grain dishes were full of nutrients and fiber. She noted that her paternal grandmother influenced her philosophy that "the right attitude, together with eating properly and keeping physically active, could dramatically contribute to well-being and longevity."

Queen Noor hints of her attraction to healthy eating in *Leap of Faith*, and another account from the time confirms this assessment. In the early 1990s, after Iraq invaded Kuwait, the American reporter Geraldine Brooks dined several times with the king and queen at the palace in Amman. In *Nine Parts of Desire: The Hidden World of Islamic Women* (see p. 303), Brooks describes the battery of small dishes that would be brought out for Queen Noor's meal, "always including the light, healthy things she liked, such as seaweed soup, grilled fish or spiced lentils with yogurt. The king rarely ate any of what he jokingly disparaged as Noor's health food."

Queen Noor graciously agreed to contribute some of her current favorite recipes for *The Book Club Cookbook*. Her Majesty's choices reflect her continued enjoyment of Middle Eastern food and her lifelong devotion to good health.

HER MAJESTY'S MUJADARA (LENTILS AND RICE) WITH CUCUMBER YOGURT

This warming lentil and rice dish, considered an everyday food in Jordan, is generally eaten in the winter. It is served as a main course, often accompanied by Cucumber Yogurt (see below) or salad.

2 cups uncooked short-grain rice, preferably Egyptian or Spanish varieties (see Purchasing Information, p. 499)
1 cup brown lentils
2 large onions
3 tablespoons olive oil

1 teaspoon ground cumin
1½ teaspoons salt
½ teaspoon white pepper
½ teaspoon allspice
2 tablespoons cornstarch
Vegetable oil for deep-frying

1. Soak the rice for about 30 minutes. Rinse and drain several times until the rice water is clear.
2. While the rice is soaking, pick over the lentils and wash them well. Place in a pot and cover with 5 cups of water. Bring to a boil, then reduce heat and simmer until lentils are partially cooked, about 12–15 minutes. Drain lentils, reserving cooking liquid.
3. Slice 1 onion crosswise in ¼-inch slices. Separate the rings and set aside. Dice the other onion. Heat the olive oil in a large skillet or Dutch oven. Add the diced onion and sauté until very soft and golden. Add the rice and cook, stirring, for 3 minutes. Add the lentils, cumin, salt, white pepper, allspice, and 3 cups of reserved lentil stock. Bring to a boil for 2 minutes, reduce heat, and cover. Let the mixture cook until the liquid is absorbed and the rice is cooked, about 20 minutes.
4. While the *mujadara* is simmering, prepare the onion garnish. Place the onion rings into a plastic bag and add the cornstarch. Close the bag and shake to coat the onions well. Heat

1 inch of vegetable oil to very hot (375°F) in a pan for deep frying. Add the onion rings in batches and fry until brown and crisp, about 2 minutes. Watch onions closely to prevent burning. Gently stir once or twice while frying to keep them from sticking together. Drain on brown paper or paper towels and coarsely chop.

5. Arrange the hot *mujadara* on a serving platter and sprinkle with fried onions. Serve with cucumber yogurt on the side.

Yield: 6 servings

CUCUMBER YOGURT

3 medium cucumbers, peeled, seeded, and diced   *2 tablespoons fresh mint leaves, chopped*
1 clove garlic, minced   *Salt*
2 cups plain yogurt

In a bowl, combine cucumbers, garlic, yogurt, and mint. Salt to taste. Refrigerate, covered, for several hours, to allow flavors to develop.

Yield: About 4 cups

HER MAJESTY'S SPINACH BÖREK (PASTRY)

These triangular spinach-filled pastries are traditionally served as part of a *mezzah*, or banquet of appetizers. The filling gets its special flavor from *sumac*, or Sicilian sumac (*Rhus coriria*), a spice made from dried, powdered berries. Although largely unknown in America, *sumac*, which imparts a sour flavor, is used commonly in Middle Eastern cooking.

For the dough
1 teaspoon active dry yeast   *1¾ cups all-purpose flour*
1 teaspoon sugar   *Dash of salt*
½ cup warm water   *2 tablespoons olive oil*

For the filling

1½ pounds fresh spinach, or 1 10-ounce package
   frozen chopped spinach, thawed

3 tablespoons olive oil

2 medium onions, diced

1 teaspoon salt

¾ teaspoon ground white pepper

1½ tablespoons sumac (see Purchasing
   Information, p. 499)

1 egg yolk

¼ cup milk

1. Preheat oven to 350°F.
2. To make the dough: Dissolve the yeast and sugar in the warm water. Let sit until foamy, about 10 minutes.
3. Mix the flour and salt. Add the olive oil and yeast mixture and knead until a soft ball forms. Cover the dough with a cloth and let it rest for 15 minutes.
4. To make the filling: If you are using fresh spinach, cook it in boiling salted water for 2 minutes. Drain fresh or frozen spinach well by pressing in a colander, squeezing out excess moisture by hand, and finally rolling in paper towels or a clean dishtowel and wringing dry. After drying, chop fresh spinach coarsely.
5. Heat the olive oil in a heavy-bottomed skillet. Sauté the onions until soft and translucent, 8–10 minutes. Add the chopped spinach, salt, white pepper, and *sumac.* Cook for 5 minutes, then remove from heat. Drain off any liquid (there shouldn't be any if you've dried the spinach), and allow to cool.
6. To make the pastries: Cut the dough into 5 equal parts and roll into balls. On a lightly floured work surface, roll out the dough balls to ¼- to ⅛-inch thickness. Place one-fifth of the filling in the center of each. Lift the three sides of the round dough and seal together on top to form a triangle (the finished pastries should be about 4 inches across).
7. Make an egg wash by lightly beating the egg yolk into the milk.
8. Arrange the pastries on a greased baking tray. Brush the top of each with egg wash and bake until the crust is lightly browned, about 20 minutes. Serve warm.

Yield: 5 servings

If there's one thing that the fifteen suburban women of Shannon Bloomstran's St. Louis–based book club share, it's pregnancy. "Since we began meeting in 2000, there have been fourteen babies born, including two sets of twins, and there are more on the way," says Bloomstran, a freelance writer and charter member of the group. "In over three years, there have been just a few months when no one was pregnant."

Sharing a common stage in life unites what was already a close-knit group. Bloomstran, originally from Nebraska, is one of only three members who didn't grow up near St. Louis. Many members attended high school or college together.

In its early stages, the group read literary fiction and memoirs. Since relaxing their paperback-only rule, members are gravitating toward more recent fiction. Some of their best discussions have accompanied Louis de Bernières's *Corelli's Mandolin* (see p. 81), Barbara Ehrenreich's *Nickel and Dimed* (see p. 300), Betty Smith's *A Tree Grows in Brooklyn* (see p. 452), and Helen Fremont's *After Long Silence,* a memoir about a Catholic woman's discovery of her Jewish heritage.

To enhance the group's appreciation of the setting and story line of certain books, members occasionally provide thematic food to accompany discussion. Pam Bulanda-Barks, a corporate meeting planner, served takeout Chinese food with Amy Tan's story of Chinese-American immigrants, *The Joy Luck Club.* For Jay McInerney's novel *Bright Lights, Big City,* which recounts drug use in New York City in the 1980s, Mimi Boyle encouraged members to dress in 1980s fashions and served Bolivian brownies, "essentially, brownies with a liberal sprinkling of powdered sugar on top," according to Bloomstran.

Even when the women's schedules leave them no extra time for culinary creativity, they always enjoy a meal at meetings. Food ranges from sandwiches, wraps, pasta, and salad to shrimp and hominy soup and cioppino, an Italian seafood stew. "And we always serve wine," says Bloomstran. "Except to the pregnant ones. They're left out."

Although meetings incorporate food and fun, the focus of group discussion remains on the book. "We don't just use meetings to vent about our families and jobs," says Bloomstran. "We do socialize, which is important, but the literary reactions are just as important."

The women expressed a range of reactions to Queen Noor's *Leap of Faith,* which generated lively discussion ranging from the nature of memoir and marriage to perspectives on the Palestinian-Israeli conflict. Although some group members did not agree with Queen

Noor's views, they welcomed her perspective on Middle East politics. "We live in a country allied with Israel, so we Americans are used to hearing the Israeli perspective. This gave the Palestinian view, which was interesting and thought-provoking," says Bloomstran.

More Food for Thought

"Leap of Faith seemed like a logical book to pair with a thematic meal," says Amy Miller of the first book that inspired her Needham, Massachusetts, book club to prepare food related to the book being discussed. Until then, members of the club, which started meeting in 2003, had served pizza, lasagna, soup, bread, brownies, and wine, but nothing related to the books. "Everyone thought that serving related foods was a lot of fun," says Miller.

Miller's *Leap of Faith* menu included falafel, tahini, hummus, stuffed grape leaves, a platter of crudités and pita triangles, chicken and veggie kabobs, couscous, Greek salad, and wine. Miller's book group colleague Lita Young topped the meal with home-baked baklava, a delicacy found throughout the Arab world. This sweet, gooey pastry of phyllo dough is spread with a sugary nut mixture and covered with syrup.

Having lived in Libya for a year in the 1960s, Marlene Davis of the Friends of the Fort Worth Public Library Book Forum in Fort Worth, Texas, had firsthand experience with Middle Eastern food. "When I went to big feasts, there was often a roast lamb as a centerpiece, surrounded by lots of little dishes, the *mezzah,* that you could sample," says Davis. For her book club's *Leap of Faith* feast, she left out the lamb but prepared baba ghanoush, couscous, and hummus.

A Lesson Before Dying

Ernest Gaines

....

KNOPF, *1994*

(available in paperback from Vintage, 1997)

A LESSON BEFORE DYING, which won the National Book Critics Circle Award for fiction, is set in the rural 1940s Cajun Louisiana of Ernest Gaines's childhood. It is a place with a bitter history and bleak prospects for African Americans. The novel centers on the relationship between Jefferson, a poor, uneducated black man, and Grant Wiggins, a discouraged university-educated plantation schoolteacher who has returned to teach in his community.

When Jefferson is sentenced to death for a crime he didn't commit, his godmother, Miss Emma, asks Wiggins to help Jefferson find dignity and meaning in life in the little time left to him before his execution. Together, Jefferson and Wiggins learn the meaning of heroism and the importance of maintaining self-respect under the most undignified of circumstances.

Southern Louisiana is rich in Creole and Cajun heritage, and this culture plays an important role in Gaines's works. He says he wouldn't set his novels anywhere else: "My characters are usually people who are really Louisianans. My folks like jambalaya and gumbo, and you can't get that everywhere."

At first, Miss Emma's gifts of food for the imprisoned Jefferson are rejected and left uneaten. Stripped of his dignity, Jefferson feels he is undeserving of Miss Emma's lovingly prepared treats, and she is heartbroken. "You want a tea cake? You don't have to eat no chicken if you don't want. You don't have to eat no old yam neither. But I know how much you like my tea cakes," Miss Emma pleads.

Edna Lewis and Scott Peacock's Old-fashioned Tea Cakes

Tea cakes have significance in Ernest Gaines's novel—and in his life. When Gaines left Louisiana in 1948 to attend school in California, he said good-bye to the aunt who had raised him and profoundly influenced his life. "My aunt, her courage and her discipline, are things that I try to put in most of my characters," he has said. His aunt packed tea cakes "wrapped in brown paper" for Gaines's journey west.

Scott Peacock spent considerable time deciding which food to re-create from the pages of *A Lesson Before Dying* when he was asked to prepare a southern meal for Oprah Winfrey's on-air book club discussion of the novel. Peacock, chef at the acclaimed Watershed Restaurant in Decatur, Georgia, was selected by Oprah's personal chef, Art Smith, to prepare what was billed as Dinner with Ernest Gaines. The program was filmed in Oscar, Louisiana, Gaines's boyhood home and the setting for *A Lesson Before Dying*.

Peacock cooked through the night to concoct smothered chicken, gumbo, cornbread, and collard greens. "I decided the food had to be extremely simple, nothing fancy or frilly," Peacock told us. "It had to fit with the somber mood of the book."

For dessert, Peacock baked Old-Fashioned Tea Cakes, also known as southern butter cookies. "Tea cakes hold a special place in the hearts of southern cooks," says Peacock.

Peacock's tea cake recipe is featured in his bestselling cookbook, *The Gift of Southern Cooking: Recipes and Revelations from Two Great American Cooks* (Knopf, 2003), coauthored with Edna Lewis. Tea cakes often have simple flavorings. In this version, a hint of lemon is the perfect complement to the sweetness of the cookie. Try serving these tea cakes with a fresh pot of "Luzianne coffee," which is enriched with roasted chicory (see Purchasing Information, p. 499).

NOTE: To make Homemade Baking Powder

Sift ¼ cup cream of tartar and 2 tablespoons baking soda together 3 times and store in a clean, tight-sealing container.

Yield: 6 tablespoons

½ cup (1 stick) unsalted butter, softened

2 cups sugar

2 eggs, lightly beaten

½ cup buttermilk, at room temperature

1 tablespoon finely grated lemon peel

4 cups unbleached all-purpose flour

4 teaspoons Homemade Baking Powder
  (see note above)

1½ teaspoons salt

Sugar for sprinkling

1. Adjust oven rack to middle position, and preheat oven to 400°F.

2. By hand or with an electric mixer, mix together the butter and sugar in a large mixing bowl. When well blended, mix in the eggs a bit at a time. Continuing to mix, gradually add the buttermilk and the lemon peel.

3. In a separate bowl, sift together the flour and baking powder. Stir in the salt. Add the flour mixture by cupfuls to the liquid ingredients, mixing well after each addition. If using an electric mixer, you may need to mix in the last of the flour by hand because the dough should be quite stiff.

4. Divide dough into 4 portions. On a lightly floured surface, roll out each section of dough to ⅛-inch thickness. Cut into 2½-inch rounds using a biscuit or cookie cutter. Place cakes ½ inch apart on a parchment-lined cookie sheet and sprinkle the surface of each tea cake lightly with sugar. Bake 8–10 minutes, just until the edges begin to turn golden brown. Transfer immediately to a cooling rack. When completely cooled, store in a tightly sealed container. Tea cakes will keep up to 1 week.

Yield: About 5 dozen cookies

LOUISIANA PRALINES

Jefferson's acceptance of Miss Emma's pralines is a turning point in *A Lesson Before Dying*. Because they play a symbolic role in the book, pralines are a fitting snack to accompany your discussion. Pronounced "prah-leen" in Louisiana, these pecan candies have a variety of textures—crisp, creamy, or chewy. You can order them from specialty stores (see Purchasing Information, p. 499).

Fifteen African-American professional women make up the Sisters Book Club of Tampa, Florida. They meet monthly in members' living rooms, in local restaurants, and occasionally in Books and Thoughts, a bookstore owned by book club member Felecia Wintons. The group enjoys a wide variety of fiction, including classics and contemporary Christian literature.

Sisters Book Club warms up with an icebreaker to put the club in the mood for discussion. They distribute a few book-related trivia questions and see who answers the most correctly. "If you haven't read the book in a while, it will help you remember details," says Wintons.

"As a historical novel, *A Lesson Before Dying* provides a wonderful learning experience for book club members who don't want to read nonfiction," says Wintons. "We discussed the sacrifices that were made so we can have better lives—sacrifices that we often forget. This novel keeps us grounded."

Sisters recommends the film version of *A Lesson Before Dying* as a complement to the book. "The film goes hand in hand with the book," says Wintons. "It's one of the best adaptations of a book to film in recent memory."

More Food for Thought

The sixteen members of the Imani Book Club of Montgomery, Alabama, generally enjoy appetizers—chicken wings (see p. 72), fruit, and veggie trays—for their meetings. But Ernest Gaines's *A Lesson Before Dying* inspired the hostess to add a spicy seafood gumbo to the menu. "We were surprised and delighted because the gumbo was the perfect food for our discussion," says Cashana Seals, who founded the Imani Book Club in 1999. "The hostess left out the okra—some members don't like it—and beef products," says Seals, "and it was delicious!"

The group followed up their book club discussion and meal with a visit, the following day, to the Alabama Shakespeare Festival, where they watched a dramatization of *A Lesson Before Dying*.

More Food for Thought

The South Florida Preschool PTA Book Club created a Louisiana-style southern buffet for their discussion of *A Lesson Before Dying*: iced tea, soft-shelled pecans, barbecued and fried chicken jambalaya, shrimp, crab, and sausage gumbo, macaroni and cheese, collard greens (see p.150), red beans and rice, green beans with bacon, cornbread, biscuits, sweet-potato pie (see p. 423), and pecan pie.

Life of Pi

Yann Martel

....

HARCOURT, 2002

(available in paperback from Harvest, 2003)

Sixteen-year-old Pi Patel, the son of a zookeeper in Pondicherry, India, is a keen observer of animal behavior. Born of agnostic parents, Pi is fascinated by spirituality, and at one point declares himself to be a Hindu, a Muslim, and a Christian. When his father decides to move the family to Canada, Pi, his parents, and his brother, Ravi, board a Japanese freighter for North America and take some of the zoo animals with them. When the ship sinks, Pi finds himself adrift on a lifeboat in the Pacific Ocean with several animals, including a 450-pound Bengal tiger. Thus begins a seven-month odyssey at sea before Pi lands in Mexico. Pi's background in zoology and animal psychology, and his father's instructions about handling tigers, become critical to his survival.

"This book was born as I was hungry," writes Pi in the opening of the novel, and hunger and starvation become a central theme in *Life of Pi*. A vegetarian, Pi is forced to compromise his principles, as he depends on fish and turtles to keep him alive. "A fish jumping out of the water was confronted by a famished boy with a hands-on, no-holds-barred approach to capturing it," writes Pi, who quickly loses his revulsion at touching sea life: "I descended to a level of savagery I never imagined possible."

Pi is able to filter seawater, and becomes an expert in gathering food for himself and his unusual shipmate, using a cargo net to lure fish. He tames the tiger by asserting his authority—letting the tiger know that he will provide food if the tiger behaves.

TANDOORI SHRIMP

Dawn Epping hosted the Dallas Gourmet Book Club's *Life of Pi* dinner meeting. When Epping hosts the group, the menu selection, a joint effort of Epping and her husband, Dennis, can begin as early as a month in advance. The Eppings selected tandoori shrimp, tying together Pi's Indian heritage and his constant craving for Indian food with the marine theme of the book. Pi's treats while floating on the Pacific included shrimp and crabs plucked from the bottom of his raft.

The tandoori shrimp was a huge success with the Dallas Gourmet Book Club: "One of our members who grew up in Bangladesh said that the flavoring was perfect and the ladies nearly licked the plates clean," says Epping.

"Timing the food for book club can be a challenge, but I am fortunate to have a husband who enjoys cooking and helping me entertain," says Epping. "The group is thrilled when I host because they know that Dennis will be cooking. Generally, we are cooking right up until people begin arriving. Then he quietly slips out and takes our children out to dinner. Within about an hour and a half, he is back to begin assembling and plating dessert."

The Eppings followed a recipe for tandoori shrimp from *The Williams-Sonoma Complete Entertaining Cookbook: The Best of Festive and Casual Occasions* (Weldon Owen, 1998). We have adapted this recipe from the Williams-Sonoma book. Because most people don't have a tandoor (a clay oven), this recipe is designed for the grill. You can also broil the shrimp if a grill is not available.

NOTE: You can use 1 teaspoon red chili powder, which can be found at Indian groceries (see Purchasing Information, p. 499), in place of ½ teaspoon ground cayenne pepper. It is bright red and moderately spicy.

NOTE: Wear plastic or rubber gloves while handling the chiles to protect your skin from the oil in them. Avoid direct contact with your eyes, and wash your hands thoroughly after handling.

For the marinade

1 tablespoon ground cumin

1 tablespoon sweet paprika

½ teaspoon cayenne pepper

½ teaspoon salt

¼ teaspoon ground turmeric

1 cup (8 ounces) nonfat plain yogurt

3 tablespoons fresh lime juice

3 tablespoons minced fresh ginger

1½ pounds large shrimp, peeled and deveined

About 12 bamboo skewers for grilling

2 serrano chiles, seeded and minced

3 or 4 cloves garlic, minced

2 tablespoons vegetable oil

Lemon or lime wedges

1. Combine all the marinade ingredients (those on p. 241 and top four above) in the bowl of a food processor and process until blended to a smooth paste. Transfer to a large, nonreactive bowl.

2. Dry the shrimp well with paper towels and toss together with the marinade. Cover and refrigerate 1–3 hours.

3. Soak the bamboo skewers in warm water for at least 20 minutes (this prevents them from burning on the grill). Prepare a fire in a charcoal grill.

4. Drain the skewers and remove shrimp from marinade. Thread the shrimp onto parallel skewers in a ladderlike arrangement (this simplifies turning them on the grill). You should get 4–5 on each pair of skewers. Leave at least ½ inch of space between shrimp. Brush the grill rack with oil and place the shrimp on the grill. Grill about 2 minutes per side. Do not overcook.

5. Serve immediately with lemon or lime wedges.

Yield: 8 to 10 servings

BOOK CLUB PROFILE

Austin, Texas, attorney Hilary Young and two friends reorganized their old book club into the New Book Club in 1999. Their six-year-old book club had dissolved because members of the old book club had varied interests that over time took most of them in different directions. "The New Book Club is a little less serious than the old book club, and we always drink wine and eat a meal," says Young. The nine women of the New Book Club include two other attorneys, a paralegal, a regulatory manager for an energy company, an environmental consultant, a saleswoman, a nurse who sings opera, and a nail technician who is the single mother of two grown sons. The diversity of their work and backgrounds adds spice to the lively discussions. They read fiction, mainly bestsellers, and the occasional classic or autobiography.

At the meetings, held every other month, the hostess provides a meal, the member who selected the book leads the discussion, and a third member brings suggestions for the next book. Sometimes the group's meals are tied to the reading selection, such as an Italian meal highlighted with Maeve Binchy's *Evening Class,* a novel about an Italian night class in Dublin.

The group pondered Yann Martel's *Life of Pi* over a catered Indian dinner that included curried chicken, lamb meatballs, and *saag paneer,* a spinach-and-cheese dish. "*Life of Pi* was a very unusual book," says Young, "with endless discussion possibilities about the themes of the story, the characters, the language, the background, and the reasons Martel wrote the book." A book such as *Life of Pi* that presents big issues, such as the existence of God, the ability of humans to survive adversity, and the nature of reality, has a lot to offer a book group, says Young. "Martel starts out by claiming, 'This is a story which will make you believe in God,' a claim that provoked much debate. Did he make us believe in God, and if not, why not?" says Young. The group concluded that the book was more about the choice to believe in God than about the compulsion to believe, and spent some time exploring the question Martel raises of what constitutes reality and how people process and interpret their experiences.

OATMEAL BISCUITS

Depleted and dehydrated during the first few days on the lifeboat, Pi dreams of *masala dosis* with coconut chutney and other Indian treats. Instead, he finds a survival kit on the lifeboat containing food: Seven Oceans Standard Energy Rations from "faraway, exotic Bergen, Norway," a far cry from the spicy Indian treats he craves. Pi's first morsel of food in days is a bite of fortified biscuits of "baked wheat, *animal fat* and glucose" designed to keep seafarers nourished. "Two nearly square biscuits, pale in colour and fragrant in smell. Lord, who would have thought? I never suspected. It was a secret held from me: Norwegian cuisine was the best in the world!" writes Pi.

Norwegian oatmeal biscuits were made with dried milk and sugar, providing sustenance for long voyages at sea. Our Oatmeal Biscuits recipe (see p. 130) for *Endurance,* the true survival story of explorer Ernest Shackleton and his crew, would also be a fitting food accompaniment to *Life of Pi.*

More Food for Thought

Silicon Valley Book Club members have a fondness for Southern Indian food and prepared an Indian feast for the group's discussion of *Life of Pi*, including *sambar* (vegetable gravy), *uttapam* (lentil crêpe topped with vegetables), chutneys, *potato masala* (potato curry), fresh figs, and ice cream. "The meal gave a flavor of the type of food that the main character was longing for throughout his days at sea, and reflected the delicious variety of food available to him as a vegetarian at home in India," said member Jan Seerveld.

Love in the Time of Cholera

Gabriel García Márquez

KNOPF, *1988*

(available in paperback from Penguin, 1999)

W IDELY PRAISED for its lyricism and artistry, Nobel laureate Gabriel García Márquez's *Love in the Time of Cholera* is an epic story of an unrequited love that survives more than five decades on a remote coast of nineteenth-century Colombia.

Spurning a proposal of marriage from Florentino Ariza following a passionate and clandestine correspondence, the enchanting and cultured Fermina Daza marries instead a wealthy physician, Dr. Juvenal Urbino. For more than fifty years, Florentino's heart remains true to Fermina, even as she builds an affectionate, if imperfect, marriage with her urbane, European-educated husband. When Dr. Urbino dies trying to retrieve his pet parrot from a tree, Florentino, now wealthy and in his seventies, attends the wake at Fermina's home.

After the guests have left, Florentino declares his undying love for Fermina. Although she dismisses him from her home in anger, she finds her thoughts returning to Florentino again and again, and he soon becomes a frequent visitor. One day Florentino and Fermina take a river cruise together and never return, determined to sail down the river for eternity.

Love in the Time of Cholera revolves around the changing fortunes and feelings of Florentino, Fermina, and Dr. Urbino. The foods mentioned in the novel not only provide a flavor of South America, they demonstrate the evolution of the relationships among the three main characters.

Fermina's carefree nature and her excitement over her youthful courtship with Florentino emerge as she strolls through the marketplace, smelling and tasting foods. She inspects pickled herring, Alicante sausage, slices of cod, and red currants in *aguardiente,* a fiery liquor made from the juice of pressed sugarcane. She crushes sage and oregano in her palms "for the pure pleasure of smelling them," and buys cloves, star anise, ginger root, and juniper, walking away laughing because "the smell of the cayenne pepper made her sneeze so much." But as she chews the offering of a fruit vendor, "a triangle of pineapple speared on the tip of a butcher's knife," she catches sight of the object of her affection, and she is instantly disenchanted. Realizing her mistake in choosing Florentino, her delight dissipates.

Soon after Fermina rejects him, Florentino takes a river trip. He returns a changed man, determined to win back the affections of his beloved. His life's new single-minded purpose is reflected, metaphorically, in his new attitude toward food. Where he formerly was indifferent toward food, he becomes "habitual and austere": His routine includes "a large cup of black coffee for breakfast, a slice of poached fish with white rice for lunch, a cup of café con leche and a piece of cheese before going to bed." Florentino continues his food regimen, like his pursuit of Fermina, until the end of his days.

MOJITOS

A delicious minty drink enjoyed throughout the Caribbean, especially in Cuba, mojitos capture the south-of-the-border flavor of *Love in the Time of Cholera*.

A refreshing concoction of rum, mint leaves, fresh lime juice, and club soda, mojitos date from the early twentieth century. Some believe they evolved from America's mint julep. It is said that, in the 1920s, Ernest Hemingway sipped mojitos on the rocks while relaxing in Havana and Key West.

America's burgeoning Hispanic population has brought a revival of mojitos, now one of America's hottest drinks. Many book clubs have joined the craze by serving mojitos when discussing Latin-themed novels. *Mojito* is the diminutive form of *mojo*, or "soul," in Cuban street slang. We know these refreshing drinks will add soul and spirit to your discussion of *Love in the Time of Cholera*.

For the best results, use very fresh mint leaves and serve the drinks right away.

NOTE: 4 teaspoons of sugar may be substituted for the simple syrup. Mash the sugar with mint leaves, then add the lime juice and stir well to dissolve the sugar.

10–12 *large fresh mint leaves, plus 1 sprig*
   for garnish
Juice of 1 lime (about 2 tablespoons)
   (reserve half of the squeezed lime)

2½ *tablespoons Simple Syrup (see p. 172)*
2½ *ounces light (golden) rum*
Club soda

In a 12-ounce highball glass, lightly mash the mint and lime juice together to extract the mint oils. Add the squeezed lime half, top with syrup, and mix well. Fill with ice and add rum. Mix well again. Top with a little club soda and garnish with a mint sprig.

Yield: 1 drink

MANGO, JÍCAMA, AND CORN SALAD

Tami Ziel, a member of the East County Mother's Club of Contra Costa County, California, prepared Mango, Jícama, and Corn Salad (from the June 1996 issue of *Bon Appétit*) for the potluck that accompanied the group's discussion of *Love in the Time of Cholera*.

"It was light and refreshing," said Cheryl McHugh, who coordinates the book club. "Some people used chips to scoop up the salad, like a salsa."

Other Latin American theme dishes rounded out the club's meal: guacamole, homemade tortillas and salsa, taquitos, and sangria. "The meal was a hit," says McHugh. "The mango, jícama, and corn salad, and the rest of the tasty offerings just hit the spot."

6 ears fresh corn, or 4 cups frozen corn kernels
1½ pounds jícama, peeled and cut into
  ¼-inch dice
6 small or 3 large ripe mangos, peeled, pitted,
  and coarsely chopped

1 cup chopped red onion
½ cup chopped cilantro leaves
½ cup fresh lime juice
Salt and ground cayenne pepper

1. Cook the corn in boiling salted water for 2 minutes. Drain and rinse under cold running water. Slice off enough kernels to measure 4 cups and place in a medium bowl. (If using frozen corn, cook according to package directions and allow to cool.)
2. In a large bowl, combine the corn, jícama, mangos, onion, cilantro, and lime juice. Season to taste with salt and cayenne. Cover and refrigerate. Serve cold. The salad may be prepared up to 3 hours ahead.

Yield: 8 servings

"Although the name of our group sounds ostentatious, we try not to take ourselves too seriously," says Alex Roel, founder of the Literary Society of San Diego, California, a reading group of six men and six women. "We purposefully chose the name as a bit of a joke to keep us in our place. Witness our motto: 'Finding meaning even where there is none.'"

Since 1997, the Society has met monthly at members' homes in the San Diego area. Roel, a web designer and software engineer, founded the club with several colleagues interested in discussing literature. Each of the founding members then invited acquaintances to expand the group beyond an existing group of friends.

Six newer members, all of whom learned of the Society through the group's website, have replaced those who have left the group over the years. The Society limits membership to twelve, but regularly fields on-line requests to join the Society. New member Jeff Thompson was a radar data analyst on a San Diego–based aircraft carrier when he contacted the Society in search of an off-ship activity. Other members include a writer, a homemaker, an apartment manager, a news reporter, a doctor, a lawyer, a student, a teacher, a law school administrator, an Internet research analyst, and a university researcher.

At each meeting, the host provides a light dinner. Society members enjoy finding gastronomic connections to the books they discuss. For George Orwell's *Down and Out in Paris and London,* detailing Orwell's exploration of living hand-to-mouth early in his life, Bill Neeper created a "soup kitchen" with homemade soup and bread. For Stewart O'Nan's *The Circus Fire,* the story of a devastating Hartford, Connecticut, circus fire, Hope Roel, Alex's wife, served circus food: popcorn, hot dogs, lemonade, and cotton candy. For David Guterson's *Snow Falling on Cedars* (see p. 403), set in the Pacific Northwest, the Society enjoyed salmon, sushi, lox, and strawberries provided by Rebecca Rauber. Rauber also hosts a lavish Mexican feast for her book club each November 1 to celebrate Día de los Muertos (the Mexican Day of the Dead). The menu includes homemade tamales, tortillas, sopas, and *muchas muchas dulces.*

The Society also enjoys reading titles recommended by other book clubs that they have met on-line. They read Wallace Stegner's *Crossing to Safety,* suggested by the Last Thursday Book Club of Albuquerque, New Mexico, and Charles Frazier's *Cold Mountain,* recommended by the Elm Street Book Club of Canby, Oregon.

Former Literary Society member Ceci Damonte, a native of Peru, introduced several Spanish and Portuguese titles to the group. "Ceci brought us Isabel Allende's *The House of the*

Spirits, José Saramago's *The Year of the Death of Ricardo Reis,* and Gabriel García Márquez's *Love in the Time of Cholera,* which became one of our favorites," says Alex Roel.

"García Márquez's richly painted characters planned, interacted, loved, and died during a catastrophic cholera outbreak," says Roel. "Despite this tragic backdrop, they were living life fully. It was a bittersweet read. García Márquez seems quite in touch with his earth, his country, and his people, describing the characters by wonderfully illuminating both their joys and their suffering."

In their discussion of *Love in the Time of Cholera,* the Society explored the book's many themes. Group members noted that decay—of the body (through cholera and aging), of relationships, of community, of the river, of the colonial regime, and of social hierarchies—played a prominent role in the novel. They also discussed the novel's many types of love: sexual, romantic, marital, parental, communal, and bestial. "García Márquez doesn't judge the quality or quantity of the relationships, but simply tells the stories," says former member Eileen Durst.

The men in the group generally did not admire Florentino, the poet. "They were not impressed by his poetry, his clothes, or his stalking skills," said Durst. "His promiscuity, especially with a youthful American, caused concern . . . or was it envy?"

Durst assumed García Márquez's writing style in closing her review of the Society's discussion.

We all looked at each other, and thought about cheesecake and coffee. La Sierra [Ceci] looked at El Principe Santiago [her infant son] in her arms and asked, "How long do you think we can keep this Literary Society of San Diego going?" Santiago smiled, showering us with his invincible power, his intrepid love. "Forever," he said.

More Food for Thought

The South Florida Preschool PTA Book Club's Michelle Dice of Miami prepared a Caribbean menu for her book club's discussion of *Love in the Time of Cholera.* Her buffet spread included mojitos, pork tenderloin with peach sauce, black beans and rice, cucumber salad, mandarin orange and almond salad, and fruit tarts for dessert.

"The book takes place in the Caribbean, and I chose a menu that was light and reflected some of the fruitiness of Caribbean cuisine," says Dice.

Mama Day

Gloria Naylor

TICKNOR & FIELDS, *1988*

(available in paperback from Vintage, 1993)

SET ON THE fictional island of Willow Springs off the Georgia coast, *Mama Day* is a depiction of a traditional African-American community in the Low Country. The residents of Willow Springs have deep roots on the sea island, dating back to the days of Sapphira Wade.

Sold to slave owner Bascom Wade in 1819, Sapphira marries Wade and is emancipated. But as legend has it, Sapphira murders Wade. She was known to be a woman with mystical powers, who could "walk through a lightning storm without being touched, grab a bolt of lightning in the palm of her hand," and heal "the wounds of every creature walking up on two or down on four."

Sapphira's great-granddaughter, Miranda, known to all as Mama Day, is now the island's matriarch. Mama Day possesses a psychic ability akin to Sapphira's, and Willow Springs residents turn to her for herbal remedies. While Mama Day heals, others on the island dabble in witchcraft and black magic.

Mama Day and her sister, Abigail, worry about the future generation, which is personified by Abigail's granddaughter, Ophelia, whom they call Cocoa. Lured from the island by the excitement and sophistication of New York City, Cocoa nevertheless returns each year for a visit. When Cocoa returns home with her new husband, a New Yorker named George who is wary of Mama Day's mysticism and psychic power, a powerful storm strikes the island and destroys its bridge to the mainland. At the same time, Cocoa becomes dangerously ill, and George and Cocoa fall prey to the island's darker forces, putting Mama Day's healing powers to their ultimate test.

Gloria Naylor uses food and its preparation to show the impact of modern life on the culture and traditions in Willow Springs. Mama Day values "food that came from the earth and the work of your own hands," food that takes time and work to prepare. She laments the loss of old culinary traditions, and she and Abigail savor the time it takes to shell peas, grate fresh coconut for coconut cakes, pick their own peaches, and roll pie crusts.

One of Mama Day's favorite rituals is the annual Willow Springs Candle Walk, where residents walk the main road and exchange homemade gifts and baked goods. Mama Day laments how the Candle Walk gift exchange tradition has changed with the changing fortunes of youth. Instead of baking homemade treats, such as Mama Day's gingerbread cookies, younger folks buy one another "fancy gadgets from catalogues," and "gingersnaps come straight from a cookie box." In contrast, Mama Day could "whip up a peach cobbler with her eyes closed."

PEACHES-AND-CREAM PIE
WITH STREUSEL TOPPING

Mama Day makes fresh peach pie to welcome George to Willow Springs. As she mixes cinnamon, vanilla, and sugar into her peaches, she has an ominous feeling. Mama Day finishes rolling out her crusts and calls Abigail to warn her that "a storm's coming." Mama Day and Abigail weather the storm of a fight between George and Cocoa, while Mama Day slices up "peach pie as calmly as if she were at a church supper." Eventually, the couple make peace, and folks jam the front yard: "Anyone with a mouth to wrap around some peach pie shows up."

Peaches have flourished in Georgia for centuries, and most Georgians have a family version of peach pie. Our peach pie is made with the same ingredients Mama Day uses in hers—cinnamon, vanilla, and sugar—with a gingery streusel topping. Take your time and savor the preparation of this southern treat.

NOTE: The pie may be served warm or cold and is wonderful topped with vanilla ice cream. Leftovers must be refrigerated to keep the custard filling from spoiling.

½ recipe Basic Pie Crust (see p. 112)

For peach filling

5 cups peeled and thinly sliced firm, ripe peaches or 5 cups frozen peaches, thawed and drained (see Purchasing Information, p. 499)

½ cup sugar
2 tablespoons all-purpose flour
⅛ teaspoon ground nutmeg
⅛ teaspoon ground ginger

For cream filling

1 egg

1 tablespoon sugar

½ cup heavy cream

¼ teaspoon vanilla extract

For streusel topping

⅔ cup all-purpose flour

⅔ cup old-fashioned rolled oats

⅓ cup granulated sugar

⅓ cup brown sugar

1 teaspoon ground cinnamon

¼ teaspoon salt

2 tablespoons finely chopped crystallized ginger

5 tablespoons butter, melted

1. Preheat oven to 400°F.
2. To make the peach filling: Place the peaches in a large bowl. Mix together the sugar, flour, nutmeg, and ginger in a small bowl and gently stir into peaches. Set aside.
3. To make the cream filling: Using a fork, beat together the egg, sugar, cream, and vanilla. Set aside.
4. To make the streusel topping: In a medium bowl, mix the flour, oats, sugars, cinnamon, salt, and crystallized ginger. Pour in the melted butter and stir until moistened.
5. Arrange the peach mixture evenly in the pie shell and cover with cream mixture. Sprinkle streusel topping evenly on top. Bake 15 minutes. Lower temperature to 350°F and bake an additional 40 minutes, until peaches are bubbly and hot. Keep an eye on the crust near the end of the baking time—it may require a foil shield to prevent overbrowning.

Yield: 1 9-inch pie, 6 to 8 servings

BOOK CLUB PROFILE

Formed in 1997 by Sandra DeBerry Watson and four other like-minded women in a Washington, D.C., church, A Moment of Peace is a Christian-based book club that reads and discusses all kinds of literature.

Founding member Sandra Jowers believes that book clubs can bring positive change to group members' lives and to the community. The fifteen African-American women members begin each meeting by sharing and speaking of a moment in their lives that has given them peace and for which they are thankful. For example, one member passed her doctoral comprehensive exams, another had a good result after a scary biopsy, and a third enjoyed calm while her children were away at camp.

This supportive start to each meeting encourages members to continue to share personal experiences when the book discussion begins. "We usually find something in the book that relates to something in our lives," says Jowers. "Everyone who comes to the meetings knows they can talk about issues that are important to them."

A Moment of Peace extends a supportive hand to the larger community, too. Every year they invite a local author to their end-of-year dinner, an act of support for the author and also a way for group members to meet and talk with the author. They support independent bookstores by buying books there and occasionally holding group meetings or events there. And Jowers, who is studying the African-American deaf community in pursuit of a Ph.D. in history, founded Booksisters, a book club for deaf teenage girls. "I believe it's important to have book clubs for all members of the community, to give people a chance to get together and communicate, while increasing their reading ability," says Jowers.

Food plays a big role in A Moment of Peace's meetings. Once a month, members clear their Sunday evening schedules. They arrive at the designated house at 4 P.M. and plan to stay "to whenever." Tables creak under the weight of dishes, including stuffed chicken, shrimp, salad, cake, barbecued ribs, and more. Sometimes members prepare foods that are related to the theme of the book, as in the case of the book *Mama Day*, when the hostess served southern cornbread.

Group members loved the wisdom and spiritual strength of the Mama Day character. "This was an older woman who *knows* things, who you go to for remedies," says Jowers. "There was a supernatural feeling to the book." They also appreciated Gloria Naylor's fine writing. Members were so taken with Naylor's vivid descriptions of Georgia that they considered taking a field trip. *Mama Day* is the only book that many members of A Moment of Peace have read more than once. "I just read the book again," says Jowers, "and it has a prominent place on my shelf."

More Food for Thought

For their discussion of *Mama Day*, the Encinitas, California, book club Book-women dined on a southern meal of fried green tomatoes and fried chicken. Hostess Cheri Caviness used the recipe for oven-baked fried chicken from *In the Kitchen with Rosie: Oprah's Favorite Recipes* (Knopf, 1994). "I looked and looked for a recipe for fried green tomatoes, and finally had to ad-lib," says Caviness, "but they were a great success."

Memoirs of a Geisha

Arthur Golden

....

KNOPF, *1997*

(available in paperback from Vintage, 1999)

W ELL, LITTLE GIRL,' Mother told me, 'you're in Kyoto now. You'll learn to behave or get a beating . . . do as you're told; don't be too much trouble; and you might begin learning the arts of a geisha two or three months from now.'" So begins nine-year-old Sayuri's life of slavery in Gion, the geisha district of Kyoto, after she and her sister were wrenched from their small Japanese fishing village and sold to an *okiya* (geisha house) in 1929.

Mother and Granny run the profitable Nitta *okiya*. There, Sayuri begins her apprenticeship under the tutelage of Hatsumomo, a successful but hateful older geisha who tries to thwart Sayuri's progress. In spite of Hatsumomo's efforts, over time Sayuri masters the subtle arts of the geisha— dance and music, elaborate makeup and hairdos, sparkling conversation and alluring body language—and learns to negotiate the competitive world of the *okiya*, where winning the affection of men, and the money that comes with it, is a matter of survival. After her apprenticeship, Sayuri starts to entertain men at local parties and teahouses, and several men want to be her *danna*, or protector. While her position requires that she submit to these sexual arrangements, Sayuri longs for a more loving and committed relationship.

Memoirs of a Geisha, Arthur Golden's debut novel, conjures the culture of the pre–World War II geisha society in rich detail and depicts the decline of that culture—and the changes in Sayuri's life—as war hits Japan.

TERIYAKI BEEF SKEWERS

During his first formal meeting with Sayuri, the Minister, an occasional patron of the Ichiriki Teahouse, enjoys skewers of marinated beef. The scene takes place at the height of Gion's vitality, when socially prominent patrons of the teahouse regularly enjoyed beer, sake, and delicacies like beef in the company of the geishas.

The Minister's humorless personality fails to impress Sayuri. When he holds up a strip of beef with his chopsticks and wonders aloud what he is holding, Sayuri teases him: "'Oh, that's a strip of marinated leather,' I said. 'It's a specialty of the house here! It's made from the skin of elephants. So I guess I should have said "elephant leather."'"

We offer our own version of teriyaki beef skewers, tender enough never to be confused with elephant leather.

About 25 bamboo skewers
1 pound round or sirloin steak

2 cups Teriyaki Sauce (see below)
Vegetable oil for the grill

1. Soak the skewers in warm water for at least 20 minutes. Slice the steak across the grain into ¼-inch slices (slicing will be easier, especially for thicker cuts, if you place the steak in the freezer until firm, but not frozen). Thread the beef onto the skewers, then lay them in a large baking dish and coat generously with 1 cup of the teriyaki sauce. Marinate, refrigerated, for at least 45 minutes or up to 4 hours. Remove the meat from the refrigerator 20 minutes before grilling.

2. Heat the remaining cup of teriyaki sauce gently in a small saucepan and keep warm. Remove skewers from the marinade, reserving extra marinade for basting. Heat the grill on the highest setting and brush with oil. Place the skewers on the grill, leaving space between them (if broiling, use a rack set 4 inches from the heat source). Cook, turning once, until the meat loses its pinkness, usually no more than 2 minutes per side. Baste with the reserved marinade once on each side while cooking. Remove and serve warm, drizzling each skewer with a bit of warmed teriyaki sauce.

Yield: 6 to 8 servings as appetizer

Teriyaki Sauce

1 cup regular or low-sodium soy sauce

¼ cup brown sugar

½ cup mirin (sweet rice wine) (see Purchasing Information, p. 499)

1 cup sake

3 tablespoons grated fresh ginger

1 scallion (optional)

Combine soy sauce, brown sugar, mirin, sake, and ginger in a saucepan. If using the scallion, discard the roots and dark green top, slice once lengthwise, then cut into 2-inch sections. Add the scallion to the saucepan. Heat gently, stirring frequently, until the sugar is dissolved, then simmer for 5 more minutes, continuing to stir. Remove from heat, and if you used the scallion, remove it now. Sauce will keep, refrigerated, for two weeks.

Yield: 2½ cups

BOOK CLUB PROFILE

After the September 11, 2001, attacks on the World Trade Center and the Pentagon, when sentiment against Arab Americans was running high, Pages and Plates was born. The book club is sponsored by the Asian Professional Exchange (APEX), an organization with more than one thousand members of East Asian descent—Chinese, Koreans, Vietnamese, Japanese, Thai, and Filipinos. APEX seeks to promote professional development, community service, and cultural vitality in the Los Angeles Asian-American community.

"This period of time after 9/11, when we knew there might be a backlash against Arabs, reminded us of World War II, when Japanese Americans were harassed," says Bonnie Lu, director of cultural affairs at APEX. "We understood why people might feel afraid, and we in the Asian-American community wanted to start talking about these issues."

Pages and Plates now convenes each month at an Asian restaurant appropriate to the book. This format supports the cultural mission of APEX and adds fun to meetings, according to Lu. Eight to ten APEX members come for dinner and discussion, although the composition of the group depends on the location.

"It's hard to find a central location in Los Angeles," says Lu. "There are a few hardcore people who will drive anywhere, and others who come depending on the location of the restaurant." Lu and APEX's associate director of cultural affairs, Charles Ferrari, choose books for the year, focusing on a variety of Asian-American ethnicities. Says Lu, "We try to diversify our reading selections so they are not focused on just Chinese or Koreans"—the groups with the largest representation in APEX—"and we also try to diversify by gender. We select books that are a bit off the beaten path," such as Wen Ho Lee's *My Country Versus Me: The First-Hand Account of the Los Alamos Scientist Who Was Falsely Accused,* about the Taiwan-born author's traumatic saga of being accused of espionage by the American government; Aimee Liu's *Flash House,* an espionage thriller set in Communist China; and Katy Robinson's *A Single Square Picture: A Korean Adoptee's Search for her Roots,* a memoir of a Korean-born girl's search for her birth parents.

The traditional Japanese culture depicted in *Memoirs of a Geisha* captivated the five men and four women who met at a restaurant in downtown L.A.'s Little Tokyo for dinner and discussion. Over fish, noodles, and teriyaki, the group discussed how cultural traditions like geishas have supported a male-dominated workplace. "Traditionally, men have visited geishas in a group; it's a way of building community among male workers," says Ferrari.

An aging population has forced the Japanese to refocus on the culture of families, according to Ferrari. "In Japan today, there are more people over sixty than under fifteen," says Ferrari. "This is an old country. The Japanese have found that they need to encourage younger families in order to spur economic growth. As a result, the culture is becoming more family-oriented."

Although the tradition of the geisha portrayed in Arthur Golden's book endures to this day, group members agreed that Japan's changing economy and culture threaten the traditional geisha roles. "Younger people are going to other types of clubs," says Ferrari. "The geisha is disappearing. But it will take a while."

More Food for Thought

Erika Gardiner made sushi party balls for her Boston-area book club's discussion of *Memoirs of a Geisha.* The recipe for the white rice balls, filled with carrots and scallions and rolled in black sesame seeds, came from Didi Emmons's *Vegetarian Planet: 350 Big-Flavor Recipes for Out-of-This-World Food Every Day* (Harvard Common Press, 1997). "I made a soy-ginger wasabi for dipping, and the rice balls went quickly," says Gardiner. The group capped their meal with green tea ice cream.

Middlemarch

George Eliot

1871

(available in paperback from Penguin, 2003)

Eliot's novel is set in Middlemarch, a fictional provincial English Midlands town, during the early 1830s, a time when manufacturing and technological progress created new sources of wealth and political reforms created broader participation in the political process. Eliot brings to life a changing community, depicting the rising middle classes of the town as well as the landed gentry of the adjoining villages. The novel presents a finely drawn portrait of social change, love, courtship, marriage, politics, and work, and of the intricate web of circumstance and coincidence that shapes the lives of Middlemarch's inhabitants.

Middlemarch is a study of human nature, and Eliot provides keen psychological portraits of many individuals, including the two leading characters: the young, moral, restless upper-class Dorothea Brooke, who yearns for intellectual growth and a role in improving the lives of those around her, and Tertius Lydgate, a struggling, highly principled young doctor, whose career is thwarted by the limitations of provincial life. Their ambitions limited by a narrow-minded society, both find themselves trapped in unsuitable marriages: Dorothea to the aging scholarly cleric Casaubon, and Lydgate to the socially inferior, ambitious, beautiful Rosamond Vincy. The wholesomeness of the family of Caleb Garth, agent for Dorothea's land, provides a contrast to characters such as the nefarious banker Bulstrode, and Fred Vincy, Rosamond's profligate brother. Eliot illustrates how individuals of different temperaments and convictions, motivated by idealistic or materialistic values, constrained by social custom, and at the mercy of circumstance and fate, live their lives.

The Garth family—Caleb, Susan, and their six children—are people of principle, proud, industrious, unpretentious, moral. The Garths live "in a small way" in a "homely place," a former farmhouse a little out of town, with an attic smelling of apples and quinces.

Hardworking Susan Garth is a former teacher who earns money instructing students and her own children at home, all the while presiding over the baking and other household chores. "Even while her grammar and accent were above the town standard, she wore a plain cap, cooked the family dinner, and darned all the stockings," writes Eliot. Susan, who is looked down upon by other women in Middlemarch because she has no servants, stands in sharp contrast to most of the other female characters, who are either wealthier or more socially ambitious.

When Fred Vincy visits the Garth home to confess that he can not repay the note Caleb Garth has signed for him, he observes Mrs. Garth carrying out several tasks at once—instructing her son and daughter and "pinching an apple-puff"—as he waits to speak to Caleb. Fred is amused by the sight of her, sleeves rolled up, "deftly handling her pastry—applying her rolling pin and giving ornamental pinches, while she expounded with grammatical fervor what were the right views about the concord of verbs and pronouns." Unlike other female characters, such as Rosamond and Dorothea, Mrs. Garth is not afraid to get flushed or to have a little flour on her nose while baking pies.

APPLE PUFFS

The apple-puff that Mrs. Garth bakes is a quintessential nineteenth-century English dessert. Recipes for puff pastry, or "paste," a light, buttery pastry used for tarts and pies, appear in many English cookbooks of the nineteenth century, including one of the most popular culinary references of the time, *Mrs. Beeton's Book of Household Management*, by Mrs. Isabella Beeton, first published in London in 1861 (Farrar, Straus & Giroux, 1977).

"Pastry is one of the most important branches of culinary science," writes Mrs. Beeton, as it "occupies itself with ministering pleasure to the sight as well as to the taste." She adds, "The art of making pastry requires much practice, dexterity and skill. It should be touched as lightly as possible, made with cool hands and in a cool place."

Puff pastry is folded and rolled numerous times to create a rich, delicate multilayered pastry. When the butter enclosed within each layer melts during baking, the moisture creates steam, resulting in puffy dough and flaky layers.

According to Mrs. Beeton, apples are "esteemed" as dessert fruits in pies and puddings, and are the "most useful of all British fruits," with an abundance and variety of apples available. Mrs. Beeton suggests using a puff pastry recipe to make treats that can be stamped out with "fancy cutters" in a variety of shapes, such as a half-moon. For our Apple Puffs, we adapted Mrs. Beeton's recipe for apple filling and enclosed it in miniature crescent-shaped puff pastry. Roll up your sleeves, and enjoy making these delicious British treats for your discussion of *Middlemarch*.

Homemade Puff Pastry (see below) or
  1 17¼-ounce package frozen puff pastry
  (2 sheets)
3 cups cooking apples, peeled, cored,
  and finely chopped
⅓ cup sugar

2 tablespoons all-purpose flour
½ teaspoon ground cinnamon
½ teaspoon finely minced lemon peel
1 tablespoon lemon juice
1 egg white, whisked into froth
Extra sugar for topping

1. Prepare puff pastry or frozen puff pastry (see below).
2. Preheat oven to 400°F.
3. In a bowl, mix together the apples, sugar, flour, cinnamon, lemon peel, and lemon juice.
4. Mound 1 heaping tablespoon of the apple mixture on half of each 4-inch round. Fold over into a half-moon shape and crimp to finish, sealing edges.
5. Bake for 15–20 minutes. Remove puffs from the oven, brush with egg white, and sprinkle with a little sugar. Return to the oven and bake for a additional 2 minutes until golden, making sure crust does not burn. May be served warm or cold.

Yield: 2 dozen apple puffs, 6 to 8 servings

HOMEMADE PUFF PASTRY

This recipe for homemade puff pastry from *New British Cooking* by Jane Garmey (Simon & Schuster, 1985) calls for chilling dough in between rolling.

NOTE: The dough can be refrigerated for four to five days, or it can be frozen for several months, if wrapped first in plastic and then in foil.

2 cups sifted all-purpose flour,
  plus extra for sprinkling
1 teaspoon salt

1 cup (2 sticks) butter
½ cup ice water

1. Sift the flour and salt into a large bowl. Cut four tablespoons of butter into small pieces and work into flour with your fingers until mixture resembles coarse bread crumbs. Add enough ice water to turn the mixture into a stiff dough. Work the dough quickly into a ball, dust lightly with flour, place in a plastic bag, and refrigerate for at least 1 hour.

2. Using your fingers, soften remaining butter and work into a 4-inch square. Place butter square between two sheets of waxed paper and roll it smooth. Remove the top sheet of waxed paper and sprinkle butter with a little flour. Wrap in fresh waxed paper and refrigerate until the butter is firm.

3. Take the dough and butter from the refrigerator and remove the waxed paper. Lightly flour a rolling surface. Roll dough into a 12x12-inch square. Place butter diagonally in the center. Bring the corners of the dough over the butter to make a closure similar to an envelope. Dust the dough with a little flour and roll into a rectangle approximately 6x10 inches, the long sides running top to bottom. Fold the top dough over all but the bottom third of the rectangle. Then fold the bottom third over the top and turn the dough so that one of the open ends is facing you. Roll the dough from the center to the edge farthest from you, stopping before the very edge so as to keep the butter in. Turn the pastry around and roll the other half out and away from you until you have a rectangle approximately 12 inches long. Fold the dough into thirds as before. Wrap in waxed paper and chill in the refrigerator for 30 minutes.

4. Remove dough from the refrigerator and take off the waxed paper. Flour work surface and the dough, and roll out exactly as before, always rolling away from you. Fold into thirds again and repeat the rolling-out process. Chill the dough for at least another 30 minutes.

5. Remove the dough from the refrigerator and roll out to ¼-inch thickness. Using a cutter or the top of a glass, cut dough into 4-inch rounds.

Yield: 12 ounces homemade puff pastry

For frozen puff-pastry sheets

Defrost puff pastry sheets at room temperature for 20–30 minutes or until pliable. Roll out one pastry sheet on a lightly floured surface to ¼-inch thickness. Using a cutter or the top of a glass, cut 4-inch rounds. Repeat rolling and cutting with second pastry sheet until you have about 24 rounds. You may have additional puff pastry.

BOOK CLUB PROFILE

"Five of us wanted to read James Joyce's *Ulysses,* but none of us dared undertake it by ourselves," says librarian Karen Traynor of the formation of the Inklings in 1998. Named after a literary society founded by C. S. Lewis and J. R. R. Tolkien for the exploration of intellectual great ideas, the Inklings continue to meet at the Sullivan Free Library in Chittenango,

New York, where Traynor works. The group now has twelve members. "*Ulysses* gave us a great sense of accomplishment," says Traynor. "We knew we could read anything. And we learned how much fun it could be to read a great work of literature with a group."

Inspired by their successful discussion of *Ulysses,* which chronicles the adventures of a Dublin advertising salesman, Leopold Bloom, on June 16, 1904, the Inklings tackled other literary classics they considered challenging, such as Homer's epic *The Iliad* and *The Odyssey,* and Geoffrey Chaucer's verse classic about a medieval pilgrimage, *The Canterbury Tales.*

"Library patrons who overhear us can't believe we are having such a good time discussing these serious works, but we don't take ourselves too seriously," says Traynor. "We don't pretend to understand these books perfectly, and we're not trying to become literary experts. We just want to come away with something we didn't know and gain a solid background in the classics, which is important to our understanding of all literature."

The Inklings are teachers, a retired high-school principal, a physician's assistant, library staff, and a computer technician, and their range of expertise brings different perspectives to the group. "There is no leader," says Traynor. "We piece together our impressions to better understand the book, and no one is afraid to speak up in this group." They use a variety of materials—reading guides, literary criticism, and a dictionary of symbols—to guide them through the tomes.

Traynor claims the Inklings will read anything, "with enough good food and drink." Usually, Inkling Debbie Rose treats her group to desserts. "It's fun to guess how the dessert ties into a book," says Traynor. Among Rose's more inventive desserts: devil's food cake for the *Inferno* section, and angel food cake and ambrosia (see pp. 308 and 444) for the *Paradiso* of Dante Alighieri's *The Divine Comedy,* an account of a journey through hell, purgatory, and heaven. The group consumed Irish soda bread (see p. 18) and scones over the months they read *Ulysses.* They often serve Pim's cookies, English chocolate-covered fruit-filled biscuits, along with tea to fit the mood and theme of the many British novels they read.

The Inklings celebrate their completion of longer works with a thematic feast, either a potluck or at a restaurant. For *Ulysses,* it was a meal with cock-a-leekie soup, a chicken-and-leek soup mentioned several times in Joyce's novel, and Irish coffee; for *The Divine Comedy,* a dinner of lasagna, veal marsala, and cavatelli at an Italian restaurant; for Seamus Heaney's translation of the epic eighth-century poem *Beowulf,* a picnic with food such as meat pies, deviled "dragon eggs," and ale from a local microbrewery; and for William Thackeray's classic novel about society in Regency England, *Vanity Fair,* a potluck dinner with grog (warm rum with spices and fruit juice), scones, cucumber sandwiches, and a variety of English ales.

Traynor had seen George Eliot's *Middlemarch,* another Inklings selection, on many classics reading lists. "But," says Traynor, "I was particularly inspired by a Barbara Kingsolver essay in which she suggests there is no need to read trash when there are books like *Middlemarch.*" The Inklings read and discussed *Middlemarch* over four months, dividing the eight hundred pages and eight books or chapters up into four parts. "*Middlemarch* provided an excellent portrait of women during the early 1800s in provincial England and provoked a discussion of the limited options available to women during a time when marrying well was the most important objective. We learned that Eliot—her real name was Marian Evans—had a very unusual lifestyle and wondered if Dorothea, the protagonist, was based on Eliot's idea of what a woman should be—intelligent, curious, and not content to limit herself to what was acceptable to the society around her," says Traynor.

The Inklings had read other nineteenth-century British novels, but found that *Middlemarch* delved deeply into the role of the church in society as well as into the politics of the time. Members were surprised to learn that clerical positions were inherited or appointed, not necessarily a matter of faith or a "calling," as in modern times. Traynor recommends watching the Arts & Entertainment network's film adaptation of *Middlemarch,* which she says is very faithful to the book. "We all enjoyed *Middlemarch* immensely, and it led us to other books of that period, such as Jane Austen's eighteenth-century comedy of manners, *Pride and Prejudice,* and Gustave Flaubert's *Madame Bovary,*" says Traynor.

The Inklings enjoyed sipping tea and eating biscuits and scones as if they were characters in *Middlemarch* during each of the discussion meetings. "We didn't have a dinner to celebrate the end of *Middlemarch,*" says Traynor. "Perhaps because we enjoyed it so much, we didn't feel the need to reward ourselves."

More Food for Thought

English Wedgwood china, cut crystal stemware, and sterling silver flatware set the mood for the Portola Hills Book Group's discussion of *Middlemarch.* "We don't usually get so fancy," says Lynne Sales of Portola Hills, California, who hosted the meeting. "But I thought that using the formal china matched the tone of the book." Sales served a typical English dessert, blueberry and peach trifle, along with chocolate and blond brownies and an assortment of English teas and coffee.

Middlesex

Jeffrey Eugenides

FARRAR, STRAUS & GIROUX, 2002

(available in paperback from Picador, 2003)

*M*IDDLESEX IS the fictionalized life story, in the form of a first-person narrative, of Cal, a hermaphrodite living in Berlin. Calliope "Callie" Stephanides appeared female at birth and was raised as a girl, but is genetically male.

During adolescence in Grosse Pointe, Michigan, in the 1970s, Callie becomes increasingly concerned when facial hair appears, and breasts and menses fail to develop. Callie develops a crush on a female schoolmate, "the Object." When Callie's parents consult with a New York specialist, Dr. Luce, and Callie learns the truth of her condition, she flees by hitchhiking across America.

Cal discovers the source of his unusual condition by tracing his family history. His grandparents are Desdemona and Eleutherios, or "Lefty," Stephanides, a brother and sister who marry en route to America after fleeing an attack by the Turks in the 1920s. In their tiny Greek village, Bithyios, families had intermarried for centuries.

As immigrants in Detroit, Desdemona and Lefty share a home with a Greek cousin, Sourmelina, and her husband, Jimmy. The women give birth to Tessie and Milton, who later marry and pass the genetic flaw that causes hermaphroditism to their daughter, Callie.

Comic and tragic, Jeffrey Eugenides's Pulitzer Prize—winning novel spans three generations of the Stephanides family against a panorama of events in American history that includes Prohibition, the Depression, World War II, and the civil rights movement.

In Detroit, Desdemona and Lefty immerse themselves in the Greek community. Soon after their arrival—and continuing into the next generation—food and cooking become their livelihood. They open a bar, which later becomes a diner, the Zebra Room. Their son, Milton, Callie's father, becomes the successful founder of Hercules Hot Dogs, a chain of restaurants in shopping malls.

Unlike Sourmelina Zizmo, Desdemona's cousin, who "erased just about everything Greek about her" in America and adopted peanut butter and lobster thermidor as favorite foods, Desdemona clings to the foods of her homeland. To combat homesickness after her arrival in Detroit, she packs lunches of feta cheese, olives, and bread for Lefty, and spends days making *pastitsio*, a baked pasta dish; *moussaka*, a casserole of eggplant, meat, and sauce; and *galactoboureko*, a custard-filled dessert. Still, Desdemona finds the American grocery store produce selections depressing and misses "the savor of peaches, figs and winter chestnuts of Bursa."

ELAINE OGDEN'S
GREEK RICE PUDDING

Desdemona's rice pudding appears in several scenes in *Middlesex*: It is served to Callie's brother and to Dr. Philobosian, the elderly physician who delivered Callie. As Callie says, restaurateurs in her family became the "technocrats of rice pudding and banana cream pie."

Elaine Ogden, of Washington, D.C., says it was no different for her father, who immigrated to America at the turn of the twentieth century. She spent years assimilating and perfecting pudding recipes handed down from her Greek elders, and here contributes her authentic Greek recipe for rice pudding. This is a favorite Greek dessert, and as you will find, the recipe will be well worth your efforts.

NOTE: Ogden recommends using short-grain rice for this recipe; its starchiness will help bind the pudding better than long-grain varieties (see Purchasing Information, p. 499). But it's fine to use medium-grain rice for this recipe. She suggests using a flat-edged spatula to keep the bottom of the pan clean while stirring the mixture and emphasizes the importance of continuous stirring to prevent the mixture from burning on the bottom and to keep the eggs from curdling.

½ cup plus 2 tablespoons uncooked
  short-grain white rice, unrinsed
  (see note above)
¼ cup water
3 cups whole milk

4 eggs
⅓–½ cup sugar, depending on taste
4 tablespoons butter
Ground cinnamon for topping (about
  1½ tablespoons)

1. Combine the rice and water in a heavy-bottomed 3-quart saucepan. Cook over medium-high heat, stirring constantly, until water is almost gone. Add 2 cups of the milk. Stir well. Reduce heat to low, cover, and simmer, stirring occasionally, until rice is very soft, about 1 hour. Take care not to let the mixture burn on the bottom.

2. Meanwhile, beat the eggs with an electric mixer on high speed until they are light yellow and thick, about 10 minutes. Add the sugar. Beat 5 more minutes. Add ½ cup of the milk and beat well.

3. Add ½ cup of the milk to the rice mixture, stir to combine, and remove from heat. While beating the egg mixture slowly, add the rice mixture, one large spoonful at a time, until it is all combined. It is very important to do this gradually so that the eggs do not curdle.

4. Return the pudding to the saucepan over very low heat and add the butter. Stir continuously to keep the eggs from curdling. Continue to cook until thick, about 20 minutes (the rice grains will rise to the top as the pudding thickens). Remove from heat and pour into dessert cups. Sprinkle with cinnamon. Allow pudding to cool before refrigerating. The pudding is also delicious warm, but allow it to cool and thicken a bit.

Yield: 8 servings

TZATZIKI

In *Middlesex*, Dr. Müller, a nutritionist conducting research on the Mediterranean diet, mistakenly believes Desdemona is ninety-one, and enrolls her in a longevity study. The Stephanides family does not reveal that the grandmother is actually seventy-one—that she confuses sevens with nines—as "they didn't want to lose out to the Italians or even that one Bulgarian" also being studied.

Dr. Müller peppers Desdemona with questions about the Greek cuisine on which she was raised, trying to determine how much yogurt, olive oil, and garlic she consumed as a child. Callie is amazed that he considers their Greek diet—including their "cucumber dressings"—to be the secret to longevity.

Tzatziki is a refreshing cucumber-and-yogurt dip enhanced by garlic and olive oil. While we don't know if this Greek dip is a "potential curative," and can't guarantee that it will prolong your life, it is certainly delicious. Try serving it with warmed or toasted pita bread, or as an accompaniment to grilled meat or fish.

Our recipe is adapted from *The Complete Book of Greek Cooking* (Harper & Row, 1990), by the Recipe Club of Saint Paul's Greek Orthodox Cathedral.

2 cups plain yogurt

2 large cucumbers

3 cloves garlic, minced or put through a press

1 tablespoon fresh lemon juice

2 tablespoons extra-virgin olive oil

Salt and pepper

1. Spoon the yogurt into a sieve or colander lined with cheesecloth. Allow to drain for at least one hour, preferably several hours or overnight.

2. Peel, seed, and coarsely grate the cucumbers. Gently squeeze excess liquid from cucumbers and drain on paper towels. In a medium bowl, stir together the cucumber, garlic, and lemon juice. Add olive oil and mix well. Season with salt and pepper to taste. Add the drained yogurt and stir to blend. Adjust seasonings. Let stand 1 hour, refrigerated, before serving. Serve cool or at room temperature.

Yield: 2 cups

BOOK CLUB PROFILE

Motivated by a desire to immerse themselves in the setting and culture of a book, members of the Book Club of the Brown University Club in New York generally head to an ethnic restaurant for their meetings.

One of the club's more memorable meals accompanied discussion of *Anna Karenina* (see p. 28), when members consumed vodka and beef stroganoff at a swanky, noisy Russian café in the East Village. For discussion of Michael Chabon's *The Amazing Adventures of Kavalier & Clay* (see p. 11), the group chose New York–style pizza. And for Jonathan Franzen's *The Corrections,* about a Midwestern family in crisis, members enjoyed typical American fare, including rotisserie chicken and potato salad (see p. 187).

The group reads books that reflect members' interest in various cultures and that honor the link that brought them together: Brown University. "We occasionally choose books that are written by a fellow Brown alum, or that involve Brown in some way, and then we invite the authors to attend discussions of their books," says John Kwok, a medical data analyst, freelance photographer, unpublished novelist, and a coordinator of the club. The group timed its reading of Ron Suskind's *A Hope in the Unseen* (see p. 186) to coincide with the author's visit to the Brown Club in New York. And the club had its second largest turnout when Brown alum Amy Sohn joined the group at a French Moroccan restaurant in the East Village to discuss her book *Run Catch Kiss: A Gratifying Novel,* about a young New York sex columnist, the author's real-life occupation.

Although 150 names fill the book club roster, meetings generally attract anywhere from a handful of members to several dozen. A loyal core of ten or so members attend three to five meetings yearly.

An intimate group of seven showed up at a Greek restaurant in Midtown Manhattan to discuss *Middlesex* over grilled Greek chicken, a spicy gyro plate, lamb, rice pilaf, and pita bread. Kwok was delighted to find a "humongous, overgrown piece of baklava" on the table for dessert.

"It was one of our best discussions," says Kwok. The group was impressed with Eugenides's skill in developing characters. "We compared and contrasted the characters in the Stephanides family, trying to see the similarities in character between the grandmother and her grand-daughter, Callie," says Kwok. "Eugenides created characters that we cared about."

Members also admired Eugenides's grasp of social and historical movements—the rise of the Nation of Islam, racial unrest, and the development of jazz. "We were trying to under-stand what was happening in Detroit in the 1920s and again during the race riots of the 1960s. I think we were all impressed with Eugenides's skill at incorporating such important historical elements into his tale," says Kwok.

The group found it useful to compare *Middlesex* to other books about the immigrant ex-perience, such as *The Amazing Adventures of Kavalier & Clay,* and books about family dynam-ics, such as *The Corrections.* "We agreed that *Middlesex* was deserving of the Pulitzer Prize," says Kwok. "It was a powerful meditation on what it means to be an immigrant in America."

More Food for Thought

The thirteen women and men of Stephanie Howard's Boston-area book club always try to match food to the books they read, though some books lend themselves more easily to thematic meals than others. "In *Middlesex*, food is a big part of the story," says Howard, who hosted her club's *Middlesex* meeting. "There are issues of cultural identity as the immigrants attempt to hold on to tradition in the midst of Detroit. Food is also a way for family to gather together and discuss the latest issues relevant to Greece and Turkey around a traditional Sunday meal. And the father eventually opens up a chain of hot-dog stands. How American can you get?"

Howard's *Middlesex* menu included hummus, baba ghanoush, tabbouleh, and dolmades (stuffed grape leafs), vegetarian moussaka with rice, Greek salad, and Greek potatoes. The potatoes were prepared with olive oil, oregano, lemon juice, and garlic, as suggested in *Recipes from Moosewood Restaurant* (Ten Speed Press, 1987).

The SeaDogs Book Club is named for the Computer Science and Artificial Intelligence Laboratory (CSAIL) at the Massachusetts Institute of Technology in Cambridge, Massachusetts, where members conduct artificial intelligence research. The doctoral candidates discussed *Middlesex* over a Greek feast at host Erica Hatch's South Boston home. The *spanakopitas*, spinach-and-feta turnovers (see p. 81), were favorites with the group. They also enjoyed mint-marinated lamb chops, Greek salad, Greek-style quesadillas filled with olives and vegetables, and marinated chickpeas, along with baklava and wine.

"*Middlesex* was well received by the group and inspired a lot of personal discussion about where our gender identity and attractions come from," says SeaDogs member Jaime Teevan. "We also talked about the different types of love, and how the love we feel for a biological family member may or may not be different from what we feel toward a partner."

Milk in My Coffee

Eric Jerome Dickey

....

DUTTON, *1998*

(available in paperback from Penguin, 2003)

Eric Jerome Dickey's third novel focuses on an interracial romance between two young Manhattanites: Jordan Greene, a young African-American professional, and Kimberly Chavers, a white artist. Despite Jordan's initial unwillingness to date a white woman, he is attracted to Kimberly's vivacious, independent spirit when the two meet in a shared cab.

The couple faces the predictable hostility of friends, former lovers, family, and even strangers as their relationship evolves. But other events test their relationship, too. Jordan's former lover, J'nette, announces she is pregnant with their child, and when Jordan is called home to Tennessee for his ex-stepfather's funeral, he becomes enmeshed in family troubles.

Kimberly contends with a former boyfriend and attempts to settle an unresolved relationship from her past, while keeping details of past connections from Jordan. Jordan and Kimberly confront long-hidden issues and obstacles as they navigate their relationship.

Jordan and Kimberly's romance is told against the panorama of Manhattan life, and Dickey fills his novel with New Yorkers' passion for eating. In *Milk in My Coffee,* characters nosh on muffins at coffee shops, lobster lunches at chic cafés, and pork and noodles at Chinese restaurants.

LEMON CHEESECAKE

One of Jordan and Kimberly's happiest moments takes place at a New Year's Eve party, where their relationship is cemented. Kimberly whispers to Jordan that she's craving "a thick slice of New York cheesecake," and the couple heads back to Jordan's apartment for cheesecake and sparkling wine.

Cheesecake is a New York tradition, and New Yorkers claim it as their own. In *The New York*

Cookbook (Workman, 1992), Molly O'Neill writes that New Yorkers dismiss historic facts about European or other origins of cheesecake and say, "Cheesecake wasn't really cheesecake until it was cheesecake in New York."

O'Neill explains that New York cheesecake was derived from an Eastern European–style cake made from cream cheese and pot cheese, a variation of cottage cheese. Many New York restaurants, including the famous Lindy's, popularized cheesecake, and the cake has been served with a variety of crusts, including cookie-crumb and graham-cracker-crumb crusts.

The Summerwood Book Club of Columbus, Ohio, savors the lemon cheesecake member Laura Seeger frequently bakes for their meetings. This is a cake for lemon lovers: the lemon-cookie-crumb crust gives it an extra citrus flavor. The recipe Seeger uses belongs to Karen Chesnut of Clarksburg, California, and won fourth place in *Country Woman* magazine's September–October 2002 recipe contest.

For the crust

1½ cups lemon or ginger-lemon cream-filled
    sandwich cookie crumbs (can be crumbled
    in food processor)
4 tablespoons butter or margarine, melted
2 tablespoons sugar

For the filling

⅔ cup plus 2 tablespoons sugar
5 tablespoons cornstarch
1 cup water
2 egg yolks, slightly beaten
⅓ cup lemon juice
2 tablespoons butter or margarine
1 teaspoon grated lemon peel

For the cheesecake

1 envelope (1 tablespoon) unflavored gelatin
½ cup lemon juice
3 8-ounce packages cream cheese, softened

¾ cup sugar
1 cup heavy cream, whipped
2 teaspoons grated lemon peel

1. Preheat oven to 350°F.

2. To make the crust: Combine the cookie crumbs, butter, and sugar in a bowl. Press into the bottom of a lightly greased 9-inch springform pan. Bake for 8–10 minutes or until the crust just begins to brown. Remove from the oven and cool on a wire rack.

3. To make the filling: In a saucepan combine the sugar and cornstarch. Add the water and whisk until smooth. Bring to a boil, then cook over medium heat 2 minutes or until thickened, stirring constantly. Remove from the heat. Stir a small amount of hot filling into the

egg yolks. Pour tempered egg mixture into the pan and, stirring constantly, bring to a gentle boil. Simmer 2 minutes. Remove from the heat and stir in the lemon juice, butter, and lemon peel. Allow to cool.

4. To make the cheesecake: In a small saucepan, sprinkle the gelatin over the lemon juice. Let stand for 1 minute, then place over low heat, stirring until gelatin is dissolved. Remove from the heat.

5. Beat the cream cheese and sugar together in a mixing bowl. Gradually beat in gelatin mixture until combined. Fold in the whipped cream and lemon peel.

6. Spoon three-fourths of the cheesecake mixture into the crust, building up the edges slightly. Chill for 5 minutes. Spoon the lemon filling over the cheesecake layer to within ½ inch of the top of the pan. Top with remaining cheesecake mixture. Cover and refrigerate overnight. Carefully run a knife around the inside of the pan and remove sides of pan. Leftovers should be refrigerated.

Yield: 12 to 16 servings

For a lemon cheesecake with an Italian twist, see our Lemony Ricotta–Goat Cheese Cake, p. 144.

BOOK CLUB PROFILE

Their slogan "Reading is knowledge!" conveys the philosophy of the Pages Readers Group of Southern California. "Pages is a group of African-American men and women who share a passion for reading and, in the process, support the efforts of African-American authors. We believe that reading enlightens the mind, body and spirit," the group states on its website.

Pages was founded in 1994 by Shannon Bush and Marsha Pradia, women who love to read and who wanted to tap into the wealth of local and national black literary talent. "I had never read exclusively African-American authors," says Cassandra Madison, a Mary Kay consultant and member for six years. "I wanted to be part of an environment where women could gather once a month and talk about these books." Members enjoy classic and contemporary fiction, including Lolita Files's *Child of God,* Bernice McFadden's *Sugar* (see p. 422), Lalita Tademy's *Cane River* (see p. 58), and Sister Souljah's *The Coldest Winter Ever* (see p. 71).

Good food always accompanies Pages discussions. The host determines the type of food, which has ranged from light appetizers (finger foods or deli sandwiches) to salads, spaghetti, and Chinese food. Sometimes the group meets at a local restaurant to enjoy classic American fare.

Beyond good food and discussion, Pages members share a strong sense of pride and group identity. Pradia embroiders the Pages logo on a line of gear—polo shirts, jean shirts, jean jackets, hats, book bags—available to members.

In August 2003, the group celebrated its ninth anniversary with a Murder Mystery Dinner, held at the Harbor House in Marina del Rey, California. The women enjoyed a warm artichoke spread on sliced baguettes (see p. 168), fresh fruit and cheese, grilled king salmon, chicken *en brochette,* and Mediterranean penne while attempting to solve "the crime of the century." "By the time we were served dessert—a sinful raspberry marquis—we pretty much thought we knew who the killer was!" says Madison.

For their 2002 Christmas celebration, they held a Gumbo Ya-Ya, complete with gumbo made by an expert southern cook, baked goods, a gift exchange, and "bone-deep massages," according to Madison.

Pages supports authors by buying and reading their books, and by inviting them as special guests to meetings. Author visits give members an "up-close-and-personal understanding of how the author develops the story," says Madison. Over the years, the group has enjoyed visits by Victoria Christopher Murray, Parry Brown, Jenoyne Adams, and—one of their favorite authors—Eric Jerome Dickey.

The group especially enjoyed Dickey's *Milk in My Coffee* for its provocative theme: interracial marriage. "We felt Dickey set up a believable situation," says Madison. "The book gave us perspective on how people see each other and pass judgment without knowing all the facts."

More Food for Thought

Southern soul food was the dinner theme when the South Florida Preschool PTA Book Club met to discuss *Milk in My Coffee.* Member Kathy Barber recalls down-home cooking, with collard greens (see p. 150), sweet-potato pie (see p. 423), and a delicious lemon-coconut cake. "And of course we had coffee with and without milk," says Barber.

Motherless Brooklyn

Jonathan Lethem

DOUBLEDAY, *1999*

(available in paperback from Vintage, 2000)

IN CONTEMPORARY BROOKLYN, Lionel Essrog, an orphan with Tourette's syndrome, contends with his tics, uncontrollable verbal outbursts, and obsessive-compulsive behavior. Lionel is one of the "Minna men"—four orphans recruited as teenagers from St. Vincent's Home for Boys for employment by small-time criminal Frank Minna. Minna has a soft spot for Lionel, affectionately calls him Freakshow, and tries to help him understand his neurological affliction.

A surrogate family for Lionel, the Minna men ostensibly work for Minna's detective and limousine agency, a front for a petty criminal operation. In reality, the boys spend most of their time moving stolen goods, although Frank does provide them with some detective training. When Minna is murdered, the boys are devastated and set out to find his killer.

Events quickly spin out of control after Minna's death. Two of the Minna men compete to fill Minna's shoes, the third ends up in jail, and Frank's widow, Julia, leaves town quickly after the murder. Determined to solve the crime, Lionel struggles to keep words straight in his head and his twisted speech under control when he speaks with associates of Minna's, two older men known as "the clients," and a police detective. Lionel follows clues through Brooklyn streets to a Manhattan Buddhist retreat, and eventually to a Japanese-owned restaurant and sea urchin harvesting operation on the coast of Maine.

Lionel presents an intimate, poignant, and humorous portrait of Tourette's syndrome. His mistreatment at the hands of some and the compassion and kindness shown him by others are at the center of this unconventional detective story.

Food "mellows" Lionel, and sandwiches are his obsession. Stakeouts are "gastronomic occasions"—opportunities to devour sandwiches, with knees tucked under the dashboard, "elbows jammed against the steering wheel, chest serving as a table, my shirt as a tablecloth."

Even Lionel's eating habits are guided by his compulsions. He chooses quantities by lucky numbers—six White Castle burgers, five Papaya Czar hot dogs—and he counts how many bites he takes of each.

Hot dogs and hamburgers will do when he has the "itch for something between two slices of bread," but what Lionel really yearns for are sandwiches from Zeod's, the fictional night market on Brooklyn's Smith Street, where he can indulge his fantasies of turkey and Thousand Island dressing on a kaiser roll, pepperoncini and provolone heroes, and horseradish and roast beef on rye. At Zeod's, the meat is sliced "extraordinarily thin" and draped to make a sandwich with the "fluffy compressibility" he craves. Ultimately, it is a Zeod's sandwich order that provides Lionel with a clue to the mystery of Frank's death.

In the novel's final pages, Lionel admits he doesn't mind driving customers to the International Terminal at Kennedy Airport for one of the "great secret sandwiches of New York," chicken *shwarma* from an Israeli food stand, "carved fresh off the roasting pin, stuffed into pita, and slathered in grilled peppers, onions and tahini." He recommends it highly, "if you're ever out that way."

Naturally, Jonathan Lethem suggested a sandwich recipe to pair with *Motherless Brooklyn* and contributed his thoughts on sandwiches to *The Book Club Cookbook* in a short essay, "Books Are Sandwiches."

Books are sandwiches. Between their bready boards lies a filling of information-dense leaves nestled together, an accumulation of layers for cumulative effect. Ratio is everything. Proportion. Too many slices of either meat or cheese can wreck a sandwich's middle passages, the overused fundamental creating a bricky, discursive dry spot in what ought to have been a moist sequence. Too much aioli or chutney or roasted red pepper (always use those soaked in olive oil, never water) can gush, drench bread, run down the hand, and destroy a wristwatch. Yet other sandwiches, the tours-de-force, thrive on excess, disunity, a peperoncino or cherry tomato bursting through the door like a character with a gun in his hand, a rant of watercress or filibuster of Brie, an unexpected chapter of flaked oregano inserted like a flashback or dream in italics.

We dislike instinctively those who turn a sandwich and gnaw vertically, against the grain, wrecking the spine and architecture of a sandwich. Their disregard for narrative sequence is as violent as spoiling the plot of a book by gossiping in advance of the outcome. In each sandwich inheres an intrinsic eating speed, shameful to violate. Eating more and understanding(?) less? Slow down!

Hors d'oeuvres on tiny crackers are poems, always seeking perfection in elusive gestures, annoying to try to make a meal of. Hot dogs, ice cream sandwiches, and Oreo cookies are like children's picture books, bright and goonish, drawing the eater's eye like a magpie's to something glinting—the clowns of sandwiches. Hamburgers are clowns too, anonymous clowns that pile out of cars, frequently dwarves. Despite the propensity to make hamburgers ever bigger, to boast of ounces, the default hamburger is a White Castle—as Wimpy knows, burgers are eaten in serial, like mystery novels, eye always on the last page, and the burger to follow.

Sandwiches are too often served in public. In fact the reader of sandwiches is essentially engaged in a private act, and becomes steadily irritable at our scrutiny. The Earl of Sandwich may have been a pool player, but the reader of sandwiches has no time for us or the ringing telephone, and only one hand free—for a book.

Zaytoon's Chicken Shwarma

Ahmad Samhan and Faried Assad, both Palestinian Americans, are co-owners of Zaytoon's, a popular Middle Eastern restaurant with two locations in Brooklyn, one on Smith Street, the location of the fictional Zeod's market in *Motherless Brooklyn*. Sahman says the chicken *shwarma*, from a recipe passed on by a Syrian friend, is their number-one bestseller: Zaytoon's sells 140 pounds of the sandwiches daily.

For the traditional Middle Eastern chicken *shwarma* sandwich, marinated chicken breasts are cooked slowly on a vertical rotisserie. The tender, flavorful meat is then shaved into thin slices and tucked into fresh pita bread with tahini, baba ghanoush or hummus, tomatoes, lettuce, onions, and Middle Eastern pickles.

While Zaytoon's prepares rotisserie chicken for their *shwarma* and serves the sandwich with homemade tahini in freshly baked pita bread, Samhan says you can easily make a delicious version with baked chicken and store-bought pita bread and tahini sauce. Samhan adds, "As Grandma always says, '*Sahtein*,' meaning, 'Eat in good health.'" We think Lionel would go out of his way for a taste of Zaytoon's *shwarma*, a perfect companion for *Motherless Brooklyn*.

NOTE: Middle Eastern pickles are sour pickles, usually made from small, cornichon-sized cucumbers, and are available at any Middle Eastern grocery (see Purchasing Information, p. 499). You may substitute good-quality dill pickles.

Store-bought tahini is often unsalted, so you may need additional salt to season the sandwiches.

For the marinated chicken

2 pounds boned, skinned chicken breasts

1 tablespoon kosher salt

½ cup white vinegar

½ cup vegetable oil

1½ teaspoons oregano

1½ teaspoons ground black pepper

1½ teaspoons paprika

1 teaspoon ground cardamom

1 teaspoon ground cumin

5 teaspoons minced garlic

For the sandwiches

4 large (10-inch) rounds pita bread

½–¾ cup tahini, hummus, or baba ghanoush

Salt

2 medium tomatoes, sliced

1 small red onion, sliced

Middle Eastern pickles (see note)

1. To marinate the chicken: Trim the chicken to remove any excess fat. Moisten the chicken slightly with water and rub well on all sides with kosher salt. Wash the salt off thoroughly with hot water. Pat the chicken dry.

2. In a large bowl, whisk together the vinegar and oil. Add spices and blend. Add the chicken and turn to coat. Cover, refrigerate, and let marinate for at least 6 hours, preferably overnight.

3. To prepare the sandwiches: Remove the chicken from the refrigerator 1 hour before cooking. Preheat oven to 350°F. Arrange the chicken breasts in a single layer in a baking dish. Pour in enough marinade to half cover the chicken. Bake until cooked through, about 25 minutes. Baste frequently with additional marinade to keep top of chicken moist.

4. Slice each pita round in half to form 2 pockets. Spread the inside of the pockets with 2–3 tablespoons tahini, hummus, or baba ghanoush. Slice the warm chicken as thinly as possible and fill sandwiches (about one-half breast, or ½ pound, of chicken per round). Sprinkle with salt to taste, and add the tomatoes, onion, and pickles.

Yield: 4 sandwiches

"Members of the club were selected on the basis of both their literary and culinary abilities," says Joseph Ginocchio of his Santa Fe, New Mexico, book club. The book club's four married couples have discussed fiction over dinner since 1984. The idea for the book club arose when one of the friends noted that they always discussed current movies, but because they hadn't read the same books, literature wasn't a topic of conversation. The group of teachers, college professors, medical and health professionals, and physicists began hosting meetings in their homes. "It seemed natural to serve dinner at home," says Ginocchio, a physicist. "These are people who like cooking, eating, and drinking wine."

The meals started out modestly, but quickly escalated to multicourse dinners. "Each successive person had outdone the last until the meeting turned into a full-course feast," says Ginocchio. When they discussed Fyodor Dostoyevsky's *The Idiot,* Ruth Kovnat served Russian peasant fare—stuffed cabbage and potato pancakes.

The book club's long-standing commitment means going the distance for a meeting. When members Byron Goldstein, Carla Wofsy, Mark Bolsterli, and Judy Costlow were on sabbatical in Washington, D.C., their fellow readers traveled cross-country twice to visit, once to discuss Margaret Drabble's *The Middle Ground,* a novel about a successful journalist, and once to discuss Milan Kundera's novel *Immortality,* which explores themes of death and immortality.

The club started with a reading list dominated by classics, but moved to more contemporary fiction. Of the more than one hundred books they have read together, they name *The Idiot,* Dostoyevsky's Russian classic about a saintly man's clash with an empty society; *The Bird Artist,* Howard Norman's story of a bird illustrator in Newfoundland who confesses to murder; John Updike's *Rabbit Is Rich,* one of a series of novels about the suburban American Angstrom family; and Jonathan Lethem's *Motherless Brooklyn* as favorites.

The book club thought *Motherless Brooklyn,* told from the point of view of an orphan with Tourette's syndrome, provided an unusual and interesting perspective. "*Motherless Brooklyn* was tremendously poignant," says Ginocchio, "and we all had great sympathy for the central character. Such human warmth among the characters appealed to us. Yet it also had a comic element and was different from many of the books we have read."

More Food for Thought

The Silicon Valley Book Club, with members in the San Francisco Bay area, enjoyed the "tiny" White Castle hamburgers hostess Karen Wynbeek purchased from a local grocery store when they discussed *Motherless Brooklyn* (see Purchasing Information, p. 499). "Lionel had a bag of White Castle hamburgers in the car," says Wynbeek, "and the description of the burgers even mentioned the square shape, the holes in them, and the onions." Wynbeek also served other New York food: lox and bagels, kosher dill pickles, and New York cheesecake.

For their discussion of Jonathan Lethem's *Motherless Brooklyn*, the Book Club of the Brown University Club in New York dined on burgers, fries, salad, and classic New York cheesecake at Junior's, a Brooklyn culinary landmark noted for its cheesecake (see Purchasing Information, p. 499). "Considering that Junior's is located close to where most of the events of *Motherless Brooklyn* occurred, we thought it was an apt choice," says John Kwok, a coordinator of the book club. "Most of the characters in the book ate burgers, so those of us who ordered hamburgers felt it was a very appropriate choice."

My Ántonia

Willa Cather

1918

(available in paperback from Penguin, 1999)

M Y *ÁNTONIA*, an American classic, is a love letter to the frontier spirit of those who fanned out across North America in the late nineteenth and early twentieth centuries to make new lives in the West.

First published in 1918, *My Ántonia* is told through the fond reminiscences of a man named Jim Burden. Jim, orphaned at age ten, is sent by train to live with his grandparents in Nebraska. On the train he meets Ántonia and her family, the Shimerdas, immigrants from Bohemia who are also looking to build a new life in Nebraska.

In their new lives, Jim and Ántonia become fast friends, spending days in the fields under the Nebraska sun, enduring harsh Midwestern winters, and weathering family tragedy together. When Ántonia's father dies by his own hand, the community pitches in to help the Shimerdas; Ántonia leaves school and takes to hard labor in the fields to help support her family.

Jim and Ántonia grow apart as they reach adolescence, but are reunited in the town of Black Hawk, where Jim's grandparents have moved so he can attend school. Ántonia, like many immigrant girls in the area, finds domestic work in the household of a Black Hawk family.

When Jim leaves for college in the East, he leaves Ántonia and the Midwest behind. He will not see her again until twenty years later when he finds Ántonia, still in Nebraska, happily married and with a large family of her own.

Jim's nostalgia for his childhood on the plains graces nearly every page of *My Ántonia,* and descriptions of food reflect his longing. On his first morning on the farm after returning to Nebraska, Jim sniffs gingerbread baking, a harbinger of the many hearty and delicious farm foods—bread, waffles, sausages, chocolate cake, chicken, ham, bacon, pies—his grandmother would cook. There is affection, even melancholy, in Jim's recollections of his grandmother's culinary nurturing: "On Sundays she gave us as much chicken as we could eat, and on other days we had ham or bacon or sausage meat. She baked either pies or cake for us every day, unless, for a change, she made my favourite pudding, striped with currants and boiled in a bag."

The food in *My Ántonia* not only mirrors their pioneering self-reliance and industry, it also reveals the kindness and hospitality of neighbors facing hardship together. After hearing that the Shimerdas are reduced to killing prairie dogs for food, the Burdens bring them a hamper of food. With nothing but frozen potatoes in her larder, Mrs. Shimerda returns the favor with a teacup full of brown chips—dried Bohemian mushrooms.

To Jim, Ántonia embodies the richness of the Nebraska land they frolicked on as children. Consistent with this image of Ántonia, as an adult Jim finds her surrounded by a richness and abundance of food. Cherry and apple orchards and gooseberry, currant, and mulberry bushes abound on her farm. In her "fruit" cave, dill pickles, chopped pickles, and watermelon rinds fill barrels, and glass jars of cherries, strawberries, crab apples, and spiced plums line the shelves.

As Jim inspects the jars of fruit, Ántonia's children inform him that she makes kolaches with the spiced plums. One of the boys snickers. Jim responds, "You think I don't know what kolaches are, eh? You're mistaken, young man. I've eaten your mother's kolaches long before that Easter Day when you were born."

DANIELA SEVER'S FAVORITE
SPICED PLUM KOLACHES

*K*olaches are yeast buns with a slight depression for fillings such as apricot, poppy seed, cherry, or prune. They were brought by Bohemian immigrants to the United States and can be found in midwestern bakeries in and around Czech immigrant communities.

Daniela Sever, a Boston area dentist, has fond memories of eating plum *kolaches* baked by her nanny, Babička (Granny), throughout her childhood in her native Czechoslovakia.

"In Czechoslovakia, we ate *kolaches* at weddings and parties," says Sever. "And I bought one every day from the local bakery on the way home from school." In the United States, Sever makes spiced plum *kolaches* for special occasions.

NOTE: To make vanilla sugar, mix 7 tablespoons sugar with several drops of vanilla extract. Or add 1–2 vanilla beans, cut into 1½-inch pieces, to a small jar of sugar. Cover tightly with lid and let sit in a cool, dark place for 2–3 weeks.

1 cup milk

3½ tablespoons (1½ packets) active dry yeast

3 cups cake flour

⅛ teaspoon salt

½ cup granulated sugar

7 tablespoons unsalted butter, softened

2 egg yolks

3–3½ pounds ripe Italian plums (about 24), quartered and pitted

7 tablespoons vanilla sugar (see note above, or Purchasing Information, p. 499)

2–3 tablespoons poppy seeds, either whole or ground (optional)

3–4 tablespoons unsalted butter, melted

1. Heat ½ cup of the milk until lukewarm. Pour into a small bowl and add the yeast. Allow to sit until yeast is foamy, about 5 minutes.

2. Sift together the flour and salt in a mixing bowl. Mix in the sugar, butter, and the yeast mixture.

3. In a separate bowl, beat the egg yolks with the remaining ½ cup milk and mix into the flour mixture. Cover with a damp kitchen towel and let rise for about 1 hour.

4. Preheat oven to 350°F. Roll out the dough into a rectangle and transfer to a shallow, greased 17x11-inch baking pan. Wet your hands and stretch the dough out to the edges of the pan. Top with the plums and sprinkle with vanilla sugar and poppy seeds, then drizzle with melted butter. Bake 25–30 minutes, or until plums are pink. Allow to cool, then slice into 3-inch squares.

Yield: 24 pieces

BOOK CLUB PROFILE

The Chicago-based Book Club of Hope Hadassah, originally part of the local chapter of this national Jewish women's organization, meets monthly at members' homes on Chicago's North Side.

"We have enjoyed our lively, opinionated, and friendly discussions over the past ten years," says Sue Edlin. "We only read fiction, but have covered quite a range of classic and contemporary literature." A favorite way for the twelve-member Hope Hadassah group to end the evening is to try to cast the book's characters for a movie. "It doesn't matter if they've cast the movie already, we don't care!" says Edlin. "Age doesn't matter, either, we can pick a young Cary Grant or an older Katharine Hepburn."

They also enjoy comparing book cover illustrations when club members have different editions of the reading selection, to see the publishers' interpretations of the story and what the publisher thought would appeal to the reader.

M&M's are the Hope Hadassah group's food mascot, says Edlin. "They're at every meeting." Lavish theme dinners are not their style, but there is usually a snack relevant to the reading selection, especially if it's an ethnic book. Members have brought Indian or Japanese snack mixes or ethnic cookies and pastries. For *The Secret Life of Bees,* by Sue Monk Kidd (see p. 398), Karen Delee served honey candies and had honey hand lotions for members to take home. Brownies and chocolate chip cookies are frequent treats. "There is always a way to convince us that the book has a tie-in to chocolate," says Edlin.

The Hope Hadassah group read *My Ántonia* when it was chosen as the One Book–One Chicago selection for fall of 2002, part of a program that encourages Chicago residents to all read the same book as a way of promoting a sense of community. "Everybody liked *My Ántonia* and had something to say about it," says Edlin.

"Some books take forever to get into, but *My Ántonia* gets you right away," says Edlin. "The severity of the summer heat and winter cold, the loneliness, poverty, and backbreaking work, as well as the town life came alive in Cather's descriptions."

The women discussed the primitive way settlers lived. "The thought of living in a room dug into the earth did not appeal to any of us," says Edlin. "It is difficult to comprehend these living conditions having existed in relatively modern times. The contrast between the prairie and life in the city was startling."

More Food for Thought

Guests of Milwaukee School of Engineering's Great Books Dinner and Discussion series in Milwaukee, Wisconsin, dined on foods from the pages of *My Ántonia* for their dinner discussion of Willa Cather's novel.

Coordinators of the series devised a menu reflecting the heritage of the novel's Shimerda family (Bohemian meatballs), the Nebraska corn farm setting (buttered corn), and Mrs. Shimerda's favorite: poppy seeds (poppy seed–green onion noodles).

My Soul to Keep

Tananarive Due

....

HARPERCOLLINS, *1997*

(available in paperback from William Morrow, 1998)

IN TANANARIVE DUE'S supernatural thriller, *My Soul to Keep*, a middle-class African-American family's domestic tranquillity is shattered when Jessica, a successful investigative journalist for a Miami newspaper and mother of a five-year-old daughter, Kira, discovers an astonishing secret about her charming and supportive husband, David.

David, she discovers, is Dawit, a five-hundred-year-old immortal. A member of an Ethiopian sect of scholars, Dawit traded his soul for eternal life by drinking the blood of Christ—a secret he must never reveal. Accounts of Dawit's former lives—as a slave and a jazz musician—are interwoven with his history as one of the immortal brethren.

Although Dawit's covenant with his immortal sect requires that he return to his order when suspicion about his identity is aroused and before his agelessness becomes apparent, Dawit is determined to remain with Jessica and Kira.

Dawit kills those close to Jessica as their suspicions are aroused. Fearing his crime spree will lead to the revelation of Dawit's true identity, his fellow immortals summon him to return to Ethiopia. When he refuses, Dawit confesses his story to Jessica, endangering the lives of the family he loves. Jessica remains with Dawit at first, but eventually flees with her daughter and is pursued by Dawit, who is determined to have his family join him in eternal life. The immortals, too, are in pursuit, determined to silence her.

Tananarive Due suggested recipes for *doro wat* and *injera*, traditional Ethiopian dishes, to pair with *My Soul to Keep*. She told us:

When I created the character of David (or Dawit) in *My Soul to Keep*, it was important to me to establish that he is a master in the kitchen. What is it about a man who cooks for you? Careful readers will note how many times David is preparing meals, serving meals, or delivering meals, like the critical evening he brings his wife a hot dinner plate at her office! David is nourishing Jessica on a very deep level.

I chose an Ethiopian recipe because of David's Ethiopian heritage. This chicken dish is never mentioned by name in the book, but my husband and I love it! We always order it when we visit Ethiopian restaurants. The book does mention David's *injera*, however, as well as his homemade honeywine!

Why doesn't Jessica leave David when she discovers he is a five-hundred-year-old immortal? The way to a woman's heart . . .

Doro Wat (Chicken Stew) with Injera (Flatbread)

The spicy stew known as *doro wat* and a flatbread, *injera*, are staples of Ethiopian cuisine. *Berbere*, hot-pepper paste, and *niter kebbeh*, a spiced butter, frequently used in soup or stew, give *doro wat* a spicy flavor. The *doro wat* is served on a large communal platter, and the *injera* is used as an eating utensil. It can line the platter on which the *doro wat* is served and it can be used to scoop up the stew. This recipe makes individual portions.

NOTE: We have included a recipe as well as Purchasing Information for *berbere* (see p. 499).

2 tablespoons lemon juice

2 teaspoons salt

1 2½–3 pound chicken, cut in pieces

2 tablespoons peanut oil

2 onions, chopped

¼ cup Niter Kebbeh (see below)

2 cloves garlic, chopped

1 tablespoon freshly grated ginger

2 tablespoons paprika

¼ teaspoon ground cardamom

¼ teaspoon ground fenugreek

½ cup Berbere Paste (see below, or Purchasing Information, p. 499)

¼ cup dry red wine

1 cup water

4 hard-cooked eggs, peeled

1. Combine the lemon juice and salt in a small bowl. Wash the chicken pieces, pat dry, and rub well with lemon juice–salt mixture. Let stand at room temperature for 30 minutes.
2. Heat the oil in a large heavy skillet or Dutch oven and sauté onions over medium heat until they begin to soften, about 5 minutes. Add the *niter kebbeh* to skillet. When *niter kebbeh* is melted, add garlic, ginger, paprika, cardamom, and fenugreek, and stir well. Add *berbere* and cook over low heat for 5 minutes, stirring occasionally. Add wine and water. Bring sauce to

a boil, then reduce the heat and simmer, uncovered, until sauce begins to thicken, about 5 minutes.

3. Add the chicken to the sauce, turning to coat well. Cover tightly and simmer 15 minutes.

4. Pierce the eggs well with a fork and add to the stew. Cover and simmer until chicken is cooked through, about 15 minutes.

5. Remove the chicken pieces and skin and bone them. Pull meat into small pieces and return to the stew. Serve atop *injera*.

Yield: 4 servings

Niter Kebbeh (Spiced Butter)

1 cup (2 sticks) unsalted butter

2 tablespoons chopped onion

2 teaspoon finely chopped garlic

1 teaspoons minced fresh ginger

¼ teaspoon turmeric

Seeds from 2 cardamom pods, lightly crushed (see Purchasing Information, p. 499)

½ cinnamon stick

1½ whole cloves

Pinch of ground nutmeg

Melt butter in a saucepan over low heat. When butter is melted, raise heat and bring to a boil until surface is foamy. Reduce heat and skim off the foam. Add onion, garlic, and spices. Simmer over very low heat for 1 hour. Pour through a strainer lined with cheesecloth and discard solids. *Niter kebbeh* will keep in the refrigerator for 2–3 months.

Yield: ¾ cup

Berbere Paste

NOTE: Wear plastic or rubber gloves while handling the chiles to protect your skin from the oil in them. Avoid direct contact with your eyes, and wash hands thoroughly after handling.

NOTE: If you choose to make the homemade version of this spice blend, see Purchasing Information (p. 499) for fenugreek seed, cardamom pods, and piquin chiles.

1 teaspoon cumin seed

¼ teaspoon fenugreek seed (see note)

¼ teaspoon black peppercorns

2 cardamom pods (see note)

½ small onion, coarsely chopped

2 cloves garlic, coarsely chopped

½ cup water

7 dried piquin chiles, stems removed (see note)

1 tablespoon ground cayenne pepper

1 tablespoon ground paprika

¼ teaspoon ground ginger

⅛ teaspoon ground allspice

⅛ teaspoon ground cloves

⅛ teaspoon ground nutmeg

1½ tablespoons vegetable oil

1. In a hot skillet, toast cumin, fenugreek, black peppercorns, and cardamom until fragrant, about 2 minutes. Shake the skillet constantly, and, when done, transfer to a bowl immediately to prevent burning. Grind to a powder using a spice mill or a mortar and pestle.
2. In a blender or food processor, purée onion, garlic, and ¼ cup of the water. Add the chiles and ground spices, and blend until smooth. With the motor running, gradually add the remaining water and the oil and blend to a smooth paste.

Yield: About 1 cup

Injera (Flatbread)

1 cup whole-wheat or buckwheat flour

1 cup unbleached white flour

½ teaspoon baking soda

2 cups club soda

Vegetable oil for the griddle

1. Combine the flours and baking soda in a large bowl. Add the club soda and stir until combined. The batter should be very thin. More club soda may be added as necessary.
2. Heat a large griddle and brush lightly with oil. Cover the surface of the griddle with a large circle of batter. The batter should be thicker than for crêpes but thinner than for pancakes. Cook for 1–2 minutes, until bread is spongy and holes appear on the surface. Remove from pan and let cool—*injera* is cooked on one side only. Repeat process until batter is used up.

Yield: 6 large rounds

Honeywine is thought to be one of the oldest alcoholic drinks known. Ethiopian honeywine, *t'ej*, is made from fermented honey and native Ethiopian hops, *gesho*. The amber-colored wine is commonly served for cocktails and with meals in Ethiopia, and the preparations are often homemade brews. *T'ej*'s sweetness makes it the perfect complement to spicy Ethiopian cuisine. (To purchase honeywine, see Purchasing Information, p. 499.)

BOOK CLUB PROFILE

"I wanted it to be real," says Adrianne Watson, founder of the STAR (Simply Thrilled About Reading) Book Club in Chicago. "Friends talked about their book clubs, but they seemed to have no rules and no structure. You didn't even have to read the book. I wanted an organized club, where everyone reads the book."

Adrianne and her mother-in-law, Karen Watson, often shared books. "I suggested we invite family and friends to form a book club," says Karen. "Adrianne took charge, and voilà, STAR was born."

When Marlon Hayes, another member's husband, expressed an interest in joining, the all-female group initially balked. "The majority thought it would change the flavor of the group, but we agreed to invite them," says Watson. "It has enhanced our group, and now we await their responses." The group now includes thirteen members, including the two men, ranging in age from twenty-four to sixty.

Each STAR meeting has two hosts. The meeting is held at the dinner host's home. The dinner host is responsible for preparing a meal, which can range from a Thanksgiving-type dinner to pizza and salad. The book host introduces the book, facilitates the discussion, and poses questions. At the conclusion of each meeting, the book host presents his or her choice for the next reading selection; that choice can be overridden only if at least one-third of the group has already read it.

To keep the group disciplined, STAR members voted to assess a one-dollar fine on those who are more than thirty minutes late to meetings, and the member with the best attendance wins a gift certificate to a bookstore. The late fee has helped members be punctual. "It shows how serious we are about our books and our club," says member Elsa Lightfoot.

Members respond to Watson's enthusiasm and organization, and her constant effort to improve the group. An annual spa retreat fosters closer bonds among members.

"A few of the single members didn't really open up until we went on the first retreat," says Watson. The retreat is also a time for reflection and organization: Goals are created, strengths and weaknesses analyzed, and new ideas generated for the coming year. The retreat has been the impetus for innovations such as joint meetings with other book clubs, conference calls with authors, and even a children's book club.

A diverse reading list is important to STAR. "Although we are all African Americans, we don't limit ourselves to African-American authors," says Lightfoot. "We joined the club to read a variety of books." The group exceeded their usual three-hour meeting time when they discussed *My Soul to Keep,* for which they had arranged a conference call with author Tananarive Due. "Much of the discussion focused on the desirability of eternal life," says Watson. "Most of us would not choose immortality if it meant an eternity without family or loved ones."

Dawit, the immortal, was a controversial character for the group. "I did not like Dawit when he killed, but in the end I was rooting for him to evade the immortals so he could give his daughter his blood to keep her alive," says Watson. STAR members agreed that Dawit's choice—leaving the family he loved or turning them into immortals—would be profoundly difficult.

STAR members were thrilled to have Due, a favorite author, join their discussion. Due answered questions about the inspiration for her book, her religious preferences, and plans for the film version of *My Soul to Keep*. "But our most important question to Tananarive," says Watson, "was whether she would choose to be immortal. She said no."

More Food for Thought

Ten members of the Sistahs About Reading, a Washington, D.C.–based book club, headed to an Ethiopian restaurant to discuss *My Soul to Keep*. "We were a little anxious about going there," says Shermonta Grant, founder of the group. "We wondered if we would like the food. And some group members worried about offending restaurant employees by eating the food in the wrong way."

The Meskerem restaurant, in the Adams-Morgan section of Washington, D.C., welcomed the visitors warmly. The group ordered a variety of Ethiopian *wat*s, or stews, including seafood, chicken, and beef. The *wat*s arrived Ethiopian-style, piled onto one large, thin, pancake-like *injera*. In true Ethiopian style, group members tore off bits of bread with their hands and used them to scoop up mouthfuls of the *wat*s.

"I can't emphasize enough what an exciting experience this was for everyone," says Grant. "Just being in that environment made us feel connected with the book. We had a wonderful discussion."

The nine African-American women of We Just Wanna Have Fun Book Club in Atlanta, Georgia, enjoyed Ethiopian fare for their discussion of *My Soul to Keep*. Members scoured the Internet for recipes and arrived at the meeting with *doro wat*, *injera*, lentils, chickpeas, and rice. "I had never cooked or eaten lentils before," says Rhonda Haney, who hosted the meeting. "This was new food for all of us, and it was fun to try it out."

Mystic River

Dennis Lehane

....

WILLIAM MORROW, *2001*

(available in paperback from HarperTorch, 2002)

In 1975, three friends—Sean Devine, Jimmy Marcus, and Dave Boyle—are playing on the street of a close-knit Boston neighborhood. A man who appears to be a cop pulls up and authoritatively orders Dave into his car. Dave goes, not to return for four excruciating days, and the lives of all three friends change forever.

Mystic River, a novel, explores the three boys' lives twenty-five years after the abduction when, as grown men, their paths once more intersect. Sean has become a homicide detective. When Jimmy's daughter, Katie, is murdered, Sean is assigned the case. He pursues several leads, but eventually Dave comes under suspicion. Since his childhood abduction, Dave has fought his own personal demons. Sean and Jimmy discover that on the night of Katie's murder, Dave had arrived home in the wee hours covered in someone else's blood. As Jimmy becomes increasingly convinced of Dave's guilt, he grows impatient with Sean's investigation and wants to exact his own revenge. But to do so would propel him back into a life of crime, a life he left long ago.

In the context of a riveting murder mystery, *Mystic River* explores loyalty, guilt, vengeance, and remorse, and the devastating effects that can ripple through countless lives from one formative event.

DREW HEVLE'S ITALIAN SAUSAGE AND PEPPERS

At a neighborhood barbecue soon after Dave's safe return from his abduction, Jimmy inhales the smell of hot dogs and Italian sausage, which reminds him of Boston's historic baseball stadium, Fenway Park. Although *Mystic River* is a fictional story, Italian sausage could not be more real. Vendors have been peddling sweet Italian sausages outside Fenway Park for years, lending a festive, if smoky, atmosphere to the streets that surround the ballpark.

Besides evoking current-day Boston, the mention of Italian sausage is a reminder of Boston's immigrant history, crucial to the development of the tight-knit neighborhood setting of *Mystic River*. Large-scale immigration to Boston in the nineteenth century shaped it into the city of ethnic loyalties and close neighborhoods astutely depicted in Lehane's book. Successive waves of English, Polish, Russian, Jewish, and Portuguese immigrants occupied areas of Boston, but the Irish came in the greatest numbers. In the early and middle decades of the 1800s, Irish immigrants flooded the city, first settling near Boston's piers. The advent of railroads allowed the Irish to fan out into outlying parts of the city. By the 1870s, Boston saw an influx of Italian immigrants, who supplanted the Irish in communities like Boston's North End, and who still dominate that part of the city today. Visitors to Boston still seek Italian delicacies in its historic North End—Italian pastries like cannoli and tiramisu, Italian cheeses and pastas, and Italian sausage.

Drew Hevle of the Houston Book Club in Texas developed this tempting recipe for Italian sausage and peppers after tasting similar dishes. "I especially like the colorful combination of red and green peppers," says Hevle.

The number and variety of Italian sausages is staggering, and the flavor overtones of this dish will depend on the type of sausage you use. Hevle prefers freshly ground spicy Italian pork sausage. If you choose a milder sausage, Hevle recommends adding a *bouquet garni* (bundle of fresh herbs) to the pan, including fresh parsley, oregano, and thyme, when you add the vegetables.

This dish can be served as a main dish, an appetizer, or a side dish. For a main course, toss cooked angel-hair pasta in heated marinara sauce. Top with vegetables and slices of sausage. As an appetizer serve with crusty Italian bread.

Hevle warns that his dish can overpower. "With the garlic, onions, and sausage, this is a strong dish, so take care what you serve it with. A bold red, such as a Chianti, will stand up to the spice."

2 pounds sweet or hot Italian sausage
  or a mixture
1 tablespoon olive oil
1 large sweet onion, cut into large pieces
3 bell peppers (1 each red, green, and yellow),
  sliced into thin strips

3 cloves garlic, crushed
Salt and pepper to taste
2 cups Denise DiRocco's Marinara Sauce
  (see below) and 1 pound angel-hair pasta

1. Place the sausage in a large, deep skillet with enough water to barely cover the bottom. Place over medium heat, cover, and cook 20–25 minutes, turning once (don't use a fork—you don't want to puncture the sausages). Check occasionally to make sure the liquid has not boiled off, and add a little more if necessary.

2. Pour off any liquid from the pan and reserve it. Brown the sausage on all sides. Remove sausage from pan, cut into bite-size pieces, and place in a large bowl. Set aside.

3. Put the olive oil, onion, peppers, and garlic in the pan. Sauté over medium-high heat until vegetables are done, but still firm to the bite. You may add some of the reserved pan liquid as the vegetables cook for extra flavor. Return sliced sausages to pan and heat through with vegetables. Season with salt and pepper to taste.

Yield: Serves 6 as a main course, 8 as an appetizer

Our friend Denise DiRocco contributed her recipe for flavorful marinara sauce. To achieve the fullest flavor, she highly recommends using Pastene "Kitchen Ready" tomatoes.

DENISE DIROCCO'S MARINARA SAUCE

3 tablespoons olive oil

1 medium onion, finely chopped

5 cloves garlic, pressed

1 6-ounce can tomato paste

¾ cup red wine

1 28-ounce can ground plum tomatoes, such as Pastene "Kitchen Ready"

1 teaspoon dried oregano

1 teaspoon dried basil

1 teaspoon dried parsley

3 tablespoons grated Parmesan cheese (optional)

Salt and freshly ground black pepper to taste

1. Heat the olive oil in a medium saucepan over medium heat. Add the onion and garlic and sauté until very soft but not browned, about 5 minutes.

2. Add the tomato paste and wine. Stir and simmer over medium heat for 3–5 minutes. Add the tomatoes. When the sauce bubbles, reduce heat and simmer for 15 minutes, stirring occasionally.

3. Add the oregano, basil, parsley, and Parmesan (if desired) and simmer an additional 10 minutes. Season to taste with salt and pepper.

Yield: About 4 cups

KERSTIN JANSSON'S
SWEDISH MEATBALLS

After Katie's death, friends and neighbors shower Jimmy and his wife, Annabeth, with food, including Irish soda bread, pies, croissants, muffins, pastries, potato salad, deli meat, ham, turkey, and Swedish meatballs.

Made of seasoned pork or beef and covered with a brown gravy, Swedish meatballs were brought to America by Scandinavian immigrants, many of whom settled in northern Midwest states. Popular in America at the beginning of the twentieth century and again in the 1950s and 1960s, Swedish meatballs are enjoying a resurgence in popularity, including among book clubs.

Jan Seerveld of the Silicon Valley Book Club in California contributed this recipe from her friend, Kerstin Jansson. Originally from Gothenburg, Sweden, Jansson remembers eating these Swedish meatballs—her mother's recipe—at smorgasbords and festive events like Christmas. Today, Jansson serves the meatballs at Christmastime with gravlax (smoked salmon with a spice rub), pickled herring, *matjes* herring (filleted and cured with salt, sugar, vinegar, and spices), sausages and ham, and Jansson's Temptation, a traditional Scandinavian side dish of potatoes, onions, and anchovies.

She also serves them as a dinner entrée. "My children's favorite is Swedish meatballs with mashed potatoes," says Jansson. "They pour the gravy from the meatballs over the potatoes. And, of course, we always have lingonberries," the traditional Swedish accompaniment to the meatballs, similar to cranberry sauce (see Purchasing Information, p. 499).

For family dinners, Jansson makes her meatballs with ground beef or with a combination of beef and pork. For festive occasions, Jansson uses veal to give the meatballs a special flavor.

As a main course, these meatballs can be served with cranberry sauce and mashed potatoes or egg noodles, and gravy on the side. For an appetizer, Jansson skips the gravy and serves the meatballs plain or with a dipping sauce made of equal parts yellow mustard and plum preserves. "This dip is not Swedish at all," Jansson tells us, "but it really jazzes up the meatballs."

For the meatballs

1 medium onion, grated

½ cup soft bread crumbs

scant ½ cup water

2 eggs

1 teaspoon sugar

2 teaspoons salt

¼ teaspoon ground white pepper

1½ pounds ground beef

½ pound ground pork or ¼ pound veal and
   ¼ pound pork

Butter or margarine for frying

For the gravy

⅓ cup flour

3½ cups beef bouillon (substitute half-and-half
   for ¾ cup of bouillon for a creamier gravy)

1–2 teaspoons beef bouillon granules

Dash Kitchen Bouquet, to color (optional)

1. To make the meatballs: In a large bowl, combine the onion, bread crumbs, water, eggs, sugar, salt, and pepper. Let the mixture sit for 5–10 minutes, until bread crumbs swell. Add the meat and mix well with a sturdy wooden spoon until well combined.

2. Form meatballs about 1½ inches in diameter (you may want to make them a little smaller for appetizers). Fry the meatballs in the butter or margarine at medium heat until cooked through, not too many at a time. Shake the pan or turn gently to keep the meatballs nicely rounded and browned on all sides. Remove from pan to a serving dish. Do not wash the pan—you will use the pan juices for the gravy.

3. To make the gravy: Heat about ¼ cup of water in the frying pan and scrape down the browned bits. Pour through a strainer and reserve.

4. In a small bowl, dissolve flour in a bit of the bouillon. In a saucepan, heat on high setting the rest of the bouillon (and half-and-half, if using) with the instant bouillon and reserved pan liquid. When it approaches a boil, whisk in the dissolved flour. Turn down heat to medium-high and cook, whisking constantly, for 3–5 minutes, until gravy is smooth and thick. Add a bit of water or milk if gravy becomes too thick. Stir in Kitchen Bouquet for color.

Yield: Serves 6 as a main course, 10 as an appetizer

Every month since 1995, the San Geronimo Lodge in Taos, New Mexico, has been opening its doors to members of Who Did It? A Grammatically Correct Mystery Book Club. "The innkeeper is a mystery buff," explains Art Bachrach, founder of the club, which limits itself to the reading of mysteries. "She's generous with her space."

Who Did It? is sponsored by the Moby Dickens Bookshop, a business that Bachrach, a former professor and director of a biomedical laboratory in Bethesda, Maryland, opened when he and his wife moved to Taos in 1984. In Taos you can "be who you want," says Bachrach. "Taos is a town where you'll go to a party and both a Navajo artist and your plumber will be there. It's a very individualistic community."

The membership of Who Did It? reflects the community's individualism. Many of the twenty to thirty people who attend meetings—mostly women over fifty—have moved to Taos from the East. They hold a wide variety of jobs, including hospital administrator, investment counselor, airline pilot, motorcycle racer, and housewife. "The one thing that binds us is that we all love mysteries," says Bachrach.

To enhance meetings, the group taps the rich reservoir of writers living in the area. By Bachrach's estimates, there are close to twenty-five mystery writers living in New Mexico, and they make frequent appearances at Who Did It? meetings. Past guests include Jake Page, Rex Burns, Michael McGarrity, Steve Brewer, Robert Westbrook, Walter Satterthwait, John Dunning, and James Doss. Who Did It? members look for books featuring strong character development when making their selections. "The writers whose characters never change from book to book lose us," Bachrach says. "We strive for a standard of great writing, good character development, and a well-crafted mystery."

Several books the club has read in past years have met this standard, including Arturo Pérez-Reverte's *The Seville Communion,* a literate thriller set in modern-day Spain, and Martin Cruz Smith's *Rose,* a detective story set in nineteenth-century England. "We still talk about these books," says Bachrach.

More recently, the group read Dennis Lehane's *Mystic River,* and found the related discussion to be particularly lively. Group members dwelled on the book's ending, some arguing that it flowed naturally from the development of the characters; others, that it was inconsistent with the characters. "Some people had hopes that everyone would live happily ever after," says Bachrach, "but others felt it was predictable that this core of malevolence would emerge."

Conversation also focused on the book's setting. "People were interested in the ethnicity depicted in the book. We felt Lehane portrayed a typical, small, closed Boston community very well. People could see how this small-town atmosphere contributed to the unhappy ending," says Bachrach.

Everyone agreed that Lehane's writing was superb. "Lehane stands out among contemporary mystery writers for his strong and sensitive character development, his sense of place in a community the reader can enter and comprehend, and his suspenseful, well-crafted plots," says Bachrach. "I recommend his writings very highly for mystery readers. *Mystic River* is one of his best."

More Food for Thought

Karen Oleson served canned vegetarian baked beans and New England clam chowder to her San Francisco–area book club, FRED (Friends Reading, Eating, and Discussing books), when the group discussed *Mystic River*. "The story took place in the greater Boston area," says Oleson, "and beans and chowder are common Boston fare."

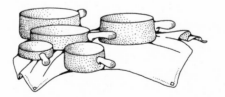

Nickel and Dimed:
On (Not) Getting By in America

Barbara Ehrenreich

METROPOLITAN, 2001

(available in paperback from Owl, 2002)

I N 1998, at the age of fifty-seven, the writer and social critic Barbara Ehrenreich was pounding the pavement looking for a low-wage job. Her goal: to discover firsthand how millions of women about to be tossed into the labor market because of welfare reform could possibly make ends meet. The result is *Nickel and Dimed,* an account of Ehrenreich's experiences working as a waitress, maid, nursing home aide, and Wal-Mart salesperson. Her descriptions of the challenges and indignities facing low-wage workers and her analysis of why, in the face of this "state of emergency," the middle class stays silent paint a frightening portrait of class inequality and indifference in America.

Ehrenreich explains one of the ironies of poverty as she feels herself slipping into its downward spiral. The less money she makes, the fewer options she has for saving money. Ehrenreich applies this principle to food choices: "If you have only a room, with a hot plate at best, you can't save by cooking up huge lentil stews that can be frozen for the week ahead. You eat fast food or the hot dogs and Styrofoam cups of soup that can be microwaved in a convenience store." Workers who lack kitchen facilities tend to buy the most convenient—and most expensive and, often, least healthy— prepared foods.

As a waitress at two restaurants in Key West, Florida, Ehrenreich falls into just such a pattern. Tabs at the low-budget restaurants where she works are low, meaning small tips for Ehrenreich. Her wages and tips amount to just minimum wage. Although she is lucky enough to find a $500-a-month efficiency with a kitchen, she is not ready to go the "lentil stew route" yet, because "I don't have a large cooking pot, potholders, or a ladle to stir with (which would cost a total of about $30 at Kmart, somewhat less at a thrift store), not to mention onions, carrots, and the indispensable bay leaf." Instead, she lunches on unlimited refills at Wendy's, or grabs a Wendy's Spicy

Chicken Sandwich from the drive-thru. Dinner is two or three mozzarella sticks, hastily eaten while standing at a restaurant counter between shifts.

But even as she immerses herself in the lifestyle of a typical low-wage worker, Ehrenreich knows that she can never fully experience the pressures around food and money that plague her coworkers. In an interview given after the publication of her book, Ehrenreich said, "I don't understand how some of the people I worked alongside could get through an eight- to nine-hour shift without eating. It took me a long time to realize that they weren't dieting. It was not that at all. They actually did not have fifty cents in their pockets."

MOZZARELLA STICKS

Rich and gooey mozzarella sticks are one of the dishes that Ehrenreich, as a waitress, serves her customers in abundance and eats during her experiment as a low-wage worker. Serve these sticks with tangy marinara sauce (see p. 295).

2 eggs

¼ cup water

1 cup Italian-style dry bread crumbs

½ teaspoon garlic powder

½ teaspoon dried basil

½ teaspoon dried oregano

¾ cup all-purpose flour

1 1-pound brick of mozzarella, sliced into finger-size sticks

½ cup vegetable or canola oil, for frying

NOTE: To save time, you can use prepackaged mozzarella sticks (string cheese) in place of brick mozzarella.

1. Beat the eggs with the water and set aside.
2. Mix the bread crumbs, garlic powder, basil, and oregano and set aside.
3. Place the flour in a plastic bag. Place the cheese sticks in flour bag and coat with flour. Remove the cheese sticks and dip them in the egg mixture. Coat each cheese stick with the bread-crumb mixture.
4. In a heavy skillet, heat the oil to 360–370°F.
5. Place mozzarella sticks carefully in hot oil and fry approximately 15–20 seconds or until golden. When golden, remove from hot oil and drain on brown paper or paper towels. Serve immediately.

Yield: Approximately 18 sticks

The economic and class issues explored in *Nickel and Dimed* sparked the interest of the League of Women Voters' Book Club, an official group of the local League of Women Voters of Corvallis, Oregon. Twelve retired or part-time working women—schoolteachers, university professors, clerical workers, research scientists, social workers, and nurses—formed a book group with a commitment to social change. Many are community activists. Although the group reads a variety of fiction and nonfiction, *Nickel and Dimed* tapped into the group's interest in social problems. Founding book club member Corrine Gobeli reports that the League of Women Voters of Corvallis encourages citizens to participate actively in government and politics, and studies the impact of public policy on people's lives. "That's what this book brought up: What happens when economic power is concentrated in a large corporation? How does this affect, for example, food security and family farms? Our discussion went way beyond Ehrenreich's experiences to larger policy issues."

The League of Women Voters' Book Club was interested in Ehrenreich's book for another reason. "She's a Reedie!" said Gobeli, meaning that Ehrenreich graduated from Reed College in nearby Portland, Oregon, where she studied biology and chemistry. Ehrenreich later earned a doctorate in biology at Rockefeller University in New York. Of her science background Ehrenreich says: "The disadvantage is that I didn't spend years studying history or political science or something that would have come in more handy. But I'm not sorry, really. It gives me a way of seeing the world, an analytical strength."

Nine Parts of Desire: The Hidden World of Islamic Women

Geraldine Brooks

DOUBLEDAY, *1994*

(available in paperback from Anchor, 1996)

WALL STREET JOURNAL correspondent Geraldine Brooks spent six years reporting on the Middle East. In *Nine Parts of Desire*, she delivers us behind the veil to capture the multifaceted face of Islam today as seen through the lives of Muslim women. Brooks introduces the reader to housewives, divorcées, athletes, career women, political activists, and other notables, including the American-born Queen Noor of Jordan and the Ayatollah Khomeini's daughter. From Egypt and Iran to Ethiopia and Saudi Arabia, Brooks takes us on a journey through the tides that influence the lives of Islamic women, and which they, in turn, are creating. Intimate, revealing, and dramatic, *Nine Parts of Desire*, though written in 1994, is relevant for anyone seeking to understand the post–September 11 world.

Brooks's meetings with Muslim women—some public, some private—frequently take place over meals. The author also sets her scenes with descriptions of foods, such as the smells of *lavosh* bread baking in the morning in Tehran: "The air carries both the sweetness of the seared crusts and the tang of the woodsmoke from the oven sunk into the bakery floor." Brooks is invited to a *rosee*—"a cross between an afternoon tea party and a religious studies class"—where women are served "fruit, tiny, crisp cucumbers, sweet cakes and tea." At an Egyptian supper in Gaza she is served "foul, tamiyya and molokiyya—mashed beans, fried chickpeas and an okra-like green" scooped on flatbread (see Mrs. Mahfouz's Mulukhiya, p. 331). At dinner with Jordan's Queen Noor, she dined on light, healthy dishes the queen liked, such as seaweed soup and grilled fish, and spiced lentils with yogurt (see Her Majesty's Mujadara, p. 230).

FRED SAIFNIA'S SALAD SHIRAZI
(TOMATO-CUCUMBER SALAD)

Cheri Caviness prepared a Persian meal for her book group, the Bookwomen of Encinitas, California, when the group discussed *Nine Parts of Desire* at her home. Salad Shirazi, served with a Persian rice dish and chicken kabobs, was the highlight.

"My husband taught me to make salad shirazi, a traditional Persian salad made with ripe tomatoes, cucumbers, onion, and mint, dressed with fresh lemon juice, olive oil, and a hint of garlic," says Caviness. "Traditionally, this light, refreshing salad is made with mint, but I've had it with other herbs as well—and I usually toss in a chopped jalapeño pepper to give it some pizzazz. If you go to an authentic Persian restaurant and order salad, salad shirazi is likely what you'll get." Adds Caviness, "This is a summer favorite at our house, and it complements almost any meal."

NOTE: Wear plastic or rubber gloves while handling the chiles to protect your skin from the oil in them. Avoid direct contact with your eyes, and wash your hands thoroughly after handling.

For the dressing
4 tablespoons olive oil
Juice of one lime (about 2 tablespoons)
1 clove garlic, minced
Salt and freshly ground pepper to taste

For the salad
3 medium-sized firm, ripe tomatoes, seeded and diced
1 large cucumber, peeled, seeded, and diced
2 scallions, coarsely chopped
⅓–½ cup chopped fresh mint leaves
1 small jalapeño chile, seeded and chopped (optional)

Whisk together the olive oil, lime juice, and garlic with salt and pepper to taste. Put all the salad ingredients in a medium-size serving bowl, add the dressing, and toss well. Refrigerate for 30 minutes before serving.

Yield: 6 to 8 servings

The Bookwomen of Encinitas, California, was born on June 25, 1992, when Cheri Caviness started a book club as a birthday present to herself. "I had always wanted to be in a book club, so I invited friends and neighbors from near and far to get one started," says Caviness, a human resources management consultant.

Caviness enjoys entertaining, and members come from all over San Diego County to meetings in her home. She creates a book-themed meal for the Bookwomen each month.

"They look forward to finding out what I've come up with," says Caviness. "We stand in the kitchen, sipping wine and eating appetizers, and catch up with one another's lives, and over dinner we discuss the books. It's quite delicious."

Caviness's meals have included South American stuffed pork loin for Isabel Allende's *The House of the Spirits* and shrimp creole for Zora Neale Hurston's *Their Eyes Were Watching God* (see p. 427). Caviness describes her group as casual about reading requirements. Members are encouraged to come even if they haven't finished reading that month's selection. "Just don't expect us not to give away the ending!" says Caviness.

Reading selections are made by mutual consensus, after a brief discussion. The group tends to favor fiction, especially by authors from other countries and cultures.

"In America we live in isolation. Until something affects us directly, we're often unaware," says Caviness. "Fiction can take you to history and introduce you to events. But some of our best discussions have come from reading nonfiction, such as Naomi Wolf's exploration of the relationship between beauty and female identity, *The Beauty Myth;* Carl Sagan's reflections on scientific thought, *The Demon-Haunted World;* and Geraldine Brooks's *Nine Parts of Desire.*

"In *Nine Parts of Desire,* Geraldine Brooks spoke with women from many different countries, cultures, and 'versions' of Islam, and did an excellent job of studying the Koran and comparing cultural practices with Islamic teaching," says Caviness. "She broke down many stereotypes Americans have about Islamic beliefs and practices. With ongoing United States involvement in Iraq and elsewhere, this book helps Americans understand Islam and the lives of women in other parts of the world."

Caviness's husband, Fred Saifnia, is from Iran and "always has something to say when we read a book about the Middle East," says Caviness. "He has lived in the United States for forty years, so he also learns new things when he reads books like *Nine Parts of Desire.*"

Having an Iranian man at the meeting provided a valuable perspective for the group's discussion.

Saifnia was surprised and pleased to learn that the Ayatollah Khomeini's daughters were educated women. "He has never lived in Iran under the present religious regime," says Caviness, "and was fascinated that even under a fundamentalist government, Iran didn't seem to be completely oppressive to women, as evidenced by large numbers of college-educated women—including women from the Ayatollah's own family," says Caviness. "He thought it was interesting that some of the women had made adjustments in their attitudes and behaviors to accommodate fundamentalism in order to maintain their position in society."

No Ordinary Time:
Franklin and Eleanor Roosevelt—
The Home Front in World War II

Doris Kearns Goodwin

SIMON & SCHUSTER, *1994*

(available in paperback from Simon & Schuster, 1995)

IN FIVE YEARS President Franklin D. Roosevelt transformed a weak, isolationist United States into the most powerful military force in the world, ready to take up arms in defense of democracy. Although his wife, Eleanor, advised and supported him in this effort, she also championed causes of her own. During her husband's presidency, Eleanor became a model of independence, intelligence, and compassion for women throughout the world.

No Ordinary Time, Doris Kearns Goodwin's engrossing history of the home front during World War II, sheds light on the personal and political lives of these two remarkable leaders, while depicting the atmosphere of fear and uncertainty in the United States during the war years and the determination of a country united in its resolve to defend its way of life.

Goodwin links the story of America's mobilization for war with the personal stories of Franklin and Eleanor. The First Couple, and the welcoming, chaotic White House they presided over, inspired hope in Americans struggling through the Great Depression and World War II.

With world peace to consider, food should have been a source of pleasure and distraction for the president. Roosevelt loved good food, being "especially fond of quail and pheasant cooked so rare as to be bloody. He loved oyster crabs, out-of-the-way country cheeses, and peach cobbler."

But Mrs. Henrietta Nesbitt, head housekeeper at the Roosevelt White House, refused to indulge the president's taste for fine cuisine. A former Hyde Park neighbor of the Roosevelts, Nesbitt had never worked outside her home before coming to the White House at age fifty-nine. She was overwhelmed. Eleanor hired her to plan meals and oversee a staff of thirty-two, but Mrs. Nesbitt's cooking proved bland and uninspired. She served the president chicken—and then sweetbreads—so relentlessly that, in a memo to Eleanor, Franklin complained, "I am getting to the point where my stomach positively rebels and this does not help my relations with foreign powers. I bit two of them today."

Academics have long speculated about why Eleanor could not bring herself to fire the headstrong Mrs. Nesbitt. In *From Hardtack to Homefries: An Uncommon History of American Cooks and Meals* (Penguin, 2002), culinary historian Barbara Haber suggests that Mrs. Nesbitt and Eleanor hoped to set an example for the nation by practicing frugality in the White House. Mrs. Nesbitt's *White House Diary* (Doubleday, 1948) offers some support for this theory. In an early entry, she writes: "Mrs. Roosevelt and I had our economy program all mapped out and we were going to stick to it. With so many Americans hungry, it was up to the head house of the nation to serve economy meals and act as an example."

In contrast to her cooking skills, Mrs. Nesbitt's baking was excellent. Eleanor and Franklin had bought Mrs. Nesbitt's pies and strudels to serve at large parties in Hyde Park. When Roosevelt was running for governor of New York, Mrs. Nesbitt supplied his campaign with baked goods. After examining Mrs. Nesbitt's collection of recipes in *The Presidential Cookbook: Feeding the Roosevelts and Their Guests* (Doubleday, 1951), Haber concludes that Mrs. Nesbitt's cooking was, at its best, "uninspired, but at its worst . . . downright bad," whereas "almost all of her recipes for cookies, cakes, and pies are appealing, and some are unusual."

Mrs. Nesbitt's Angel Food Cake with Lemon Cream

Henrietta Nesbitt's recipe for angel food cake, Eleanor's favorite, falls into the latter category. The addition of almond extract gives this cake a distinctively delicious flavor and smell, and distinguishes it from most other angel food cakes, which commonly call for vanilla extract. If you prefer vanilla, though, feel free to substitute. Just don't forget to add a dollop of our Lemon Cream, which turns an old-fashioned favorite into a delicious new deal.

1¼ cups egg whites (10–12 eggs)
1½ teaspoons cream of tartar
1½ cups granulated sugar

½ teaspoon almond extract
1 cup sifted cake flour
¼ teaspoon salt

Lemon Cream for topping (see below)

1. Preheat oven to 375° F. Beat the egg whites until foamy. Add the cream of tartar, then gradually add 1 cup of the sugar, beating continually, until the whites stand up in peaks. Beat in the almond extract. Sift flour. Sift together the remaining ½ cup sugar, flour, and salt. Gently fold flour mixture into egg whites, ½ cup at a time, just until flour is moistened.
2. Pour the batter into an ungreased 10-inch tube pan and bake 30–35 minutes, until the top feels springy to the touch. Invert the cake pan and stand it on a bottle to cool.
3. When the cake is completely cooled, loosen its edges by running a spatula or thin knife around the edge of the pan. Gently shake the cake onto a serving plate. Top with Lemon Cream and garnish with strawberries.

Yield: 8 to 10 servings

LEMON CREAM

½ cup heavy cream
¼ cup confectioners' sugar

½ cup lowfat lemon yogurt

1. Beat the whipping cream and confectioners' sugar until soft peaks form.
2. Fold in the lemon yogurt. Serve immediately.

BOOK CLUB PROFILE

Dedicated to promoting women in careers in history, the Institute for Research in History launched a variety of initiatives in New York City in the 1970s. One of those initiatives—helping women to organize book clubs around their interests in history—spawned the Urban and Women's History Book Club. Even after the Institute for Research in History closed its doors, the book club endured. Today, fifteen women of the Urban and Women's History Book Club continue to meet monthly in homes and apartments in and around New York City to discuss historical nonfiction.

To choose books, the club consults the Bancroft Prize in American History list of winners. They have tackled Ira Berlin's *Many Thousands Gone: The First Two Centuries of Slavery in North America* and Joseph J. Ellis's *Founding Brothers: The Revolutionary Generation.* "We read books that we wouldn't otherwise read, and we get to discuss them with people who have good ideas and superb critical thinking skills," says Edith Gordon, a member since 1988. "This is a very stimulating group."

Gordon and other members are clearly dedicated to the group. A former elementary-school teacher and independent historian, Gordon joined the group after she met a member at a historical conference they both attended. Now a resident of Long Island, Gordon travels one hour and forty minutes each way to attend monthly meetings.

Members of the Urban and Women's History Book Club are middle-class women in their forties through seventies who share "a liberal outlook." Many teach or are retired from teaching at city colleges. Their professional backgrounds and interest in history make them discriminating readers. "We pay a lot of attention to footnotes," says Gordon. "We look for whether quotes are attributed to primary sources, and we are very critical of secondary source attributions."

Their interest in footnotes came in handy when they read *No Ordinary Time,* a book they characterize as "extraordinary." "We read the book before Doris Kearns Goodwin got into trouble," says Gordon, a reference to charges of plagiarism leveled against Goodwin in 2001. The charges initially concerned Kearns's 1989 book, *The Fitzgeralds and the Kennedys: An American Saga* (which the group also read), although *No Ordinary Time* also came under close scrutiny. "We looked closely at the footnotes and felt she had done a good job," reports Gordon.

Group members who had lived through World War II found a special thrill in reading the detailed information about the period supplied by Goodwin. "This book gave us insight into what was going on during those years beyond our personal experience. It gave us an added dimension," says Gordon.

The club has read other texts about the period, including Blanche Wiesen Cook's volumes on Eleanor Roosevelt, so their discussion has often returned to *No Ordinary Time.* "Other readings have been more critical of FDR," says Gordon. "If we read *No Ordinary Time* today, maybe we would be more critical of the work. But we found that we could push beyond Goodwin's personal opinions about FDR and appreciate the book for its wealth of information."

In addition to monthly meetings, the women of the Urban and Women's History Book Club take an annual "June Jaunt" to places of historical interest. These direct encounters with historical sites and materials enhance members' understanding and appreciation of historical events, and give them a chance to socialize. They have visited the Rockefeller Estate in Tarrytown, New York; the William Sidney Mount Collection on Long Island; and neighborhoods such as historic Harlem and the meatpacking district of New York City, which are gentrifying. Their excursions always end with lunch at an upscale restaurant.

The No. 1 Ladies' Detective Agency

Alexander McCall Smith

ANCHOR, *1998*

(available in paperback from Anchor, 2003)

M MA PRECIOUS RAMOTSWE's calling is to help her people solve the mysteries in their lives, so she becomes the first female private detective in Botswana. African-born Alexander McCall Smith introduces Mma Ramotswe in *The No. 1 Ladies' Detective Agency*, the first in a series of novels about the private investigator.

Following a disastrous marriage to an abusive husband and the death of her father, middle-aged Mma Ramotswe sets out to rebuild her life. She invests her inheritance in a home on Zebra Drive in Gaborone, Botswana's capital, and purchases an abandoned store on the edge of town, where she sets up her detective agency. Although she has no formal training for the job, she learns in a private detection manual that hunches and intuition, which she possesses in abundance, are the real requirements for a successful detective. What her office lacks in physical assets it makes up for in its magnificent view of acacia trees and the hills on the horizon—and in the keen intellect of its only detective.

Mma Ramotswe soon finds clients at her door, all with seemingly ordinary problems: a wife searching for her vanished husband; a father seeking knowledge of his daughter's boyfriend; a hospital investigating a doctor's questionable performance. Mma Ramotswe quickly proves her skills at cracking cases by relying on her feminine intuition, wisdom, logic, and her inherent understanding of people. Mma Ramotswe is most preoccupied with the moral questions behind each case, and often offers direct and practical advice to her clients in addition to solving their crimes. She quickly resolves most of her cases, but the solution to a more serious mystery, the disappearance of a young boy, eludes her.

Mma Ramotswe enjoys life's simple pleasures: a pot of tea, which she shares with clients and friends, and a pot of stew. A teapot and three mugs are a few of the items on the small inventory list for her detective agency.

"Bush tea is very important to Mma Ramotswe and her assistant, Mma Makutsi," explains McCall

Smith. "It is a reddish tea, caffeine-free, which is also known as *rooibos*, or red bush tea. It is an acquired taste, and may be drunk with honey, in which case it is called honeybush tea."

Mma Ramotswe offers her own advice about bush tea. When asked if bush tea is better with honey or without, she responds:

If anybody says to you: You should not add honey to bush tea! You can reply: The people who grow that tea add honey, so why can't I? That should end the argument. If the people continue to argue, then you should tell them to quiet.

PUMPKIN SOUP

Mma Ramotswe prepares her favorite comfort food, a pot of stewed pumpkin, as she contemplates her cases. "She loved standing in the kitchen, stirring the pot, thinking over the events of the day," writes McCall Smith. Pumpkin gives her food for thought:

It was time to take the pumpkin out of the pot and eat it. In the final analysis, that was what solved these big problems of life. You could think and think and get nowhere, but you still had to eat your pumpkin. That brought you down to earth. That gave you a reason for going on. Pumpkin.

We created a delicious Pumpkin Soup that we think Mma Ramotswe would savor. Make a pot of the soup when you're in need of contemplation. Honey makes a nice topping for this soup, along with peanuts. And if anyone argues, tell them to "quiet."

3 tablespoons butter
2 large shallots, chopped
1 large red onion, chopped
1 carrot, diced
1 29-ounce can puréed pumpkin
3 tablespoons tomato paste
3 cups chicken or vegetable broth
2 cups water
3 teaspoons chili powder

1 teaspoon ground coriander
¼ teaspoon cardamom
¼ teaspoon ground cloves
1 teaspoon ground cumin
1 teaspoon sugar
Salt and pepper
1 cup chopped roasted salted peanuts
2½ tablespoons honey (optional)

1. Melt the butter in a stockpot. Add the shallots, onion, and carrot and sauté until soft, about 10 minutes.

2. Add the pumpkin, tomato paste, broth, water, chili powder, coriander, cardamom, cloves, cumin, and sugar. Bring to a boil over medium heat, stirring occasionally. Reduce heat and simmer, covered, 30 minutes. Add salt and pepper to taste.

3. Ladle into bowls. Sprinkle liberally with peanuts and top each serving with 1 teaspoon honey if desired.

Yield: 8 servings

BOOK CLUB PROFILE

The Four Major Food Groups and Literary Society of Anchorage, Alaska, began as a dinner club but quickly evolved into a book group. The nine-member club has its own definition of the four major food groups—salt, sugar, fat, and chocolate—and all four are in abundance when the club meets.

Group member Dana Stabenow, an Edgar Award–winning mystery author, cohosts Alaska Public Radio's *Book Talk Alaska* with Janice Weiss, the book group's founder. Stabenow enjoys the escape from crime fiction offered by her book club, which reads women's fiction, science fiction, biographies, and history. They made an exception, however, for *No. 1 Ladies' Detective Agency,* a mystery that quickly became a club favorite. "Alexander McCall Smith has a wonderful you-are-there descriptive style. Now we all want to visit Botswana," says Stabenow.

The Four Major Food Groups and Literary Society includes four teachers, two corrections officers, a software writer, and a potter. They all admired McCall Smith's detective, Mma Ramotswe, for "her strength, her humor, and for embracing private investigation as a way of bringing people's lives into order," says Stabenow. "Yet even she can be snookered," she says, referring to one case where Mma Ramotswe is outwitted. The group also explored whether the episodic structure of the book worked, as compared to one overall story arc, and agreed that it did.

Suspense was in the air the night the group met to discuss *No. 1 Ladies' Detective Agency*: They turned themselves into food detectives and created a mystery-ingredient dinner to complement their discussion. "We had to solve the mystery of the key ingredient in each dish," says Stabenow, "and one member's was pumpkin, a favorite of Mma Ramotswe."

More Food for Thought

Kathy Barber's menu for the South Florida Preschool PTA Book Club's discussion of *The No. 1 Ladies' Detective Agency* featured foods mentioned in the mystery: pumpkin seeds, candy pumpkins, pumpkin pie, pumpkin bars, brown rice with small chunks of honeydew and cantaloupe melon, and a fruit and melon salad. For drinks, Barber created her own South African Lion Beer by placing Lion stickers on cans of Budweiser and served South African wines. She also served the red bush tea Mma Ramotswe adores and gave each guest red bush tea as a party favor.

The African feast was served on a blue cloth, because Mma Ramotswe's wedding dinner was served on one. To create the atmosphere of a detective agency, the board game *Clue* was displayed, along with large magnifying glasses, and a chalk body outline was drawn on the tile floor.

Taking the mystery theme to another level, book group members came dressed as their favorite detective or crime fighter, including Nancy Drew, Sherlock Holmes, Dr. Watson, Miss Marple, Magnum PI, and Mma Ramotswe. Barber, attired in a trench coat and a fedora and carrying a stuffed eagle, was Sam Spade of *The Maltese Falcon*.

BUSH TEA

Bush tea is made from the tips of leaves of red bush, or *rooibos*. Discovered thousands of years ago, *rooibos* remains one of the most popular herbs in South Africa, commonly used for food coloring or flavoring as well as for tea. Grown in the Western Cape region of South Africa, the naturally caffeine-free tea is thought to have health-giving properties. Red bush tea is now widely available in the United States at grocery stores or can be ordered directly from distributors (see Purchasing Information, p. 499).

October Suite

Maxine Clair

RANDOM HOUSE, 2001

(available in paperback from Random House, 2002)

SEPARATED FOR THE first time from her childhood friends and family in Ohio, October Brown arrives in Wyandotte County, Kansas, in 1950 to begin her first teaching job. October finds lodging in a boardinghouse for teachers. Despite the strict moral code for the boarding-house—no smoking, no drinking, and no men allowed in the rooms—October falls in love and becomes pregnant by a married man. She returns home to Chillicothe, Ohio, to have the baby.

In Chillicothe, October's two aunts and her sister, Vergie, support her through pregnancy and childbirth. Once the baby, David, is born, October cannot seem to warm to him. Vergie and her husband, Gene, are unable to conceive and are desperate for a child. They wait breathlessly for the unimaginable to occur, and it does: October gives the baby to Vergie and Gene to raise and returns to her life in Kansas.

The consequences of simple decisions are never simple, of course. *October Suite* is the story of October's struggle to live with her fateful decision, her troubled and evolving relationship with Vergie, and her desire to be close to her son. October's story is subtly intertwined with a terrible childhood secret that the sisters share as it follows them hauntingly into adulthood.

Maxine Clair's novel immerses readers in the Midwest of the 1950s, complete with racial segregation, moral strictures, and the excitement of an emerging jazz scene. *October Suite* resonates with jazz and blues riffs as the music gradually makes its way from New York to midwestern clubs.

Hearty down-home cooking fills the pages of *October Suite*. October and her friends enjoy barbecue, meatloaf, potato salad (see p. 187), rib sandwiches, cole slaw, fried catfish, biscuits, cornbread, beans, baked ham, and sweet-potato pie (see p. 423).

Most interesting are the ways that food seems to reflect or play a role in the relationships between the characters. October's deep longing for a relationship with David sometimes expresses itself in food. For Christmas she prepares him mincemeat cookies. The foods she prepares for David's weeklong stay—"a freezer full of hamburger patties she had seasoned herself, corn on the cob she had blanched herself, baked chocolate-chip cookies, and a jar full of quarters for Popsicles"—reveal her anxiety and anticipation of his visit, and her desire to please him.

KATHY GALLIGAN'S DEVILED EGGS

Deviled eggs have graced American picnic baskets and party spreads throughout the twentieth century. Some have suggested that the portability of deviled eggs played a role in their popularity, providing a quick meal for travelers when restaurants were sparse. "And for African Americans in the age of Jim Crow," writes John T. Edge, director of the Mississippi-based Southern Foodways Alliance, "a shoebox stuffed with good eats was not so much a gustatory choice as a matter of practicality," because blacks were often denied seating beside white diners.

When Vergie, Gene, David, and October head out for a picnic, Vergie brings—what else?—deviled eggs.

Kathy Galligan served these deviled eggs to her book club, the Novel Women of Wenham, Massachusetts. "I had never made deviled eggs before, so I created my own recipe," says Galligan. She served the eggs with other pickups, like veggies and dip, turkey and cheddar cheese kabobs, and cherry preserves and cream cheese on crackers.

This recipe is devilishly simple, but the taste is heavenly.

6 hard-cooked eggs, peeled
2 tablespoons mayonnaise
1–2 teaspoons Balsamic Vinaigrette
  (see below)

Salt and pepper
Capers or green olives,
  for garnish

1. Slice each egg in half lengthwise and remove the yolks. In a bowl, mash together the egg yolks, mayonnaise, and vinaigrette. Season to taste with salt and pepper.
2. Stuff egg whites with yolk mixture. Top each egg with a caper or a halved green olive. Serve slightly chilled.

Yield: 6 to 8 servings

Balsamic Vinaigrette

5 tablespoons extra-virgin olive oil

2 tablespoons balsamic vinegar

½ teaspoon Dijon-style mustard

Salt and pepper

Mix the first three ingredients well. Season with salt and pepper.

Yield: ⅓ cup

Pink Lady

The Lovely Ladies Book Club of Bryan–College Station, Texas, adopted pink as their color in 1998 when member Dianne Stropp crafted pink and black book bags as Christmas gifts for the group. So it was fitting that the ladies celebrated the Christmas 2003 season with this recipe for a Pink Lady, a drink made with gin, cream, and a splash of rosy grenadine.

"The Pink Lady is a drink just like us: a little tart, quite smooth, and very pretty," quips member Susan Parker. "It's a drink that makes a festive beginning to a special evening."

In *October Suite*, October's boyfriend, Leon, serves Pink Ladies to October and Cora, her friend, as Miles Davis's "Someday My Prince Will Come" plays in the background. What could be more 1950s?

As you discuss *October Suite*, let a Pink Lady transport you.

NOTE: Sour mix is a bartending staple consisting of lemon juice mixed with a sugar syrup. You can buy a premade sour mix or easily make your own, which will taste much better, with our recipe.

1½ ounces (3 tablespoons) gin

3 ounces (6 tablespoons) sour mix (see below)

1 ounce (2 tablespoons) light cream

Splash of grenadine

Fill a cocktail shaker with ice. Add all the ingredients, shake well, and strain into a martini glass or other festive glass.

Yield: 1 drink

Sour Mix

½ cup Simple Syrup (see p. 172)   ½ cup fresh lemon juice

Mix syrup and lemon juice. That's it!

Yield: 1 cup

BOOK CLUB PROFILE

"We look beyond relationship books," says Pat Houser, associate editor of *Black Issues Book Review* and founder of the Ebony Book Club of Brooklyn, New York. "We look for books that are different."

The Ebony Book Club (EBC), founded by Houser in 1996, now has seventeen members, all African-American women in their twenties through sixties, including retired school-teachers, editors, clerical workers, a nurse, and an aspiring actress. As a board member of the National Book Club Conference, an organization that promotes reading by creating "the world's largest book club meeting once a year," Houser brings many reading ideas to her group. The members read serious fiction, literary fiction, mysteries, biographies, and social commentary, all by African-American authors. "The quality of the writing makes a big difference to our group," says Houser. "We look for well-written books." Favorites include Bernice McFadden's *Sugar* (see p. 422), Sister Souljah's *The Coldest Winter Ever* (see p. 71), and Solomon Jones's *Pipe Dream,* about four Philadelphia crack addicts wrongly accused of murder.

Group members share a love of good books—and of food. After the discussion they sit down to a full meal provided by the host, including appetizers (Swedish meatballs [see p. 296], deviled eggs, pigs-in-a-blanket), entrée (honey-glazed chicken, red beans and rice, macaroni and cheese), dessert (banana pudding, cheesecake [see pp. 144 and 271], rum cake), and drinks (iced tea, pink lemonade, mixed fruit punch).

The EBC aspires to be much more than just a reading and eating club. Since 1996, the EBC has evolved into a force for promoting a love of literature in the greater Brooklyn African-American community. It has brought authors and community members together to exchange ideas, build networks, and celebrate the authors' work. The EBC's April 2003 anniversary literary luncheon, which was open to the entire community, brought authors Bernice McFadden, Solomon Jones, and Denene Milner to the Two Steps Down Restaurant in Brooklyn, where they discussed their books over French toast and banana pancakes. For their November 2002 Open House, which was designed to introduce the EBC to prospective members and other book clubs, author Shawne Johnson presented her debut novel, *Getting Our Breath Back,* about three sisters growing up in Philadelphia in the 1960s and 1970s.

The EBC enjoys more intimate meetings with guest authors, too. Their first pre-anniversary luncheon, for members only, was held in March 2002 at the Brooklyn Marriott Hotel. There members ate and talked with Martha Southgate, author of *The Fall of Rome,* the fictional story of a young black boy attending an all-white prep school. "This was an enlightening event," recalls Houser. "The fact that Southgate attended a prep school similar to the one depicted in *The Fall of Rome* led members to recount their own educational experiences." Houser revealed how, as an elementary-school student, she had been bused from an all-black school to a gifted program in a predominantly white neighborhood. "I especially identified with the isolation felt by Rashid Bryson, the black adolescent in Southgate's book," she says. "Our discussion of the book's racial issues coupled with our own personal experiences emphasized how differently blacks and whites view even the simplest things."

Some of the group's most meaningful interactions with authors happen over the phone, on conference calls. "Some members of our group prefer conference calls to visits by the author," says Houser. "The telephone acts as a barrier and helps shy group members relax. People speak up more." The group names its chat with Maxine Clair, author of *October Suite,* as one of its most memorable evenings.

Before the call, group discussion focused on the book's mother-daughter relationship. According to Houser: "Most members of our group are mothers, so October's dilemma really hit home. We talked about whether, if in need, we would be able to give up a child. And would we want the child back?" Group members also enjoyed learning about the lives of midwestern schoolteachers in the 1950s, including the boardinghouse conditions, marriage regulations, and definitions of morality.

When Clair spoke with the EBC, conversation turned to the origins of the main character, October Brown. She had first appeared as a minor character in one of Clair's short stories in her collection, *Rattlebone,* which the EBC had read. "We wanted to know how Clair managed to capture events that appeared in *Rattlebone* and seamlessly integrate them into the scenes that she presented in *October Suite,*" says Houser. Had she revisited the pages of *Rattlebone,* pondering the detailed sequence of events as she wrote *October Suite*? Had she reread the original text in its entirety? We were truly amazed to discover that she hadn't." Clair also shared with the group how her life experiences—her relationship to her sister, her career as a teacher—influenced the writing of *October Suite*.

"Some members had wanted to read a racier book than *October Suite*," says Houser. "But after talking to the author, the whole group went back and reread sections of the book. We all loved it."

One Thousand White Women:
The Journals of May Dodd

Jim Fergus

ST. MARTIN'S, *1998*

(available in paperback from St. Martin's, 1999)

JIM FERGUS's inventive novel is based on a true historical incident: the 1854 proposal by a Northern Cheyenne chief that the United States Army trade one thousand white women (to be wives for his warriors) for one thousand horses, to assist with the Cheyenne's assimilation into white culture. In *One Thousand White Women: The Journals of May Dodd*, Fergus imagines that President Ulysses S. Grant approves the deal.

The women sent to the Cheyenne are a collection of misfits, criminals, and the mentally ill. Among the volunteers for the Brides for Indians program is May Dodd, who records the journey west in her journal. Raised in an affluent Chicago home, May was sent by her father to an asylum after she became the mistress of one of his employees. May pens the adventures of the colorful group of new brides and shares intimate accounts of her new life as the wife of Chief Little Wolf. Through May, Fergus gives a sometimes whimsical, often tragic portrait of Native American history, politics, and religion in the old American West.

Jim Fergus offered his thoughts on the role of food in *One Thousand White Women*:

I suppose it's been done, but it seems unimaginable to me that anyone could write a novel that did not include at least some mention of food. To me this would be like writing a novel without weather, or landscape. For my part, I'm always worried about what my characters are going to eat, which is a metaphoric as well as an actual concern. On the most fundamental level, if they don't eat, how can they live, either in the imagination (both the author's and the reader's) or in the world they inhabit?

The matter of food and sustenance seemed particularly acute in the case of *One Thousand White Women*. In sending May Dodd and the other women into the wilderness to live with Cheyenne Indians, I felt a responsibility to understand intimately how they would be fed and nourished. At the same time,

May and her friends were charged with instructing the Cheyennes about the white world; they had a responsibility to teach their hosts a little something about our culinary arts. So food and the conviviality inherent in the activities of cooking and eating serve as a great common denominator and cultural bridge.

But of course, food is much more than that. All hunter-gatherer societies lived in constant fear of a sudden scarcity of game and wild fruits and legumes as a result of drought and other natural disasters. For this reason, the acquisition, preparation, and consumption of food held tremendous spiritual and practical significance to Native Americans. It is important to remember that the Plains Indian tribes were subdued, finally, not so much by the white man's superior military strength, as the decimation of the great buffalo herds they depended on for their livelihood. *One Thousand White Women* describes a brief summer of bounty in those last days of the free Cheyennes. Knowing how things must end for them, and for my women, I wanted them at least to eat well.

As Fergus describes, food is a significant part of the cultural exchange in *One Thousand White Women*.

At first, Cheyenne food does not suit May's palate. She writes that sometimes the "cooking scents are actually appetizing, at other times, the stench rising from the pot is so perfectly revolting that I can hardly bear it." At a wedding feast for May and other brides, the Cheyenne wives prepare boiled dog, much to the horror of the new brides. But May soon becomes accustomed to regular meals of buffalo, deer, and antelope.

She is also initially reluctant to participate in the tribe's communal cooking activities. Although she has an interest in culinary arts, she envisions preparing a "lovely little French dish" such as *coq au vin* for her tentmates. But she soon forgets such fancies. May's new life means constant physical effort. Food preparation for the tribe involves digging roots, and May becomes "competent in all aspects of skinning, butchering, scraping and tanning hides, drying meats and cooking over the fire."

INDIAN FRY BREAD

Brother Anthony, a Benedictine monk sent to live with the Cheyenne, teaches the white women and the native women to bake bread, and their passion for bread leads to calamity, and important realizations. When Quiet One, a wife of Little Wolf's, bakes bread, she confuses arsenic powder with baking powder. The mix-up is not fatal, but many tribe members fall ill, and the event is the catalyst for a tribal council to discuss arsenic, which the tribe had been using to poison predatory wolves. At the end of the meeting, Chief Little Wolf, who has consumed the bread, proclaims his belief that the Great Medicine Man himself delivered the poison so Little Wolf would understand its perils, and he bans use of arsenic in the camp.

Food writer and culinary historian Mary Gunderson, author of *American Indian Cooking Before 1500: Exploring History Through Simple Recipes* (Blue Earth Books, 2000), told us that corn was the grain most often grown and used by Native Americans over the centuries. As settlement pushed west, the United States claimed more land, and by the late 1800s, most Indian tribes were moved to reservations. In place of traditional hunting and gardening, tribes were given such commodities as wheat flour and lard.

"Indian tribes across the country hadn't grown wheat," says Gunderson. "It was an Old World grain. Tribal people figured out ways to use the commodities, and fry bread was a marrying of American Indian and European food cultures."

Fry bread is a staple of Native American meals. The bread is fried until it's crispy and brown on the outside, yet soft on the inside. Fry bread can be served hot with sugar, honey, or jam, as a complement to stews or soups, or used to make tacos with a variety of fillings.

3 cups all-purpose flour
2 teaspoons baking powder
1 teaspoon salt

1⅓ cups warm water
Canola oil for frying

1. Combine the flour, baking powder, and salt in a mixing bowl.
2. Add 1 cup of the water, and then additional water as needed to make a soft dough. Knead the dough until smooth. Roll and then pull the dough into a 16x16-inch square. Cut into 8 square pieces, each approximately 4x4 inches.
3. Pour approximately 1 inch of oil into a heavy skillet. Heat the skillet to 400°F.
4. Fry dough pieces on both sides until golden, approximately 30–45 seconds for each side. Drain bread on brown paper or paper towels. Serve the bread hot or warm with jam, honey, or confectioners' sugar, or fill with meat and vegetables for Indian tacos.

Yield: 8 servings

Stacy Alesi started the Boca Bibliophiles, a contemporary-fiction reading group, in 1998 while working for Borders Books and Music in Boca Raton, Florida, where the group originally met. As a bookstore employee, Alesi was constantly being asked by new residents where they could find a book group.

"I thought it would be fun to sponsor a book club at a local bookstore," says Alesi. Within a few months, word had spread. Attendance peaked in an unprecedented turnout of seventy readers to discuss Arthur Golden's *Memoirs of a Geisha* (see p. 255). "The community seemed happy to have a place to drop in and discuss contemporary fiction and learn how to set up their own book groups," says Alesi.

A library associate with the Southwest County Regional Library, Alesi maintains a website (www.bookbitch.com) devoted to book reviews and promoting new authors, facilitates a mother-daughter book club, conducts book talks for local nursing homes every month, and reviews books for *Library Journal*.

When Borders stopped hosting the group, the Boca Bibliophiles began meeting in various public spaces, and membership is fluid, with anywhere from ten to twenty people attending meetings. "We don't have the continuity of membership that some groups have, but we often get very different perspectives because we don't all know one another," says Alesi, who believes that familiarity can thwart good discussion because "you pretty much know what is going to set some people off, and where their passions lie."

In selecting titles, Alesi avoids popular trends to concentrate instead on less well known books and chooses fiction that is multicultural, historical, or has interesting religious, political, or relationship-related themes. To ensure variety, she occasionally includes other genres, such as mystery or chick-lit.

Coffee and cake are provided for the evening meetings, but occasionally Alesi will select a dessert or beverage that complements the book. Tea was served when the Bibliophiles met to discuss *Memoirs of a Geisha*, scones were on tap for the British-based *White Teeth* by Zadie Smith, and there was baklava for Louis de Bernières' *Corelli's Mandolin* (see p. 81), set in Greece.

A voracious reader, Alesi devours several books a week and regularly scours the Internet, publishing-industry journals, and publishers' catalogs to find new authors or unusual books to introduce to her book club. Jim Fergus's *One Thousand White Women* was one of these "virgin" novels that appealed to Alesi. "The novel's journal format is unusual—worthy of discussion in and of itself," says Alesi.

The Boca Bibliophiles discussed the clearly delineated roles for women in 1875. "Women were good or bad, wives or whores, and that's the way they were treated by society and the men in their lives," says Alesi. "For instance, the main character, May Dodd, was committed to an insane asylum by her family because she was living with a man without the benefit of marriage." Learning about the lives of Native Americans, how they treated their women, and how whites treated them fascinated the group. The Bibliophiles also speculated on whether the events depicted could really have taken place.

Alesi frequently recommends *One Thousand White Women* to other book clubs. "It has everything a good discussion book should have," says Alesi, "an intriguing premise, fascinating characters, a diverse culture, and an historically interesting time period and setting. And it's well written and a fast read. It's a book club winner!"

More Food for Thought

For their discussion of *One Thousand White Women*, the Bookwomen of Encinitas, California, enjoyed a meal similar to one May Dodd might have eaten: Indian fry bread, dandelion greens salad—made with scallions, fresh dill, olive oil, and lemon juice—and roasted chicken. "Our group likes the adventure of trying new things and is always open to experimentation," says Cheri Caviness, who hosted the group's discussion. "But I thought it wise to stop short of serving buffalo, rabbit, or roasted rattlesnake! One of our members had a Native American cookbook, which inspired the menu for our dinner."

The Optimist's Daughter

Eudora Welty

....

1973

(available in paperback from Vintage, 1990)

O F EUDORA WELTY's generous body of fiction, nonfiction and essays, *The Optimist's Daugh-*
ter is perhaps her best-known work; it won the Pulitzer Prize in 1973. *The Optimist's Daughter*
tells the story of Laurel McKelva Hand, a middle-aged woman who travels to New Orleans from
her Chicago home to nurse her ailing father. When Judge McKelva dies, Laurel boards a train for
her hometown of Mount Salus, Mississippi. There, her six bridesmaids, as they still call themselves, and old family friends embrace her in her grief. Her time in Mount Salus triggers childhood memories and thoughts of her mother and husband, both gone. Embraced by friends and by
the place that she knew as a child, Laurel mulls her past, gaining new understanding of memory
and loss and fresh insight into the relationships she now must negotiate.

The importance of place infuses the pages of *The Optimist's Daughter.* Laurel's mother, Becky,
reminisces lovingly of her childhood "up home" in West Virginia and dies in despair, believing that she was "somewhere that was neither home nor 'up home,' that she was left among
strangers."

Fay, Judge McKelva's second wife, feels alienated and alone away from her home state of Texas,
declaring in tears in the hospital waiting room, "I'm *not* from Mississippi. I'm from Texas!" And
Laurel feels torn between the pull of her childhood home in Mississippi and her adult home in
Chicago. The womenfolk of Mount Salus understand the implications for Laurel of her decision to
leave for Chicago rather than set down roots in Mount Salus. As Mrs. Pease, a family friend,
warns, "Once you leave after this, you'll always come back as a visitor."

It is no wonder that Mississippi plays an important role in Eudora Welty's work. She never
really left home. Born in Jackson in 1909, Welty spent her entire life in that town, aside from a few
years of college, and died in a Jackson hospital in 2001. She traveled throughout rural Mississippi
between 1933 and 1936 as a publicist for the Works Progress Administration (WPA), part of a fed-

eral government effort to chronicle American foodways, collecting recipes "gleaned from ante-bellum homes." Welty weaves the scenes and smells and tastes of her beloved Mississippi throughout the pages of *The Optimist's Daughter.*

SOUTHERN CHEESE STRAWS

It is in honor of Welty's ties to her home state of Mississippi that we include a quintessentially southern treat. Cheese straws, a rich and flaky appetizer, are a fixture at southern parties. In her biography of Welty, Ann Waldron notes that cheese straws were served at the "flurry" of graduation parties given for "every girl in the senior class." They were invented in the South before refrigeration as a way for people to avoid wasting food: After breakfast, folks would mix leftover biscuit dough with cheese, form them into "straws," and bake them in an oven that was still hot from the morning meal.

Edna Earle, a character in Welty's novel *The Ponder Heart* (1954), claims that beating the batter three hundred times is the secret to the success of cheese straws.

¾ cup grated medium or sharp cheddar cheese

4 tablespoons unsalted butter, softened

1–2 tablespoons ice water

¾ cups all-purpose flour

⅛ teaspoon salt

⅛ teaspoon cayenne pepper

1. Stir the cheese and butter together. Add the ice water and blend.
2. In a separate bowl, combine the flour, salt, and cayenne. Stir into the cheese mixture until blended. Wrap the dough in plastic and chill until very firm, at least 2 hours.
3. Preheat oven to 350°F. Cut the dough into 4 equal pieces. Using your hands, on a lightly floured surface roll each piece of dough into ¼-inch-diameter cylinders. If the tubes get unworkably long, just cut them into more sections. Cut dough into straws 7–8 inches long.
4. Place the straws on an ungreased cookie sheet. Bake for 12–15 minutes until golden brown.
5. When cool, store in airtight container.

Yield: Approximately 40 straws

MINT JULEP

As a Depression-era WPA worker, Eudora Welty collected recipes from various parts of Mississippi for the Mississippi Advertising Commission, generously noting that "Yankees are welcome to make these dishes. Follow the directions and success is assured." One recipe she included in this study was the mint julep, a classic southern drink. Welty collected the recipe from Mrs. T. C. Billups, a premier hostess from Columbus, Mississippi, who commented that the drink "is refreshing and carries with it all the charm of the Old South when life was less strenuous than it is today, when brave men and beautiful women loved and laughed and danced the hours away." Try our own concoction (on p. 172), meant to conjure the days of Welty's youth.

BOOK CLUB PROFILE

The members of Judy Schroeder's Bloomington, Indiana, book club almost all have some association with Indiana University. Schroeder recently retired as editor of the university's alumni magazine; others are active or retired faculty and staff.

Schroeder's book club reads fiction, personal memoirs, and historical nonfiction, and prefers directed, purposeful meetings. "This group is extremely focused on the book," says Schroeder. "We don't do a lot of chitchat." Meetings start promptly at 7 P.M. and end at 9:00, a discipline that works well for the busy group members, all in their fifties, sixties, or seventies.

Schroeder's group admired *The Optimist's Daughter* for its hidden depth. Members at first believed the book was a straightforward telling of a daughter's loss, but through discussion came to appreciate the book's complex rendering of class issues and the father-daughter relationship. "We saw how carefully crafted it was, something we hadn't really seen when we first read it," says Schroeder. "It made us think about how we have coped with losses in our own lives."

Palace Walk

Naguib Mahfouz

DOUBLEDAY, *1990*

(available in paperback from Anchor, 1990)

Published in 1956, *Palace Walk*, the first volume of Naguib Mahfouz's acclaimed Cairo trilogy, takes readers into the Cairo neighborhood and home of an upper-middle-class merchant, al-Sayyid Ahmad, his long-suffering wife, Amina, and their five children. It is a critical time in the history of Egypt: the early twentieth century during and immediately following the First World War, when Egyptian nationalists are struggling to shake free of the British Protectorate.

Al-Sayyid Ahmad's authority over his family parallels British authority in Egypt. Inside the household, it is a pivotal time in the lives of family members, who yearn for freedom from the father's tyrannical, narcissistic governance. A series of domestic crises unfold: Amina, an obedient, submissive wife, contends with her husband's nightly debauched revels. The older sons, the lustful Yasin and the idealistic, patriotic Fahmy, behave in ways their father views as shameful, and conflicts arise around appropriate marriages for the daughters; their untraditional behavior later challenges Ahmad's authority. Outside the Ahmad household, the focus shifts to the streets and Fahmy's involvement in the nationalist movement.

Against this backdrop of Egyptian modernization and the struggle for independence, Mahfouz details his characters' fears, passions, and ambivalence, portraying universal themes of family life: birth, death, courtship, marriage, career, generational conflict, sibling rivalry, obedience, and rebellion.

Mahfouz carefully details the daily routines and rituals that shape the lives of the characters in al-Sayyid Ahmad's home.

Amina's domain is the oven room—the ground-floor bakery where she kneads dough—her early-morning sanctuary. For Amina, who feels she is "a deputy or representative of the ruler" in the upper levels of household, she is the "queen, with no rival to her sovereignty." Though her husband praises her only when she has prepared food to his liking, in the oven room Amina is the "mother, wife, teacher, and artist everyone respected."

The oven fire and conversation contribute to the warmth of the oven room. In preparation for Ramadan, the Muslim holy month, the room comes alive with the cooking of delicious foods, sweet fruit compotes and doughnuts and, later, the cakes and pastries for Id al-Fitr, which marks the end of Ramadan.

In contrast to the cozy atmosphere below, the top-floor dining room is the setting for the brothers' daily breakfast with their father, always a formal and strained affair reflecting the household's social hierarchy. For Yasin, Fahmy, and Kamal, this meal is their only meeting with al-Sayyid Ahmad each day, but the atmosphere keeps them from enjoying the food. Ahmad examines his sons critically before Amina delivers breakfast, and frequently scolds them as they chafe under the military atmosphere. Meanwhile, Amina stands by, ready to obey any order, after delivering fried beans and eggs, loaves of flat bread, cheese, and pickled lemons and peppers, all of which her husband greedily devours.

In contrast to the rigid breakfast scene, Amina presides over the coffee hour with the entire family, except Ahmad, who is usually out at that hour. The children gather with Amina in the first-floor sitting room, filled with colored mats and cushions, before sunset. The coffee hour is a "well loved time" to enjoy conversation and refreshments, and, in the winter, a chance to get warm by the fire.

MRS. MAHFOUZ'S MULUKHIYA
(GREEN SOUP)

Naguib Mahfouz's wife, Atiyyatallah Ibrahim, contributed a recipe for her husband's favorite dish: *mulukhiya*, or green soup. We are honored to include Mrs. Mahfouz's recipe, a tribute to a true literary giant.

The soup is made from the leaves of the *mulukhiya*, a leafy green plant unique to Egypt that has been a staple of Egyptian cooking for centuries. The plant has long been thought to have medicinal properties and has been used to treat a variety of ailments.

Popular among Egyptians, *mulukhiya* can be difficult to obtain outside the region. Mrs. Mahfouz's version calls for frozen *mulukhiya*, which is available from specialty stores and Middle Eastern grocers.

Traditionally, the *mulukhiya* leaves are chopped, stewed in chicken stock, and served in a soup. The soup is often served with meat, rice, or bread.

NOTE: The *mulukhiya* should not boil, or it will sink to the bottom of the pan.

3 cups chicken broth

1 14.1-ounce package frozen mulukhiya
   (see note)

Salt

3 tablespoons vegetable oil

15–20 garlic cloves, finely chopped

2 tablespoons ground coriander

1. Bring the broth to a boil in a medium saucepan. Reduce the heat and add the frozen *mulukhiya* and stir until thawed. It is important to keep the soup below a boil or the *mulukhiya* will become bitter. Season to taste with salt.
2. Heat the oil in a skillet and stir in garlic. Add coriander and sauté until golden brown. Stir the garlic mixture into the soup and simmer 1–2 minutes. Serve hot.

Yield: 4 to 6 servings

Mrs. Mahfouz's Labaneya
(Spinach Soup with Yogurt)

This Egyptian spinach soup, *labaneya*, makes a delicious alternative if *mulukhiya* is not available.

1 pound fresh spinach, or 1 10-ounce package
   frozen spinach

2 tablespoons vegetable oil

1 medium onion, chopped

1 leek (or 3–4 scallions), thoroughly cleaned
   and finely chopped

½ cup uncooked rice

Salt and pepper

½ teaspoon turmeric (optional)

1½ cups plain yogurt

1 clove garlic, put through a press

1 tablespoon lemon juice

1. Wash the spinach in water. Remove tough stems. Drain and slice into wide ribbons. (If using frozen spinach, thaw, wrap in paper towels to squeeze out excess moisture, and chop coarsely.)

2. Heat the oil in a large, deep skillet or Dutch oven. Add the onion and sauté until soft. Stir in the spinach and sauté gently. Add the leek or scallions, rice, and 4 cups of water and season with salt and pepper. Bring to a boil, then reduce heat and simmer gently for about 15 minutes, until the rice and spinach are cooked. Add turmeric, if using.

3. Beat together the yogurt and garlic. When the rice and spinach are done, add the yogurt mixture to the soup and stir well to combine. Heat through, but do not allow soup to boil or the yogurt will curdle. Stir in lemon juice. Serve hot.

Yield: 4 to 6 servings

BOOK CLUB PROFILE

Sharon Conway's West Hartford, Connecticut, book club began in 1989 when a group of psychotherapists started meeting to read and discuss articles about their work.

When women with other professional interests joined, the club evolved from a professional reading group to a more traditional book club. "It was an opportunity to expand our reading interests," says Conway, the only original member of the group. The group still tends to enjoy more psychologically based titles, such as Amy Bloom's *Come to Me* and Ethan Canin's *The Palace Thief,* short story collections from two contemporary authors.

Conway says the group tries to have "multimedia experiences." They seek out speaking appearances by authors whose works they have recently read and have attended lectures by Nathan Englander, author of the short-story collection *For the Relief of Unbearable Urges,* and J. M. Coetzee, author of *Disgrace* (see p. 106). When they read Mark Salzman's *Lying Awake,* about a middle-aged nun, Sister John, suffering from temporal lobe epilepsy, Conway's husband, Steve, a prominent Hartford neurologist, explained the etiology of epilepsy to the group. "Understanding the medical history behind Sister John's seizures explained her transformation," says Conway.

The group has enjoyed reading classics over the summer when they have more free time and can invest in a longer read. Favorites include nineteenth-century British novels, such as Thomas Hardy 's *Jude the Obscure* and Emily Brontë's *Wuthering Heights.*

Conway says her group generally prefers books that "take them elsewhere"—fiction or nonfiction set in another country or culture. Books that have deepened their knowledge and understanding of other cultures include Jung Chang's *Wild Swans: Three Daughters of China* (see p. 486), Jhumpa Lahiri 's *Interpreter of Maladies* (see p. 204), Ann Patchett's *Bel*

Canto (see p. 46), Rohinton Mistry's *A Fine Balance* (see p. 137) and Naguib Mahfouz's *Palace Walk*.

"Many of us felt we would love to travel to Egypt after reading *Palace Walk*," says Conway. "Mahfouz portrayed the country and culture so vividly."

Conway's group had an interesting discussion of women's rights and cultural attitudes toward women after reading *Palace Walk*. "It forced us to evaluate the female characters' roles in light of their own culture and heritage and not judge them based on our own expectations as women here in America," says Conway.

Many of the members of the group have struggled with the challenges of balancing career and family, and Conway says *Palace Walk* contributed to a charged discussion about the choices they have made, especially in contrast to Amina, the novel's female protagonist, who had so little choice in her life.

"*Palace Walk* took us into Egyptian culture," says Conway. "This book truly met the criterion of transporting us out of our suburban lives and into another culture. We recommend it highly to other book groups."

More Food for Thought

Judy Bart Kancigor of the Second Wednesday Dinner Book Club, a gourmet book club in Fullerton, California, says her group's *Palace Walk* meal was both delicious and memorable.

One member's husband is Syrian, and though *Palace Walk* was set in Egypt, he helped create a Middle Eastern meal to accompany the discussion, a meal that included tabbouleh, a bulgur salad with parsley and tomatoes; *kibbe*, a ground lamb and bulgur dish; and baklava, a pastry layered with phyllo dough, honey, and nuts.

Peace Like a River

Leif Enger

....

ATLANTIC MONTHLY, *2001*

(available in paperback from Grove, 2002)

Tʜᴇ ꜰɪʀꜱᴛ ᴍɪʀᴀᴄʟᴇ Reuben Land experiences is the gift of life itself: At birth, he gasps for air. When his father, Jeremiah, commands him to breathe, his lungs fill with life-giving air. Miracles and faith are at the core of *Peace Like a River,* Leif Enger's debut novel, a book filled with biblical references, stories of the Old West, and allusions to American literature and folklore.

From his perspective as an adult, Reuben recounts the story of his childhood in rural Minnesota in the 1960s. As eleven-year-old Reuben struggles with asthma, his younger sister, Swede, writes rhymed poetry about a hero named Sunny Sundown. Reuben and Swede share a love of cowboys and a passion for stories of the Old West.

Jeremiah, now a widower, works as a janitor to support Reuben, Swede, and their older brother, Davy. In spite of Jeremiah's station in life, he continues to perform miracles in Reuben's eyes. But when Jeremiah rescues Davy's girlfriend from two attackers, the assailants seek revenge against the family.

Davy kills them in self-defense; nevertheless he is convicted for the killings. He escapes from jail and disappears into the Badlands of North Dakota. His family soon follows, with the FBI in close pursuit. *Peace Like a River* follows the Lands' journey west and brings their story to a shattering climax.

During their search for Davy, the Lands find refuge with Roxanna Cawley, a woman who sells them gas and offers them rooms in her farmhouse in Grassy Butte, North Dakota. In Roxanna's home, the Lands leave a lifetime of meager meals behind them. Roxanna takes the chill off the North Dakota winter and nourishes the family with warm hearty meals and tales of the Wild West.

MRS. ENGER'S CINNAMON ROLLS
WITH COFFEE FROSTING

Roxanna tells the Lands about her great-uncle Howard, a gunsmith and doctor in Casper, Wyoming, who baked cinnamon rolls almost every morning. When you entered his home "you smelled pastry and coffee and oilswabbed steel," Roxanna recalls. Howard met and befriended the famous outlaw Butch Cassidy when Cassidy appeared on his doorstep and asked Howard to repair his revolver, which had been run over by a train. Cassidy's revolver was beyond repair, but Howard offered Cassidy freshly baked cinnamon rolls and "after several rolls, the young man's spirits lifted."

Roxanna loves to bake, and Howard's cinnamon rolls are a favorite. Roxanna teaches Swede to bake Howard's recipe, showing her how to thin the frosting "with coffee and a little warm butter." Roxanna describes the care Howard took with the frosting: "His especial pride was the frosting—he ordered back East for confectioner's sugar, fifty pounds at a time, and he added melted butter and a potion of strongbrew coffee and a dried vanilla bean ground fine with mortar and pestle."

The story of Roxanna's great-uncle Howard's cinnamon rolls has inspired many book clubs to re-create the pastries, including the Silicon Valley Book Club in California, the Lemmings of Rochester, Minnesota, and the Adult Book Discussion Group at the Richmond Public Library in Batavia, New York.

Author Leif Enger contributed his thoughts on the pastries to *The Book Club Cookbook*, along with his mother's recipe for cinnamon rolls. We think her version would have lifted Butch Cassidy's spirits, too.

Following is my preferred recipe for Mr. Cassidy's favorite breakfast, the cinnamon roll. Of course, given the restrictions of his lifestyle he often had to make do with certain substitutions, sweetening the dough with molasses instead of honey, for example, but the rolls taste best made this way, and I feel confident they propped up Mr. Cassidy's spirits on many a frosty Wyoming morn. The coffee was a closely guarded secret until my brother Lin stumbled over it while doing research; none have tasted this without profound gratitude.

If you set the dough to rise by 6 P.M., it's ready to knead before bedtime. You may need to get up early to bake—these sometimes overrise—but cinnamon rolls taste best at 5 A.M., and Butch was known to roll out well before dawn.

¾ cup honey

½ cup vegetable oil or lard

1 scant tablespoon yeast

2 beaten eggs

2 teaspoons salt

8 cups all-purpose flour

Melted butter

6 tablespoons ground cinnamon

2 cups sugar

For the frosting

Coffee

2 cups confectioners' sugar

2 tablespoons melted butter

1. Bring to boil 2 cups of water, honey, and oil or lard. Allow to cool.

2. Dissolve yeast in ½ cup water, with a dab of honey to hasten proofing. Put cinnamon and sugar in a bowl and mix.

3. Place cooled water-honey-oil mixture in a large mixing bowl and add the eggs and salt. Add the yeast mixture. Stir in flour; you want a fairly stiff dough, so you may need to adjust the amount.

4. Turn the dough out onto a floured surface and knead well for 15–20 minutes, until smooth and elastic. Shape into a ball, place in a greased bowl, cover, and set aside to rise for at least 3 hours.

5. Punch the dough down and knead for a few minutes. Roll the dough out thin—it will make two or three large flats. Brush the top with melted butter, then lay on a heavy coat of cinnamon and sugar. Roll flats up into tight cylinders and pinch the edges together to seal. Slice cylinders into three dozen rolls, place on jellyroll pans, and allow to rise overnight, covered.

6. Preheat oven to 350°F. Bake rolls for 18–20 minutes.

7. To make the coffee frosting: While the first batch bakes, set up a pot of strong coffee. Have a cup, then splash ½–¾ cup in a bowl containing confectioners' sugar and melted butter. Stir until smooth and not too thin. Drizzle over the warm cinnamon rolls, or spread it on with a knife.

Yield: 4 dozen 3-inch rolls

BOOK CLUB PROFILE

Mary Gay Shipley's vision was to create a true community bookstore when she opened That Bookstore in Blytheville (TBIB) on Main Street in Blytheville, Arkansas. It was 1976 and Shipley just couldn't seem to find the right name for her shop. "We couldn't decide on a name," says Shipley, "and customers would call and say, 'Oh, you're that bookstore.' Pretty soon everyone knew us as 'that bookstore' on Main Street, so we took the name formally." Shipley has created a friendly, relaxed atmosphere, where browsers can sip a cup of That Bookstore in Blytheville's Special Edition coffee, a robust Colombian blend, or relax in a rocking chair near the wood stove.

That Bookstore in Blytheville, which Shipley describes as the "cultural center for a small town in Arkansas," is decorated with tiles designed by customers, illustrating their favorite books, and the guest book is a collection of folding wood chairs signed by visiting authors. The backroom is a community center of sorts, a site of constant activity, including concerts, author lectures, programs for children, and book groups.

Since 1998, Cookie Coppedge, a friend of Shipley's and a frequent customer of That Bookstore in Blytheville, has led That Bookgroup of Cookie's in the store's backroom one night a month. The group consists of men and women in their fifites and sixties, but Shipley says, "We often have younger folks join us and we welcome their participation." Paul Shipley, Mary Gay's husband, is a member of the group, and usually contributes egg salad (see p. 458), or pimento cheese (see pp. 133–135), two group favorites, to the informal potluck buffets they serve.

That Bookgroup of Cookie's focuses on fiction. In 2003 faith was a central theme, with reading selections such as Mary Doria Russell's *The Sparrow* (see p. 407), Yann Martel's *Life of Pi* (see p. 240), and Leif Enger's *Peace Like a River*. "It was a topic we seemed to return to again and again," says Coppedge. "The nature of faith, the manifestation of the divine in each individual, and the hopelessness that results in those whose faith is crushed.

"*Peace Like a River* was like a breath of fresh air," says Coppedge. "It was good for the soul. It provided such a good balance for all of the books we read that had at their core a crisis of faith. It was an unabashed affirmation of faith and it made a wonderful ending to the year's reading."

Methodist minister Robert Armstrong, a member of the group, proved very helpful to the group's understanding of the novel. Armstrong explained details that casual readers might not have noticed, says Coppedge. "For example, the meaning behind the name of character Jeremiah Land. The biblical Jeremiah bought land outside of Jericho to encourage people to look beyond tragedies. Jeremiah Land is looking to the future and is hopeful."

The nature of miracles and faith were key to the group's discussion of *Peace Like a River*. "Reuben, the sensitive eleven-year-old narrator, is asthmatic and moves between life and death for the duration of the novel," says Coppedge. "We discussed the effect of Reuben's poor health on the narrative and traced the changes in his character as the narrative unfolded. He is a witness with a faith equivalent to that of the saints of old. As Reuben says again and again, 'Make of it what you will.'"

More Food for Thought

Peace Like a River was the 2003 reading selection of the Tale for Three Counties program, which encourages residents of Genesee, Orleans, and Wyoming counties in rural western New York State to read and discuss the same book.

"*Peace Like a River* was a perfect choice, and people are still reading and talking about it," says Leslie DeLooze, the librarian at the Richmond Memorial Library in Batavia, New York, who created the program.

"The selection for A Tale for Three Counties should have literary merit, address issues that deal with rural family life, appeal to teenagers as well as adults, and not be well known, and this novel met all of those criteria. At the time we chose *Peace Like a River*, it had not been published in paperback and was not yet widely known," says DeLooze.

Author Leif Enger visited each county to discuss his novel, and the Adult Book Discussion Group DeLooze facilitates at the Richmond Memorial Library attended his presentations. "We were enthralled by his story of how he came to writing, and how he developed the characters in the book," says DeLooze.

The group enjoys breakfast foods for their early-morning meetings, and when they met to discuss *Peace Like a River*, member Esther Marone made cinnamon rolls from a recipe she found on the Internet.

"Food is a metaphor in *Peace Like a River*, showing both the desolation of the family, such as the canned beans they eat, as well as the comfort provided by friends who care about them and prepare huge home-cooked meals for the family," says DeLooze. "Cinnamon rolls are connected to the character of Roxanna, who becomes the mother figure to the motherless children and the wife to their father."

The Perfect Storm: A True Story of Men Against the Sea

Sebastian Junger

W. W. NORTON, *1997*

(available in paperback from HarperTorch, 2000)

IN OCTOBER 1991, an unprecedented confluence of extraordinary meteorological factors created a storm off the Nova Scotia coast of such power and fury it became known as "the perfect storm." Caught in the maelstrom was the *Andrea Gail,* a swordfishing boat out of Gloucester Harbor in Massachusetts that had become known as "one of the best sword boats on the East Coast."

Bobby Shatford was a crew member on the *Andrea Gail.* Born and raised in Gloucester, Bobby hoped the money he earned from swordfishing would pay off his child support, freeing him to marry his girlfriend, Chris. Their life together was full of hard drinking, violence, devotion to each other, and, for Chris, the constant angst of waiting for Bobby's boat to pull safely into the harbor.

In *The Perfect Storm,* an account of the *Andrea Gail*'s final hours and the storm that consumed it, journalist Sebastian Junger describes the unique circumstances that created the perfect storm, the difficult and frequently tragic lives of those whose loved ones set out to sea to put seafood on the nation's tables, and the courage of those often called upon to rescue them.

What actually happened aboard the *Andrea Gail* on the howling night she went down can only be imagined, and Junger does just that—vividly. But Junger also gives the reader real-life characters like Bobby Shatford, a journalist's-eye view of the perilous lives of North Atlantic swordfishermen, and a harrowing description of what it must be like to face death on a cold and angry sea.

SWORDFISH KABOBS

It is only fitting that we included a recipe for swordfish with *The Perfect Storm*. As you enjoy the fruits of their labor it is worth contemplating the lives of swordfishermen: the risks they take when they set out to sea and the ultimate sacrifice they are too often forced to make.

2 pounds fresh swordfish
½ cup fresh lemon juice
½ teaspoon salt
¼ teaspoon dried oregano
⅛ teaspoon freshly ground black pepper
⅛ teaspoon cayenne pepper

1 teaspoon Dijon-style mustard
1 tablespoon minced garlic
2 cups Tzatziki (see recipe p. 267), thinned
   with juice of 1 lemon (about 3 tablespoons)
Bamboo skewers

1. Trim skin and dark meat from the swordfish and cut into 1½-inch cubes.

2. In a large bowl, combine the lemon juice, salt, oregano, black pepper, cayenne, mustard, and garlic. Add the fish cubes and turn to coat. Cover bowl or transfer to a plastic bag and refrigerate at least 2 hours.

3. If using bamboo skewers, soak in warm water 20 minutes before threading. Remove fish from marinade and thread onto skewers. Pour any extra marinade into a small saucepan and simmer for 2 minutes. Set aside.

4. Preheat grill or broiler, and lightly oil cooking surface. Lay kabobs on grill and cook until firm to the touch, about 8 minutes, turning to grill all sides. Baste with reserved marinade halfway through cooking time. Do not overcook. Serve accompanied with bowls of *tzatziki*. Served as an entrée, the kabobs go well with rice pilaf.

Yield: serves 5 as a main coarse, 10 to 12 as an appetizer

BOOK CLUB PROFILE

Members of the men's Pandora Book Club of Philadelphia favor nonfiction works rich in content. They also enjoy current fiction. "Sometimes you get the best discussion with fictional, controversial books," says Rudi Lea, a retired high-school teacher and administrator, who founded the group in 1996. All fifteen original members—active and retired educators, lawyers, and a physician—remain with the group today. They value the friendships the book club has spawned, and the knowledge they have gained from discussing the books. All of the members are over fifty and college-educated. Their religious orientations differ. "One of my aims was ecumenical: to bring together a mixed group of friends," Lea says, "but we try to avoid books with a religious theme."

The members of the Pandora Book Club serve simple fare at their meetings. "We do men-kind-of-food" like hoagies and pizza, says Lea. Once a year, spouses are invited to attend. At these meetings, menu offerings become distinctly more varied and upscale, encouraging longer periods of socializing before book discussion begins.

The Perfect Storm appealed to the Pandora Book Club's thirst for vivid content and real-life adventure. The superstorm described in the book, a unique and tragic convergence of several severe weather systems, fascinated the group. Marty Cohen, who hosted the meeting, played a recording of a National Public Radio interview with Sebastian Junger.

"Junger knew very little about meteorology before writing the book," says Cohen, "but he learned so much, and was able to transmit his knowledge of weather systems so clearly." The group also liked *The Perfect Storm*'s character development and tragic story line, but their discussion kept circling back to the awesome power of natural forces. Everyone tried to visualize a thirty-four-story-high wave as it was described in the book. Some of the recreational fishermen in the group recalled how it felt to set out on "iffy" days, only to find themselves facing difficult weather. "This book really got us talking," says Cohen. "It did just what a book is supposed to do: get everyone involved."

More Food for Thought

The South Florida Preschool PTA Book Club gathered at the Miami home of Donna Lyons to discuss *The Perfect Storm*, a book selected for the club's annual Couples Night, when the members invite their husbands to a potluck dinner and book discussion. "In the book, Junger discussed the rescue of sailors by Coast Guard swimmers who jump out of helicopters," says Barber, "and Donna Lyons's husband, Phil, who had served in the Air Force, explained the rigorous training that the Coast Guard who fly rescue and that Navy SEALs undergo to learn this type of open-sea recovery."

The group's *Perfect Storm* menu included a smoked seafood dip appetizer, grilled mahimahi, and New England corn pudding. "One couple came dressed in full weather gear just like the picture of the fisherman on the Gorton's Seafood packages," says member Kathy Barber. "They were singing 'Blow the Man Down' and various other sea shanties."

Personal History

Katharine Graham

....

KNOPF, *1997*

(available in paperback from Vintage, 1998)

When Katharine Graham assumed control of *The Washington Post* in 1969, she became one of the most powerful and influential women in America. In *Personal History*, Graham recounts her extraordinary life, from her privileged childhood in Washington, D.C., to her marriage to a brilliant but mentally ill husband, to her dealings, as a publisher, with labor strikes, assassinations, and presidential cover-ups.

Graham was no stranger to the newspaper business. Her father, Eugene Meyer, bought the *Post* in 1933 and worked relentlessly to increase profits. Both Graham and her mother worked in various capacities at the paper. After Katharine—or Kay, as she was known—married Phil Graham in 1940, Meyer gradually turned over operations of the paper to him, while Kay stayed home and raised their children.

Kay and Phil Graham spent the next twenty years involved in politics, the *Post*, and child-rearing. But Phil gradually fell victim to a debilitating mental illness that eventually claimed his life.

After his 1963 suicide, everyone—including Graham herself—assumed she would sell her interest in the paper. But Graham found herself reluctant to part with an enterprise that both her father and husband had spent decades building. With the advice and encouragement of friends, Graham overcame her gnawing lack of confidence and, in 1963, took over as publisher of the *Washington Post*.

In the ensuing years, Graham guided the paper through the upheavals of the Vietnam War, the assassinations of both Robert Kennedy and Martin Luther King, Jr., and the Watergate break-in and cover-up. She courageously supported reporters Bob Woodward and Carl Bernstein as they investigated and exposed the Watergate scandal. Their report rocked the nation, brought down a president, and catapulted the *Post* to international prominence.

With its depth, scope, and unique voice, *Personal History* tells the story of a formative time in American history through the eyes of a perceptive, powerful woman.

Throughout her life, Katharine Graham traveled in exclusive intellectual circles. She attended private schools and colleges and made her debut at eighteen. As a publisher's wife and then a publisher herself, she dined with some of the world's most powerful leaders, including presidents, prime ministers, and generals. One might assume high-quality food was served at such auspicious occasions, but Graham makes little mention of specific foods in *Personal History*. She focuses instead on the substance of these meetings rather than the culinary details.

One notable exception was author Truman Capote's Black-and-White Ball. In November 1966, Capote hosted an extravagant, star-studded costume ball and invited Katharine Graham to be the guest of honor. Widely considered the social event of the century, the ball attracted 540 of the wealthiest, most powerful people in the country.

Although Graham reported that the "very good, simple food" made for a relaxed affair, others were less charitable, claiming the party succeeded in spite of the "unremarkable" food. Guests enjoyed their best food, it seems, before the party began, during the dozens of pre-ball dinners that Capote had arranged.

Capote asked Graham to bring the food for their private picnic dinner before the ball. Guessing Capote's culinary preferences, Graham ordered champagne and caviar, but her life as an intellectual ill prepared her for such a purchase. "Having never lived this kind of life, I'd never bought caviar before and, when told its price, decided on a quarter of a pound, which was barely a couple of spoons for each of us," she writes. In spite of the meager portions, Graham claimed that Capote left to greet guests in high spirits.

CAVIAR PIE

With a caviar pie, you can enjoy the opulence of the Black-and-White Ball at your next book club meeting.

When her Dallas Gourmet Book Club discussed *Personal History*, Nancy Primeaux prepared this caviar pie, a recipe contributed by her mother, Eleanor Ricards of Houston. Ricards found the recipe in the Gamma Phi Beta newsletter, attributed to member Billie Lasater. "I tried to envision the parties at Katharine Graham's house, with people standing around with flutes of champagne. I thought the caviar pie would represent the era," says Primeaux.

NOTE: Primeaux makes the pie the night before and tops with caviar at the last minute before serving, but it can be made further in advance. Just cover with plastic wrap and refrigerate.

3 tablespoons mayonnaise

8 ounces cream cheese, softened

6 hard-cooked eggs, peeled and chopped

1 small red onion, chopped

⅔ cup sour cream

3 ounces red caviar, drained

1. Butter the sides of an 8-inch springform pan. In a bowl, stir together the mayonnaise and cream cheese until smooth.

2. Spread the chopped egg across the bottom of the pan. Sprinkle the onion evenly over eggs and press down gently. Cover this layer with the mayonnaise–cream cheese mixture, press down carefully, and smooth.

3. Gently spread sour cream over the top. Spoon drained caviar over the top and spread out in an even layer (take special care not to stir up the sour cream). Refrigerate 3 hours or overnight. Serve with plain crackers, such as toast crackers or water crackers.

Yield: 12 to 15 servings

BOOK CLUB PROFILE

"Our group has a lot of history," says Alice Haddix, an independent consultant and founder of her Tucson, Arizona, book club. "When people want to join the group, I always tell them the stories."

One story involves author Barbara Kingsolver, a fellow Tucson resident. At the club's first meeting in 1990, twenty women gathered in Haddix's living room to discuss Barbara Kingsolver's *The Bean Trees,* about a young woman who settles in Tucson. This started a tradition of reading a Kingsolver book each January. Several years later, Kingsolver, at the request of a neighbor who was a member of Haddix's group, agreed to attend their club meeting. Her visit was thrilling.

"She was funny and forthright," Haddix remembers. "At this point, we've read most of what she's written."

Another of the group's literary traditions evolved from Tucson's blistering summers. "The temperature in Tucson is nearly unbearable in the summer, so we always read a 'cold' book," says Haddix, meaning a book set in a cold climate or with a climactic scene involving cold weather. Some of their frosty choices: Ursula K. Le Guin's science-fiction tale, *The Left Hand of Darkness,* about a lost planet, Winter; Louise Erdrich's *Tales of Burning Love,* which is set during two North Dakota blizzards; and David Guterson's *Snow Falling on Cedars* (see p. 403).

One year, for lack of a better idea, the group read *The Masters,* a novel set at an English university, which has no relation to cold weather save the name of the author: C. P. Snow. "This was the nadir of our creativity!" says Haddix, who occasionally serves ice cream to accompany "cold" discussions.

In general, Haddix, who always hosts the group at her house, serves soft drinks, wine, and beer, but rarely food. "I grew up watching my mother participate in Saturday afternoon book groups, and I wanted to avoid the aroma of competition I sensed in their displays of hospitality," says Haddix.

There are exceptions, though. The group celebrates birthdays with cake. And every December, Haddix serves sweet sherry, dry sherry, and fruitcake. Haddix hoped to prepare fried green tomatoes when the group read Fannie Flagg's book by that name, but she had trouble finding any. "I made a coconut cream pie from a recipe in the back of the book instead," says Haddix. "And later, when my friend had an overabundance of green tomatoes in her garden, I took some and was at last able to cook them for the group."

At least two members must read and recommend a book to qualify it for consideration by the group. Group members, who range in age from their forties to their seventies and who have worked outside the home (although some have retired), prefer literary fiction, memoirs, and feminist nonfiction. Favorites include John Irving's *A Prayer for Owen Meany* (see p. 363), Wallace Stegner's *Angle of Repose* (see p. 22), Jane Smiley's *A Thousand Acres* (see p. 432), and Katharine Graham's *Personal History.*

The women were most impressed by Graham's strength of character. "We have a group memory of more than thirteen years," says Haddix, "and we liked adding Katharine Graham to our pantheon of strong women," which includes Jill Ker Conway, author of *The Road from Coorain* (see p. 383), and the fictional heroine Smilla, who investigates a young boy's death in Peter Hoeg's *Smilla's Sense of Snow.* "We've encountered a goodly number of women whose behavior and attitude toward the world struck us as strong and admirable," says Haddix. "Katharine Graham is one of them. Rather than being a victim of history and personal experience, she's a woman who triumphs, makes her peace, and overcomes."

Graham's triumphs seemed all the more remarkable in light of the obstacles she faced. As her husband, Phil, descended into mental illness, Graham had to cope without the benefit of modern-day psychiatric information and destigmatizing. "We were all taken aback by the inaccurate and harmful treatment of mental illness during that time," says Haddix. "The world around her made it much harder for Graham to deal with mental illness than it would be today. She just didn't have the proper tools."

Discussion of Graham's personal plight roused "strong emotional memories" in members, which they shared with the group. "One member's husband was afflicted with mental illness for some months before dying; another's father experienced something similar to an event in the book," says Haddix. While some members identified with the tragedies in Graham's life, all of them marveled at Graham's phenomenal life story. "There are not a whole lot of us who could have done what she did, keeping such an enormous enterprise running with such a huge public profile," says Haddix. "She led an amazing life."

More Food for Thought

Nancy Primeaux of the Dallas Gourmet Book Club tried to re-create the ambience of an elegant party à la Katharine Graham for her group's discussion of *Personal History.* Her menu included champagne and wine, caviar pie, sausage pinwheels, shrimp curry supreme, saffron rice, green bean bundles, chocolate-raspberry tarts, and coffee, all served on Royal Doulton fine china and sterling silver. Guests sipped champagne from crystal flutes and dabbed their lips with linen napkins.

"My goal was to provide an elegant dinner in the style that would do justice to the kind of dinner parties that I imagined Katharine Graham would have hosted," says Primeaux. "Members wore period dresses and long gloves, which was quite fitting for a dinner that started off with champagne and caviar."

Plainsong

Kent Haruf

(available in paperback from Vintage, 2000)

T HE PROSE in Kent Haruf's novel about the interconnected lives of seven people in a small rural town is as spare and haunting as the eastern Colorado landscape where *Plainsong* is set. A finalist for the 1999 National Book Award, *Plainsong* is the story of people whose lives come together after a series of heartbreaks, conflicts, and tragedy.

At the center of *Plainsong* is a high-school teacher, Tom Guthrie, who loses his wife to a deep depression and must raise his two sons, Ike and Bobby, alone. Tom finds support, and romance, in the arms of a colleague, Maggie Jones.

When seventeen-year-old Victoria Robideaux becomes pregnant and is thrown out of the house by her abusive mother, it is Maggie, the emotional touchstone for all of Haruf's principal characters, who arranges for Victoria to get room and board in exchange for chores at the ranch of two elderly bachelor brothers, the McPherons. After an awkward and wary beginning, an abiding mutual affection develops between the childless McPherons and Victoria. Perhaps the most memorable of all of the novel's vivid characters, the McPheron brothers become fierce protectors of Victoria's interests and her dignity.

Each of Haruf's characters has a desperate, if unarticulated, emotional void that is filled, often in the most unexpected way, by one of the others and, eventually, by the extended family they become. *Plainsong* is, ultimately, a book about families, the ones we are born to and the ones we create.

Haruf uses food to represent the nurturing that the characters in *Plainsong* give to one another. When asked about his use of food in *Plainsong*, Haruf told an interviewer:

One of the ways you show love is to prepare food for somebody. The father is doing that at the beginning of the story. At the end, Victoria feels confident enough and secure enough in her place out there so that she is the one who has begun to do the cooking and she's the one who presents the food to the boys when they come out to the McPherons'. At the very end of the book there is the suggestion that soon they will all go in and eat supper together.

CHEWY OATMEAL COOKIES

The Attic Salt Book Club, based at the Sullivan Free Library in Bridgeport, New York, enjoys serving a dessert related to the theme of their reading selection, and the group's leader, Karen Traynor, baked oatmeal cookies to accompany the discussion of *Plainsong*.

"In *Plainsong*, the two young boys, Ike and Bobby, go to visit an elderly neighbor, Iva Stearns, shortly after their mother leaves them," says Traynor. "It's obvious that the boys need some mothering, and Iva Stearns, out of despair of anything better to do, sends them to the store to buy the ingredients for oatmeal cookies. The boys help her bake them and it's a memorable scene in the book.

"When the book group met I had the oatmeal cookies on the table," adds Traynor, "but I told them they couldn't eat them until someone figured out why I made those particular cookies. It took a few minutes of furious page turning, but someone found the scene and we all enjoyed the cookies."

Traynor's favorite recipe for oatmeal cookies can be found on the Crisco shortening package or at the Crisco website, www.crisco.com. For the *Plainsong* discussion, she divided the batter and made half a batch with ½ cup of raisins and ½ cup of walnuts. For the other half, she made a favorite combination, replacing the walnuts and raisins with ½ cup each of milk chocolate chips, pecans, and dried cherries.

1 ¼ cups firmly packed light brown sugar
¾ cup butter-flavored vegetable shortening
*   (such as Crisco)*
⅓ cup milk
1 ½ teaspoons vanilla extract
1 egg
3 cups rolled oats, quick or old-fashioned

1 cup all-purpose flour
½ teaspoon baking soda
½ teaspoon salt
¼ teaspoon ground cinnamon
1 cup raisins
1 cup coarsely chopped walnuts

1. Preheat oven to 375° F. Using an electric mixer at medium speed, mix together the brown sugar, shortening, milk, vanilla, and egg until well blended. In a separate bowl, combine the oatmeal, flour, baking soda, salt, and cinnamon. Add to the shortening mixture, beating at low speed just until blended. Stir in the raisins and walnuts.

2. Drop dough by rounded tablespoons on a greased baking sheet, 2 inches apart. Bake, one sheet at a time for 10–12 minutes, or until the cookies are lightly browned. Do not overbake. Allow to cool on the baking sheet for 2 minutes, then transfer to a wire rack to cool completely.

Yield: About 2½ dozen cookies

BOOK CLUB PROFILE

Book-related food has become an increasingly important part of Wuthering Bites, a group of eight thirty- and forty-something women in the Seattle, Washington, area. "We used to serve chips and salsa, but we wanted to make it more fun," says Sue Gray, a charter member of the club, which started in 1992.

In 2002, with ten years of book club experience behind them, Gray and fellow member Stephanie Koura decided to create a website that would combine their mutual interests in literature and food. Koura is a culinary arts school graduate, former professional cook, and web design student. Early 2003 saw the launch of their website, Wuthering Bites (www.wutheringbites.com), where the group's creative pairing of books and menus, including Scandinavian comfort foods for Anita Shreve's *The Weight of Water* (see p. 477) and pie recipes for Yann Martel's *Life of Pi* (see p. 240), can be found.

It was books, not food, that first brought the group together. When a group of friends who worked in the same company discovered their mutual love of reading, they started meeting monthly in their Seattle homes. They enjoy current fiction, classics, and nonfiction dealing with women's issues.

Some of their favorites include books by John Irving, especially *A Prayer for Owen Meany* (see p. 363) and *The Cider House Rules,* about an abortionist and his surrogate son; Michael Chabon's *The Amazing Adventures of Kavalier & Clay* (see p. 11); Alexandre Dumas's swashbuckling adventure classic *The Count of Monte Cristo*; and Kent Haruf's *Plainsong*.

Group members loved the character development and writing of *Plainsong*. "I came away from this meeting with a deeper appreciation of the book than I had walking in," says Gray. "Haruf's writing is so beautiful, it doesn't matter if you know where the story is going. You just go along with the ride and soon you find you've begun to care about these characters."

Several of the "simple but real characters" in *Plainsong* particularly appealed to the group, according to Gray. "My personal favorites were the two young boys. The chapter where they befriend an old and lonesome lady on their paper route is very touching." The McPheron brothers, two aging bachelor farmers, also inspired the group's admiration, especially in the scene where they are chopping and removing ice from the horses' water tank as they decide to take a pregnant teenager into their home. "We thought this moment, when they are making a decision to change their solitary lives, was beautifully captured," says Gray. "Our group found the central themes of the novel—the connection between people in need and those that can help them, and life in a small town—very compelling."

More Food for Thought

When Britta's Book Club of Irvine, California, discussed *Plainsong*, Britta Pulliam prepared food from the pages of the novel: peppered beefsteak, boiled potatoes, green beans, a chocolate cake, and coffee.

For the *Plainsong* dinner discussion for her Chicago-area book club, Rose Parisi prepared all-American comfort food: her grandmother's recipe for oven-fried chicken, accompanied by steamed green beans, mashed potatoes, cornbread, and strawberry shortcake for dessert.

The Poisonwood Bible

Barbara Kingsolver

HARPERFLAMINGO, *1999*

(available in paperback from Perennial, 1999)

A T T H E E N D of her first day in Kilanga, the Congolese village where her evangelist father has come to redeem the souls of the natives, Rachel Price weeps "for the sins of all who had brought my family to this dread, dark shore." So begins the story of the Price family, told in turn by Rachel; her sisters, the twins Leah and Adah; five-year-old Ruth May; and their mother, Orleanna, in Barbara Kingsolver's ambitious novel, *The Poisonwood Bible*. The story follows the Price family from 1959, when they arrive in the Congo, to 1998. As Orleanna and the girls age, their storytelling reflects their changing perspectives. The family's complex saga is set against the backdrop of Congo's fight for independence from Belgium and American intervention in the country's fledgling government.

From the start, Congolese food troubles the Price girls. Goat stew, prepared by the villagers to welcome the newcomers, leaves Rachel miserable and disgusted. Orleanna wonders how she will feed her family from the scant resources, and Ruth May watches as tarantulas infest their bananas. As they settle into life in a foreign culture, the Price family's relationship to food brings out the different anxieties and types of alienation that each member feels.

But the start of a new life also brings excitement and wonder. These emotions, too, are expressed through food. Leah marvels at the strange and wonderful names of the living things around her: "*Nguba* is peanut (close to what we called them at home, goober peas!); *malala* are the oranges with blood-red juice; *mankondo* are bananas. *Nanasi* is a pineapple, and *nanasi mputo* means 'poor man's pineapple': a papaya. All these things grow wild! Our very own backyard resembles the Garden of Eden."

SALADI YA MATUNDA
(TROPICAL FRUIT SALAD)

O͟ur *Poisonwood Bible* recipe harvests the bounty of fresh fruit that Leah celebrates. A traditional African fruit salad, *saladi ya matunda* can be made from a variety of tropical fruits. Feel free to experiment. Book club member Helena Puche of the South Florida Preschool PTA Book Club served a menu of Congolese food to her group, but called the *saladi ya matunda* "the magisterial dish" that book club members enjoyed most. "The two special touches, shredded unsweetened coconut and sweet water as dressing, gave us a combination of flavors that the members are not accustomed to tasting," says Puche (see p. 499 for purchasing information).

NOTE: Make this recipe a few hours ahead and refrigerate. It doesn't keep for long.

2 oranges, peeled and sectioned,
membranes removed
2 mangos, peeled, pitted, and diced
1 medium papaya, peeled, seeded, and diced
½ fresh pineapple, cored, rind removed,
and diced
½ cantaloupe, seeded, rind removed,
and diced

4 bananas, peeled and sliced
Juice of 1 lemon (about 3 tablespoons)
Simple Syrup (see p. 172)
Grated coconut to taste
Roasted peanuts, chopped, to taste

1. Cut the orange sections in two. In a large bowl, gently combine the oranges, mangos, papaya, pineapple, and cantaloupe. Fold in bananas. Stir in the lemon juice and add the Simple Syrup to bring the salad to desired sweetness. Cover the salad and let stand at room temperature for 30 minutes, stirring gently once or twice. Refrigerate until ready to serve.
2. Serve in individual bowls and top with coconut and peanuts.

Yield: 8 to 10 servings

The Boston-Area Returned Peace Corps Volunteers provides a support network for local Peace Corps volunteers going overseas and for those who have returned. The nonprofit group also works to fulfill the Peace Corps' stated goal of "bringing the world back home to promote a better understanding of other people on the part of the American people."

Founders of the Boston-Area Returned Peace Corps Volunteers Book Group wanted to connect with others on a monthly basis, and since 1995 a group of eight to twelve members, including book-loving friends, neighbors, and spouses, meets each month at a member's home or at a local restaurant. Mary Knasas, who now works for Boston's Department of Neighborhood Development, served as a Peace Corps volunteer in Togo from 1980 to 1982. Fellow book club members are returnees from India, Honduras, Tuvalu, Lesotho, Iran, and many other countries. "Coming home can be a culture shock, and it helps to spend time with those who have had similar experiences," says Knasas.

"Naturally, as Peace Corps volunteers we are interested in social issues and the politics of the developing world," says Knasas, "but we have no boundaries." Memoirs and novels set in regions of the world where members have served are of special interest, such as *River Town: Two Years on the Yangtze,* by Peter Hessler (a returned Peace Corps volunteer), and *The God of Small Things,* by Arundhati Roy (see p. 157). Their readings cover a wide spectrum of fiction and nonfiction and reflect the broad taste and experience of the group.

Once a year, long-distance member Beth Segers hosts the group at her home in Maine for a discussion of a book set in Maine or by a Maine author, such as Richard Russo's *Empire Falls* (see p. 125). The group takes a long walk together; has a potluck barbecue, often including lobsters and blueberry pie; and camps out on futons, air mattresses, and beds scattered throughout the house. Members agree that the sleepover is reminiscent of the sense of camaraderie typical of the Peace Corps experience. "When I was in the Peace Corps, volunteers often traveled to each other's villages and cities. We would often crash at one another's homes, reflect on our shared experiences, and talk about the foods we missed," says Knasas.

Today the Boston-Area Returned Peace Corps Volunteers Book Group often connects literature and food. "Our refreshments often reflect the theme of the book," says Knasas. "It just adds to the meeting by getting us into the mood of the book." The group enjoyed Indian vegetarian stew with Jhumpa Lahiri's *Interpreter of Maladies* (see p. 204) and an elegant spread of appetizers featuring oysters and champagne with F. Scott Fitzgerald's *The Great Gatsby* (see p. 171).

Barbara Kingsolver's *The Poisonwood Bible* resonated strongly for many of the Peace Corps returnees. "I could smell the earth. It was describing Africa as I lived it," said Knasas. "The father was so rigid. He was going to do everything as he would have at home. As a Peace Corps volunteer, you learn you just don't bring materials and ways of doing things from the United States to another continent without ever learning why they may be doing things differently, whether it's planting crops or observing family traditions. For example, where are you going to get replacement parts for a highly mechanized tractor? Seeds from our soil do not take root and flourish on another continent," says Knasas.

More Food for Thought

In Miami, Helena Puche hosted the South Florida Preschool PTA Book Club's discussion of *The Poisonwood Bible*. She looked for simple but authentic Congolese foods to complement the discussion, especially foods that could be chopped and scooped up with the plantain and yucca chips or the cassava crackers she served. Her menu for the group of thirty included chicken in peanut and tomato sauce, grilled tilapia, red beans with shrimp (*ukali*), sweet potato salad with bacon and peanuts, and *saladi ya matunda* with Belgian chocolates for dessert.

Marilyn Christensen and Sharon Murr of the Book Bags of New Prague, Minnesota, shopped at an African market in downtown Minneapolis to prepare for their discussion of *The Poisonwood Bible*. The shopkeeper, who greeted them in colorful Nigerian clothing, advised them on foods to serve to their group.

They hoped to serve *fufu*, a paste made of the ground-up powder of the manioc root and one of the staples of the Kilanga diet. Although in *The Poisonwood Bible*, Orleanna describes *fufu* as "a gluey paste" with "the nutritional value of a brown paper bag," the Book Bags were undaunted. "The thud of *fufu* being processed, along with stirring to the limits of your endurance; these descriptions from the book were interesting to the group," says member Ann Prchal. The storekeeper suggested quick-cooking yam powder, so no pounding or heavy stirring was needed.

The Book Bags' *Poisonwood Bible* menu also included groundnut stew (*hka-tenkwan*) and mango snow, a dessert of steamed mangos and sugar, both from *The Africa News Cookbook: African Cooking for Western Kitchens* (Viking Penguin, 1986), and fried plantains and fresh-squeezed blood-orange juice.

Hostess Marilyn Christensen greeted guests in traditional African garb. Inside the house, she arranged tropical plants and African artifacts and played the taped sounds of tropical birds and animals to create a jungle atmosphere. The meal was served on a number of "thoroughly sterilized" hubcaps, a reference to the "metal bowls or hubcaps or whatnot" the villagers in *The Poisonwood Bible* held up to receive food at the feast.

Pope Joan

Donna Woolfolk Cross

CROWN, *1996*

(available in paperback from Ballantine, 1997)

Donna Woolfolk Cross, an English professor and author of books on language, became fascinated by references to a female pope in a French novel and spent seven years researching accounts of Pope Joan in ancient manuscripts. Although the Catholic Church denies it, Cross found a solid historical record of Pope Joan, a woman who disguised herself as a man and became Pope in the ninth century. It was impossible, however, to determine details of Joan's life. Cross chose to write a fictional account of Pope Joan, interweaving historical events and figures of the Middle Ages.

Joan, the daughter of a tyrannical canon and his pagan Saxon wife, shows an early intelligence and aptitude as a scholar. At a time when a learned woman was considered to be unnatural and even dangerous, and women were forbidden to learn how to read and write, Joan persists in her quest for an education. Her older brother, Matthew, teaches her basic skills, and a visiting Greek scholar, Aesculapius, recognizing Joan's gifts, instructs her in languages and in the classics. Aesculapius also arranges for Joan to be schooled along with another brother, John, at the palace of the bishop of Dorstadt. At Dorstadt, Joan meets and falls passionately in love with Gerold, a knight.

When John is killed during a Viking attack at Dorstadt, Joan assumes his identity and is initiated into the brotherhood of the Benedictine monastery of Fulda in his place, taking the name Brother John Anglicus. Joan distinguishes herself as a scholar and a healer at the monastery. When an outbreak of plague strikes, Joan escapes and survives. She is drawn to Rome, where she becomes enmeshed in the religious conflicts and political battles of the day. In Rome, she is also reunited with Gerold, unleashing a struggle between her passion for Gerold and her faith.

For her bravery, wisdom, and determination, Joan, in her male identity, is made Pope and sits on the papal throne for two years.

CORMARYE (ROAST PORK WITH CORIANDER-CARAWAY SAUCE)

Donna Woolfolk Cross meticulously researched details of culinary life in the Middle Ages for *Pope Joan*. She suggested we include a medieval pork roast recipe, *cormarye*, to accompany a discussion of her novel, a recipe based on the meal Joan's family serves to Aesculapius, an honored guest in their home. "The meal was splendid," writes Cross in *Pope Joan*, "the most lavish the family had ever prepared for a guest. There was a haunch of roast salted pork, cooked till the skin crackled, boiled corn and beetroot, pungent cheese, and loaves of crusty bread freshly baked under the embers."

Cross explained to us her decision to use meat in this important scene:

The presence of meat reflects the visitor's great importance, for in the ninth century meat was not an everyday item on the tables of poor families. Note that the pork is salted, a common method of preservation back then. Salted meat could be stored for several months, guaranteeing a supply of food during the lean winter months.

I get more reader feedback than most authors, for I chat by speakerphone with reading groups all over the country several times a week. During these fun and lively conversations, someone inevitably comments on the inclusion of corn in the meal, pointing out that corn is a New World, not an Old World, food.

But in truth, what we Americans refer to as corn is actually maize—a grain that is indeed native to North America and not Europe. *Corn*, on the other hand, is an ancient word that means grain or seed.

However, considering the number of readers I have confused in this way, I certainly wish I could go back in time and write that the dish was boiled barley!*

Our recipe for *cormarye* is based on a fourteenth-century English recipe and adapted from *Pleyn Delit: Medieval Cookery for Modern Cooks*, by Constance B. Hieatt (University of Toronto Press, 1996). Cross suggests preparing any grain, such as barley, to accompany this medieval pork roast,

*To arrange a conversation with Cross for your book group, visit her website: www.popejoan.com.

should readers wish to reproduce the entire meal. You may prepare this dish using a larger roast—just increase the amount of marinade proportionately and allow a longer cooking time.

1 teaspoon coriander seed

1 teaspoon caraway seed (see Purchasing
Information, p. 499)

5 cloves garlic, pressed or mashed

1 cup red wine

½ teaspoon salt

¼ teaspoon freshly ground black pepper

1 3-pound boneless pork loin roast

Pork or chicken broth for deglazing pan juices

Dry bread crumbs (optional)

1. Grind the coriander and caraway seeds as finely as possible, using a spice mill or mortar and pestle, and place in a medium bowl. Add the garlic, wine, and salt and pepper and stir to combine.

2. Prick the pork loin all over with a fork and place in a resealable plastic bag. Pour the prepared marinade into the bag, squeeze out as much air as possible, and seal. Make sure the marinade coats the meat well. Refrigerate at least 3 hours or overnight.

3. Preheat oven to 325° F. Place pork loin in a metal roasting pan with half the marinade and roast until done, basting occasionally with remaining marinade and pan juices. Cooking time should be about 1 hour, but will vary with the size and shape of the roast. A meat thermometer inserted in the thickest part of the roast should register at least 160°F. (Some people prefer a more well-done roast, up to 180°F. At 160°F, the roast should be done but slightly pink in the center.)

4. Transfer the roast to a serving dish. Place the roasting pan on a burner over medium heat and add a small amount of broth. Bring to a boil, scraping browned bits from bottom of pan with a spatula. Thicken with bread crumbs if desired, and serve as a sauce alongside pork.

Yield: 6 servings

BOOK CLUB PROFILE

A Room of Her Own Book Group is named for a separate section of the Frugal Frigate Bookstore in Redlands, California, a room dedicated to books by, for, and about women, where the book group meets monthly.

A Room of Her Own is housed in a livery stable dating from the 1800s with old brick, wood, and high beams opening into the cathedral ceiling. Katherine Thomerson, owner of the Frugal Frigate Bookstore, teaches women's and children's literature at local Crafton Hills Community College and facilitates the book group. Thomerson says the group had always enjoyed discussing books over tea and cookies, but in February 2003, they noticed the store's men's book group having a smorgasbord at their meeting. The women were inspired, and since then have brought a variety of finger foods, appetizers, and wine to meetings. Sometimes they enjoy foods to complement their readings, such as salsa and chips for Víctor Villaseñor's *Rain of Gold,* a story about a Mexican family, and Middle Eastern foods, including tabbouleh and hummus, with Jean Sasson's memoir *Princess: A True Story of Life Behind the Veil,* set in Saudi Arabia. Thomerson baked her family recipe for Irish Brown Soda Bread (see p. 18) for their discussion of the Irish novel *Gracelin O'Malley,* which included a phone conversation with author Ann Moore.

Depending on the month and the book, between ten and thirty members meet in A Room of Her Own. Each member is encouraged to recommend a book and has an opportunity to sell it to the group before they vote on the next several titles. Designated reading categories, such as a book written by or about an African-American woman for February, a work about a notable woman or a women's issue in March, and a classic in August, help them diversify the list. In December, when members are busy with the holidays, they read young-adult novels. "Most readers are amazed at the power in young-adult fiction," says Thomerson. "Young-adult writers, such as Karen Hesse, who wrote *Witness,* raise interesting issues and get to the point quickly, and we enjoy these writers."

Many members enjoy historical fiction, says Thomerson, and they loved Donna Woolfolk Cross's *Pope Joan.* "What I love about literature is when the author gives you fiction that causes you to talk about truth, and this was the case with *Pope Joan,*" says Thomerson.

Pope Joan provoked a "hot discussion," says Thomerson, as many members didn't realize it was a fictional episode until they read the author's notes at the end, and some felt they had to reread the book.

"This was a period of history members were unfamiliar with," says Thomerson. "We were amazed that this episode was passed over in Catholic history. During the ensuing discussion of religion and politics, we explored what other events the Church might have hidden."

More Food for Thought

"I wanted to include a few items that were on the feast table," says Myra Anderson of the snacks she prepared for her book club, Wine, Women, and Words, when they discussed *Pope Joan* at her home in the Boston suburbs. Anderson served chicken drumsticks from a local grocery store, dried figs, apricots, dates, and spiced nuts. "There were several places in *Pope Joan* where the author described food on banquet tables such as fruits and nuts," says Anderson. "While I couldn't exactly put out a stuffed goose or suckling pig, chicken drumsticks seemed a symbolic substitute." Anderson did devise an appropriate table centerpiece: a stuffed animal in the form of a moose with a pig's nose.

Wine, Women, and Words enjoyed having author Donna Woolfolk Cross join them via speaker phone. "Her enthusiasm and wit sparked quite a lively conversation," said member Ann Marie Gluck. "We came into the meeting somewhat skeptical that Joan could have hidden her gender for decades, but after speaking with Donna Cross, we were convinced that a woman could indeed have successfully deceived so many people by hiding her gender in the ninth century."

A Prayer for Owen Meany

John Irving

RANDOM HOUSE, *1989*

(available in paperback from Ballantine, 1990)

I AM A CHRISTIAN because of Owen Meany," declares narrator Johnny Wheelwright in the opening pages of John Irving's novel. His friend Owen Meany, tiny and self-assured, considers himself a vehicle for God's will. And Johnny's lifelong friendship with Owen convinces him that Owen is indeed a messenger of God.

The son of a quarry owner in Gravesend, New Hampshire, Owen has a strange, high-pitched voice, a dwarfish body, and an ability to "see" things before they happen. At age eleven, during a Little League game, Owen hits a hard foul ball that strikes and kills Johnny's mother. He is racked with sadness and remorse, although he believes that God has used him to express his will. Owen later wangles the part of the Baby Jesus in the Gravesend Christmas pageant. He plays the role with commanding presence, and chooses Johnny to be Joseph.

In keeping with their pageant roles, Owen and Johnny stick together throughout high school at the local private Gravesend Academy and college at the University of New Hampshire. At Gravesend, the subjects of women and sex occupy countless hours. Owen's somewhat inexplicable sex appeal—he dates Johnny's alluring cousin, Hester, known to some as Hester the Molester—inspires envy in Johnny, who cannot seem to get a date. Throughout their teenage and young adult years, Johnny wonders about his sexuality, the identity of the father he never knew, and his mother's secret life. Together, the friends seek to resolve some of these mysteries.

Owen attends college on a ROTC scholarship, and when he leaves for basic training in Indiana after graduating in 1966, he and Johnny separate for the first time. But Owen Meany has had visions of his own death, a moment for which he has prepared his whole life. When he meets Johnny again, he knows his time has come.

BANANA-PINEAPPLE SMOOTHIE

Owen's determination to fight in Vietnam infuriates his girlfriend, Hester; she sees his departure as a rejection. One day her fury spills over. She tackles and pummels Owen, splitting open his lip, which needs four stitches. Owen's diet is restricted to liquids. Johnny's grandmother prepares "something nourishing for him in the blender: a fresh pineapple, a banana, some ice cream, some brewer's yeast."

A smoothie is a nonalcoholic drink made by puréeing fruit with yogurt, ice cream, or milk. There is some disagreement as to when the term "smoothie" arose, although most agree the drink is a product of the twentieth century. Popular in the 1960s, smoothies have enjoyed a resurgence since the 1980s with the coming of the modern sports and fitness craze.

Although Owen drinks an ice cream–based smoothie, our recipe uses nonfat yogurt frozen for several hours. The cold, creamy frozen yogurt balances the sweetness of the bananas and pineapple to make a refreshing fruit drink without all the calories.

1 cup nonfat plain yogurt

1½ ripe bananas, peeled and sliced

1¼ cups unsweetened pineapple juice

½ cup cubed fresh or drained canned pineapple

10 ice cubes, crushed (approximately 1 cup)

3 tablespoons light brown sugar

Place the yogurt in small bowl; cover and freeze at least 6 hours or up to 2 days. When ready to make smoothies, let the yogurt sit at room temperature until it can be pried out of the bowl, about 30 minutes. Transfer the yogurt to a blender. Add the remaining ingredients and blend until smooth.

Yield: About 4 servings

BOOK CLUB PROFILE

At the first meeting of Cheryl Haze's Philadelphia, Pennsylvania, book club in 2002, members were given surveys as a way to break the ice. Patterned after a weekly feature in the *Philadelphia Business Journal,* the questionnaire asked each member about her current job, the kind of car she drives, her best and worst decisions, her first job, and her favorite restaurant, book, movie, car, and vacation spot. Each person summarized her own "biography" aloud.

"We discovered that more than half of us had lived overseas," says Haze, a venture capitalist and cofounder of the group. "One member was born in Poland, lived in Israel a number of years, and then came to the United States. Another is British and was the first member of her family to finish high school—and now she has a Ph.D. and an MBA. Another lived in Germany during her early years. The surveys brought out all kinds of details that helped us find common ground as a group and also exposed some unknown hobbies: sports cars for midlife crises and watching gory murder shows on TV."

In addition to foreign living experience, group members share an unusually high level of education. The eight women are all either current or past senior executives in the pharmaceutical industry or in venture capital investment, and hold advanced degrees in various fields—business, law, chemical engineering, veterinary medicine, accounting, and pharmaceutical sciences. Many members hold multiple degrees.

High-powered careers mean busy lives. This affects the group's book selection. For the most part, the club reads paperbacks, "not because of expense, but because many of our members travel, and paperbacks are easier to carry," says Haze. Long, "vague" books and books with limited potential for discussion are nixed, according to Haze. Other than these criteria, though, anything goes.

Group discussions often take place at restaurants linked to the theme of the book. For example, the group discussed Anchee Min's *Becoming Madame Mao,* about the wife of the Chinese leader, over a twelve-course banquet in Philadelphia's Chinatown during the Chinese New Year. The meal—and the fact that one member has adopted two babies from China—inspired the group to tackle other books with Chinese themes, such as Dai Sijie's *Balzac and the Little Chinese Seamstress* (see p. 37).

When group members read British author Nick Hornby's *How to Be Good,* about a woman struggling to maintain happiness within her marriage, they met at Philadelphia's Four Seasons Hotel for a brunch with an English flavor. After their discussion of Bharati Mukherjee's *Jasmine,* about a young Indian woman who immigrates to America, they went out for Indian food.

The club gathered at a member's house for pizza and a movie when they discussed John Irving's *A Prayer for Owen Meany,* one of the group's favorites. "This was one of our best discussions because this was such a meaningful book," says Haze. "We loved Owen Meany's efforts to figure out his significance to the world as he grew up." Group members found many topics for discussion in the book's themes, including religion, the Catholic Church, family relationships, and life's deeper meanings. The book's symbolism also intrigued the group, particularly the dressmaker's dummy that belonged to Johnny's mother, which Owen carries around and places at the foot of his bed.

After pizza, the group watched *Simon Birch,* a movie based in part on *A Prayer for Owen Meany*. According to Haze, the movie highlighted similarities between Owen's life and the life of Jesus from conception to death, a parallel that fascinated group members.

More Food for Thought

In tribute to Owen Meany's small stature, Cheri Caviness of Encinitas, California, served "tiny" finger foods to her book club, the Bookwomen, when they discussed *A Prayer for Owen Meany*. Caviness says she made some favorite stand-bys: dolmades (stuffed grape leaves), *tzatziki*, a yogurt-cucumber dip (see p. 267), and baby vegetables and pita chips served with hummus. "Who says good things don't come in small packages?" asks Caviness.

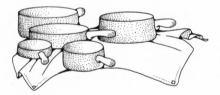

Reading Lolita in Tehran:
A Memoir in Books

Azar Nafisi

RANDOM HOUSE, 2003

(available in paperback from Random House, 2003)

A S A WOMAN and an intellectual in postrevolutionary Iran, Azar Nafisi is forced to live a bifurcated existence. She veils herself, resentfully, to comply with government edicts and to keep her university position. She meets covertly with a male intellectual friend—she calls him "my magician"—so as not to arouse the suspicions of the police. And she restrains her natural impulse to clap a male student on the back whose religious beliefs forbid physical contact with women other than his wife.

Out of frustration and rebellion, Nafisi withdraws from her university post and convenes a literature class of seven young women—her prize students—to discuss the works of F. Scott Fitzgerald, Vladimir Nabokov, Henry James, and other Western authors held in contempt by the Iranian fundamentalist theocracy. In *Reading Lolita in Tehran*, Nafisi recounts the story of this literature class, describing how it came to be and introducing us to the "girls," as she calls them, mostly in their twenties, who attend regularly, peeling off their veils and chadors upon entering the sanctuary of Nafisi's apartment; and re-creating the discussions of literature and its relationship to the women's personal lives and to Iran under Islamic fundamentalist rule.

Nafisi's account includes flashbacks to the early days of the revolution, to her teaching position at the University of Tehran, and to the Iran-Iraq War. Nafisi provides a sweeping view of the profound changes in Iranian society since the revolution, especially for women. Her ultimate decision to leave Iran is tinged with sadness for herself and for the students who look up to her, as they must face the indignities and hard choices of living as women in Iran without her counsel.

The food in *Reading Lolita in Tehran* offers sanctuary, comfort, and the promise of intimacy in a cold, unpredictable, sometimes hostile society. The moment the women, tense and uncertain, enter their teacher's apartment, they are offered a "calming distraction" of tea and cream puffs.

So begins a weekly ritual of sharing tea, coffee, and pastries, which the women provide in turn. As the group's comfort level grows, so does the abundance of their meals. Several weeks into the class, deep into discussion of Gustave Flaubert's *Madame Bovary*, Nafisi's students bring a feast of special dishes. As Nafisi writes, "*Madame Bovary* had done what years of teaching at the university had not: it created a shared intimacy."

In countless situations, Nafisi shares intimacies with students and colleagues over food. With two tall cafés glacés between them, Nafisi's student Yassi reveals her confusion about veiling herself and her negativity toward marriage. When Nafisi and her colleague Laleh brood over the evisceration of the Persian and Foreign Languages and Literature Department at the University of Tehran, their appetites are "insatiable." And when Nafisi meets her magician, they conspiratorially call their ham-and-cheese sandwiches *croques-monsieurs*, a French term likely repugnant to the government. With laughter and raised glasses, they revel in their rebellion. "One could write a paper on the pleasure of a ham sandwich," her magician says.

We asked Azar Nafisi to share her thoughts on the role that food has played in her life. Her response:

Some of my most intimate memories of childhood and early youth are associated with the many celebratory rituals in our family and country involving the preparation and eating of food, which was always a communal affair. Preparation, serving, and eating food can be very sensual, evoking pleasure through senses of sight, smell, and taste, and I can still evoke my past through aromas and colors of food. The images of those days are associated with the memories of different finely chopped herbs—cilantro, tarragon, rosemary, sage, basil—and scented and poetically named spices—saffron, cardamom, cumin, turmeric—and rice and sauces cooked over very slow fire, spreading their aroma hours before the food was served.

On Fridays my family usually ate out with close friends. Eating out was a carefully planned, much-anticipated, and noisy event. The Tehran of my childhood was filled with great restaurants, and at least once a week during summer we ate at some favorite open-air place, where we sat in a garden filled with scents of jasmine and roses, and ate a cold soup made of yogurt and cucumber mixed with finely chopped herbs, walnuts, and raisins. During these occasions everybody from children to grown-ups participated in singing and dancing that continued well past the children's bedtime. More than anything else I miss these luminous moments when the pure and unadulterated joy of living took precedence over the usual considerations that separated us through age, rank, or gender.

After the Islamic revolution, eating out lost its sense of joy. The regime negated and banned everything original and individual, imposing repressive laws to ensure the uniformity and conformity that are the trademark of every totalitarian mind-set. Pleasure was considered sin and therefore forbidden. Dancing and singing were banned, men and women could not go out together in public unless they were married or related by blood. Women had to wear the mandatory veil in restaurants, and laughing and other expressions of joy were forbidden. I remember one friend saying that whenever she ate at a restaurant she felt as if it were raining because of the long robe and large scarf she had to wear. Coffee shops and restaurants that became popular with the youth were raided and often closed down. Persians could not give up their appreciation of life, and when they were deprived of these joys publicly they had to create them privately, transferring most of their public entertainment and pleasure to their homes.

This is why in my book food is related to the idea of style, of retrieving those rituals that give color and shape to an otherwise shapeless and drab reality. At home we compensated for what we lacked in public by spending a great deal of time and effort over the preparation of food. In the private class I describe in my book, we looked forward to our tea and pastry. We took turns bringing the pastry, which ranged from delicate homemade Persian pastries to cream puffs made with real cream to elaborate cakes.

As we became more intimate, we added to our eating rituals, which gradually became very elaborate and innovative. I introduced my students to my favorite concoction: vanilla or coffee ice cream with a little coffee poured over and topped with walnuts or almonds. Later, as our discussions stretched far beyond the customary three hours, we sometimes organized feasts, to which everyone made a contribution. Soon there was a great competition among my students over who made the tastiest and most elaborate dish. Our table on such occasions, in which my family now and then participated, was graced with dishes such as duck with pomegranate and walnut sauce; saffron rice with herbed beef sauce; saffron rice with lentils, raisins, dates, nuts; cumin rice with chicken; and of course various desserts accompanied by my mother's thick and creamy-looking Turkish coffee served in small, delicate china cups.

As I write these lines, evoking the sensual and forbidden scents and sights of our innocent yet guilty pleasures, I am once more struck by the way we were able to keep our sense of identity and community through gestures that might seem so trivial, but are so central to human existence, like the care and inspiration that go into the creation of one small dish and the pleasure that is evoked through sharing it, reminding us that no authoritarian power can take away from a people their sense of joy and pride in the simple and yet complex act of living.

KOLUCHEH YAZDI (CAKE)

As happened with the women in Nafisi's group, delicious pastry sustained members of the Daughters of Abraham Book Club in Cambridge, Massachusetts, when they discussed *Reading Lolita in Tehran*.

Gay Harter, a retired social worker, drew on her knowledge of Iranian foods to prepare for the meeting. In the 1980s and 1990s, Harter worked with immigrants, including Iranian men and women fleeing political persecution, at the U.S. immigration detention center in Boston. "I made an effort to learn about their culture and even studied Farsi for a while," says Harter. "During that time I found a Persian cookbook and tried some of the recipes."

The cookbook Harter found, *Persian Cuisine, Book One: Traditional Foods* by M. R. Ghanoonparvar (Mazda, 1982), contains a recipe for moist, delicious *koluceh Yazdi*. Although translated as Yazdi cookies, the dessert more closely resembles a cake. "I've been told by an Iranian friend that a more appropriate name for the recipe would be *keik-e-Yazdi*, or cake from the city of Yazd, because it comes out more like cake than cookies," says Harter. She highly recommends using rose water rather than vanilla to give this sweet an authentic Persian flavor. Serve with hot coffee or tea.

4 eggs, well beaten
1 cup sugar
¾ cup (1½ sticks) unsalted butter, melted
2 cups all-purpose flour
1 cup plain yogurt
1 teaspoon baking powder
1 teaspoon baking soda
½ teaspoon ground cardamom

1 tablespoon rosewater (see Purchasing Information, p. 499), or substitute 1 teaspoon vanilla extract
1 cup raisins
½ cup slivered almonds, blanched (see Purchasing Information, p. 499)
4 teaspoons chopped pistachio nuts

1. In a large bowl, combine the eggs, sugar, and butter. Mix well. Gradually add the flour, mixing after each addition. Add the yogurt and mix well.

2. In a separate bowl, combine the baking powder, baking soda, cardamom, and rosewater. Add to the flour mixture and let the dough rest, covered, for 1 hour.

3. Preheat oven to 325° F. Stir the raisins and almonds into the dough. Transfer the mixture

into a 13x9x2-inch baking pan, sprinkle pistachios over the top, and bake 25–30 minutes, until golden brown. Allow to cool in the pan, then cut into squares.

Yield: 10 to 12 servings

BOOK CLUB PROFILE

After the September 11, 2001, attacks on the World Trade Center and the Pentagon, First Church in Cambridge, Massachusetts, organized a memorial service led by spiritual leaders of various denominations. Standing in the crowd was First Church member Edie Howe, who found herself wedged among women of all faiths, some wearing traditional Muslim head scarves. Many were sobbing. "I thought to myself, This is crazy! We're all daughters of Abraham," says Howe, a former lawyer and student of theology who hopes one day to do interfaith work. "I started thinking that I had to respond to the powerful feeling in this church, and to the humanity in all its diversity that was standing there that day."

A year later, the Daughters of Abraham—a book club bringing together women of the three Abrahamic faiths, Judaism, Christianity, and Islam—met for the first time. "The goal of our group is to get people to be aware of others' faith traditions," says Howe. "I hope that learning about others' beliefs and practices will lead to greater understanding and tolerance."

The group boasts a core of members who attend virtually every meeting. But the busy lives of the members, many of whom hold professional jobs or attend school, mean that sometimes membership fluctuates. Five Muslim members initially joined the group, but now only fifteen Christians and five Jews regularly attend meetings. "We're focused on recruiting Muslim members, as their presence is essential to our discussions," says Howe.

Monthly book selections reflect the three Abrahamic faiths. "We're not focusing directly on issues of faith," says Howe, "but we're trying to lay the groundwork for dialogue." To establish a common background for their dialogue, for the first meeting, in September 2002, members read chapters on Islam, Christianity, and Judaism from Huston Smith's *The World's Religions: Our Great Wisdom Traditions.* Subsequent books have explored one of the three faiths each month. Books that have sparked lively discussion include Anita Diamant's *The Red Tent* (see p. 374); Faye Kellerman's *The Ritual Bath,* the first in a detective series featuring an orthodox Jewish woman and her Baptist love interest; Leila Ahmed's *Border Passage,* a memoir of an Egyptian woman who comes to America; and Anne Lamott's *Traveling Mercies: Some Thoughts on Faith,* a lighthearted account of the author's spiritual awakening.

Food at Daughters of Abraham meetings is generally simple—fruit, cheeses, desserts, coffee, tea, juice, and seltzer—but is always kosher (consistent with Jewish dietary laws), and, when Muslim members attend, halal (consistent with Muslim dietary laws). The group was inspired to match foods with the theme of the book for the first time upon reading Azar Nafisi's *Reading Lolita in Tehran,* a book that triggered one of the group's most intense discussions.

What particularly struck the Daughters of Abraham was what Margaret Gooch, a librarian and charter member of the group, afterward called "the survival value of literature. . . . These women faced hardship, deprivation, and danger as a tyrannical regime gradually—and unbelievably—took hold of the country," says Gooch, summing up the comments of many group members. "We talked about how literature offered them an outlet for their imagination, a way of envisioning a different future for themselves, a source of truth apart from their daily reality."

To group members, a trial of *The Great Gatsby* (see p. 71), conducted to determine the worthiness of the book to society, reenacted by Nafisi's literature students, demonstrated most vividly the crucial role that literature played in their lives. "I would have been a terrible defense attorney because I never thought much of *The Great Gatsby,*" says Jenny Peace, a Ph.D. candidate in comparative religions. "But Nafisi shows her students that it is not the morality of the characters that should be on trial. Great literature exposes great human truths. The insight illuminated in *Gatsby* is the danger of imposing one's perfect and complete ideal on a messy, ever-changing reality. This is why Gatsby speaks to a group of Muslim women in wartorn Tehran: they are experiencing firsthand how it feels to live in someone else's dream." The commitment of Nafisi's students to distill truth from literature gave the Daughters of Abraham renewed appreciation for something that Americans tend to take for granted: the freedom to read.

Group members explored many other facets of Nafisi's memoir, including her relationship with her "magician," and the meaning of his decision to withdraw from society; the little-known effects on Iranians of the Iran-Iraq War; and Nafisi's decision to wear—or not to wear—the veil. "When the government took away women's right to choose to wear the veil, the act became submission rather than celebration," observes Jeanette Macht, a lawyer. Several group members, who, as former nuns, used to wear habits, talked about the physical limitations of wearing a head covering. "You can't feel the wind on your neck," says Anne Minton, an Episcopal priest and professor of history who spent seven years as a cloistered nun. "It's remarkable what you miss."

More Food for Thought

The Cambridge, Massachusetts–based Daughters of Abraham had their first taste of thematic food for their discussion of *Reading Lolita in Tehran.* Their menu included *kolucheh Yazdi,* cream puffs, baklava, pistachio nuts, and pomegranates.

"I think the food stimulated people's taste buds and their spirits, and brought us into the mood of going to the Middle East," says Edie Howe, a cofounder of the group. "It also paralleled what we were reading about. The women in the book always had wonderful things to eat during their meetings, and we did too. It was a case of life imitating art."

The five members of the suburban New Jersey Alcott Society served a tea with dates, dried fruits, pistachio nuts, and cream puffs for their discussion of *Reading Lolita in Tehran.* The members felt that just as Nafisi bonds with her friends and students by sharing refreshments, their bond with Nafisi became deeper as they shared the same type of foods.

The Red Tent

Anita Diamant

....

ST. MARTIN'S, *1997*

(available in paperback from Picador, 1998)

THE COMPRESSED STORIES and images in the Bible are rather like photographs," explains *Red Tent* author Anita Diamant. "They don't tell us everything we want or need to know." Diamant longed to know more about the circumstances surrounding the rape of Dinah, Jacob and Leah's only daughter. Recounted in only one line of the Bible from Genesis, chapter 34, the story of Dinah's rape by Shechem is followed by a longer account of vengeance visited on Shechem's people by Dinah's six older brothers.

"The drama and Dinah's total silence—she does not utter a single word in the Bible—cried out for explanation," says Diamant. "I decided to imagine one." *The Red Tent* gives voice to Dinah—her feelings of betrayal, grief, and ambition—while illustrating the daily existence of biblical women. *The Red Tent*'s depiction of women—their daily chores, monthly rituals (retiring to the red tent during menstruation among them), and momentous life events—focuses attention on the Bible's peripheral, often silent characters, conjuring lives of sisterly bonding and deeply felt emotions.

Food and its preparation figure prominently in the daily lives of the women of *The Red Tent* and with good reason, according to Diamant:

> Food is front and center in *The Red Tent* because food preparation took so much time in a traditional or premodern society. The growing, processing, cooking and clean-up must have taken so many hours every day. Yet another reason I am not at all nostalgic for the ancient world of my imagination.

Because their roles were strictly defined by a patriarchal society, women had little bargaining power. They ruled the kitchen, though, and food became a useful tool. Leah hopes her meal, which she "suffered over . . . like nothing else I had ever cooked," will win Jacob's heart, and she gains confidence from his approval: "I knew how to please his mouth. . . . I will know how to please the rest of him."

The women comfort one another with food, as when Inna, the midwife, feeds Rachel bits of bread dipped in honey and mead while whispering "secret words of comfort and hope" into her ear.

The richness and variety of food in *The Red Tent* is striking. The book's pages are laden with references to produce, grains, meats, and spices of the ancient world—figs, dates, quince, melon, pomegranates, mulberries, cucumbers, barley, olives, lamb, goose, fish, coriander, and mint. Anita Diamant tells us that she chose foods "self-defensively," making sure that no modern-day items slipped into the book. "I didn't want there to be any anachronisms—foods that would not have been part of the diet in that place or at that time. So no tomatoes—they're New World. And no chickens—as 'Jewish' as chicken seems to us today."

Readers can learn something about biblical chronology by attending to food in *The Red Tent*. As Diamant told us:

> Readers may have noticed that there was liberal mixing of meat and milk in the cooking in *The Red Tent*. That was intended as a signal that this book is historical and not religious in its bones. The first strictures against boiling kids in their mother's milk comes in Exodus, after Moses gets the Torah. Milk and yogurt are effective and standard marinades for meat in the Near East to this day, after all.

Fig Spread and Goat Cheese Toasts

To make use of the bounty of fruits, nuts, and grains available in the ancient Middle East, we adapted the Dried Fruit, Cinnamon and Red Wine Compote recipe in Kitty Morse's *A Biblical Feast: Foods from the Holy Land* (Ten Speed Press, 1998) for the fig spread here. The Bible mentions figs at least fifty times—a testament to their popularity. Both figs and dates are among the seven foods listed in the Bible in praise of the Promised Land. Prized for their sweetness and long shelf life when dried, in ancient times figs were used by the poor in place of honey, which was reserved for the wealthy. Dates enjoyed popularity at all levels of society.

The fruit compote came to our attention when Judy Bart Kancigor, book club member and cookbook author, made it for her *Red Tent* "biblical feast." She served the sweet, intensely flavored compote as a dessert. Here, we pair it with toasted pitas and a goat cheese topping to make an ancient world appetizer for a modern discussion of *The Red Tent*.

½ cup dried apricots (about 3 ounces)

¾ cup pitted dates, chopped (about 4 ounces)

⅓ cup dried Mission figs, coarsely chopped
(about 2 ounces)

⅓ cup raisins

¾ cup port wine (or sweet kosher wine)

½ teaspoon ground cinnamon

⅓ cup almonds, pistachio nuts, or walnuts

Juice of ½ lemon (about 1½ tablespoons)

16–20 2-inch pita triangles, toasted

4 ounces goat cheese

1. Place the apricots in a bowl and cover with warm water. Let soak until plump, about 30 minutes. Drain and finely chop.

2. Place the chopped apricots, dates, figs, raisins, wine, and cinnamon in a saucepan. Cook over medium heat, stirring, until mixture thickens. Remove from heat.

3. If using almonds or walnuts, toast them briefly in a hot frying pan until fragrant but not browned. Spread the nuts on a flat surface and crush (the flat side of a cleaver or flat end of a knife handle is good for this).

4. Add the crushed nuts to the compote and stir to blend. Stir in the lemon juice, a little at a time, to taste. Allow to cool.

5. Spread a thin layer of the compote on a toasted pita triangle, put a dollop of goat cheese on top, and serve.

Yield: 8 to 12 servings

BOOK CLUB PROFILE

"We started as a much younger group," claims Carol Morrissey, one of the core of faithful charter members of the Beaufort, South Carolina, Les Livres Book Club. Meeting since 1991 with an open-door policy, Les Livres has swelled to more than thirty members. The club has an elected president, who serves as the group's administrator and often facilitates the meetings, which usually draw twelve to eighteen women monthly.

Food and drink help catalyze the discussion for Les Livres. When they meet, each member brings either a bottle of wine or an appetizer. "We drink too much wine at our meetings," admits member Debbie Pate, "but we're very weight-conscious." At times, members spontaneously decide to bring thematic food: honey for Sue Monk Kidd's *The Secret Life of Bees* (see p. 398), chocolate for Laura Esquivel's *Like Water for Chocolate,* and French food and wine for Sandra Gulland's *The Many Lives and Secret Sorrows of Josephine B.*

Les Livres members pay annual dues, which are donated to charity. In 2001, the group donated to the Literacy Volunteers of the Lowcountry, which sponsors literacy programs for adults, children, and new Americans. The following year, they purchased a Christmas tree to benefit a local hospice, decorating it with bookmarks they had made and bought, and with decorative angels holding books made out of noodles.

The women of Les Livres found much to discuss in *The Red Tent,* especially the issues it raises about women's physical and emotional health. With three obstetrician-gynecologists and several nurses in the group, much of their discussion focused on giving birth. In *The Red Tent,* Leah's sisters attend her difficult labor and delivery, while Inna, the midwife, offers herbs, oils, and massage to ease her pain. "We've taken something that's supposed to be so natural, childbirth, and made it so clinical," says Morrissey, a former critical-care nurse. "Coming into womanhood was celebrated in *The Red Tent,* but modern Western society has taken all that away. Even the ob-gyns in our group agreed that women have lost control of the birth process."

Group members also mourned the passing of a time that nurtured close female bonding. Rachel and Bilhah "strained and reddened together, and they cried out with a single voice" when Bilhah's baby was born. "In the world today, we feel like we have a couple of close friends, but the sisterliness of those times is just not around anymore," says Morrissey.

More Food for Thought

Cookbook author Judy Bart Kancigor assembled a gourmet biblical feast for her book club's discussion of *The Red Tent*. Her Second Wednesday Dinner Book Club of Fullerton, California, enjoyed a menu of bread dipped in toasted ground almond and sesame dip or pomegranate molasses; salad (arugula, thinly sliced onions, olives, and cucumbers) with olive oil and wine vinegar dressing; and Jacob's pottage (a hearty lentil stew). Kancigor found most of her recipes in Kitty Morse's *A Biblical Feast: Foods from the Holy Land* (Ten Speed Press, 1998), a cookbook that uses only the approximately eighty ingredients mentioned in the Bible to create dishes appealing to the modern palate.

Bonnie Kulke, of the Bethel Bookwomen, in Madison, Wisconsin, baked molasses-seed cookies, an original creation, for her book club's discussion of *The Red Tent*. Kulke, an herb grower, especially enjoys cooking with herbs and sharing her knowledge of their history.

"Some of the seeds in this recipe were discussed in the book, so I thought it would be fun to tell everyone some of the interesting history and uses of these herbs and spices," says Kulke. "For example, coriander was thought to have been an ingredient in the Old Testament manna. Caraway was so treasured that Egyptians were buried with it. Fennel was eaten in ancient times by women to prevent obesity, and anise is helpful for soothing colic in babies and to stimulate the milk supply in nursing mothers," says Kulke.

A River Sutra

Gita Mehta

NAN A. TALESE, *1993*

(available in paperback from Vintage Books, 1994)

A WORK OF FICTION, *A River Sutra* is set on the banks of India's Narmada River. Pilgrims who walk for two arduous years, following the course of the river from the mountains to the ocean in search of redemption, believe this holy river to be the daughter of the god Shiva. Assuming a personality of her own, sometimes human, sometimes godlike, the Narmada flows ceaselessly through *A River Sutra,* and the book's narrator leaves behind his life of privilege as a high-ranking bureaucrat to manage a rest home where he "can hear the river's heartbeat pulsing under the ground." On the Narmada's banks he encounters ascetics, spurned lovers, courtesans, musicians, and madmen. It is through their stories of love, desire, violence, and enlightenment that the protagonist begins to understand the complex mysteries of humanity and the significance of his own place in the world.

GITA MEHTA'S GANGA-JAMNA DAL (LENTILS)

A River Sutra brings to mind other great Indian rivers. Gita Mehta suggests pairing dal, a classic Indian lentil dish, with the reading and discussion of *A River Sutra,* as a metaphor for the several holy rivers that wind through the Indian subcontinent. Here is how Gita Mehta explains her recipe, which we present below:

Made from a combination of red and brown lentils, I call this dish the Ganga-Jamna Dal, after the two great north Indian rivers, the Ganges and the Jamna. The two rivers rise from a common source in the

Tibetan plateau, but one side is muddy and the other side, flowing over rocks, is clear. I am told by those who have been there that the two strands of water do indeed look gold and silver in the sunlight, perhaps explaining why, in India, combinations of gold and silver colors in any form are named after these two holy rivers.

Mehta chose a dal recipe for practical reasons, too. "Dal is the great staple of the Indian diet," she tells us, "a whole food high in protein and low in fat, impossible to overcook, excellent for re-heating, able to be expanded for unexpected guests with the addition of more water, and so versa-tile it will accommodate the addition of almost any vegetable from aubergines to spinach to mushrooms to green beans." Not only that, Mehta finds the dish perfectly suited to her life as a writer, as it "eliminates the boring necessities of shopping more than once a month; cooking more than once a week (maximum); and deciding what to eat."

Brown lentils, or *masoor dal,* and red lentils are the same bean (see p. 499 for purchasing in-formation). The difference is that brown lentils are unskinned and therefore cook more slowly. Soaking the brown lentils in cold water for one hour will even the cooking time. Mehta instructed us to leave the seeds in the chiles so they can leak into the sauce, adding flavor and heat. If you prefer a milder dal, you can remove the seeds from the chiles before adding them to the sauce.

In India, dal is always eaten as an entrée or as an accompaniment to an entrée. If you serve it as an appetizer, note the varying yields.

NOTE: Wear plastic or rubber gloves while handling chiles to protect your skin from the oil in them. Avoid direct contact with eyes, and wash hands thoroughly after handling.

2 tablespoons vegetable oil

2 teaspoons whole cumin seed

1 small onion, finely chopped

¾ cup brown lentils, soaked in cold water for 1 hour and drained

1 cup red lentils, washed and drained (see Purchasing Information, p. 499)

3½ cups water

¼ teaspoon turmeric powder

4 large cloves of garlic, peeled and slightly crushed with flat edge of knife

1 1-inch piece of ginger, peeled

2 plum tomatoes, skinned and chopped

2 serrano or other hot green chiles (or more to taste), sliced lengthwise

1 teaspoon salt

Lime or lemon wedges

Suggested accompaniments

Basmati rice or pita bread

Yogurt (may add chopped cilantro and salt)

Sweet mango chutney, such as Major Grey's
   (see Purchasing Information, p. 499)

Mango pickles

Chicken or lamb kabobs

1. Heat the oil in a large saucepan or Dutch oven over medium heat. Add the cumin and sauté 2 minutes, stirring. Add the onion and cook for a few more minutes, until it begins to soften. Add the brown and red lentils and cook for another minute.

2. Add the water, turmeric, garlic, and ginger. Increase the heat and bring to a boil. Stir well, reduce heat to low, and simmer, covered, for 15 minutes.

3. Add the tomatoes, chiles, and salt. Simmer, covered, an additional 40 minutes. If the dal begins to stick to the bottom of the pan or is too thick, stir in a little warm water.

4. Remove the garlic, ginger, and chiles (seeds may remain in sauce). Whisk the dal to the consistency of a thick soup. Add additional salt to taste. Serve with lime or lemon wedges and accompaniments, as desired.

Yield: 6 to 8 servings as an entrée, 12 servings as an appetizer

BOOK CLUB PROFILE

The Sage Sisters Book Club of Cody, Wyoming, formed in 2002 when the young mothers in a toddlers' playgroup realized that they shared an interest in books as well as children. The twelve women started meeting at night, sans kids.

The Sage Sisters love the food connections in books and try to prepare thematic foods for all of their meetings, but they are particularly drawn to ethnic foods. Cofounder Jessie Wagner spent her junior year of college in Cuba and recently cooked a Cuban feast, complete with chilled avocado soup, empanadas de picadillo, green salad with mango and bananas, rum custard, and *mojitos* (see p. 246), for a discussion of Cristina García's Cuba-based novel *The Agüero Sisters*. Even the Sage Sisters' "extracurricular" events involve food. At their *Big Fat Greek Wedding* party, where members looked through one another's wedding albums, watched the eponymous movie, and ate gyros, baklava, and hummus, they talked extensively about marriage, a common bond among the women.

It was religious differences, though, that enriched the book club's discussion of *A River*

Sutra. The Sage Sisters represent a variety of religions—Catholic, Methodist, Baptist, Jehovah's Witness—and have a couple members who are interested in Buddhism and Quakerism. *A River Sutra*'s exploration of asceticism inspired members to draw on their own religious backgrounds to delve into issues of faith, belief, the pull of monasticism, and, as Wagner put it, "what's really important." This was "one of the few books where our discussion got personal but also stayed relevant to the book," says Wagner. "Our discussion of *A River Sutra* was very deep and spiritual."

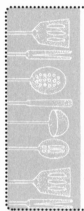

More Food for Thought

True to form, Sage Sisters member Liz Campbell prepared an Indian feast to complement her group's discussion of *A River Sutra*. The menu included samosas, spicy cabbage slaw with cilantro, tandoori chicken, cucumber sauce, and mango. Says Campbell, "I have a few close friends from India, and I vividly remember the amazing food they have cooked for me and the evenings dining with them. This was the mood I tried to re-create."

The Road from Coorain

Jill Ker Conway

KNOPF, *1989*

(available in paperback from Vintage, 1990)

In *THE ROAD FROM COORAIN*, Jill Ker Conway, former president of Smith College, in Northampton, Massachusetts, chronicled her childhood growing up on a remote sheep farm on the western plains of Australia.

In 1930, Conway's parents moved their family of two young boys to the land granted to them by the government. They named it Coorain, the aboriginal word for "windy place." With efficiency and discipline, the hardworking couple set about furnishing their simple bush house, setting in fences, and acquiring animals. Their youngest child, Jill, was born in 1934. Jill's early childhood days were spent teaching herself to read and acting as her father's station hand: mustering sheep, checking fences, and cleaning water troughs. The family was content, and the farm prospered.

Disaster struck in 1941 with the arrival of a devastating five-year drought. The subsequent death of Conway's father, possibly by his own hand, further traumatized the family. In 1945, with her brothers away at boarding school, Conway and her mother moved to Sydney, a seaport city, where her mother managed the farm from a distance and Conway attended school with peers for the first time.

Conway's academic studies at private schools and the University of Sydney ignited her interest in literature and history. Her increasing awareness of the limitations of the Australian educational system, then influenced heavily by British colonial rule, as well as the increasing demands and dependency of her mother, precipitated Conway's application to Harvard University. She soon sets off to begin a new phase of her life in America.

The foods in *The Road from Coorain* sprang from life in the Australian bush in the 1930s and 1940s. Conway's family ate a "standard bush diet" of homegrown meat, potatoes, pickles, eggs, homemade butter, and wild spinach, along with doses of cod liver oil and lime juice to compensate for lack of fresh produce. With the installation at Coorain of a windmill and a forty-thousand-gallon water tank came the joy of fresh fruit. Conway reveled in "the scent of orange and lemon trees, the taste of fat green grapes, and the discovery of salads."

The bounty of the garden, however, did not alter the staples of the diet, a source of adolescent friction and rebellion. At age seventeen, Conway realized that her swollen ankles and extra weight were due, at least in part, to her mother's "generous hand with salt." She rejected her mother's cooking, steadfastly refusing to eat much of the "daily fare of meat and potatoes."

But Conway also fondly recalls her mother's efficient and industrious character, reflected in her cooking. On Thursdays—baking day—Conway's mother would make scones, cupcakes, sponge and pound cakes, tarts, flans, and meat pies, all in the oven of a woodstove. She gave "a quick test of the hand to determine whether the oven temperature was 'just right' to brown pastry or make a sponge cake rise." Conway also reminisced about her mother's Christmas specialties: "succulent roast turkeys and ambrosial plum pudding."

VICKI LEE BOYAJIAN'S
ANZAC COOKIES

If nothing else, *The Road from Coorain* is a tribute to the rugged beauty of the Australian outback. No food is more quintessentially Australian than ANZAC (the acronym for Australian and New Zealand Army Corps) biscuits, which were made by women in Australia and New Zealand for their brothers, husbands, and sons fighting in World War I. Originally called Soldiers' Biscuits, these oat-and-coconut concoctions were designed to keep well during naval travel and provide the fighting men with needed nutrition. The binding agent for the biscuits is Lyle's Golden Syrup, a liquid sweetener popular in England, rather than eggs, most likely because poultry farmers' enlistment in the service caused a scarcity of eggs.

Vicki Lee Boyajian, a former bakery owner and caterer in the Boston, Massachusetts, area, contributed her legendary recipe for ANZAC "cookies," as she calls them. She originally learned the recipe from her boss, Billie Merrill, a bakery owner in Concord, California. Boyajian brought the recipe east and introduced it in series of suburban bakeries bearing her name, including the Vicki Lee Boyajian bakery in Needham, Massachusetts. Although Boyajian sold the bakery in 1999, her reputation for yummy ANZAC cookies followed her.

"Everywhere I go, people associate that cookie with me," says Boyajian. "The recipe itself is like the American flag, or apple pie. It's a national symbol of a country."

In addition to the traditional ingredients, Boyajian's cookies incorporate walnuts to make a deliciously chewy, nutty treat. Boyajian tells us that the key to good ANZAC cookies lies in using Lyle's Golden Syrup, a readily available brand of the sweetener. "There really is no substitute," she says (see p. 499 for purchasing information).

This treat from Down Under will have your book club standing at attention.

1 cup all-purpose flour	1/4 teaspoon salt
1 cup sugar	1 teaspoon baking soda
1 cup old-fashioned rolled oats	2 tablespoons boiling water
1 cup coarsely chopped walnuts	1/2 cup (1 stick) unsalted butter
1 cup unsweetened shredded coconut (see	3 tablespoons Lyle's Golden Syrup (see
Purchasing Information, p. 499)	Purchasing Information, p. 499)

1. Adjust oven rack to center position and preheat to 350°F.
2. Combine the flour, sugar, oats, walnuts, coconut, and salt in a bowl. Set aside.
3. Measure the baking soda into a small bowl. Pour a splash of the boiling water in and stir until mixture stops fizzing. Repeat until you use all the water and the fizzing stops.
4. In a small saucepan, melt the butter. Remove from heat. Add the syrup to melted butter and stir.
5. Pour the butter-syrup mixture and the baking soda–water mixture into the flour mixture. Stirring by hand, combine well.
6. Use an ice cream scoop to form rounded balls of batter and arrange on an ungreased baking sheet. Using your palm, press batter into disks about 3 inches in diameter. Bake until edges are golden, 8–10 minutes. Do not overbake. Allow to cool on the baking sheet.

Yield: About 1½ dozen cookies

BOOK CLUB PROFILE

The twelve members of Bethel BookWomen, a book club of the Bethel Lutheran Church in Madison, Wisconsin, have been meeting since 1994. They read historical fiction, biographies, and classics. Although the group began when their pastor, Laura Nelson, formed a club to read works by female authors, their reading has evolved to include works by male authors, too.

The BookWomen are women readers of all ages who enjoy the fellowship of the group and share news about themselves, their friends, and family. "We respect our differences regarding personal interpretation and learn from one another," says member Norma Hereen.

Members occasionally bring treats to share to the monthly meetings. For their discussion of Anita Diamant's *The Red Tent* (see p. 374), member Bonnie Kulke brought cookies that incorporated herbs and spices described in the novel.

Each spring the group meets at Borders Books in Madison to pore through titles and compile the coming year's reading list. Hereen says the yearly book selection ritual contributes to the group's cohesiveness. "Members have the opportunity to promote the book they may especially want the group to read." Favorite authors, such as Wallace Stegner and Willa Cather, are reconsidered during this meeting, and the BookWomen look for new titles to promote variety.

Author Jill Ker Conway's experiences growing up as a "bush" girl on a sheep station in Australia, chronicled in her memoir *The Road from Coorain,* fascinated the Bethel BookWomen. "Many areas of Australia are often dry and bleak," says Hereen, "but Conway wrote of the beauty and color she found in the country, providing a vivid picture of New South Wales."

The BookWomen discussed the role the Australian government played in encouraging citizens to move to the bush and the motivation for Conway's parents to move there. They also explored Conway's mother's role in creating a positive family environment and educating her children.

Hereen says the BookWomen often enrich the discussion by relating themes and events in books to personal experiences. One of the members compared the aloneness and hardship faced by her Norwegian grandmother, who had immigrated to the United States without the support of family members, to the loneliness faced by Conway's mother. Another member contrasted the drought and dust on the sheep station where Conway was raised to her mother's stories about living through the Great Plains Dust Bowl in the 1930s, when a prolonged drought and soil erosion combined with heavy winds to create huge dense clouds of dust. She recounted tales of losing the family vegetable garden and stuffing rags around the windowsills to try to prevent the fine dust from coming into the home, says Hereen.

"*The Road from Coorain* clearly depicted what ingenuity and hard work can accomplish," says Hereen. "It also tells a fascinating story of a family's happiness and times of failure, conflict between mother and daughter, tragedy, and intellectual quest."

The Samurai's Garden

Gail Tsukiyama

ST. MARTIN'S, *1995*

(available in paperback from St. Martin's, 1996)

Sent off from college to his parents' beach house in the small Japanese village of Tarumi to recover from tuberculosis in 1937, Stephen, the young Chinese protagonist of Gail Tsukiyama's *The Samurai's Garden*, finds the town devoid of young people. Most of the men have been drafted into the army. The young women shy away from any Chinese men. And so, isolated, Stephen turns to his art for comfort and to the taciturn caretaker of the beach house, Matsu, for companionship.

Stephen has limited though frightful memories of Matsu from childhood visits to the beach house. But as Matsu slowly nurses Stephen back to health, Matsu's initial reticence yields. Matsu introduces Stephen to his friends Sachi, a leper living in a mountain village, and Kenzo, Sachi's former boyfriend.

Through these characters, *The Samurai's Garden* explores the many faces of beauty. Sachi's deformed appearance masks an irrepressible inner kindness. Her rock garden ripples with a simple, quiet elegance. "Beauty can be found in most places," Matsu says, and Stephen's experience in Tarumi reveals this, along with more painful truths about loyalty and prejudice.

Food first begins to melt the frosty relationship between the newly arrived Stephen and his host, Matsu. Although language and personality keep the two from talking much, Matsu extends a welcome by preparing a breakfast of rice with pickled vegetables and miso soup on Stephen's first morning in Tarumi. Although the men exchange only six words over breakfast, later in the day Stephen recalls the breakfast: "Matsu was certainly a good cook, even if he wasn't much of a talker."

Later, Matsu uses a tray of food as a vehicle to convey approval. He interrupts Stephen's painting with a tray of "noodles sprinkled with green onions and thin slices of fish, a rice cake, and tea." After slurping his noodles, Stephen notices another box containing several beautiful paintbrushes that once belonged to Stephen's grandfather. Matsu's offering, brought in subtly on a tray of food, is a sign of approval of Stephen's beloved pastime, and brings the two closer.

Matsu and Sachi also nurture each other with food. After Sachi's attempt to take her life, Matsu brings her food and tea. "Even though the tea tasted cold and bitter, I have never been more grateful for anything in my life. He also brought along some rice cakes and a package of dry seaweed which I ate hungrily," says Sachi. In turn, many years later, Sachi tries to please Matsu with food. With few options to openly enjoy their relationship, their moments of pleasure often take place in Sachi's hut in the mountain village, where Matsu and Stephen visit her. After serving Matsu marinated eel, tofu, and rice, "she stood quietly to one side, and watched him take his first mouthful, chew, then nod his head approvingly as her lips curved upward just slightly into a smile."

HIYASHI UDON (COLD UDON NOODLES) WITH DIPPING SAUCE

Of the many dishes peppering the pages of *The Samurai's Garden,* noodles are a staple of the Japanese diet. Popular lunch spots, Japanese noodle houses serve both soba, thin brown noodles made from buckwheat flour, and udon, thick, round wheat noodles. Our recipe calls for udon, as Matsu prepares for Stephen, but you can substitute soba if desired.

The Japanese consider the noisy slurping of noodles to be a sign of gastronomic satisfaction. Let members of your book club fill small bowls with noodles and toppings. Then offer chopsticks, so they can dip small portions of noodles into the sauce and slurp as loudly as they please.

NOTE: Udon noodles are available either dried or precooked and refrigerated. Either will work fine.

NOTE: Dashi is a soup stock made with dried bonito tuna flakes, used widely in Japanese cooking.

For information on purchasing specialty ingredients, including dashi, mirin, udon noodles, nori, and wasabi paste, see Purchasing Information, p. 499.

For the sauce
2 cups dashi (see note)
¾ cup soy sauce
6 tablespoons mirin (sweet rice wine) (see note)
1½ teaspoons sugar

For the noodles
2½ pounds precooked udon noodles, or 2 10-ounce packages dried udon noodles (see note)

Garnishes

½ *pound silken (soft) tofu*

2 *sheets nori (seaweed sheets) (see note)*

½ *cup chopped scallions*

1 *tablespoon wasabi paste (see note)*

1. To make the sauce: Combine the dashi, soy sauce, mirin, and sugar in a small saucepan. Bring to a boil over medium heat, stirring to combine, and remove from heat. Let the mixture cool. If making ahead of time, refrigerate until needed. Sauce may be served cool or at room temperature.

2. To make the noodles: If using dried noodles, prepare according to package directions. For precooked noodles, cook in boiling water for 1½ minutes. Drain udon well under cold running water, then place in a bowl filled with ice water for a few minutes. Drain again before serving.

3. To make the garnishes: Slice the tofu into ½-inch slabs and place between paper towels for 10 minutes to remove excess moisture. Cut into ½-inch cubes and keep refrigerated until ready to serve. Toast the nori briefly over an open flame until it flakes apart easily. Do not let it blacken. If no gas flame is available, toast in a toaster oven for a few seconds or in a dry skillet. Crumble into small pieces.

4. Fill individual plates with udon and serve accompanied by chopsticks and bowls of dipping sauce. Arrange tofu, scallions, nori, and wasabi on a plate or in small bowls and serve with the noodles.

Yield: 10 to 12 servings

BOOK CLUB PROFILE

When Debby Saltzman and her fellow book club members meet in Westborough, Massachusetts, there is always a feast for the senses. "We use food, scenery, costumes from the book—whatever it takes to transport us to the time and place of the book we're reading," says Saltzman, a member since the group's beginning in 1997. About twenty at-home moms and working women, all in their late thirties or early forties, belong to the group, and about a dozen members attend any given meeting. The group reads and discusses mostly current fiction, with an occasional memoir or classic.

According to Saltzman, often the hostess will decorate her house—or herself—to re-create the mood of the book. For *The Red Tent* by Anita Diamant (see p. 374), hostess Noel Foy draped tapestries over the doorways to simulate the feel of a tent and scattered pillows on the floor. She dressed in a toga, approximating desert wear, and even placed a deer ornament on the table as a symbol of animal sacrifice. When they discussed *Girl with a Pearl Earring* by Tracy Chevalier (see p. 153), hostess Mary Kate Reid dressed as the Dutch servant girl, donning a large turban and an earring. Along with the elaborate decorations, thematic food and drink are also staples for this creative group.

Marjorie Ashton went to great lengths to prepare her house for the group's discussion of *A Samurai's Garden,* a book the group highly recommends. To simulate the book's Japanese setting, she moved furniture out of her living room, set up a large, low table on cinder blocks, and decorated the table with straw mats and paper lanterns. She served Japanese food from a local restaurant, including sushi, miso soup, and Japanese beer.

The group appreciated the unusual subject matter of *A Samurai's Garden.* They admired Sachi, "a beautiful person who has leprosy," and marveled at Matsu's devotion to her. "Taking care of Sachi the way Matsu did shows an unbelievable amount of compassion," says Saltzman. "We liked the emotion of this book." They felt Gail Tsukiyama established a strong sense of place in the book, especially in Sachi's garden, where "the sense of peacefulness that the author created was very satisfying." Finally, the group enjoyed the novelty of a book about a Chinese man living in Japan during the war. "We just appreciated the exotic nature of this book," says Saltzman.

More Food for Thought

The Sage Sisters of Cody, Wyoming, enjoyed home-cooked Chinese food—fried wontons, beef with green onions, fried eggrolls, white rice, stir-fried broccoli with egg, and fortune cookies—for their discussion of *The Samurai's Garden.* "I don't know how to cook Japanese food," explains Liz Campbell, who hosted the meeting, "so I cooked my own version of some Chinese dishes," a fitting tribute to the protagonist's Chinese heritage. "The smells really transported us. Eating the meal was a fun way to end the evening," says Campbell.

Seabiscuit:
An American Legend

Laura Hillenbrand

....

RANDOM HOUSE, 2001

(available in paperback from Ballantine, 2002)

Despite his legendary lineage, no one expected Seabiscuit, a sleepy colt whose body "had all the properties of a cinder block," to go far. *Seabiscuit* tells the true story of this unlikely hero, and the three men whose lives were inextricably linked with one of the greatest Thoroughbreds of all time. Seabiscuit rose to fame during the Depression, when Americans desperately needed both heroes and distractions from the burdens of their daily lives. In 1934, Seabiscuit was languishing in an obscure stable, losing races, when veteran trainer Tom Smith spotted him. "I'll see you again," murmured the taciturn Smith. Two years later, Smith convinced his boss, stable owner and self-made millionaire Charles Howard, to buy the colt. Under Smith's tutelage—and the hand of jockey Red Pollard—Seabiscuit captivated a nation and galloped into sporting history.

PUMPKIN BISCUITS

In keeping with her book group's tradition of preparing desserts connected with the reading selection, Ruth Kolbe wanted to combine biscuits with another thematic ingredient to complement her club's discussion of *Seabiscuit*. She settled on pumpkin, the name of the former cow pony that trainer Tom Smith housed with Seabiscuit as a way of soothing the unhappy Thoroughbred. Pumpkin, who was "broad as a Sherman tank and yellow as a daisy," had a calming effect on Seabiscuit. The two remained steadfast friends and stablemates for the remainder of their lives.

Kolbe adapted a recipe for pumpkin biscuits to her taste. The resulting biscuits, served with clotted cream, were an odds-on favorite at her book club gathering.

2 cups all-purpose flour, plus extra as needed
    to form dough

¼ cup sugar

1½ tablespoons baking powder

1 teaspoon salt

½ teaspoon ground cinnamon

¼ teaspoon ground nutmeg

¼ teaspoon ground ginger

¼ teaspoon ground allspice

5⅓ tablespoons cold butter

¾ cup canned pumpkin purée

¾ cup half-and-half or equal parts milk
    and light cream

¾ cup finely chopped roasted pecans

1. Preheat oven to 450°F.
2. Place the flour, sugar, baking powder, salt, cinnamon, nutmeg, ginger, and allspice in a medium-size mixing bowl and stir well to combine.
3. Cut butter into flour mixture with a pastry blender or fork until the batter resembles coarse crumbs.
4. Add the pumpkin, half-and-half, and pecans and stir just until moistened and a soft dough forms. More flour may be added here if needed, but just enough to make the dough easy to handle.
5. On a lightly floured surface, roll the dough out to ½-inch thickness. Cut into approximately 2½-inch rounds with a floured biscuit or cookie cutter and place 1 inch apart on a lightly greased cookie sheet.
6. Bake for 8–12 minutes or until golden brown. Serve hot with butter, honey, and jam.

Yield: Approximately 12 biscuits

BOOK CLUB PROFILE

Mary Ann Oldfield describes her book club as "pure joy—it's the best thing outside of family." The group formed when Oldfield and other mothers in a neighborhood playgroup confided they missed reading and keeping up with the latest titles. Two men later joined the group. The group's passion for reading and the bond they share has endured: Twenty-two years later the members live in various Massachusetts communities but continue to meet monthly.

Oldfield attributes the group's longevity to their disciplined focus on the book discussion. "It has never been a book club of just good friends. We're not too chatty. There will always be an intellectual discussion about the book," says Oldfield. She also credits the choice of "good books, not just bestsellers, but quality literature," for the group's success and longevity. "This is in no small measure due to the contributions of two of our earliest members, a successful publishing professional and a librarian."

Group members also are cooking enthusiasts. The host always prepares a dessert that has been mentioned in the reading selection or is symbolic of a theme or element in the book. The host mulls over the choice of dessert while reading the book, leaving the rest "to wonder what treat the host has prepared," says Oldfield. The group celebrates the end of the reading season in June, with a dinner that complements that month's selected book's theme.

Oldfield's book club rates each book they read, with the high scores going to books that tell a compelling story with strong character development. "But the biggest points go to someone who can really write, and those are books that don't just resonate for days but for years," says Oldfield. Favorites have included *The Killer Angels* by Michael Shaara (see p. 216), *The Great Gatsby* by F. Scott Fitzgerald (see p. 171), and *Seabiscuit*.

Laura Hillenbrand's meticulous research and her exploration of the lives of horse trainers and jockeys made a deep impression. "We all had many dog-eared pages in *Seabiscuit*," says Oldfield. The group discussed the importance horse racing held for so many people in the Depression. "We wondered if this could happen now and whether any current activity unites our nation or captures its imagination."

Discussion of *Seabiscuit* reminded Oldfield of a board game, Kentucky Derby, that she had played as a child. She searched for it on eBay, and bought the vintage game. "Sure enough, Seabiscuit was in a post position," says Oldfield.

More Food for Thought

The Novel Women, readers from several of Massachusetts' North Shore communities, had a Kentucky Derby–themed book club meeting for their *Seabiscuit* discussion. Andi Galligan's Hamilton, Massachusetts, home provided the perfect backdrop for the meeting. Home to the prestigious Myopia Hunt Club, one of the country's oldest existing hunt clubs, Hamilton is horse country. "We have horses grazing on three sides," says Galligan, who served buttermilk biscuits with jam, mint juleps (see p. 172), and "big, gorgeous" strawberries dipped in confectioners' sugar.

The Secret History

Donna Tartt

....

KNOPF, *1992*

(available in paperback from Ballantine, 1993)

*T*HE SECRET HISTORY is the tragic tale of six college friends who immerse themselves in the classical Greek world. Their secret performance of an ancient ritual leads to violence, more secrets, and a gradual unraveling of their friendship.

Richard Papen narrates the story. Newly arrived at tiny Hampden College in Vermont, Richard is determined to continue his study of classical Greek. He registers for a class with Julian, an eccentric instructor, who insists that his tiny collection of students drop all classes other than his own. By signing on, Richard enters an elite but isolated world of Grecophiles delving deeper and deeper into ancient Greek language, ritual, and practice.

Particularly intriguing to the group is Dionysus, the Greek god of fertility, ritual dance, mysticism, altered states, ecstasy, terror, wildness, and deliverance. Four of the friends—Henry, Francis, and the twins, Charles and Camilla—hold a bacchanal, or spiritual frenzy, achieving a state of ecstasy and, as they had hoped, seeing Dionysus. They also commit murder.

Neither Bunny, another group member, nor Richard attends the bacchanal. When Bunny learns of the murder, though, he becomes a threat to the group's secrecy. The group must respond; in so doing it cascades further into violence and remorse.

A gripping murder mystery, *The Secret History* revolves around college relationships shattering under the weight of shifting allegiances, myriad sexual liaisons, and communal responsibility for certain brutal acts.

Notable throughout *The Secret History* is alcohol. Whether it's scotch, whiskey, gin, champagne, stout, Campari, Bloody Marys, beer, or wine, at almost any time of day and in almost every setting, at least some of the friends can be found drinking. Drunken revelry accompanied celebration of Greek Dionysian festivals, in which the friends show a keen interest. But the group's drinking throughout the book is more likely related to the freedom of college and a means of escaping reality than to a libation to the greatness of classical Greek civilization.

Food in *The Secret History* generally involves basic college fare—eggs, bacon, omelets, pizza, peanut-butter sandwiches, orange juice, and tea. As is typical for college students, the friends savor a home-cooked meal. On one occasion, Julian prepares dinner—roasted lamb, new potatoes, and peas with leeks and fennel—that "had a sort of Augustan wholesomeness and luxuriance which never failed to soothe."

At this meal, Richard notices that a fourth course has also appeared: mushrooms. Although benign-looking, the dish actually carries with it malevolent implications. Earlier, Henry had revealed to Richard his intent to kill Bunny, who threatens to expose the group's murderous secret, by feeding him *Amanita phalloides*, or death-cap mushrooms. By serving the benign mushrooms to Julian, Henry is laying the groundwork for his plot to prepare and serve the poisonous variety to Bunny.

Mushrooms are an apt choice for Henry because of their role in the ancient world. Agrippina, Claudius's wife, is believed to have poisoned the emperor by slipping him some deadly amanitas. In fact, the Romans ate a benign variety, *Amanita caesarea*, quite frequently, which facilitated the implementation of Agrippina's plot.

The ancients also appreciated the hallucinogenic properties of mushrooms, which are believed to have played a role in bacchanals. The wine of bacchanals was often diluted with the juice of deadly nightshade plant, which Henry names as the antidote to *Amanita phalloides*. It is said that during Dionysian orgies, the eyes of fanatic female worshippers under the influence of belladonna ("beautiful lady"), derived from deadly nightshade, would dilate as they fell into the arms of male worshippers, or fell upon them to tear them apart.

NORTHERN TRUST BANK'S GRILLED PORTOBELLO MUSHROOMS

To help put you in an ancient frame of mind, we offer below a mushroom dish of the nonpoisonous variety.

Jennifer Stein, head chef at Northern Trust Bank of Florida in Miami, prepares these grilled portobello mushrooms for meetings of the Brickell Avenue Literary Society, one of many literary clubs sponsored by Northern Trust Bank, a venerable private banking, trust, and investment institution.

"The mushrooms are delicious and have become regular fare at the meetings of the Brickell Avenue Literary Society," says Bill Murphy, vice president at Northern Trust Bank and secretary and treasurer of the Literary Society. "There are plenty of vegetarians, as well as dieters, in the group." Murphy says the mushrooms make a nice alternative, or an accompaniment, to grilled fillet of beef.

At the Society's luncheons, the mushrooms are typically served as part of a buffet, with salads—Caesar, Greek, or Caprese—smoked salmon, smoked whitefish spread, fruit salad, rice pilaf, sautéed mixed vegetables, grilled fillet of beef with horseradish sauce, grilled mahimahi with mango-papaya salsa, or turkey breast with fresh cranberry relish.

For the marinade

¼ cup minced fresh garlic

¼ cup balsamic vinegar

¼ cup light soy sauce

¼ cup olive oil

1 tablespoon minced fresh thyme

6 portobello mushrooms, stems removed and gently cleaned with a damp paper towel

1. Mix all the marinade ingredients together in a shallow bowl. Add the mushrooms and let sit at room temperature for 2 hours.
2. Grill or broil mushrooms on medium-hot grill or broiler for 3–4 minutes per side. Slice and serve immediately.

Yield: 6 servings

BOOK CLUB PROFILE

The nine women of the Movie Stars Book Club of Portland, Oregon, believe that you have to know a person to trust his or her judgment about books. So they introduce themselves on their website (www.geocities.com/moviestarbookclub) and hope that visitors to the site like what they see. "We hold a wide array of opinions and enjoy various personality traits, so maybe you will find one of us to whom you can relate," reads their site.

To help visitors to the site get to know members, each Movie Stars member suggests an actress who might portray her "if our book club was a movie." They also list their occupations and favorite books and movies.

The nine Movie Stars—in their late twenties and early thirties, and all college-educated professionals—have been meeting monthly since 1995 to discuss books ranging from classics to contemporary fiction and nonfiction. Some of their favorites include John Irving's *A Prayer for Owen Meany* (see p. 363); Margaret Atwood's *Alias Grace,* based on a sensational 1843 murder trial; and Anne Fadiman's *The Spirit Catches You and You Fall Down* (see p. 410). October is always devoted to a scary book, like Vincent Bugliosi's *Helter Skelter: The True Story of the Manson Murders,* a prosecuting attorney's account of those chilling crimes, which the group found "creepy but completely fascinating."

One of the best books the Movie Stars ever read, Donna Tartt's *The Secret History,* captivated the group with its riveting plot. Six members ranked it among their top five favorite books. "This was our favorite book collectively," says Blythe Butler, an associate dean of admissions at Lewis and Clark College and cofounder of the Movie Stars. "It was such a page-turner, but it was also a really smart book. We liked the combination of murder mystery and classical text. We were captivated by the author's storytelling skill: the characters are thoroughly despicable, the setting is depressing, you learn whodunit on page one, and still we couldn't put it down!"

Dinner, including book-related foods, always accompanies Movie Stars Book Club discussions. The group enjoyed baked potatoes for Frank McCourt's *Angela's Ashes* (see p. 16), Asian food for Arthur Golden's *Memoirs of a Geisha* (see p. 255), and candy "soma" for Aldous Huxley's *Brave New World,* in which citizens of a futuristic society take drugs, or soma, daily to fight depression. "Cooking and eating are almost as much fun as talking about the books, and with each meeting we learn to love a new kind of cuisine," says Butler.

More Food for Thought

The Movie Stars Book Club brought the classical Greek theme of *The Secret History* into the modern era. Their ethnic Greek menu included homemade *tzatziki* (see p. 267), hummus, and Greek salad and store-bought pita bread, falafel, and ouzo, a Greek liquor. "While most of us had eaten Greek food in restaurants, we hadn't made it ourselves before. We were surprised at how easy and delicious it was," says Blythe Butler. "Although it wasn't exactly the bacchanal portrayed in *The Secret History,* it put us in the mood."

The Secret Life of Bees

Sue Monk Kidd

VIKING, 2003

(available in paperback from Penguin, 2003)

THIS DEBUT NOVEL, set in South Carolina after the passage of the 1964 Civil Rights Act, weaves the coming-of-age story of Lily Owens with themes of race relations, feminism, and divinity. Fourteen-year-old Lily, who lives with her abusive father on his rural peach farm and is cared for by Rosaleen, her sage African-American nanny, is haunted by her own role in the mysterious death of her mother ten years earlier.

When Rosaleen becomes the victim of a racist attack, she is arrested while trying to defend herself; Lily helps her escape from the law. Together they flee hatred and racism to the Black Madonna Honey sanctuary—an apiary run by three black beekeeping sisters. There they find a community of wise women who celebrate the female spirit and find healing in a nurturing, powerful sisterhood.

HONEY CAKE

In the biblical story of the Exodus, manna tastes like "honey cakes." In *The Secret Life of Bees*, honey cakes symbolize the body of Mary. The beekeeping sisters, May, June, and August, bake them for their Daughters of Mary annual Mary Day celebration, where their sisterhood gathers to pay tribute to their own Our Lady of Chains and give thanks for the honey crop.

Gathered in a circle, the women take turns placing the cakes on their tongues. Lily's cynicism (she is sure the "pope would have keeled over if he'd seen this") melts when it's her turn to receive a cake: She feels the "sweetness of honey cake spread through" her. *The Secret Life of Bees* drips with honey, and it's hard not to crave a taste of it while devouring the book.

Sue Monk Kidd savored the taste of honey while writing her book. "Long ago, honey was regarded as a magical, sacred substance" and was also thought to contain a 'resurrection potency,'" Kidd has written. Kidd ate honey "religiously" and kept a jar of honey on her desk while writing *The Secret Life of Bees*.

When the novel was finally published, even Kidd's husband got into the act. Kidd told us:

When a friend threw a party to celebrate the publication of *The Secret Life of Bees*, my husband, who loves to cook, made this scrumptious honey cake, using a beehive mold, and speckled it with almond-paste bees. Later, I convinced him to bake another one when my friends and I decided to throw a Mary Day party similar to the Mary Day I wrote about in the novel. People all over Charleston, South Carolina, are still talking about how good those honey cakes were!

Sue Monk Kidd shared her husband's secret: a delicious honey cake recipe he found in the Martha Stewart catalogue. Originally written for a beehive mold, we have adapted the recipe for a tube or bundt pan.

For the cake
3⅓ cups sifted cake flour, plus extra for pan

1 tablespoon baking powder

¾ teaspoon baking soda

¾ teaspoon salt

2¼ teaspoons ground cinnamon

⅛ teaspoon ground cloves

¾ cup (1½ sticks) unsalted butter, plus extra
    for preparing pan

1¼ cups firmly packed light brown sugar

⅔ cup honey

2 teaspoons vanilla extract

1½ cups milk

6 egg whites

¼ teaspoon cream of tartar

For the honey-caramel glaze
5⅓ tablespoons unsalted butter, melted

⅔ cup honey

¼ cup light brown sugar

1 teaspoon vanilla extract

For the sugar glaze
¼ cup water

1¼ cups confectioners' sugar

1. Place rack in center of oven. Preheat to 350° F. Butter a 10-inch tube or bundt pan. Dust with flour, tap out excess, and place the pan in the freezer until ready to fill.
2. To make the cake: Sift together the flour, baking powder, baking soda, salt, cinnamon, and cloves in a large bowl.

3. In the bowl of an electric mixer, cream together the butter and brown sugar. Gradually drizzle in honey, continuing to beat until light and fluffy. Add the vanilla and beat to combine. On low speed, alternately add small amounts of the flour mixture and the milk, mixing until just blended after each addition, and ending with the flour mixture.

4. In another mixing bowl, beat the egg whites and cream of tartar until stiff, glossy peaks form. Fold whites into the batter.

5. Fill the tube pan with batter, distributing evenly, and bake 40 minutes. Cover with aluminum foil and bake an additional 15–20 minutes, until a toothpick inserted in the center comes out clean. Cool on a wire rack for 20 minutes.

6. Turn the cake out of the pan, supporting the bottom with your hand. Allow to cool completely on a wire rack. When cool, wrap in plastic and refrigerate at least 1 hour.

7. Remove the cake from the refrigerator. Place the cake on a rack with a tray underneath to catch drips.

8. To make the honey-caramel glaze: Melt the butter in a small saucepan. Add the honey and brown sugar and bring to a boil, stirring continuously. Stir until sugar dissolves completely. Add the vanilla. Remove from heat and cool 1 minute or until slightly thickened. Spoon warm honey-caramel glaze over the cake to cover completely. While the glaze sets, prepare the sugar glaze.

9. To make the sugar glaze: Bring the water to a boil in a small saucepan. Add the sugar and stir until dissolved. Remove from heat and cool 1 minute. Then, spoon half the sugar glaze over cake so it drizzles down the sides. Allow to set, then spoon the remaining sugar glaze on top. Transfer the cake to a plate to serve.

Yield: 12 to 16 servings

BOOK CLUB PROFILE

The Southern Cultural Heritage Foundation in Vicksburg, Mississippi, was founded to preserve and understand the diverse cultural heritage of Vicksburg, the Mississippi Delta, and the American South. The foundation's Southern Book Club, seventeen men and women, some native southerners and some transplants, is devoted to the works of southern writers. They meet at the foundation's headquarters in a historic building in downtown Vicksburg or in the home of Rod and Linda Parker, original members of the club. Linda's signature snack is tamari-coated nuts, almonds, or peanuts she heats, coats with tamari sauce, and then cools. They have become a group favorite.

The Southern Book Club chooses books that will first and foremost enhance their understanding of the South. But they also look for entertaining titles that will provoke interesting discussions, such as Michael Johnston and Robert Coles's *In the Deep Heart's Core,* about teaching in rural Mississippi, and Clifton Taulbert's *When We Were Colored,* describing the author's childhood in the Mississippi Delta in the 1960s. The group praised both books for their positive and honest portrayals of the South.

The group relished the cultural authenticity of Sue Monk Kidd's *The Secret Life of Bees.* "The author captured the southern feeling," said Parker, "the soft voices, the close relationships between African Americans and whites that others never expect from the South, the love and the hospitality. It's all in *The Secret Life of Bees.* The characters were very real, which is not true of every book we read."

More Food for Thought

Members of the Northwest Passages, a Seattle-area book club, feasted on fried chicken salad with honey-mustard dressing, oven-fried okra, sliced tomatoes, biscuits with honey, honey cake, and banana cream pie (see p. 116) for their discussion of *The Secret Life of Bees.* "The menu brought the flavor of the South to the Pacific Northwest and set the mood for our discussion," says member Lois Gelman.

BANANA CREAM PIE

Sister May spends her mornings in search the perfect, unbruised banana. Lily notes that next to honey, bananas were the most plentiful food in the sisters' house. During the vigil after May's death, Rosaleen bakes banana cream pie as a tribute to May. Try our recipe for Banana Cream Pie, p. 116, to enhance your *Secret Life of Bees* discussion.

More Food for Thought

The Basehor Community Library in Basehor, Kansas, provides desserts or other snacks tied to the books' themes for their Culinary Book Club's monthly meetings. "It's alway something we can pass around and eat as we discuss the book," says Jenne Laytham, the club's coordinator. When the club read *The Secret Life of Bees*, they enjoyed biscuits with honey and honey-kissed chocolate drop cookies. "We also drank Coke from bottles to which we added peanuts, as the characters in the book do," adds Laytham. "I thought it tasted fine."

Snow Falling on Cedars

David Guterson

....

HARCOURT, *1994*

(available in paperback from Vintage, 1995)

O N A F O G - S H R O U D E D night in the waters north of Puget Sound, a local salmon fisherman, Carl Heine, meets his death aboard his fishing boat under circumstances that are shrouded in mystery. It is less than a decade after the end of the Second World War, and a fisherman from the same small island, Japanese-American Kabuo Miyamoto, is charged with Heine's murder.

In David Guterson's richly atmospheric debut novel, *Snow Falling on Cedars,* the snow-limned landscape of the Pacific Northwest is the backdrop for the tale of a small community bound together by the enclosing perimeter of their island, San Piedro, yet divided by prejudice and suspicion.

At the center of this haunting novel is Ishmael Chambers, a local journalist who in his youth dared to cross the island's unspoken racial divide to love a young Japanese-American girl, Hatsue. Chambers, haunted by love lost, is drawn back to those days as he observes Hatsue at the murder trial of her husband, Kabuo. Unlike many on the island, Chambers is unwilling to jump to the conclusion that Kabuo is guilty of Heine's murder.

As the trial proceeds, the island community must reckon with its past, when Japanese-American residents were sent to detention camps as their neighbors watched in silence and sometimes even appropriated land that had belonged to their exiled neighbors.

MRS. SHIBAYAMA'S
FRESH STRAWBERRY PIE

S *now Falling on Cedars* is infused with the aroma and flavor of ripe strawberries and descriptions of lush, colorful strawberry fields. San Piedro Island, modeled on Puget Sound's Bainbridge Island, where Guterson resides, was home to many strawberry farmers of Japanese ancestry. In the novel, Kabuo appears to have a motive for killing Carl Heine: While Kabuo's family was interred in the detention camps, Heine's family appropriated their strawberry fields.

"*Snow Falling on Cedars* provides an excellent history lesson about the little-discussed internment of Japanese-Americans during World War Two," says Stephanie Koura, a trained cook and website developer who read Guterson's novel with her Wuthering Bites book club in Seattle. "Sometimes I think it's hard to believe that such a violation of human rights could have happened so recently. *Snow Falling on Cedars* is not an overtly political book, but it handles the subject of cultural differences and racism with sensitivity and grace."

Koura's father and his family owned a strawberry farm on Bainbridge Island for several decades before and after World War II, and her aunts and uncles still live on the original property. "My father is a Nisei, or second-generation Japanese American, and I'm Sansei, or third-generation," says Koura. While there is no longer a farm on the property, there is a Koura Road where the farm once stood. "Growing up on the farm, my dad's favorite way of eating strawberries was simply to slice fresh strawberries and eat them with real cream," says Koura.

Stephanie Koura adapted this recipe from one created by Mrs. Eiko Shibayama, whose family were also strawberry farmers on Bainbridge Island. Mrs. Shibayama's recipe originally appeared in a Japanese Baptist church cookbook in Seattle.

1¼ cups finely processed chocolate wafer crumbs (about 18 cookies)

5 tablespoons unsalted butter, melted

1 cup heavy cream

⅓ cup confectioners' sugar

1 3-ounce package cream cheese, softened

½ teaspoon vanilla extract

⅓ cup smooth apricot, apple, or red currant jelly

3 cups fresh strawberries, hulled and sliced

1. Preheat oven to 325°F. Using a fork, stir together the chocolate wafer crumbs and butter in a small bowl until well blended. Transfer the mixture to a 9-inch pie pan and press the crumbs evenly into the bottom and up the sides of the pan to form an even crust. Even out the crust by pressing with the bottom of a flat glass. Bake until set and fragrant, 10–12 minutes. Place the pan on a wire rack and allow to cool to room temperature.

2. Beat the whipping cream until medium-firm peaks form; do not overbeat. In another bowl, beat together the confectioners' sugar, cream cheese, and vanilla until smooth. Gently fold the whipped cream into the cream cheese mixture until thoroughly combined. Pour into the cooled chocolate crust.

3. Heat the jelly in a small saucepan over low heat until melted. Cool slightly. Arrange the sliced strawberries over the cream cheese filling, starting from the outer edge, with the strawberry tips pointing outward. Slightly overlap layers as you work toward the center. Using a pastry brush, gently coat strawberries with melted jelly. Refrigerate until ready to serve.

Yield: 1 9-inch pie, 6 to 8 servings

BOOK CLUB PROFILE

The ten women of Book-A-Nons meet monthly in their homes in St. Louis, Missouri, to share their love of reading, friendship, and some wonderful food. Their broad reading interests contribute to their eclectic reading list, which includes classics, historical fiction, mysteries, contemporary fiction, and spiritual works.

"Our diversity has been our hallmark, and our camaraderie our glue," says member Janet Edwards, a freelance writer. Edwards says her group doesn't explore a book's every nuance, theme, writing style, and character. Edwards finds the members' personal histories to be the more interesting aspects of their discussions. "We still have major revelations from members when there are personal connections to the literature," says Edwards.

Mothers who met in a playgroup formed Book-A-Nons when they realized they shared a passion for reading and wanted to stay in touch after the children outgrew the playgroup. Their varied careers—writers, social workers, teachers, real estate sales agent, and marketing professionals—keep the discussions lively.

To keep in touch with former members who have moved from St. Louis, as well as friends, family, and even strangers, they share book reviews, recipes, a top-ten list, and recommended reading on their website, www.novelreaders.com.

The Book-A-Nons get together after dinner for appetizers and wine. "Book club wouldn't be book club without a big bowl of M&M's and a glass of red wine," said member Suzie Florent. Their favorite book club night recipes include Amy's Best-Ever Bruschetta and Nora's Famous Black Bean Salsa, which has become a staple at book club meetings.

Jhumpa Lahiri's *Interpreter of Maladies* (see p. 204) and Nancy Turner's *These Is My Words*, a fictionalized diary of an Arizona woman at the end of the nineteenth century, as well as David Guterson's *Snow Falling on Cedars,* are among their favorite titles.

"*Snow Falling on Cedars* seemed to have all the elements of a lasting story," says Edwards, "including forbidden love, murder, courtroom drama, prejudice, flashbacks, a memorable setting, and wonderful writing."

Edwards says members had known little of Japanese internment camps during World War II before reading the novel. "We discussed how the emotions from the internment-camp experience still permeated the community Guterson described," says Edwards.

A lasting impression of the novel, she adds, was not so much the characters, but the small community, and how their shared history shaped the unfolding story. "I love the book's title," she says. "I envision how much tension seeps into the soft image of snow falling."

More Food for Thought

Literary Society of San Diego member Rebecca Rauber often serves her book club a dinner that reflects the reading selection on tap for the evening. "*Snow Falling on Cedars* presented some challenges," says Rauber. "Much of the action was in a courtroom, on a boat being ripped up by thirty-foot waves, or in a relocation camp. But we're creative."

Rauber served lox (smoked salmon), bagel bites, fresh strawberries, and sushi, foods she says were all gastronomically relevant to the selection and helped animate their discussion. "We go to some extremes to make our food relevant, and take our task seriously," adds Rauber.

The Sparrow

Mary Doria Russell

VILLARD, *1996*

(available in paperback from Ballantine, 1997)

*T*HE *SPARROW* is the story of Jesuit priests and scientists sent to explore the planet Rakhat, home of an alien culture whose music has been detected by astronomers on Earth. When the expedition's sole survivor, Emilio Sandoz, a native of Puerto Rico and a Jesuit priest and linguist, returns to Earth, he faces questioning from his church superiors about criminal acts he allegedly committed on Rakhat. Physically and emotionally scarred by the loss of his friends and his harrowing experiences, Sandoz painfully recounts details of life on Rakhat and the expedition's demise. *The Sparrow,* Russell's literary debut, is a journey through time and space, and an exploration of ethical issues in science, anthropology, and religion.

The explorers' passion for fine cuisine is evident in the foods they bring aboard their craft, the *Stella Maris.* Tubes of lobster bisque, spaghetti with red sauce, and reconstituted Chianti concentrate are among their provisions. On Rakhat, they immediately set out to test consumption of native plants and animals to see if they can shift their dependence on Earth food to Rakhat's native offerings. On Rakhat, the explorers also plant seeds they have brought with them, and soon Earth vegetables are plentiful. But this act will ultimately prove disastrous for the planet's inhabitants and the explorers.

TEMBLEQUE (COCONUT PUDDING)

*B*efore the expedition's departure from Earth, Ann Edwards, the mission physician, prepares meals for her colleagues as they all become acquainted. She enjoys surprising them with foods from their native countries, including a Puerto Rican dessert, *tembleque,* for Emilio Sandoz.

Tembleque is a coconut pudding traditionally served at Christmas; the word literally means "trembling." This tropical pudding should quiver when it is served.

NOTE: If possible, use a heavy-bottomed pan. Also, if you don't have a heavy saucepan, try sifting the cornstarch first. To toast coconut, spread the coconut in an ungreased pan. Bake in a preheated 350°F oven 5–7 minutes, stirring occasionally, or until golden brown.

7 tablespoons cornstarch
¼ teaspoon salt
3 13.5-ounce cans unsweetened coconut milk
¾ cup sugar
3 tablespoons canned cream of coconut

1 teaspoon vanilla extract
Ground cinnamon for topping
¾ cup shredded dried coconut, toasted
  (optional) (see note)

1. In a measuring cup, mix the cornstarch and salt with ½ cup of coconut milk, whisking until completely smooth. If the mixture has the consistency of paste, add a few more tablespoons of milk until it becomes smooth. Set aside.
2. In a large heavy-bottomed saucepan, combine the sugar, remaining coconut milk, and the cream of coconut, and bring to a rolling boil over medium-high heat, stirring frequently. Reduce heat and add cornstarch mixture a little at a time, whisking constantly to avoid lumps. Simmer, uncovered, for 5 minutes, stirring constantly. Stir in the vanilla.
3. Remove from heat and pour into a 1-quart mold or 8 custard cups or dessert bowls. Allow to cool, then cover with plastic wrap and refrigerate at least 4 hours or overnight.
4. To serve, loosen *tembleque* by running a knife around the edge of the mold or bowl and invert onto a serving dish. Dust with ground cinnamon. If desired, sprinkle toasted coconut around the base of the *tembleque* before serving.

Yield: 8 servings

BOOK CLUB PROFILE

The Aunties Brigade of Santa Cruz, California, chose their unusual name when group members started having children "and we all became unofficial aunties," says Storey La Montagne. La Montagne's partner, Ann Hubble, started the group in 1993 with college friends who live in the Santa Cruz area. She wanted to get out of her "mystery genre rut," begin reading new types of literature, and reconnect with friends who attended the University of

California at Santa Cruz. The Aunties are technical writers, librarians, and teachers. "We're a version of a sewing circle, but we do books," says La Montagne.

The ten Aunties decided to enliven book club meetings by making dinners with relevance to the books. "Now, as I read the book I think about the kind of meal I might make to share with the group, and this sets the tone for the discussion," says La Montagne. The Aunties created a Middle Eastern feast for Anita Diamant's *The Red Tent* (see p. 374) and Mexican fish tacos with black beans and rice for James D. Houston's *Snow Mountain Passage,* a novel about the Donner party, set against the backdrop of the Mexican–American war.

Although the Aunties read all kinds of literature, La Montagne is a self-described "science fiction nut" and recommended Mary Doria Russell's *The Sparrow* to the group. Although there was some resistance to science fiction, the group unanimously praised *The Sparrow.*

"We were fascinated by the combination of science fiction, spirituality, and religion, which makes for compelling reading," says La Montagne. Auntie Martha Brown enjoyed the "big questions raised in *The Sparrow*: communication with other types of 'intelligent' organisms, the role of religion, Catholicism, and appropriate environmental actions. *The Sparrow* was remarkably creative and really put me in the moment in a place and society I couldn't have imagined," says Brown.

More Food for Thought

When the South Florida Preschool PTA Book Club read *The Sparrow*, they decided to step into the roles of the central characters and created a dinner theater of sorts. Several members came attired as characters in the book, and host Jennifer Wollman prepared the same dishes Anne Edwards prepared for Emilio Sandoz before the ill-fated expedition: *asopao* (a soupy rice), *bacalaito frito* (fried codfish), and, for dessert, *tembleque.*

The Spirit Catches You and You Fall Down: A Hmong Child, Her American Doctors, and the Collision of Two Cultures

Anne Fadiman

....

FARRAR, STRAUS & GIROUX, *1997*

(available in paperback from Farrar, Straus & Giroux, 1998)

Anne Fadiman's *The Spirit Catches You and You Fall Down* tells the true story of Lia Lee, an infant born with epilepsy to Hmong immigrants in Merced, California. Without taking sides, Fadiman explores the clash of two worldviews, as cultural miscommunication between parents and doctors has tragic consequences for Lia.

Lia's doctors, Neil Ernst and his wife, Peggy Philip, view Lia's seizures through the eyes of Western medicine. To them, the cause of Lia's seizures can be reduced to the misfiring of neurons in the brain. Treatment is pharmacological. But to Lia's parents, her ailment, and its cure, is not simply physiological, but spiritual and cosmological as well. To her parents, Lia's seizures are the result of a wandering soul: The spirit is catching Lia and she is falling down. Lia cannot be cured with medicine alone.

What makes this story so heartbreaking is that there are no villains to blame for Lia's tragic fate, and Fadiman lodges no indictments. The doctors are devoted, compassionate, and tireless. Lia's parents are loving, caring, and desperate for their child to get better. But the cultural barriers go deeper than language, causing a chasm that eventually proves uncrossable.

Differences between Hmong and American culture can be seen vividly in food. A fiercely independent ethnic group from Laos, the Hmongs brought to America a diet that included somewhat familiar Asian cuisine—pork, chicken, beef, steamed rice, steamed bananas, green vegetables—and many unfamiliar dishes, too. For example, the Lees prepare a stew, *kua quav*, to welcome Lia home after a stay in foster care. Fadiman asks Lia's sister, May Ying, about the dish.

She said, "It's made out of cow's intestines and the heart and the liver and the lungs, and you chop it up really fine, and there is a part that is what is inside the intestines, and you chop that up too. Then you boil it all up together and you put lemon grass and herbs in it. It has a really bad name when you translate it. I guess you could call it, oh, doo-doo soup." (The literal translation of *kua quav* is liquid excrement.) "It's a classic."

It is not just the food, but the way it is prepared and, more fundamentally, the attitude of the Hmongs toward the food and its preparation that separates them from their American neighbors. The Hmongs believe in a connection between the souls of animals and humans. According to Fadiman, the sacrifice of animals—chickens, pigs, the occasional cow—is a regular occurrence in Hmong homes in America, despite ordinances banning such activity. The Hmongs believe that animal sacrifice can cure illness by "offering the souls of slaughtered animals as ransom for fugitive souls." After an animal is sacrificed, the Hmong respect for animals and traditions of hospitality demand that they prepare a feast that incorporates ninety-eight percent of the animal, including its brain and intestines, for consumption.

It's easy to see how the Hmongs' food preparation and eating habits, so alien to American culture, could lead to misunderstanding and prejudice. In *The Spirit Catches You and You Fall Down*, Fadiman describes misperceptions and rumors about Hmong eating habits in Merced, including a rumor that the Hmong sacrificed and consumed dogs.

KAB YOB (HMONG EGGROLLS) WITH KUA TXOB (HOT DIPPING SAUCE)

Lia's doting mother, Foua, prepares a birthday feast for her daughter, complete with an American birthday cake, Doritos, freshly sacrificed chickens, steamed bananas with rice, and Hmong eggrolls.

A fried dish similar to Chinese eggrolls, our Hmong eggrolls are made with mung bean sprouts, vegetables, meat and *saifun*, or bean-thread noodles (see p. 499 for purchasing information). You can substitute pork for the chicken. They are served with a hot dipping sauce, *Kua Txob*.

The Hmongs use very hot Southeast Asian peppers. Habañeros or serranos are acceptable substitutes and are readily available in supermarkets. Adjust the amount of chiles, depending on your personal taste.

NOTE: Wear plastic or rubber gloves while handling the chiles to protect your skin from the oil in them. Avoid direct contact with your eyes, and wash hands thoroughly after handling.

1 5.3-ounce package bean-thread noodles (saifun)	¾ cup shredded carrots
1–1¼ pounds ground turkey or chicken, or 1 14-ounce package tofu, drained and crumbled	2 eggs, lightly beaten
	1 teaspoon salt
	¼ teaspoon black pepper
¼ pound mung bean sprouts, coarsely chopped	1 egg white
½ cup cilantro leaves, chopped	1 pound eggroll or wonton wrappers
3 scallions, chopped	Oil for deep-frying (3 to 4 cups, depending on size of pan)

Kua txob dipping sauce (see below)

1. Pour boiling water over the noodles and soak until tender, 15–20 minutes. Drain and coarsely chop.

2. In a large bowl, combine the noodles, ground meat, bean sprouts, cilantro, scallions, carrots, beaten eggs, salt, and pepper. Mix thoroughly.

3. Place the egg white in a small bowl and have a brush handy (small art paintbrushes work well). Place an eggroll wrapper on a work surface with one corner pointing toward you. Place 3 tablespoons of the filling near the bottom corner in an oblong shape. Fold the bottom corner of the wrapper up to the center. Brush the unrolled edges with egg white. Fold the left and right corners to the center. Squeeze gently to give it a cylindrical shape, then roll up all the way. (If using wonton wrappers, place 1 tablespoon of the filling in the center, brush the upper 2 edges with egg white, and fold over, pressing gently to seal.) Repeat with remaining filling and wrappers. *Do not* form the eggrolls more than 30 minutes before cooking, or the filling may seep through the wrapper dough.

4. Pour at least 3 inches of oil into a pot for deep frying and heat to 375°F. Add eggrolls in small batches and fry until light brown, about 3 minutes. Drain well on brown paper or paper towels. Serve with Kua Txob.

Yield: Makes 20 eggrolls or 60 wontons

Kua Txob (Hot Dipping Sauce)

To make a version of this without fish sauce: Increase lime juice and sugar by 2 teaspoons each, and add soy sauce or salt to replace the saltiness of the fish sauce.

2–4 fresh hot chiles (habañeros or serranos, seeds included), minced

¼ cup cilantro leaves, minced

1 scallion (bulb and some stem), minced (optional)

1 tablespoon sugar

¼ cup fish sauce (see Purchasing Information, p. 499)

2 tablespoons fresh lime juice

2 tablespoons water

Mash together the chiles and cilantro using the flat handle of a cleaver or other blunt object. Place in a bowl and add the scallion, if using, and the sugar, fish sauce, lime juice, and water. Adjust sugar to desired sweetness. If the sauce is too strong for your taste, add up to 1 additional tablespoon of water.

BOOK CLUB PROFILE

Patricia Coleman-Burns, director of the Office of Multicultural Affairs (OMA) at the University of Michigan School of Nursing, wanted an open dialogue about sensitive issues confronting the school community. So in 1998 she founded the OMA Book Club Discussion Group, designed to promote communication and understanding among staff, faculty, and students around issues of diversity, including race, class, ethnicity, religion, disability, and sexual orientation.

"We started the group because we wanted to give people a nonthreatening environment in which to talk about issues facing the school community," says Coleman-Burns. "The group allows people to read and discuss literature and nonfiction as a way of increasing their awareness and cultural sensitivity."

The group's diverse membership prompts lively discussion. Although mostly women, the fifteen-member core group includes African Americans, Asians, Latinas/Hispanics, Caucasians, and people of mixed race. The group also includes people of various sexual orientations, classes, educational backgrounds, religions, and abilities.

OMA selects titles for the year based on a theme. For the theme of social change in the academic year 2002–2003, book club coordinator Anu P. Whitelocke chose Harper Lee's *To Kill a Mockingbird* (see p. 444); Hari Kunzru's *The Impressionist*, a novel about an Indian boy who constantly reinvents himself in order to survive; and Audre Lord's *Zami: A New Spelling of My Name,* an autobiographical account of a black lesbian woman's struggle with identity. To fulfill their next theme, "Looking Back to Move Forward," the group will read historical works relevant to today's society. Selections include Doris Pilkington and Nugi Garimara's *Rabbit-Proof Fence,* the true story of three young Aboriginal girls who cross the Australian outback on foot, and Kiran Desai's *Hullabaloo in the Guava Orchard,* a comedic story of a young Indian boy who unexpectedly becomes a famous holy man.

Also appearing on the list each year is one children's book. "Reading children's literature reminds us how early reading experiences can affect us," Whitelocke says. Children's books the group has enjoyed include two works by Christopher Paul Curtis: *Bud, Not Buddy,* a novel about a ten-year-old boy searching for his father during the Great Depression, and *The Watsons Go to Birmingham—1963,* a fictional account of an African-American family during the summer of 1963, when the Sixteenth Street Baptist Church in Birmingham, Alabama, was bombed and four girls died inside. Often, a child moderates these discussions, as when eight-year-old Amber, the daughter of a former book club coordinator, facilitated discussion of *The Watsons Go to Birmingham.*

"I think most of us were impressed by how much our youth know about tensions in our society, about discrimination, and about our troubled past as it relates to racial relationships between African Americans and whites," says Coleman-Burns. "Amber was so well prepared and had all her questions lined up. She gave us confidence that the next generation's future is in competent hands, and that perhaps they will handle these sensitive relationships a lot more justly and wisely than we do."

The OMA Book Club celebrates special events by reading a book and hosting a potluck meal related to the culture portrayed in the book. In February 2003, the group celebrated Black History Month by reading Lalita Tademy's *Cane River* (see p. 58). After the discussion, members enjoyed a diverse array of dishes representing their various cultures. For the group's March Asian Celebration, OMA staff member Dr. Mei-Yu Yu led discussion of David Wong Louie's novel, *The Barbarians Are Coming,* about a Chinese-American family struggling with alienation from their culture and one another, followed by a meal of Asian dishes from Thailand, China, Japan, and Vietnam. Other March books included Arthur Golden's *Memoirs of a Geisha* (see p. 255) and—one of their favorites—*The Spirit Catches You and You Fall Down.*

Anne Fadiman's book added fuel to the fire of discussion already crackling in nursing-school classes. The vast cultural divide between the Lee family's and the American doctors' concept of illness and treatment fascinated the group. The story served as a useful case study for nursing students trying to understand how to bridge these differences. "We used this book as a model of cultural sensitivity," says Coleman-Burns. "The book made it absolutely clear how disparate the care provider and the family can be in their views of what's going on. These are textbook issues, but when you see them in narrative form, you can really understand what they mean."

The book brought home to many of the students the importance of taking accurate and complete case histories from patients. "After reading the book, some group members said, 'Oh, so *that's* why it's so important to ask patients questions like what does your illness mean to you?'" says Coleman-Burns. During the discussion, students shared personal stories about confronting impenetrable cultural differences. The book provided insights into ways to deal with similar obstacles in the future.

Some faculty members assign *The Spirit Catches You and You Fall Down* to undergraduates. Says Coleman-Burns, "This book helps students understand what illness means from the patient's perspective."

Stones from the River

Ursula Hegi

SIMON & SCHUSTER, *1994*

(available in paperback from Touchstone, 1997)

*S*TONES FROM THE *R*IVER is a fictional story of an ordinary German village in an extraordinary time. The villagers of Burgdorf are a microcosm of Germany during Hitler's rise to power, and *Stones from the River* follows the course of their lives through World War II as the residents make wrenching decisions and contend with the awful consequences.

At the center of the story is Trudi Montag, a *Zwerg*, a dwarf, born in 1915. As Trudi grows up, her identity is defined by her small stature and her mentally ill mother, sources of shame and secrecy. Over time, Trudi discovers that her neighbors also have secrets that make them different. By listening to their stories and harboring their secrets, Trudi gains power.

As Nazism takes hold in Germany, the villagers of Burgdorf feel the pressure to conform under the threat of violence. Some, like Trudi and her father, Leo, quietly resist. Others, whether through fear and guilt or through principle, support Nazism. In *Stones from the River*, Ursula Hegi demonstrates how Nazism could take root in an entire nation by examining its impact on one small village.

Descriptions of food fill the pages of *Stones from the River*, as Hegi captures the details of village life. Villagers bring food—glazed buns, *Brötchen* (rolls), pigeon stew, potato soup, and Christmas *Stollen* (sweet bread with raisins, candied fruit, and almonds)—to their bedridden neighbors. Women vying for Leo's attention after the death of his wife bring him plum cake, vanilla pudding with strawberry syrup, lentil soup with pigs' feet, and egg cakes filled with fruit preserves. Villagers welcome guests to their homes with pastries—*Schnecken* (a snail-shaped pastry), *Streuselkuchen* (crumb cake), and *Bienenstich*.

BIENENSTICH (BEE STING CAKE)

*B*ienenstich appears several times in *Stones from the River*, most notably when Trudi first meets her lover, Max Rudnick. Angry and hurt after Klaus Malter, her love interest, has married another woman, Trudi scours the marriage advertisements in the newspaper for amusement. She pens a note to one of the men, Max—Box 241—suggesting that she is a tall, slender, "extraordinarily beautiful" woman with auburn hair and would like to meet him. She sets up a date and then goes to a local restaurant to observe what happens.

At the restaurant, Trudi watches "Box 241" as he waits, looking for the tall woman.

Trudi was one of two women who sat by themselves—the other tables were occupied by couples or families—but the man's eyes kept shifting past her as if she were not there, returning to a heavy, dark-haired woman who was devouring a piece of *Bienenstich*, scooping out the custard filling and spreading it on top of the glazed almond topping.

As Max seems to look through Trudi to the woman eating *Bienenstich*, Trudi "was filled with an ancient rage at him and every other man who simply dismissed her." She writes a cruel note from the "other woman," and delivers it to Max as he sits waiting. Their introduction in the restaurant launches their friendship and eventual love affair.

When reading *Stones from the River* for the Lemmings Book Club of Rochester, Minnesota, Jennifer Bankers-Fulbright immediately recognized the *Bienenstich* as the cake her German-born grandmother used to make. "I knew I had to make it for the club," says Bankers-Fulbright, who often serves the cake to her own family during the holidays. "I always think I'm so American, yet I have a strong German heritage," she said. "I realized, reading *Stones from the River*, that I had been so surrounded by my family's German culture when I was little and hadn't even known it. I made the cake for my book club friends as a way to share some wonderful memories."

Bee Sting Cake is so called because, legend has it, the baker who first made the cake used a honey topping that attracted a bee, and the baker got stung. Jennifer Bankers-Fulbright's sister, Christine Bankers, adapted the following recipe for *Bienenstich* from www.joyofbaking.com.

For the custard filling

1½ tablespoons cornstarch

1 cup milk

3 egg yolks

¼ cup granulated sugar

Pinch of salt

⅓ cup heavy cream

For the topping

¾ cup blanched sliced or slivered almonds
   (see Purchasing Information, p. 499)

½ cup granulated sugar

4 tablespoons unsalted butter, softened

2 tablespoons heavy cream

Confectioners' sugar, for dusting

For the cake

1¾ cups all-purpose flour

2 teaspoons baking powder

¼ teaspoon salt

½ cup (1 stick) unsalted butter, softened

⅔ cup granulated sugar

2 eggs

½ cup milk

1. To make the custard filling: In a bowl, whisk the cornstarch into ⅓ cup of the milk until dissolved. Whisk in the egg yolks. Set aside.

2. Combine the sugar, salt, and remaining ⅔ cup of milk in a small, heavy saucepan and bring to a boil over medium heat, stirring frequently.

3. Vigorously whisk a small amount of the hot milk into the egg mixture. Then, whisking constantly, pour the eggs into the saucepan.

4. Bring to a boil over medium heat, whisking constantly. Reduce heat and simmer 1 minute.

5. Remove from heat and pour immediately into a bowl. Lay plastic wrap directly on the surface of the custard to prevent a skin from forming and refrigerate until chilled.

6. To make the topping: Combine the almonds, sugar, butter, and 2 tablespoons cream in a small saucepan and cook over moderate heat until butter is melted, stirring to combine.

7. To make the cake: Preheat oven to 350°F. Butter a 9-inch springform pan, then flour the pan and tap out excess flour.

8. Sift together the flour, baking powder, and salt into a medium bowl. Set aside.

9. Cream the butter in a large mixing bowl with an electric mixer on high speed until light. Add the sugar gradually, continuing to beat, until light and fluffy. With mixer on medium speed, add the eggs one at a time, beating well.

10. On low speed, alternately add small amounts of the flour mixture and milk, mixing until just blended after each addition. Continue until all ingredients have been added, ending with the flour mixture.

11. Pour the cake batter into the prepared pan and smooth the top. Add the topping and spread gently. Bake about 40 minutes, until cake is golden and has pulled away from the sides of the pan. A wooden skewer inserted in the center should come out clean. Set the cake pan on a wire rack and cool for 20 minutes. Run a sharp knife around the inside of the pan to loosen the cake, then carefully remove the pan. Allow the cake to cool completely.

12. Beat the $\frac{1}{3}$ cup heavy cream on high speed until it forms soft peaks. Fold a large spoonful into the chilled custard, then gently fold in the rest.

13. Using a long serrated knife or cake slicer, slice the cake in half crosswise. Place the bottom half, cut side up, on a serving platter and gently spread with custard filling. Place the other half on top, cut side down. Refrigerate the cake until ready to serve. Dust lightly with confectioners' sugar just before serving.

Yield: 8 servings

BOOK CLUB PROFILE

"I've thought about calling us the 'Journeys' book club because our members are all on journeys, reading books we normally wouldn't have read on our own, but also sharing our joys and pains, interests and concerns," says Louis Hemmi, a real estate appraiser and senior member of the Houston Book Club of Texas.

Hemmi was working at Enron Corporation when he was invited to join the relatively new book club formed by a colleague in 1991. Most of the club's members were Enron employees, although only one member was working at Enron when the energy company collapsed, leaving thousands without jobs and without their retirement savings. "Enron was always a topic of discussion," says Hemmi. "We talked about the stock prices and the political intrigue during the run-up in value before Enron's demise; and of course, we worried together about the fate of our retirement funds."

Hemmi reports that over the last decade, "several book club members have died, others have moved on or away, and as people drop out, others drop in. We all have great affection for one another, and really enjoy sharing our interest in literature and culture in general." The club now has six members, three men and three women, which Hemmi believes is an ideal number and an ideal gender mix.

Every six months, the group votes on a theme that will connect their reading selections for the next six meetings. Themes have included the occult, Japan, science fiction, Hispanic writers, romantic literature, Nobel Prize–winners, and the Civil War.

Rather then wrangling over the specific selection for the next meeting, the host is empowered to choose a book on the agreed-upon theme and is required to purchase a copy for each member before the meeting. "We try not to let on so that each month the selection is a surprise to the group," says Hemmi. "It adds an element of mystery."

The Houston Book Club initially munched on chips and dips, but with meetings starting right after work, they began serving dinner. "For the last twelve years, we've had fabulous food," says Hemmi. "Linda often serves Middle Eastern food. Drew loves Italian. I almost always serve my grandmother's *arroz con pollo*. It's the best in Texas! And John is into nouvelle, so we eat before going to his house," says Hemmi with a chuckle. "We enjoy sharing our homes and hospitality."

The Houston Book Club discussed the unusual perspectives of Ursula Hegi's *Stones from the River* at length. "Many World War Two stories address the Holocaust or the corruption of German morality," says Hemmi. "Hegi's book chronicles the reaction of a largely passive German community to the rise of Nazism and the orderly removal of many Jews to camps. While some books make all Germans look like bad people, Hegi depicts ordinary Germans as just that—ordinary.

"Hegi also gave us upper-middle-class characters that were realistic and intriguing and the unusual perspective of the protagonist, Trudi, who was a dwarf," says Hemmi. "It was a fresh look that concentrated on feelings rather than events and ghostly happenings."

More Food for Thought

The German pastries mentioned throughout *Stones from the River* provided sweet inspiration for book clubs. Patty Rullman's Between the Lines book discussion group enjoyed a German chocolate sauerkraut cake and a German cherry chocolate cake when they discussed *Stones from the River* at the Aurora Public Library in Aurora, Indiana. And Kathy Hayes baked a German apple tart and a Bavarian crème cake for the Bookenders Book Club in Lee's Summit, Missouri.

Sugar

Bernice L. McFadden

DUTTON, 2000

(available in paperback from Plume, 2001)

I T IS 1955, and the small town of Bigelow, Arkansas, is reeling. Sugar has arrived.

The protagonist of Bernice McFadden's novel is a young prostitute with a tragic past; Sugar Lacey has come to Bigelow to start anew. Abandoned by her mother, her father unknown, Sugar was raised by three women in nearby Short Junction. In spite of possessing a promising singing voice, Sugar offered the only thing of value the world told her she possessed: her body.

In Bigelow, Sugar settles at 10 Grove Street, next door to Joe Taylor and his wife, Pearl. Although the town gossips and snickers over Sugar's past and present lifestyle, Pearl recognizes something in Sugar that others miss. The friendship that develops between Pearl and Sugar changes both women: As Pearl comes to appreciate Sugar's humanity and fun-loving nature, Sugar warms to a mother figure she never had.

The past weighs heavily on Sugar, though. In spite of Pearl's friendship, Sugar cannot transcend her feelings of degradation. Her sojourn in Bigelow sheds light on the tragic intertwined stories of Sugar, Joe, Pearl, and Pearl's murdered daughter, Jude.

Home—at its best, a place of acceptance, warmth, and security—has always eluded Sugar. It is only when she arrives at 10 Grove Street that she is offered a real home to enjoy, full of the smells and flavors of comfort foods. Pearl invites Sugar to participate in her family life, and the women bond as they cook: "They laughed together in Pearl's kitchen and put an extra cup of sugar in the last batch of lemon pound cake."

At Thanksgiving, Pearl and Sugar work together, filling the kitchen with smells and the table with food:

The kitchen oozed cinnamon and nutmeg aromas; with each whip of the large wooden spoon through the sweet potato mixture, the smell became stronger.

The table creaked beneath the weight of heavy ceramic bowls filled with sweet sausage dressing, collard greens, potato salad, macaroni salad, chitlins, candied yams, and roasted potatoes. A turkey, baked to golden perfection, sat beside a glazed ham adorned with bright red cherries. Biscuits, so light and flaky they threatened to rise to the ceiling if not for the melting sweet butter that dripped and ran across their swollen bellies, restraining their flight.

Great-Grandma Olivia's Sweet-Potato Pie

Although Pearl and Sugar eventually grow close, their initial encounter—over a sweet-potato pie—is disastrous. A quintessential comfort food, sweet-potato pie appears throughout the novel as an offering of hospitality, friendship, and consolation. Mary Bedford, a boarding-house matron with whom Sugar lives at one point, sends her boarders away with slices of sweet-potato pie on Thanksgiving. When Mary falls ill, folks in the neighborhood—"the former hustlers, pimps and prostitutes"—bring her casseroles filled with all sorts of offerings, including sweet-potato pie.

It is not surprising, then, that Pearl bakes a sweet-potato pie to welcome Sugar to the neighborhood. Pearl brings it over to Sugar's, but she appears to be out. As Pearl rests on Sugar's porch rocker, she is startled by Sugar emerging from the house, and the pie lands facedown on the porch. "Leave it be, the ants will take care of it," says Sugar, and the women enter Sugar's house for their first, awkward, conversation. Several weeks later, a second sweet-potato pie offering ends up all over Pearl's face, with the women reduced to fits of laughter. Their friendship is born.

Bernice McFadden told us that sweet-potato pie conjures up memories of her own family celebrations:

Sweet potato pie has always been a staple at my family holiday gatherings. And while pie is usually viewed as a dessert food, we often consume it alongside our entrée.

For me, sweet potato pie represents family and the stories that are told during its preparation and consumption and at the end of the night, when some elder leans back, unbuckles his belt and declares, "You sure did put your foot in that pie. I ever tell you 'bout the time when . . ."

Cessa Heard-Johnson, coordinator of the DRUM Book Club at South Seattle Community College, sent us her Louisiana great-grandmother's recipe for sweet-potato pie. Serve it with Sweetened Whipped Cream or vanilla ice cream, and let the sweet tastes and smells transport you to the Deep South of the 1950s.

1 recipe Basic Pie Crust (see p. 112)
2 cups sweet potatoes, peeled, boiled, and mashed
½ cup (1 stick) butter, melted
1 cup granulated sugar
½ cup brown sugar

3 eggs
1 cup evaporated milk
1 teaspoon ground nutmeg
1 teaspoon ground cinnamon
1 teaspoon vanilla extract

1. Preheat oven to 375°F. Place pie crusts into 2 9-inch pie pans and crimp edges. Set aside.
2. Using an electric mixer, combine the sweet potatoes with melted butter. Add the sugar, brown sugar, and eggs. Beat until smooth. Add the evaporated milk, nutmeg, cinnamon, and vanilla. Beat well.
3. Pour the filling into the pie shells. Bake for 1 hour, until the filling is set and a sharp knife inserted near the center comes out clean.

Yield: 2 9-inch pies, 12 to 16 servings

SWEETENED WHIPPED CREAM

1 cup heavy cream
2 tablespoons sugar

1 teaspoon vanilla extract

NOTE: For best results, chill a medium-size metal bowl and beaters from electric mixer for at least one hour before using.

With mixer, beat together cream, sugar, and vanilla in bowl until stiff peaks form. Do not overbeat. Serve immediately.

In 2001, two friends in their thirties wanted to expand their reading selections beyond romance novels and push themselves to read at least one book every month. "We wanted to broaden the scope of our reading," says Kotanya Kimbrough, of Bakersfield, California. Kimbrough overheard guests at a home decorating party talking about Beverly Jenkins, her favorite author, and she invited them to join. The REAL (Readily Embracing African-American Literature) Book Club was born.

Five core members and several "floaters" meet monthly in the same member's home on Sunday evenings, alternating responsibility for bringing refreshments. Food ranges from finger foods to full meals, including chicken, biscuits, and salad. Dessert is a constant. With one vegetarian in the group, members cook creatively, aiming for foods that the vegetarian can eat and that everyone else will enjoy too.

In keeping with the group's mandate to read a broad range of African-American literature, members select books from different genres each month, such as mystery, erotica, health, business, contemporary fiction, and classics. These genres ensure various and unusual reading selections. "When one member was assigned the health genre, she wanted a book with a health-related theme rather than a self-improvement book," explains Kimbrough. The group ended up choosing Toni Cade Bambara's *The Salt Eaters,* about a community of black faith healers who are looking for the healing properties of salt. "The book was hard to find, and the writing style was difficult," says Kimbrough, "but we struggled through it." Another offbeat selection, this one in the business genre, was *Think and Grow Rich: A Black Choice,* by Dennis Kimbro, in which the author tailors Napoleon Hill's 1937 classic, *Think and Grow Rich,* to a black audience. Some of the group's favorite authors include Zora Neale Hurston, Tracy Price-Thompson (who twice spoke with their group), and Bernice McFadden.

Although the women of the REAL Book Club read several of McFadden's books, *Sugar* stands out. "Normally we eat and discuss around the dining room table," says Kimbrough. "We only move into the living room, away from the food, when the discussion get heated. We moved away for *Sugar*! The discussion got very intense."

Group members appreciated McFadden's vivid portraits of troubled characters, complex relationships, and painful losses. "The opening chapter of this book was one of the most moving things we've ever read," says Kimbrough, referring to the scene in which Pearl discovers that her daughter has been murdered. "We felt such anguish for Pearl." The various relationships between the characters also captivated them. "We liked watching the way Pearl and Sugar opened up to each other. And we felt that Joe had to love Pearl very much to stick by her after she shut him out." The group explored other relationships, too, like the one between Sugar and Seth, Pearl and Joe's son. "There were so many things going on in this book," says Kimbrough. "Some of us had read the sequel to *Sugar*, *This Bitter Earth*, which takes up where *Sugar* leaves off, and we had to restrain ourselves from talking about it, because we got so caught up in the story."

As a founding member of United California African-American Book Clubs (UCAAB), an organization that promotes communication among African-American book clubs throughout California, the REAL Book Club hopes to focus attention on West Coast African-American readers. Kimbrough laments that most large literary events, such as the annual Harlem Book Fair in New York City, happen on the East Coast. "The ultimate goal of the UCAAB is to become a real force in the literary world. What we're trying to say is, 'Pay attention to us!' We feel neglected. There are plenty of African-American readers on the West Coast, and we want to focus some attention out here."

More Food for Thought

The fifteen women of A Moment of Peace in Washington, D.C., discussed *Sugar* one evening in November. Fitting for the time of year—and to the book—hostess Sandra DeBerry Watson prepared a Thanksgiving feast, complete with turkey, ham, sweet potatoes, greens (see p. 150), rolls, ice cream, cake, and pie.

The foods triggered discussion of Thanksgivings past, and the meaning of cooking and eating together. "We talked about how, in our homes growing up, only the most important woman in the house cooked the turkey or ham," explains book club cofounder Sandra Jowers. "Other dishes could be 'assigned' and your place in the hierarchy decided who did what. If you were a guest, your only requirement was eating—but that's how you knew you weren't real family. If you had some hand in the cooking, you were family." Pearl's invitation to Sugar to cook with her clearly carried special meaning. "Sharing a meal allowed us to see again how important it is to belong and have a family that will accept us," says Jowers.

Their Eyes Were Watching God

Zora Neale Hurston

....

1937

(available in paperback from Perennial, 2003)

ZORA NEALE HURSTON's classic novel traces the life of Janie Crawford, granddaughter of an ex-slave, as she seeks love and fulfillment in the 1930s. Janie's quest takes her from western Florida to the south Florida Everglades and through two loveless marriages. When she finally finds happiness in her marriage to Tea Cake, she loses it again through tragedy, although she gains valuable knowledge about herself.

Written in 1937, *Their Eyes Were Watching God* came out of the Harlem Renaissance, a period from the end of World War I through the 1930s when African-American artists and writers were voicing new ideas and prolifically creating art and literature. Although the book was not widely applauded, and was even derided by African-American critics and writers when it first appeared, by the early 1970s African-American intellectuals were reading *Their Eyes Were Watching God* with new appreciation. Pulitzer Prize–winning author Alice Walker was instrumental in resurrecting the book when, in 1973, she sought out Hurston's unmarked grave in Fort Pierce, Florida, and placed a marker there that read, "Zora Neale Hurston, 'A Genius of the South.'" The book's popularity continued to surge; between 1990 and 1995, *Their Eyes Were Watching God* sold over 1 million copies.

BLACK-EYED PEA CAKES WITH JALAPEÑO-AVOCADO SALSA

In the early decades of the 1900s, migrant workers flooded south Florida's Lake Okeechobee region looking for work. It is here, during the winter vegetable season, that Janie and Tea Cake arrive to harvest beans. We soon discover that the pair "had friended with the Bahaman workers in the 'Glades," and the African-American and Caribbean cultures start to mingle. Janie boils "big pots of black-eyed peas," a staple of Caribbean cuisine. Hurston herself spent several years in the Caribbean. She wrote *Their Eyes Were Watching God* in seven weeks while doing anthropological research in Haiti. The following recipe pays tribute to the Caribbean influences in Hurston's life and in the stories she created.

NOTE: Cakes may be cooked one day ahead, then chilled, covered. Bring to room temperature before reheating in a 400° F. oven.

2 15.5-ounce cans black-eyed peas, drained
4 cloves garlic, minced
⅔ cup dry bread crumbs
4 large eggs, lightly beaten
2 teaspoons ground cumin
¼ cup thinly sliced scallions

1½ teaspoons coarse salt
1½ cups yellow cornmeal, plus additional for dusting
1½ cups vegetable oil
Jalapeño-Avocado Salsa (see below)

For garnish
½ cup chopped tomato

¼ cup chopped cilantro leaves

1. In a mixing bowl, mash half of the peas with a fork until a paste is formed. Stir in the remaining peas, garlic, bread crumbs, half the beaten eggs, the cumin, scallions, and salt. Form by hand into patties, using 2–3 tablespoons per patty. Place patties in a single layer on a tray or baking sheet and refrigerate at least 1 hour.

2. Remove the patties from the refrigerator. Dredge each patty in the remaining beaten egg and then in cornmeal, turning gently to coat, and transfer to a tray lined with waxed paper and dusted with cornmeal.

3. Heat 3 tablespoons of the oil in a 12-inch nonstick skillet over moderate heat until hot but not smoking, then fry the cakes until golden, about 3 minutes on each side. As the cakes are finished, put them in a large shallow baking pan. Between batches, carefully wipe skillet clean with paper towels and keep it well oiled.

4. If necessary, reheat cakes in a preheated 400°F. oven. Top each cake with Jalapeño-Avocado Salsa, sprinkle with tomato and cilantro, and serve.

Yield: 20 to 25 small cakes

Jalapeño-Avocado Salsa

NOTE: Wear plastic or rubber gloves while handling the chiles to protect your skin from the oil in them. Avoid direct contact with your eyes, and wash your hands thoroughly after handling.

1 medium avocado

⅔ cup sour cream

2 tablespoons seeded and minced jalapeño chiles

1 tablespoon finely chopped red onion

2 teaspoons fresh lime juice

Salt

Halve the avocado lengthwise and remove the pit. Scoop out the meat with a spoon and coarsely chop. Place all the ingredients in a mixing bowl and combine with a wooden spoon. Add salt to taste. This will keep, covered, several hours in the refrigerator.

Yield: 1¼ cups

BOOK CLUB PROFILE

A book club called Denver Read and Feed has been meeting more or less monthly since 1988. Barb Warden, and her husband, Frank Blaha, are the only remaining charter members, but the rest have been in the group for several years now.

The group meets over a full dinner that generally reflects the theme of the month's reading selection. The group rates each book on a scale of 1 to 10. "If the host thinks everyone is going to hate their book, they had better make a really good dinner to compensate for it," says Warden.

Warden, a web designer, has recorded the group's book ratings and dinner menus for over 150 books and posted them on their book club's website (www.denverreadandfeed.org). Some of their favorite books have been Gloria Naylor's *Mama Day* (see p. 250); Erich Maria Remarque's *All Quiet on the Western Front,* a classic account of a German soldier's experiences during World War I; Dorothy Allison's *Bastard Out of Carolina,* about sexual abuse in a rural Southern family; and J. K. Rowling's *Harry Potter and the Sorcerer's Stone* (see p. 176).

"This group is more focused on having fun than on serious literary discussion," says Warden, but there are guidelines that are strictly adhered to: The reading selections must be paperback fiction, less than four hundred pages, and still in print. The host generally creates a dinner to complement the subject of the book, and lately group members have developed "an odd habit of sculpting butter to match the book," says Warden.

Denver Read and Feed members sometimes travel long distances to celebrate certain milestones. For example, in honor of their fiftieth book, Wallace Stegner's *Crossing to Safety,* about a lifelong friendship between two couples, the group traveled to the Sylvia Beach Hotel, an Oregon coast bed-and-breakfast where each room is named after an author. For their one hundredth book, Anne Lamott's *Hard Laughter,* about a family's struggle to maintain humor during hard times, they met in Santa Fe. For their 150th book, Lisa Michaels's *Grand Ambition,* about newlyweds who disappear while rafting down the Colorado River, they met at a waterfront resort in Grand Lake, Colorado.

"It was nice going to a restaurant for a change," says Paul Potts of the meals they ate during their travels, "but we all missed the opportunity to watch Frank start one of his spectacular kitchen fires while preparing dinner."

Frank Blaha remembers Zora Neale Hurston's *Their Eyes Were Watching God* as one of the best books the group has read. Many aspects of the book—character, dialect, the author's history—intrigued the group. Blaha was particularly impressed with protagonist Janie's rebelliousness and self-possession, describing her as a character before her time. "She was yearning for something out of life so she gets into this journey," Blaha says. "This was a personal rebellion, well beyond the pale of what a woman of the early 1900s would do. This is not so much about the black experience. It's more about a woman's experience." He and Warden both found the dialog beautifully crafted and compelling. Finally, the story behind the book—it was written during the Harlem Renaissance by an author whose talent went largely unacknowledged during her lifetime—fascinated group members. Recalls Warden, "I enjoyed learning about Zora Neale Hurston's life; how she was able to get this and other books published during that Renaissance period, but ended up in poverty, working as a maid. It's an interesting piece of American history."

More Food for Thought

Cheri Caviness served shrimp creole for her Bookwomen of Encinitas, California, when they discussed *Their Eyes Were Watching God.* Her recipe is "an old standby," one she copied down from a magazine twenty or thirty years ago. "Cooking anything southern is usually a weakness for me," says Caviness, "and this recipe has been a family favorite for years. The tender shrimp are added at the last moment to a lovely stew of tomatoes, peppers, and onions and served atop a bed of fluffy white rice . . . yum."

The Sistah Girl Reading Club of Miami capitalized on the region's surplus of citrus with a key lime pie for their discussion of *Their Eyes Were Watching God.* "We read the book in October," says Annette Breedlove, a charter member of the group, "and at that time of year it's sometimes hard to get that 'twang' in the limes needed for a good key lime pie. But I remember that pie because everyone commented on how delicious it was."

A Thousand Acres

Jane Smiley

....

KNOPF, *1991*

(available in paperback from Anchor, 2003)

OVER SEVERAL GENERATIONS the Cook family consolidated a parcel of a thousand acres of Iowa farmland. The rich soil yields abundant corn crops, enough to support Larry Cook, his three daughters, and their families. But along with prosperity the family farm has brought misunderstanding, broken relationships, and environmental contamination. Jane Smiley's *A Thousand Acres* tells the tragic story of an American family struggling to cope with its legacy.

At the center of *A Thousand Acres* lie the complex relationships between Cook and his three daughters, Rose, Ginny, and Caroline. The story begins with Cook's decision, shortly after retirement, to transfer ownership of the farm to his three girls. This simple act results in a flurry of accusations—Caroline questions Ginny and Rose's motives in supporting the decision—and countercharges. As Cook's behavior grows increasingly erratic and demanding, Ginny and Rose alternately appease and reject him, struggling to reconcile memories of past abuse with their obligations to their father. The feud over the family farm has ripple effects on Ginny's relationship with her hardworking husband, Ty, who hopes to expand the farm's hog operation, and on Rose's husband, Pete, and their two young daughters.

Ginny and Rose also suffer physically from pesticides used on the farm. A contaminated water supply devastates Ginny's chances of bearing children and is perhaps responsible for claiming Rose's life. *A Thousand Acres* portrays women who live their lives at the mercy of forces beyond their control.

Hearty farm foods weigh down the tables in *A Thousand Acres*, suggestive of a closeness that never existed. The Cook family enjoys breakfasts of bacon, French toast, sausages, fried eggs, hash browned potatoes, English muffins, strawberries, bananas, and coffee and home-cooked suppers of tuna-and-mushroom-soup-with-noodles casserole, hamburger noodle casserole, roast beef with gravy, mashed potatoes, string beans, strawberry rhubarb pie, and ice cream. The foods themselves conjure the warmth of small towns and the security of idealized family life. In *A*

Thousand Acres, though, these ample meals often serve as a backdrop for criticism, degradation, and public humiliation.

Nothing illustrates the disturbing dynamic between Ginny and her father better than their breakfasts together. Since her mother's death and Rose's illness, it has been Ginny's job to prepare breakfast each morning at her father's house. Ginny knows that her father wants breakfast "slap on the table at six." When she arrives at his house several minutes late, he greets her with an accusing tone, which Ginny reads as "I'm hungry, you've made me wait, and also, you're behind, late, slow." As Ginny realizes that she has forgotten to bring the eggs, she faces a test: run home for the eggs or prepare just toast, cereal, and bacon. "My choice would show him something about me, either that I was selfish and inconsiderate (no eggs) or that I was incompetent (a flurry of activity where there should be organized procedure)," says Ginny. Her decision to go home for the eggs typifies her attitude of appeasement and submission at the expense of her self-respect.

Further humiliation is visited upon Ginny and Rose at an annual church potluck supper, again over food. As Ginny tries to connect with her father, he rebuffs her: "[Daddy's] plate looked like mine—ribs, potato salad, corn, macaroni and hamburger, more ribs. I said, in a friendly voice, 'Well, Daddy, it looks like we picked all the same things.' He ignored me." Ginny focuses on the food, the carrot slaw on her husband's plate, the ribs and corn on her own plate. A few minutes later, neighbor Harold Clark launches into a loud, vicious diatribe against Ginny and Rose and their treatment of their father. They leave in disgrace, heading home "as if there were no escape, as if the play we'd begun could not end."

BAKED CORN CASSEROLE

Corn is a fitting food to eat while discussing *A Thousand Acres.* Ty and Pete spend much of their time planting and harvesting their Iowa corn crop, and at one point Ginny looks out her window to see the "monochromatic green" of the burgeoning stalks.

Iowa leads the states in corn production, in 1998 growing 22 percent of the nation's corn and 8.5 percent of the world crop. Our recipe comes to us straight from the heart of corn country—Ames, Iowa. Dawn Hayslett, librarian of the Ames Public Library and facilitator of the Let's Talk About It Book Club, discovered this recipe on the Internet. She recommends it as a side dish, especially at Thanksgiving, and loves it perked up with the onion and jalapeño chile.

NOTE: Wear plastic or rubber gloves while handling the chiles to protect your skin from the oil in them. Avoid contact with your eyes, and wash your hands thoroughly after handling.

1 small onion, diced	*1 cup yellow cornmeal*
½ cup seeded, diced jalapeño chiles	*2 teaspoons baking powder*
1 tablespoon butter	*1 cup sour cream*
1 15-ounce can of creamed corn	*½ cup (1 stick) butter, melted*
1 15-ounce can of corn, drained, or 2 cups fresh corn	*1 egg, beaten*

1. Preheat oven to 350°F. Sauté onions and jalapeños in 1 tablespoon butter until soft.
2. Combine sautéed vegetables with all the other ingredients and pour into a well-greased 9x13-inch baking dish. Bake for 1 hour. Allow to cool. Cut into squares and serve.

Yield: 10 to 12 servings

BOOK CLUB PROFILE

The family dynamics of farming life depicted in *A Thousand Acres* resonated with members of the Let's Talk About It book club in Ames, Iowa. "Many members have farming backgrounds themselves," says librarian and book club facilitator Dawn Hayslett. "The issues raised in this book are close to their hearts."

Let's Talk About It, a group sponsored by the Friends of Ames Public Library, has met monthly at the library since 1988 to discuss fiction, memoirs, mysteries, and detective novels. Hayslett, who has facilitated the group for twelve years, sets a theme each semester (for example, memoirs from around the world, historical mysteries, or multicultural detectives) and chooses books accordingly.

The theme "Spirit of Place: Contemporary Regional Fiction by Women" inspired Hayslett's choice of *A Thousand Acres.* "We looked for novels that exhibited a keen sense of place and thoroughly described the character of a region and its people," says Hayslett. "We also wanted novels that portrayed the challenges and choices facing women at various levels of American society."

A Thousand Acres fit all of these criteria. "Smiley addresses both environmental and feminist concerns in *A Thousand Acres*," says Hayslett, including stewardship of the land, chemical runoff, breast cancer, miscarriage, and incest. "Group members were particularly interested in the health effects of pesticides. Many members were shocked that the effects of pesticides were so severe they could cause repeated miscarriages, as Ginny Cook experienced. Other members expressed concern about water quality in rural America."

Group discussion also centered on the similarities between the pitiful father in *A Thousand Acres* and Shakespeare's King Lear. Let's Talk About It meetings always begin with a short presentation by local scholars or other experts. For *A Thousand Acres*, two Shakespearean scholars from the University of Iowa opened the meeting with a short talk on the subject, which group members explored further during discussion.

More Food for Thought

The Denver Read and Feed book club read *A Thousand Acres* at the suggestion of Barb Warden, a member who has close personal ties to the state of Iowa. Both of her parents grew up in Iowa, and she followed in their footsteps to attend Iowa State University.

"I was at school during the farming crisis," says Warden, referring to the period in the late 1970s and early 1980s when thousands of families lost their farms to overwhelming debt and competition with large corporate-owned factory farms. "I was in classes with the children of families who were losing their farms. The characters in *A Thousand Acres* were doing what a lot of families at the time were doing: gearing up, trying to become a bigger operation."

Ty's attempt to save the farm by expanding the hog operation inspired Warden's main dish: glazed ham. She also served corn on the cob, mashed potatoes, cornbread, and apple pie, "because it seems so down-home and all-American."

More Food for Thought

At the Milwaukee School of Engineering's Great Books Dinner and Discussion Series, the dinner menu for the discussion of Jane Smiley's *A Thousand Acres* included Merry Old England royal potatoes, Yorkshire pudding, and steak-and-kidney pie.

"*A Thousand Acres* is *King Lear* in Iowa," says Judy Steininger, who led the discussion in Milwaukee, "and our intention was to draw the correlation to Shakespeare's play. We could have created a meal from a dinner on an Iowa farm, but we wanted to be inventive and glamorous."

Three Junes

Julia Glass

PANTHEON, 2002

(available in paperback from Anchor, 2003)

JULIA GLASS's debut novel is an exploration of family dynamics. How do families communicate? How do the complexities of sibling relationships play out over time? How do coincidences bring family and friends together—or divide them? Does family hinder or help when we struggle to cope with our most profound losses and regrets? *Three Junes* traces the lives of the McLeod family in three distinctive settings in the month of June over a decade.

In the first, the patriarch, Scottish widower Paul McLeod, travels to Greece, where he reflects on his troubled marriage to a woman he once adored. There, a young American artist, Fern Olitsky, captivates him. Six years later Paul's sons—Fenno, a gay bookstore owner in Manhattan, and twins David, a veterinarian, and Dennis, a chef in the South of France—come together at the family home in Scotland for Paul's funeral. The third setting is New York's Long Island shore, where an impromptu dinner party brings Fenno and Fern together.

In the second June, when the McLeod brothers reunite for their father's funeral, Dennis dominates the kitchen, nurturing his family with delicious and elaborate meals. For his brother Fenno, the novel's main protagonist, Dennis's cooking changes the entire atmosphere of their home, filling it with "extravagant odors" and suffusing it with warmth.

Because the house never smelled like this when we were small—because our mother, though she made a dependable joint, spent as little time indoors as possible—this has transformed my homecoming for the past several years. I feel as if I'm visiting a home in a dream. Where everything yet nothing is the way it should be, where the best of what you have and what you wish for are briefly, tantalizingly united.

WHITE CHOCOLATE MOUSSE

Julia Glass suggested several exquisite desserts from her novel for our *Three Junes* recipe selections. She also has a passion for soufflés and mousses—and apparently for white chocolate. When Dennis meets Mal, a friend of Fenno's, he offers to make dessert, giving Mal a choice of three chocolate soufflés, one of them made with white chocolate. In another scene, Fenno describes Dennis's white chocolate mousse as "worthy of a dinner on Mount Olympus."

For a recent New Year's Eve feast, Julia Glass made the white chocolate and pear mousse from *The Open House Cookbook* by Sara Leah Chase (Workman, 1987). "It's the best dessert I've ever made," says Glass. We adapted Chase's recipe to create a pure white chocolate mousse, similar to the one Dennis serves.

6 eggs, separated

1 cup sifted confectioners' sugar

⅓ cup pear brandy

10 ounces best-quality white chocolate, chopped or broken into small pieces

4 tablespoons unsalted butter

2 cups heavy cream

Mint sprigs and fresh berries for garnish

1. Combine the egg yolks, sugar, and pear brandy in a small mixing bowl. Beat with an electric mixer on high speed until the eggs become light yellow, about 5 minutes (the mixture should fall in ribbons when beaters are lifted). Transfer to the top of a double boiler over simmering water or place the mixing bowl in a saucepan of simmering water. Heat, whisking constantly, until quite thick, 4–5 minutes. Transfer to a large mixing bowl and set aside.

2. Melt the chocolate and butter in a saucepan over low heat, stirring constantly until smooth. Remove from heat and add the chocolate to the egg mixture, stirring until smooth. Let cool to room temperature.

3. Meanwhile, in a chilled bowl beat the cream until quite stiff. Wash and dry beaters. Beat egg whites until stiff peaks form but mixture is not dry. Fold the egg whites into the chocolate mixture, then gently fold in the whipped cream.

4. Spoon the mousse into 8 large wine goblets or other dessert glasses. Place in refrigerator and chill until set, at least 2–3 hours. Garnish with mint sprigs and fresh berries before serving.

Yield: 8 to 10 servings

GREG CASE'S FROZEN LIME SOUFFLÉ

Frozen lime custard caps off the first meal Dennis prepares for his siblings after their father's death. "Lime is one of my favorite flavors in the entire world," Julia Glass told us. "I'm crazy about margaritas, key lime pie, and those delicious Thai soups that include lime juice. I can't think of any food with lime I don't adore." Glass suggested a recipe for lime soufflé for *The Book Club Cookbook*, and Greg Case, a pastry chef and owner of G. Case Baking in Somerville, Massachusetts, was happy to share his recipe, a sublime creation.

1½ teaspoons unflavored gelatin
1 cup fresh lime juice
Grated peel of 6 lemons
6 eggs, separated

1¼ cups sugar, divided in half
2 cups heavy cream
Chopped pistachio nuts or Raspberry Sauce for
*   topping (see below)*

1. Combine the gelatin, lime juice, and lemon peel in the top of a double boiler. Allow to set 5 minutes before heating. Heat to dissolve gelatin; the mixture should be smooth, not granular. Remove from heat and set aside to cool completely.

2. Beat the egg yolks with half the sugar until thick, about 5 minutes. Fold into the cooled lime mixture.

3. Beat the egg whites until frothy. Gradually add the remaining sugar, beating continually, until stiff peaks form. Fold into the lime mixture.

4. Beat the heavy cream until soft peaks form. Fold into the lime mixture. Ladle the mixture into individual ring molds or ramekins (allow about ¾ cup per serving). Freeze for 4 hours or overnight.

5. To serve, dip molds in hot water for several seconds to soften. Run a knife around the inside edge and turn onto a serving plate. Garnish with pistachio nuts or top with Raspberry Sauce.

Yield: 8 6-ounce servings

Raspberry Sauce

1 pint fresh raspberries, or 8 ounces frozen
    raspberries, thawed

2 teaspoons lemon juice
2–3 tablespoons sugar

Purée raspberries, lemon juice, and sugar in food processor and pass through fine sieve or strainer.

TZATZIKI

When Dennis visits his widowed father in Greece, he teaches him to make a few dishes for a dinner party, including *tzatziki*, a Greek cucumber and yogurt dish, which can be served as a dip for pita bread or vegetables or as a side dish to complement grilled fish or meat. To add a taste of Greece to your *Three Juices* discussion, serve our recipe for *tzatziki*, p. 267.

Julia Glass offered this meditation on food, fiction, and the culinary perquisites of a writer's life for *The Book Club Cookbook.*

A few years ago, while I was visiting Chicago, a friend took me out of the city to an event at one of those world-in-an-oyster bookshops, Town House Books in Saint Charles, Illinois. The shop occupies a creaky antique house along with an adjoining café, and the event we attended was a dinner to celebrate the publication of a bestiary created by a woman who was an artist, poet, and singer. We ate a down-home southern dinner (chicken and biscuits), and then she talked about the book and showed her prints, even sang a little. I had just finished writing my first novel, and I remember thinking, *If it's ever published, I want an evening just like this.* A grandiose wish I kept to myself.

Over the next year and a half, a great deal happened in my life, things both terrible and wonderful: cancer, chemotherapy, an attack on my city . . . yet also the birth of my second son and, finally, the publication of my novel. I went on tour to half a dozen cities, and I was treated to some fine evenings in a fine variety of bookshops, but none quite like that delicious evening in Saint Charles.

I adore food, and I do not take for granted the privilege of being well and diversely fed. As a New Yorker, I revere restaurants—some simple, some elegant—the way so many other people revere museums, tall buildings, and operas. I love restaurants almost as much as I love bookstores. Mostly, however, I eat in, so I love reading recipes, and as much as I enjoy cooking (rarely anything fancy), I like feeding people even more. A splendid dinner party can move you as deeply as a splendid novel; in the right company, a good meal can open up a soul. I also find enormous pleasure in the culinary lexicon: words like *souvlaki, tapenade, carpaccio, farfalle, paella, oshitashi, Reine de Saba*. From *Gewürztraminer* to *Maytag blue*, pronouncing such words is almost as delightful as tasting what they represent. (Did I say how much I like *eating*?)

Inescapably, my fiction is full of food. It doesn't matter whether or not I'm hungry while I'm writing; reveries of things to eat drift in and out of my imagination along with reveries of character and setting. In *Three Junes*, rather shamelessly, I just went right ahead and made one of my principal characters, Dennis McLeod, a chef. At one point, he prepares a luncheon for dozens of people who gather after his father's death, and I remember writing about that food, because I remember faking it all. Dennis claims to make his vichyssoise with buttermilk, garlic, and nutmeg. He soaks figs in red wine for a chicken tajine; he poaches peaches in crème de cassis and lavender. But did the author test these recipes? Never. This was food designed for the delectation of the mind, never intended to leave the page. ("Don't try this at home," I might have joked in a footnote.)

The year after *Three Junes* was published, the book and I had many adventures; it was a year of good fortune (and, I should add, good eating). And then, for the paperback, another tour was planned. This time the tour included Chicago, and so—because all that good fortune gave me the hubris to do it—I wrote to the owner of Town House Books and asked if he would like to host a reading. Graciously, he said yes.

Just before I left for the Midwest, my publicist sent me an e-mail telling me how excited she was about this event; she had just heard from Town House that (as I had hoped) they planned to make it a dinner and—get this!—to re-create Dennis McLeod's menu from the funeral luncheon. Well, I panicked: That poor chef out in Saint Charles had no idea my food was all phony! Nutmeg and leeks? Peaches and lavender? Make-believe, every bit of it! And then I thought, But wait, he's a chef. A lucky man whose *job* is food.

And that is how I came to have a positively Alice in Wonderland evening, nothing short of intoxicating, in which I got to taste my very own fiction—with, of course, the creative license involved in all translations. Together, the owner of the bookstore and the chef concocted a vichyssoise with garlic and nutmeg; their tajine was composed of chicken and fruit of various kinds; and they did not omit Dennis McLeod's palate-freshening salad of greens. The dessert they invented was a peach pie in two sauces: raspberry (they apologized for skipping cassis) and a crème anglaise infused with lavender. It was something else. We ate every bit of it, we talked and laughed and drank wine, and then I read from my book. I stood up before a crowd of happily sated readers under the comforting beams of that fine old creaky house and I thought, You need not *always* be careful what you wish for.

BOOK CLUB PROFILE

Elinor Hellis is a connoisseur of books—and book clubs. As book club adviser at the Tattered Cover Book Store in Denver, she gives talks about the classics and modern books, ranging from Leo Tolstoy's *Anna Karenina* (see p. 28) to Charles Baxter's novel about modern relationships, *The Feast of Love*. Hellis also arranges book club seminars and recommends reading selections to book clubs that patronize the Tattered Cover Book Store.

Hellis's own book club members are women who met through the homeowner's association in Denver's Cherry Creek area. "We began as virtual strangers," says Hellis. The group of eight is mostly "professional working women over fifty, diverse more in personality than ethnicity," says Hellis. "But our book club has made us good friends."

"Some of us care mightily what we read, and some are happy to be told what to read," adds Hellis. "A few of us are always on the lookout for a new book club selection, mostly fiction, and others welcome the chance to discover something unexpected."

Hellis finds the relaxed atmosphere of her book club a welcome change from her role as a book club adviser. Reading selections emerge as members share recent discoveries or old favorites. Hellis believes most readers crave books that elicit an emotional connection with the characters. "*Three Junes* makes an excellent book club choice because of its emotional realism," says Hellis. "It's about families that share fears and secrets and a strong need to connect with one another."

Members of Hellis's group responded to Glass's portrayal of family interactions where much is left unsaid. "Even when we feel most alienated from family or love, those powerful family ties remain," says Hellis. "At the same time, sometimes the defining relationships in our lives, the ones that matter, are entered into almost haphazardly."

Hellis's group admired Glass's skill at creating empathy for her characters. "The main character, Fenno, is idealistic and decent yet scared, and this makes him so affecting," says Hellis. "Glass also writes scenes where we empathize with the human need to relate to powerful, painful events. When the father, Paul, visits the scene of the Lockerbie plane crash, he takes a lipstick from the wreckage. The humanization of this major disaster was deeply touching."

More Food for Thought

The LunaChics Literary Guild of Tallahassee, Florida, enjoyed a *Three Junes* meal that captured the spirit—and the flavors—of the book. Hostess Jan Keshen served vichyssoise, a green salad with fresh mushrooms and herbs, and French cheese, all "in keeping with the French feel of the oft-mentioned cuisine." For dessert, Keshen served her own "morsels of divinity": a berry-mascarpone tart with a chocolate crumb crust, and a peach tarte Tatin. "There were lots of oohs and aahs at the table that night," says Keshen. "We felt that the lushness of our meal echoed the richness of the food and the prose in *Three Junes*."

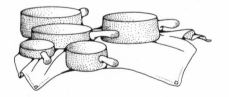

To Kill a Mockingbird

Harper Lee

....

1960

(available in paperback from Little, Brown, 1988)

Harper Lee's Pulitzer Prize–winning book, *To Kill a Mockingbird*, is one of southern literature's great works, set in the fictional town of Macomb, Alabama, in the 1930s. Atticus Finch, a local lawyer, is asked to represent Tom Robinson, a young black man falsely accused of raping a poor white girl. The story is told through the eyes of Atticus's six-year-old daughter, Scout, as she and her older brother, Jem, and their friend Dill gradually come to recognize the prejudices and injustices of small-town Alabama.

First published in 1960, at the dawn of America's civil rights movement, the book was an immediate success. It won a Pulitzer Prize in 1961 and was adapted for the screen in 1962. The book's popularity continues to this day. More than forty years after its publication, nearly half a million copies of *To Kill a Mockingbird* sold in 2002, and *Book* magazine ranked it fourth on its list of best-selling classics.

Soon after publication of her book, Harper Lee returned to her hometown of Monroeville, Alabama, refusing to grant any interviews. Today, at age seventy-seven, she divides her time between Monroeville, where she lives a quiet life with her sister, and New York City.

AMBROSIA

A traditional southern holiday dessert, ambrosia is often enjoyed around Christmastime, when Florida citrus fruits are in season. At a Christmas dinner given by Atticus's sister, Aunt Alexandra, Scout and Jen enjoy ambrosia. After being forced to converse with her boring cousin Francis and isolated at the kiddie table for dinner, Scout asserts that Aunt Alexandra's meal "made up for everything." We think the ambrosia had a lot to do with raising Scout's spirits.

½ large fresh pineapple, cut lengthwise

4 large navel oranges

2 small (or 1 large) pink grapefruit

½ cup orange juice

¼ cup honey

¼ cup dry sherry (optional)

¼ cup pecan pieces, coarsely chopped

½ cup shredded coconut

1. Using a serrated knife, remove the skin from the pineapple, and cut in half lengthwise again. Slice out the tough inner core and discard. Cut the pineapple meat into bite-size cubes and place in a large bowl.
2. Peel and section the oranges and grapefruit and cut into bite-size pieces, removing any seeds. Add to the pineapple and mix gently to avoid breaking the fruit sections.
3. In a separate bowl, mix together the orange juice, honey, and sherry (if using). Pour over the fruit and toss gently to coat each piece. Let salad stand for an hour or so before serving.
4. When ready to serve, place the fruit in a serving bowl and top with pecans and coconut. Store ambrosia in the refrigerator if you are not serving it soon.

Yield: 8 to 10 servings

BOOK CLUB PROFILE

Book clubs throughout the country keep returning to Harper Lee's classic, *To Kill a Mockingbird*. Many book club members have read the book during their high school years and are pleasantly surprised by the new insights they gain as adult readers.

The Silicon Valley Book Club, composed mostly of couples living and working in Northern California's high-tech belt, rediscovered *To Kill a Mockingbird* in 1994. The group was formed twenty-one years ago by recent graduates of Calvin College in Grand Rapids, Michigan, who had relocated to the Bay Area. They hoped to re-create their "shared experience" of reading and discussing literature in college classes. Since then, many members have married—some with each other—and most attend the same Bay Area church.

According to member Jan Seerveld, the Silicon Valley Book Club's shared experience and values helped the group appreciate the small-town life portrayed in *To Kill a Mockingbird*. "We tend to like stories about small communities because we are part of one," says Jan. They liked reading and discussing how large issues impact small communities, "how one side of the tracks affects the other side of the tracks." To Jan, this mirrors "the close-knit nature of our group."

Because the group shares a commitment to active Christian life, the Silicon Valley Book Club felt a special affinity for protagonist Atticus Finch. "We don't necessarily look for faith-based heroes," Seerveld says, "but we are always attracted to morally fine heroes."

LANE CAKE

In San Francisco, Lisa Ryers's book club reads Pulitzer Prize–winning novels, in chronological order, starting all the way back in 1918. Ryers formed the club as part of her personal pilgrimage to read the entire Pulitzer Prize list. The club likes to prepare meals that will take them to the time period and setting of the book. "The meal is a platform for creativity," says Ryers. "Otherwise you end up going to your old standbys."

When they read Harper Lee's *To Kill a Mockingbird*, they created a meal that would take them to the Deep South in the 1930s. Their menu included cornbread, chicken and dumplings, collard greens (see p. 150), and pecan pie. "But everyone was really impressed by the Lane Cake," recalls Ryers.

A beautiful multilayered cake with white frosting and a filling of coconut, nuts, bourbon and candied fruit, Lane Cake is said to be named after Emma Rylander Lane of Clayton, Alabama, who first published her award-winning recipe in her cookbook, *Some Good Things to Eat* (1898), under the name "Prize Cake." The first time Miss Maudie Atkinson makes the cake in *To Kill a Mockingbird*, Scout declares it "so full of shinny [whiskey] it made me tight." On the second occasion, Miss Maudie plans to bake a Lane Cake for a neighbor, but only when her other neighbor, Stephanie Crawford, is not looking. "That Stephanie's been after my recipe for thirty years," she complains, an example of the petty jealousies that make Macomb seem like any small American town.

Member Liz Amaral baked the Lane Cake for the group's dinner meeting. "I researched recipes and created my own version," she says, which included seven layers of cake with a coconut-caramel-raisin-bourbon sauce between each layer and on top.

You can find a good holiday Lane Cake recipe at www.epicurious.com/run/recipe/view?id-102695.

The Tortilla Curtain

T. Coraghessan Boyle

VIKING, *1995*

(available in paperback from Penguin, 1996)

WHEN DELANEY MOSSBACHER swerves his car into Cándido Rincón as Rincón runs across the road in Topanga Canyon, California, two alien worlds collide: affluent California meets the precarious existence of the illegal Mexican immigrant. In *The Tortilla Curtain*, T. C. Boyle weaves a story of two couples who inhabit these separate worlds and the fateful intersection of their lives.

Delaney and Kyra Mossbacher are Southern Californians preoccupied with their jobs, raising their son, socializing with friends, and maintaining their health and fitness. But threats from outside his gated community of Arroyo Blanco Estates worry Delaney. There are coyotes who mangle his dogs and Mexican immigrants who, residents suspect, squat in the surrounding hills and ravines, waiting for opportunities to steal. Even liberal-minded Delaney and Kyra, who want these immigrants to have their rights, feel overwhelmed.

Cándido and América Rincón are two Mexican immigrants who came to the United States with dreams of a better life. They end up fighting starvation in a makeshift shelter they have built in a ravine just outside the walls of Arroyo Blanco. They suffer almost unbearable indignities—abuse, hunger, and the despair of chronic unemployment—at the hands of a population that increasingly fears and scorns them.

After the car accident, the parallel lives of the two couples continue to veer menacingly close, until their fates finally intersect in an ironic and unexpected way.

Food symbolizes the couples' vastly different circumstances. Delaney grills tofu kabobs "with his special honey-ginger marinade." Kyra insists that her son eat healthy granola for breakfast, over his protests, and the couple enjoys veggie curry and samosas at an Indian restaurant. For Kyra and Delaney, food serves as a vehicle to a healthy life, enriched by exotic combinations of flavors. As they eat, Kyra and Delaney discuss other matters—Kyra's real estate deals, for example. Food comes easily to the Mossbachers; they never have to worry about their next meal.

By contrast, Cándido and América never know where—or whether—they will find dinner. Their deprivation—and perhaps their culture—leads them to a heightened enjoyment of food: its tastes and smells, the experience of picking it off the store shelves, and anticipating its consumption. The joy of shopping together and anticipating the meal fortifies Cándido against the burdens of life and fills him with love for his wife. As he watches América select eggs, feelings for her mingle with his fantasies of food: "She was selecting a carton of eggs—*huevos con chorizo, huevos rancheros, huevos hervidos con pan tostado*—flicking the hair out of her face with an unconscious gesture as she pried open the box to check for fractured shells. He loved her in that moment more than he ever had, and he forgot that Mercedes and the rich man and the *gabachos* in the parking lot assailing him like a pack of dogs, and he thought of stew and tortillas and the way he would surprise her with their new camp and the firewood all stacked and ready."

Tostadas with Green Chile Salsa

Chile peppers are enjoyed throughout the world, but no one employs them more passionately than cooks in the plant's homeland. Mexican farmers grow more than 140 varieties of chile peppers, and Mexicans are legendary for adding "the hots" to a vast assortment of dishes.

Cándido and América's cooking—when they can afford groceries—generally includes chiles. The meal they cook at their camp works physical changes on the couple: "the knots in their stomachs pulled tighter and tighter by the smell of it, the *hamburguesa* meat working with the onions and *chiles* to enrich the poor neutral breath of the canyon." Cándido and América also throw chiles into *cocido* (stew), fried eggs, and an onion, tomato, and rice dish.

Chile peppers made their way into the build-your-own tostadas served by the Second Wednesday Dinner Book Club of Fullerton, California, for their discussion of *The Tortilla Curtain*. Tostadas are typical Mexican street snacks, made by piling shredded ingredients such as lettuce, cheese, and chicken on a fried tortilla, and topping it off with sour cream and salsa.

To make our green chile salsa, use whatever varieties of chile peppers are available in your area. But be forewarned: Even the tamer version of our recipe makes a medium-hot salsa that will add heat to the mildest book club meeting.

NOTE: To reduce fat, toast the tortillas in a pan oiled with cooking spray. They will not achieve the crispiness typical of a tostada, but they can be folded over with ingredients tucked inside, similar to a quesadilla.

1–1½ pounds skinned, boned chicken breasts
¾ teaspoon salt
1 teaspoon onion powder
½ teaspoon garlic powder
Vegetable oil for frying
12 small flour tortillas
1 15-ounce can refried beans
2 teaspoons olive oil
1 onion, sliced

2 cloves garlic, minced and soaked in
* 1 tablespoon water*
½ cup chicken broth
1 teaspoon chili powder
2 cups shredded lettuce
1 cup shredded Monterey Jack cheese
½ cup sour cream
Green Chile Salsa (see below)

1. Arrange the chicken in a single layer in a large saucepan or skillet and add water or chicken broth to cover. Sprinkle with salt, onion powder, and garlic powder. Bring to a boil, reduce heat and cover with a sheet of wax paper, and simmer until chicken is cooked through, approximately 20 minutes.

2. Preheat oven to 200°F. While chicken is cooking, heat ¼ inch of vegetable oil in a skillet over medium heat. Drop in a tortilla and fry until crispy, about 1 minute on each side. Remove and drain on paper towels. Repeat with remaining tortillas, then remove to a platter, cover with foil and keep warm while preparing toppings.

3. Remove chicken and discard poaching liquid. Allow the chicken to cool enough to handle, and then shred with your hands.

4. Heat beans and keep warm until serving time.

5. Heat olive oil in a skillet. Sauté the onion over medium heat until yellow and soft. Add the garlic and its soaking liquid and cook for another minute or so until aromatic. Add chicken broth and chili powder and stir to combine. Add shredded chicken, mix well, and heat through.

6. In a shallow casserole dish, layer the lettuce, hot chicken mixture, and shredded cheese. Place beans, sour cream and salsa in small bowls. Spread some beans on a warm tortilla, then use tongs to add the lettuce/chicken mixture, finishing with the salsa and sour cream.

Yield: 6 servings

Green Chile Salsa

NOTE: Wear plastic or rubber gloves while handling chiles to protect your skin from the oil in them. Avoid direct contact with your eyes and wash your hands thoroughly after handling.

8 fresh mild green chiles (a mixture of
   Anaheim, poblano, and pasilla)
1 fresh serrano chile (optional)
2 fresh jalapeño chiles (optional)
¾ cup chicken broth
½ teaspoon dried oregano

2 cloves garlic, minced
1 teaspoon sugar
¼ teaspoon salt
2 teaspoons fresh lime juice
⅓ cup plain yogurt

1. Roast chiles directly on a gas burner set to medium low, turning as needed with tongs until the skin is black and blistered on all sides. If no gas burner is available, place chiles on a broiler pan and broil approximately 4 inches from the heat, turning as needed with tongs, until the skin is black and blistered on all sides. Remove each chile as it is done and place in a plastic or paper bag, keeping the top folded to seal in heat. Allow the chiles to cool in the bag for 15 minutes.

2. Peel the skins off the chiles and remove and discard stems and seeds (running water is very helpful for removing seeds, but use as little as possible, to retain flavor). Purée the chiles with the broth in a blender or food processor. Transfer to a small saucepan and add the oregano and garlic. Bring to a boil, then reduce heat and simmer 20 minutes, stirring frequently. Remove from heat and stir in the sugar and salt. Allow to cool.

3. Before serving, stir in the lime juice and yogurt. Adjust seasonings.

Yield: Approximately 1¼ cups

BOOK CLUB PROFILE

Elaborate dinners that reflect the monthly reading selection are the norm for the Second Wednesday Dinner Book Club of Fullerton, California. "Sometimes we choose the book based on its potential for a good meal," jokes Judy Bart Kancigor of her group of gourmet readers.

When the club first organized, Kancigor, a cookbook author, food writer, and cooking instructor, was dubious about serving dinner at meetings. "I thought it would become complicated, but the food has become an integral part of the book club experience. We have quickly become a real sisterhood over dinner and book discussion."

The seven members have a game plan for their monthly dinner: the host makes the main dish and each member contributes salad, vegetable dishes, starch, or dessert. "Our rule is we can brag about our grandchildren during dinner, but when dinner is over, we discuss the book," says Kancigor.

The setting and subject of T. C. Boyle's *The Tortilla Curtain* had special resonance with the group. Kancigor especially admired Boyle's ability to see the world from the perspectives of both illegal Mexican immigrants and of those who often benefit from their labors—the wealthy denizens of gated communities, where illegal aliens often work as domestics and gardeners.

"Being south of Los Angeles, we have a large Mexican population," says Kancigor. "We discussed how we often see crowds of Mexican men on street corners or in parking lots waiting for strangers to pick them up and give them work. Before reading this book, they were just a part of the landscape and we never gave them much thought. We all agreed that after reading *The Tortilla Curtain,* we will never look at them the same way. Boyle portrayed them in such a sympathetic light, but the besieged homeowners are sympathetically portrayed as well. Boyle does not pass judgment, but allows the reader to sympathize with both groups."

More Food for Thought

Capitalizing on the ever-present tortillas in *The Tortilla Curtain*, Lynne Thissell of the Portola Hills Book Group in Portola Hills, California, served tortilla pinwheels (sliced turkey or roast beef, scallions, sour cream, and green chiles spread over a flour tortilla, rolled, then chilled and sliced), taquitos (corn tortillas filled with shredded beef or chicken, rolled and deep-fried), chips and salsa, and sangría for her group's discussion of the book. "Like other meetings where we've served theme-based foods," says Thissell, "the foods for our *Tortilla Curtain* meeting seemed to add an extra flair to the evening, creating yet another avenue of conversation."

Members of the Cultures Club, a program of the Park Forest Public Library in Park Forest, Illinois, read about, research, and discuss a different culture at each monthly meeting. For their discussion of *The Tortilla Curtain*, facilitator Leslie Simms bought Mexican candies at a Latino grocery. She described one candy as "a strange, spicy taffy sold on plastic spoons, sort of like suckers."

A Tree Grows in Brooklyn

Betty Smith

....

1943

(available in paperback from HarperPerennial, 1998)

Betty Smith drew on her childhood to depict the slums of the Williamsburg section of Brooklyn in the early part of the twentieth century in *A Tree Grows in Brooklyn*.

Smith's bestselling novel chronicles the lives and struggles of the Nolan family. Uneducated and poor and the children of immigrants, Katie and Johnny marry and then struggle to raise their children, Francie and Neely. Katie is self-reliant and proud (from a line of women "made of thin invisible steel"). As she scrubs floors and works odd jobs to keep her family afloat in the face of her husband's bouts with alcoholism and unemployment, Katie is sustained by her dream of a better life for her children.

Francie, a budding writer with a passion for reading, is at the center of the novel. Francie's imagination provides an escape from the hardships of her life in Brooklyn: poverty, hunger, alcoholism, violence, prejudice, and the death of her beloved father. Through her wisdom and perseverance, she achieves her mother's dream: success through education.

Smith vividly portrays the scarcity of food for the Nolan family. As the novel begins, Francie and Neely scavenge the streets of Brooklyn for odds and ends to trade to the junk man for pennies, which they use to buy food. Most of their meals are derived from "amazing things" their resourceful mother could make with stale bread: bread pudding, fried bread, bread and meatballs.

The Nolans' one luxury is coffee, which Katie flavors with chicory and reheats throughout the day. Francie prefers the smell and warmth of the coffee to drinking it. Seeing the untouched coffee poured down the drain, Francie's aunts criticize her mother for being wasteful. Katie explains that she allows her children to throw away coffee so they won't feel so poor:

> If it makes her feel better to throw it away, rather than to drink it, all right. I think it's good that people like us can waste something once in a while and get the feeling of how it would be to have lots of money and not have to worry about scrounging.

Francie longs for fruits and sweets, but obeys her mother's rule: "Don't buy candy or cake if you have a penny." When the Nolans had bread and potatoes too many times at home, Francie's thoughts were of sour pickles, dripping with flavor. She would buy a large pickle from the Jewish pickle vendor, which she nibbled on throughout the day. "After a day of pickle, the bread and potatoes tasted good again," says Francie.

"The neighborhood stores are an important part of a city child's life," writes Smith in *A Tree Grows in Brooklyn*. "They are his contact with the supplies that keep life going; they hold the beauty that his soul longs for; they hold the unattainable that he can only dream and wish for."

At the window of a bakery in her neighborhood, Francie likes to stop and admire "beautiful charlotte russes with red candied cherries on their whipped cream tops for those who were rich enough to buy."

When Francie writes stories about her father and his shortcomings, her teacher, Miss Garnder, suggests that Francie write about less "sordid" topics—that "poverty, starvation and drunkenness are ugly subjects to choose." Francie crafts a new story featuring Sherry Nola, a "girl conceived, born and brought up in sweltering luxury." In her story, Francie's new heroine asks her maid what the cook is preparing for dinner. "I'd like to see a lot of simple desserts and choose my dinner from among them, please bring me a dozen charlotte russes, some strawberry shortcake and a quart of ice cream . . ." As Francie writes these words, a drop of water falls on her paper: "It was merely her mouth watering. She was very, very hungry."

Finding sustenance in stale bread and coffee in her kitchen, Francie rereads the passage and discovers that she has written another story about being hungry, only "twisted in a round-about silly way," and she destroys her new novel.

CHARLOTTE RUSSE

For Francie, a charlotte russe is an unattainable dessert, ogled through fancy bakery windows or served in elegant homes. Charlotte russe is made in a mold lined with liqueur-soaked ladyfingers and filled with Bavarian cream. According to Lyn Stallworth and Rod Kennedy, Jr., authors of *The Brooklyn Cookbook* (Knopf, 1991), charlotte russe, "Brooklyn's ambrosia," was ubiquitous in Brooklyn during the early part of the twentieth century—sold from pushcarts on the corners as well as in bakeries. "To old time Brooklynites, a charlotte russe was a round of sponge cake topped with sweetened whipped cream, chocolate sprinkles, and sometimes a maraschino cherry, surrounded by a frilled cardboard holder with a round of cardboard on the bottom," write Stallworth and Kennedy. Charlotte russe had a variety of pronunciations in Brooklyn, among them "charley roose" and "charlotte roosh."

Historians debate the origin of the dessert. Some say the French chef Marie Antoine Carême created the dessert for his Russian employer, Czar Alexander, while others say the dish was named for Queen Charlotte, wife of George III. Either way, our charlotte russe is a treat fit for a king (or queen). This recipe, from the Larchwood Inn in Wakefield, Rhode Island, is adapted from *Best Recipes from New England Inns*, compiled by Sandra Taylor (Yankee Press, 1991).

¼ cup kirsch (cherry brandy)	½ cup sugar
2 tablespoons juice from maraschino cherries	1 teaspoon vanilla extract
2 3-ounce packages ladyfingers	1 teaspoon almond extract
3 tablespoons instant coffee	1½ cups heavy cream
½ cup boiling water	Maraschino cherries for garnish
12 ounces semisweet chocolate	Sweetened Whipped Cream for topping
6 eggs, separated	(see p. 424)

1. Combine the kirsch and cherry juice in a small bowl, then brush the flat side of the ladyfingers with the mixture. Line the sides of a 9-inch springform pan with ladyfingers, brushed side facing in. Line the bottom with the remaining ladyfingers, brushed side up (overlapping them if necessary).

2. Dissolve the instant coffee in the boiling water. Set aside. Melt the chocolate in the top of a double boiler and set aside.

3. Beat the egg yolks with an electric mixer at high speed until foamy, then add the sugar gradually, beating until thick. Reduce the speed and add the vanilla and almond extracts, coffee, and melted chocolate.

4. In a large mixing bowl, beat the egg whites until they form stiff peaks. Stir 1 cup of egg whites into the chocolate mixture, then fold in the remaining whites.

5. In another bowl, whip the heavy cream until soft peaks form, and fold it into chocolate mixture.

6. Pour the mixture on top of the ladyfingers in the prepared pan. Freeze until firm, 4–6 hours. Before serving, garnish with a ring of maraschino cherries. Serve each piece with a dollop of lightly sweetened whipped cream.

Yield: 10 servings

During a babysitting job in 1998, Christy Sommerhauser shared Janice Graham's *Firebird,* a romantic novel set on a Kansas ranch, with her employer, Sydney Costello, and asked if they could discuss this book. "My friends in their twenties wanted to read Harlequin romances and *Bridget Jones's Diary,*" says Sommerhauser, "and the books I wanted to read and discuss had more adult themes—titles that might not interest my peer group." A first-grade teacher in Wichita, Kansas, Sommerhauser soon thereafter joined a book club Costello had formed with other educators, nurses, and stay-at-home-moms whose goal was to read books they might not pick up on their own.

At twenty-eight, Sommerhauser remains the youngest member of the group, which has met monthly since 1998. "I can't compare it to any other forum in my life," says Sommerhauser. "These women have teased me about my youth, but also taught me to be more accepting, less judgmental, and more informed all around."

Books club dinners are fun and casual. Often the host asks each member to bring an ingredient for a dish and together the group will build a Cobb salad, taco salad, or pizza. "It's easier on the hostess; the guests can bring an ingredient they like to eat; and it's fun. If someone cut cucumbers fancy, we have to give them a hard time because they didn't just chop them," says Sommerhauser. For the winter holidays, each member brings a dessert with copies of the recipe for the group.

Betty Smith's *A Tree Grows in Brooklyn,* a book Sommerhauser had always wanted to read, is "an older book that feels modern," she says. It became her favorite, as it did for many others in her group.

"*A Tree Grows in Brooklyn* reminds us why we love reading, how empowering it can be, and how it takes you places by letting you escape the reality of everyday life—exactly what I try to teach my first-graders about the pleasures of reading," says Sommerhauser. The novel provoked a discussion of relationships with parents, spouses, and significant others, and attitudes toward education. "Francie put great value in education, which appealed to our group," says Sommerhauser.

"Most of us grew up middle class," says Sommerhauser, "and few of us experienced the extreme poverty that these characters did. We discussed how poverty made Francie stronger and more determined to take control of her life."

Sommerhauser did find several similarities between herself and Francie, the book's protagonist. Like Francie, Sommerhauser didn't own many books as a child and spent hours in the library. "As second oldest of ten children, my visits to the library and time spent reading offered escape, just as they did for Francie," says Sommerhauser.

Sommerhauser's group thought Betty Smith was "forward thinking" and the voice of the book felt modern. "Even though it was written many years ago, in 1943, you could tell Smith believed in the power of women!" says Sommerhauser.

Tuesdays with Morrie: An Old Man, a Young Man, and Life's Greatest Lesson

Mitch Albom

DOUBLEDAY, *1997*

(available in paperback from Broadway, 2002)

WHEN SPORTSWRITER Mitch Albom learned that one of his favorite college professors, Morrie Schwartz of Brandeis University, was dying of amyotrophic lateral sclerosis, better known as Lou Gehrig's disease, he paid what he thought would be a last visit. That last visit turned into a weekly series of meetings, or tutorials, at Schwartz's Newton, Massachusetts, home, in which Albom and Morrie discussed topics both elemental and profound. Throughout it all, Morrie remained charming, impish, and uncommonly upbeat, and from his appearances on ABC's *Nightline* with Ted Koppel, he became a familiar face and comforting presence to millions.

Albom and Morrie spoke about love, death, success, fame —about the meaning of life and living a life with meaning. Morrie approached death with equanimity and grace, and saved his final lessons for Albom, who shares those lessons with readers.

Tuesdays with Morrie is a kind of comfort food for the soul, and food plays a significant role in Albom's relationship with Morrie. Through gifts of food, Albom nurtures Morrie and indulges him in his favorite activity aside from dancing: eating.

Albom arrives each Tuesday with bags of prepared comfort foods from Bread and Circus, a local whole-foods market: pasta with corn, potato salad, apple cobbler, chicken salad, tuna salad, carrot soup, and baklava. Morrie enjoys Albom's spirited delivery: Albom holds up the grocery bags and announces his arrival by bellowing, "Food man!"

Morrie's tastes are simple. When Albom asks Morrie what he would do with one perfectly healthy day, Morrie's fantasy includes food: a "lovely breakfast of sweet rolls" and for dinner "some great pasta" along with duck, a favorite dish. Albom marvels at the simplicity of Morrie's choices and is surprised that Morrie "would not try every exotic thing he could think of."

As Morrie's condition deteriorates, his diet becomes restricted to soft foods and liquids. Yet, to avoid hurting his feelings, Morrie doesn't tell Albom to stop bringing groceries. Even when Morrie's death is imminent, and Albom knows Morrie hasn't chewed food in months, he brings food anyway. "Sometimes when you're losing someone, you hang on to whatever tradition you can," writes Albom.

PAUL SHIPLEY'S EGG SALAD

Recalling the days he and Morrie had energetic, passionate discussions over sandwiches in the Brandeis cafeteria, Mitch Albom realizes how he missed the "long discussions over egg salad sandwiches about the meaning of life." Albom suggested that it would be appropriate to include a recipe for egg salad, which he associates with Morrie, in *The Book Club Cookbook*.

We were enticed by the description of Blytheville, Arkansas, book club member Paul Shipley's egg salad. Shipley often contributes the dish to the potluck dinners that accompany book club meetings at That Bookstore in Blytheville, owned by his wife, Mary Gay. "When he brings egg salad it's hard to settle into the book discussion," she says. "We're all circling the table."

12 large hard-cooked eggs,
* peeled and chopped*
6–10 pimento-stuffed green olives,
* chopped*
2 tablespoons finely chopped onion

2 small sweet pickles, finely chopped
1 tablespoon sweet pickle juice
4–8 tablespoons mayonnaise,
* depending on taste*
Salt and pepper

Mix the first six ingredients in a bowl, adding olives and mayonnaise according to taste. Season to taste with salt and pepper. Serve with bread or crackers.

Yield: 4 cups

"Food is almost a requirement for our meetings," says Cheryl McHugh of the East County Mothers' Club Book Club, part of a mothers' group serving nine communities in Contra Costa County, California. "As many of us are stay-at-home moms of young children, we need the opportunity to be with adults again. We can't really separate the social opportunity and the book discussion from food, which just makes it more festive."

The group started meeting in a local Starbucks, but quickly realized they had outgrown the coffee shop. Meeting in members' homes offered the opportunity to try to share new recipes, which they now e-mail to each other after meetings. The host selects the type of meal: breakfast, lunch, brunch, dinner, appetizers, desserts, wine tastings, or teas. Theme meals have included an English-style tea for Laura Hillenbrand's *Seabiscuit* (see p. 391), a California spread of taco-style appetizers, grapes, wine, and margaritas for John Steinbeck's *The Grapes of Wrath* (see p. 167), and Latin American dishes with Gabriel García Márquez's *Love in the Time of Cholera* (see p. 245).

A speech and language pathologist and mother of six-year-old Maddy, McHugh is the heart and soul of the club and devotes countless hours to the enterprise. Any of the one hundred members of the East County Mothers' Club may attend the book club, but there are seventeen active members. For each book, McHugh writes and sends out a synopsis, discussion questions, and relevant websites for members to peruse, such as a virtual tour of the house in Nathaniel Hawthorne's *The House of Seven Gables*.

McHugh selects the meeting locations, leads the discussions, and designates a reviewer to summarize the group's thoughts and assign a rating for each book they have discussed (1 to 5, with 5 being the highest rating). She also organizes group excursions to author readings and to theaters to watch film versions of books they have read.

"I really get excited about sharing my love for books and reading," says McHugh. "I love finding that extra tidbit that will help make the reading of the current book even more special for our members."

The East County Mothers' Club Book Club gave Mitch Albom's *Tuesdays with Morrie* their highest rating. "This was a book that touched many of our members very deeply," says McHugh. "It provided the catalyst for deep introspection about the life lessons it contained. What if today were the last day of our lives? How would we want to live it? What would we do? Whom would we want to be with? We talked about contacting important people in our lives that we had lost contact with or have not been in contact with as much lately."

The group openly discussed lost opportunities to learn from those who have been through life and learned what is important. But the discussion took a positive turn when they shared ideas about making changes in their lives. Some said they would stop worrying about whether the house was spotless and spend more time playing games with their children or going to the park. "The time you have with your children goes so fast," says McHugh. "Family members are increasingly isolated from one another. Mitch was given such a gift to have Morrie and to continue to learn from him. We were lucky to be able to benefit from this gift as well."

More Food for Thought

The NBA (No Boys Allowed) Book Club in Miami, Florida, enjoyed Jewish comfort food as they discussed *Tuesdays with Morrie*: homemade brisket and potato pancakes with apple sauce and sour cream, and for dessert, rugelach, Jewish pastries.

"There are millions of brisket recipes, but a good brisket melts in your mouth, and this one did," said NBA member Jacqueline Valdespino. Although most group members are Cuban or Cuban American, they were familiar with and adore Jewish cuisine. "Living in Miami, even if you are not Jewish, you are exposed to Jewish foods and traditions all the time," say Valdespino.

For their *Tuesdays with Morrie* discussion, Cheri Caviness served a brisket dinner to her book club, the Bookwomen of Encinitas, California. "The recipe is a special one from my friend Deborah Haygood's late mother," says Caviness. "It has a marinade made with orange juice and coffee that sounds unusual, but tastes delicious, and I served the brisket pot roast style, with potatoes and carrots, and a

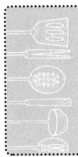

delicious gravy made from the marinade. It's just the type of dinner we all love to eat but never cook anymore."

Caviness says she brought the leftovers to Deborah at work the next day. "She took one look and started to cry," says Caviness. "She shared wonderful memories of her mom with me over lunch."

Undaunted Courage:
Meriwether Lewis, Thomas Jefferson,
and the Opening of the American West

Stephen Ambrose

....

SIMON & SCHUSTER, *1996*

(available in paperback from Simon & Schuster, 1997)

*U*NDAUNTED COURAGE is the late historian Stephen Ambrose's riveting historical account of Lewis and Clark's epic journey from St. Louis to the Oregon Coast and back at the behest of President Thomas Jefferson.

It was Jefferson who selected the young Meriwether Lewis for the ultimately futile task of finding the Northwest Passage—a water route that would connect the Mississippi to the Pacific Ocean. Jefferson personally assumed responsibility for training Lewis, and having others train him, in the many disciplines Lewis would need to make the journey a success: botany, geography, cartography, and medicine, among others.

At a time when news could travel no faster than the speed of a horse, Lewis and Clark led the Corps of Discovery, including the indispensable young Indian woman, Sacagawea, over often dangerous, uncharted terrain and through territory inhabited by Native American tribes, some of whom had never seen a white man and whose disposition toward the explorers was unpredictable.

The characteristics of the interior American West were so poorly understood that, as Lewis and Clark approached the Continental Divide on the modern-day border of Idaho and Montana, they were expecting hills no larger than the Appalachians and a view straight down to the Pacific Ocean. At the summit they saw nothing but a series of snow-capped peaks as far the eye could see.

Undaunted Courage is the story of Jefferson's vision, the perseverance of brave people in remarkably difficult circumstances, and the trove of information Lewis and Clark collected about the flora, fauna, and peoples of what become the western United States.

In addition to documenting the geography of the West, Lewis and Clark recorded their daily culinary adventures in their journals. Although the members of the Corps of Discovery relied in part on provisions they brought with them, their survival also depended on hunting, fishing, Lewis's knowledge of edible plants, and advice from various Indian tribes they encountered.

Before their departure in May 1804 from Camp Dubois in St. Louis for their journey up the Missouri River, Lewis and Clark secured a variety of provisions, including pork, hominy, and cornmeal as well as salt, wheat flour, sugar, coffee, beans, peas, portable soup (a reduced stock made into a bouillon cube), and, of course, whiskey.

During their first month on the river, the explorers were subsisting on wild game, pork, flour, and cornmeal. "Only on the rarest of occasions did the party get fresh vegetables, such as watercress, and there was no ripe fruit as yet," writes Ambrose. In June 1804, with nearly four hundred miles behind them, Lewis and Clark arrived at the mouth of the Kansas River. There was reason to be hopeful: fruit was ripening.

During their journey, the explorers enjoyed sampling berries, wild plums, and currants. Clark pronounced the plums the "'most delisious' he had ever tasted" and "the grapes 'plenty and finely flavored,'" reports Ambrose.

Mary Gunderson's *The Food Journal of Lewis & Clark: Recipes for an Expedition* (History Cooks, 2003) is a gastronomic tour of the expedition, with recipes and commentary based on the food notes in Lewis and Clark's journals (www.historycooks.com). According to Gunderson, a culinary historian, fruit was essential to the Corps members' diet as a source of vitamin C. "It was excellent that they were able to eat as much fruit as they were," says Gunderson. "Fruit, along with the roots they ate, prevented gum problems, and kept scurvy, a disease caused by vitamin C deficiency, at bay." Gunderson explains that it was critical to determine if fruit was edible, as there was much concern about poisonous berries. "These were remarkable men in terms of the breadth of their knowledge," she adds. "Lewis's mother, who was very knowledgeable about plants, gave him invaluable expertise."

By early August 1804, says Gunderson, "they were walking into the prairie's abundance of ripe summer fruits."

MACEDOINE OF RED FRUITS

Whenthe Corps of Discovery celebrated Clark's thirty-fourth birthday on August 1, 1804, Lewis wrote in his journal that to mark the occasion: "I order'd a Saddle of fat Vennison, an Elk flece & a Bevertail to be cooked and a Desert of Cheries, Plumbs, Raspberries, Currents and grapes of a Supr. Quality."

Our Macedoine of Red Fruits is a birthday tribute to Captain Clark and consists of the same fruits he enjoyed when he marked his thirty-fourth birthday on the trail: cherries, plums, raspberries, currants, and grapes. We think you'll enjoy the discovery.

1½ cups pitted, sliced red plums
1½ cups seedless red grapes, halved
¾ cup pitted cherries
or ½ cup currants
1½ cups fresh raspberries

1 tablespoon sugar
⅛ teaspoon ground cinnamon
2 tablespoons good quality balsamic vinegar
Sweetened Sour Cream (see below) or
Sweetened Whipped Cream (see p. 424)

1. Place the plums, grapes, cherries or currants, and raspberries in a serving bowl.
2. Combine the sugar and cinnamon and sprinkle over the fruit mixture. Drizzle with the vinegar.
3. Mix gently and let stand for 20 minutes. Serve with Sweetened Sour Cream or Sweetened Whipped Cream.

Yield: 8 to 10 servings

SWEETENED SOUR CREAM

4 tablespoons light brown sugar
2 cups sour cream

1 teaspoon vanilla extract

Stir together the sugar and sour cream until the sugar is dissolved, then add vanilla.

In 1995, Nancy Miller went to Barnes & Noble in Seattle to hear Nancy Pearl, director of the Washington Center for the Book, speak about starting book clubs. After the meeting a dozen audience members went to the bookstore's café to discuss the lecture. "We sized each other up and decided to form a book group," says Miller.

The group's spontaneous formation gives it great diversity, says Miller, a high school social studies teacher in Bellevue, who is joined by a fellow teachers, a psychiatrist, a librarian, a homemaker, an insurance consultant–lobbyist, a doctor, a math professor, a graduate student, a nurse, and a guardian ad litem in Booked Wednesdays, the name the club took to enable it to register for a discount at a local bookstore. Married and single men and women make up the group, which ranges in age from twenties to seventies.

"Our racial makeup has varied as people come and go, but we've never been homogeneous," says Miller. "We feel that this diversity adds to our conversation and to what we might gain from sharing about the book."

Booked Wednesdays reads from a variety of genres. Favorite titles include Michael Cunningham's *The Hours* (see p. 192), Jung Chang's *Wild Swans: Three Daughters of China* (see p. 486), Ann Fadiman's *The Spirit Catches You and You Fall Down* (see p. 410), and Stephen Ambrose's *Undaunted Courage*.

Miller says members enjoy a broad range of topics, but history has a strong appeal. "We are all of curious mind, so learning more about how our world evolved and about people's experiences in it interests the entire group," she adds.

When they discussed *Undaunted Courage*, topics included the vastness of the land, the scale of the undertaking, and the breathtaking vision and bravery of the expedition members.

Booked Wednesday members were fascinated by the roles of women and race on the expedition. "The outbreak of democracy on the banks of the Columbia River was wonderful," says Miller. Sacagawea, the Indian guide for the Lewis and Clark expedition, and Toussaint Charbonneau, her husband, a French-Canadian fur trapper who was hired for his language skills, intrigued them. "Charbonneau was hired and Sacagawea went along," says Miller. "But her knowledge was what became central to the success of the expedition. Along the way, she found trails and campsites, helped the expedition to acquire horses. While doing all this, she managed to keep an infant alive while hiking the wilds of North America and the Rocky Mountains in winter."

Miller says she is a "shirt-tail" cousin of Meriwether Lewis and had heard family versions of Meriwether Lewis's death on the Natchez Trace while en route to Washington, D.C. "That mystery was of much interest to the group," says Miller. Most of us concluded it was a suicide, based on the reactions of Thomas Jefferson and William Clark."

Several members brought books with photographs showing the land Lewis and Clark had traveled, and some had camped or traveled through the area themselves and recounted their experiences, says Miller. Many members had visited Lewis and Clark's winter camp, Fort Clatsop, near Astoria, Oregon, and the Lewis and Clark Museum in Ilwaco, Washington. "This gave physical presence and dimension to the descriptions in the book," says Miller.

After reading *Undaunted Courage,* Miller and her husband drove the Lolo Pass on the Montana-Idaho border, along a forest service road that follows the original expedition trail, and visited three other Lewis and Clark museums along the route: Fort Mandan and Knife River Indian Encampment, in North Dakota, and Pompey's Pillar in Montana, where Clark's signature can be seen carved in a rock.

The Mandan village where Lewis and Clark spent the first winter especially intrigued Miller. "The village isn't usually described in school textbooks," says Miller. "I envisioned a tribe's small encampment as one might see in a movie. It wasn't a small nomad encampment, but a city larger than many East Coast cities, with established trade and transportation. It's amazing what history texts omit."

More Food for Thought

The wine and dinner series at the Ida and Cecil Green Faculty Club on the University of California at San Diego (UCSD) campus explores haute cuisine with historic themes.

"Instead of hosting the usual winery dinner, we thought our membership would enjoy a dinner with an academic twist," says Tom Mignano, the club's director. "Our Thomas Jefferson and Ernest Hemingway dinner themes add an intellectual dimension to our excellent wine and food program."

For the Lewis and Clark Gastronomic Expedition Dinner, faculty club staff and volunteers created a menu based on extensive research of the many accounts of the expedition, including Stephen Ambrose's *Undaunted Courage*. They also drew on the vast resources of UCSD's Geisel Library, which houses the largest collection of cookbooks in California. "We took some culinary license in creating dishes, and of course the chef puts his signature on the dishes, too," says Mignano.

The Lewis and Clark Gastronomic Expedition menu featured wild mushroom bouchée; endive salad with pear, honey pecans, and blackberries; rum-soaked dried currants and tomatoes; buttermilk-chive dressing; fresh sweet corn cakes with duck confit; mild jalapeño beurre blanc and crispy tortilla strips; campfire cassoulet; pan-seared salmon; smoked chicken and apple sausage; duck roulade with blackberry sauce; and, for dessert, blueberry pandowdy. While guests enjoyed a culinary tour of dishes featuring ingredients Lewis and Clark sampled on their cross-country journey, Roger Showley, a writer for the *San Diego Union-Tribune*, history expert, and UCSD alumnus, spoke about the famous expedition.

Waiting

Ha Jin

....

PANTHEON BOOKS, *1999*

(available in paperback from Vintage, 2000)

*W*AITING IS the story of a modern Chinese couple, Lin Kong and Mannu Wu, who wait eighteen years to marry, until Lin Kong can divorce his wife.

Dr. Lin Kong, in his late forties, handsome, reserved, and honorable, is stationed at an army hospital in northern China, where he meets Manna Wu, a nurse. As a medical student, Lin had agreed to an arranged marriage so that his new wife could care for his ailing mother. From the outset, though, Lin found Shuyu, faithful wife and caregiver, unappealing, with her aged appearance, bound feet, and traditional ways. In the seventeen years since the birth of their daughter, Hua, they have slept separately. In each of those years, Lin's twelve-day military leave is devoted to returning to his home in rural Goose Village to seek a divorce from his wife, but each year Shuyu refuses. Army regulations provide that after eighteen years of separation, a divorce may be granted without spousal consent.

The lengthy courtship of Lin and Manna during these eighteen years takes place in several interrelated contexts: the coming and passing of the Cultural Revolution, the punctilious hierarchies and constraints of military life, the psychological interplay of lovers in an unconsummated relationship, and the pervasive sense of lost opportunity. With its painfully long periods of delay, Ha Jin's novel raises many questions: To what extent does the anticipation of an event become a way of life? When a dream is finally realized, can the reality ever match the expectations that have grown around it?

The characters in *Waiting* eat a striking variety of foods. In the countryside, Shuyu cooks elaborate meals. In the city, Lin Kong and Manna go to restaurants, buy food from street vendors, and eat hospital staff dinners. The resulting array of dishes gives readers a sense of the great variety in contemporary Chinese cuisine—fried carp, stewed pork, tomatoes sautéed with eggs, steamed taro, scrambled eggs with onions, sautéed pole beans, fried peanuts, cabbage, scallion pancakes, pork liver and heart cooked in aniseed broth, beef pies, sugar buns, fried dough sticks, smoked flounder, sweet and sour ribs, and sautéed pork with bamboo shoots.

For Lin Kong the pleasures of eating contrast with his anguish over a life in suspension. The ties of family, represented by food, trouble Lin; throughout the book he is torn between two families, never feeling fully a part of either. Even as he tries to divorce her, he savors Shuyu's cooking—her "soft and delicious" multigrain porridge, her eggs sautéed with leeks or scallions that leave him with redolent belches, and her steamed string beans seasoned with sesame oil that he eats with no thought to his garlicky breath.

With the same ambivalence, Lin Kong eats at a restaurant with Manna and a friend. During the ample meal of pork head, pickled mushrooms, baby eggplants, salted duck eggs, dumplings stuffed with pork, dried shrimps, cabbage and scallions, Lin Kong is overcome with melancholy, realizing that this outing marks the first time he and Manna have ever eaten out together. The futility of his situation overwhelms him, even as he is surrounded by delicious food.

Spicy Shrimp in Black Bean Sauce

Perhaps the scene that best reflects Lin Kong's paralysis takes place after another unsuccessful attempt to divorce Shuyu. After leaving the courthouse, Lin is met by an angry mob of villagers, led by Shuyu's brother, Bensheng, intent on violence had the divorce been granted. Lin is filled with hatred for Bensheng.

They return to Lin's house and are joined by Lin's brother, Ren Kong. Bensheng has bought a package of shrimp, which neither he nor Ren has ever tasted. The men clown around in front of Hua, laughing as they pretend to eat live creatures that bite their tongues. Lin instructs them all on the proper way to shell and eat shrimp. At the end of the evening, Lin realizes that he cannot cut his ties with his brother-in-law: "His mind returned to the shrimp dinner. He remembers that he had decided not to speak to Bensheng again, but somehow he had forgotten his decision."

Rosemary Lowther of Cody, Wyoming, prepared this spicy shrimp dish for the Meeteetse Book Group's discussion of *Waiting*. The menu also included stir-fried steak and broccoli, scallion fried rice, bok choy salad, and fruit for dessert. "The spiciness of the shrimp complemented the mild flavors of the other dishes," says Lowther. "We wanted to have a variety of dishes, as that seemed traditionally Chinese."

We have adapted Lowther's recipe, which came from *Hot Woks* by Hugh Carpenter and Teri Sandison (Ten Speed Press, 1995).

1 pound medium-sized raw shrimp

1 red bell pepper

1 green bell pepper

1 yellow bell pepper

4 cloves garlic, finely minced

1 large shallot, finely minced

1 tablespoon finely minced fresh ginger

3 fresh serrano chiles (seeds included),
    finely minced

¼ cup Chinese rice wine, sake, or dry sherry

1 tablespoon sugar

2 teaspoons cornstarch

1 tablespoon light soy sauce

1 tablespoon dark sesame oil, plus a dash
    for cooking

1 tablespoon black bean sauce

1 tablespoon red wine vinegar

3 tablespoons vegetable oil

Salt and freshly ground black pepper to taste

1. Preheat oven to 200° F.
2. Shell and devein shrimp, then butterfly. Cover and refrigerate.
3. Discard the stems and seeds from the bell peppers, and slice into matchsticks, about 1 inch long and ¼ inch wide. Toss peppers together in a bowl. Cover and refrigerate.
4. Combine the garlic, shallot, ginger, and serranos in a small bowl. Set aside.
5. In another small bowl, combine the rice wine, sugar, cornstarch, soy sauce, 1 tablespoon sesame oil, black bean sauce, and vinegar. Set aside.
6. Place a wok over highest heat. When the wok is very hot, add half of the vegetable oil. Tilt the wok to spread the oil up the sides. When the oil just begins to smoke, add the bell peppers and stir-fry about 2 minutes. During the final seconds, add a dash of sesame oil and salt and black pepper to taste. Immediately transfer peppers to a heated ovenproof serving platter, or to individual ovenproof dinner plates. Spread peppers out in an even layer, and place in oven.
7. Return the wok to highest heat. Add the remaining vegetable oil and again roll oil around sides of wok. When it begins to smoke, add the garlic-shallot mixture. Stir-fry for just a few seconds, then add the shrimp. Stir-fry and toss shrimp until outsides become white, about 2 minutes.
8. Give the rice wine mixture a stir to dissolve any cornstarch on the bottom, and add to the wok. Stir and toss until shrimp are glazed and cooked through, about 1 minute. Taste and adjust seasonings. Spoon hot shrimp into the center of platter or dinner plates. Serve immediately.

Yield: Serves 4 as a main course, 6 as an appetizer

Every month since 1998, seven women in the ranching town of Meeteetse, Wyoming, population 341, have gathered for a book discussion and related feast. The group enjoys books—and accompanying meals—with an "international flavor" and has enjoyed varied cuisines: Mexican, Indian, African, Chinese, Egyptian, Italian, and western American.

Group members would welcome the same diversity in their group that they enjoy at the table. "We'd welcome people of other ethnicities in our group," says Rosemary Lowther, a charter member of the group. "But there is very little ethnic diversity here."

Group members—all women in their thirties, forties, and fifties—left behind lives in various parts of the country to come to Wyoming, attracted to the region's lifestyle and beauty. A former production director for a magazine in New York City, Lowther now weaves and works in an art gallery. Other members work in typical western industries, such as ranching and the railroad, and for the U.S. Forest Service. They share a devotion to their club and an appreciation of good books and ethnic food. One member travels fifty miles to attend meetings.

The theme of the books they read determines each month's menu. For African selections such as Barbara Kingsolver's *The Poisonwood Bible* (see p. 353) and J. M. Coetzee's *Disgrace* (see p. 106), the group served shrimp *piri-piri*—spicy barbecued shrimp with a marinade, from Mozambique—and *boboti,* a traditional South African casserole of ground lamb, curry, and raisins. For Harriet Doerr's Mexico-based *Stones for Ibarra,* the group hosted a Sunday afternoon Day of the Dead party, complete with tortilla soup, chicken burritos, and a seven-layer Mexican dip of refried beans, avocados, scallions, jalapeño peppers, tomatoes, cheese, and a sour cream–mayonnaise dressing. Books with Indian themes—*Interpreter of Maladies* by Jhumpa Lahiri (see p. 204) and *The God of Small Things* by Arundhati Roy (see p. 157)—inspired spicy shrimp curry, chicken curry, and rice.

To add ambience to their discussion of Nevada Barr's *Blind Descent,* the sixth book in a mystery series featuring national park ranger Anna Pigeon, the group camped out in Kirwin, an abandoned mining town. They explored the still-standing buildings and imagined the town in its heyday, when, legend holds, Amelia Earhart vacationed there. The women bonded during the candlelit evening discussion and over their discovery, the following morning, of fresh grizzly bear tracks near their campsite.

The group originally chose to read Ha Jin's *Waiting* as an excuse to prepare and eat Chinese food. But group members found the book discussion as satisfying as the meal. In spite of the book's "unhappy theme," particularly Lin Kong's self-destructive inability to take action, members appreciated the peek into what Lowther calls "the constraints and mind-set of another culture."

The Meeteetse Book Club found that *Waiting* resonated with a universal theme. "We felt 'be careful what you wish for' applied very much to this story," says Lowther. "Maybe in waiting and wanting you make your dream into something it is not. Waiting too long makes you idealize your desire into something that can never be realized, and if you finally achieve your wish, what you end up with is disappointment."

More Food for Thought

The Book Club of the Brown University Club of New York recorded its best attendance in its history—twenty-four people—for its discussion of Ha Jin's *Waiting*, held at a Chinese restaurant, Wo Hop, in downtown Manhattan. Menu selections included vegetarian dim sum dumplings; egg rolls; Cantonese rice, meat, and vegetable dishes; and beef chow fun, a rice noodle dish. "The beef chow fun is a favorite of mine," says John Kwok, a coordinator of the book club.

A Walk in the Woods: Rediscovering America on the Appalachian Trail

Bill Bryson

....

BROADWAY, *1998*

(available in paperback from Broadway, 1999)

I n *A Walk in the Woods*, veteran travel writer and humorist Bill Bryson takes to the wilderness, chronicling his attempt to hike from Georgia to Maine on the famed 2,100-mile Appalachian Trail. Bryson's trail companion is his childhood buddy from Iowa, the underprepared and overfed Stephen Katz. This wry account of their sundry misadventures and the characters they meet is interwoven with the history and geography of the trail. Bryson makes a powerful case for conservation of the American wilderness along the way, too.

Katz shows up for the hike in miserable physical condition, with apparently no clue about the arduous journey ahead. His main provision is Snickers bars. But Bryson isn't exactly trail-savvy himself, and together they hit the trail with backpacks full of pepperoni sausages, beef jerky, and "imperishable cakes and doughnuts" to round out their trail diet. They quickly learn that "the central feature of life on the Appalachian Trail is deprivation," a condition that instills an appreciation for such ordinary foods as Coca-Cola and white bread.

Bryson and Katz aren't out of Georgia before they head off in search of a nearby restaurant to fulfill their "savage lust for food." Bryson fills up on chicken, black-eyed peas, roast potatoes, "ruterbeggars," and iced tea, and tops it off with a dessert that makes rare appearances in camp-sites, the dessert he claims most Appalachian Trail hikers spend hours daydreaming about as they slog on, mile after food-deprived mile. Bryson writes:

Everyone on the trail dreams of something, usually sweet and gooey, and my sustaining vision had been an outsized slab of pie. [The waitress] brought me a vast viscous, canary-yellow wedge of lemon pie. It was a monument to food technology, yellow enough to give you a headache, sweet enough to make your eyeballs roll up into your head—everything, in short, you could want from a pie so long as taste and quality didn't enter into your requirements.

Very Yellow Lemon Meringue Pie

Our version of lemon meringue pie is everything you could want from a pie, with the addition of great taste and excellent quality. And it won't give you a headache.

½ recipe Basic Pie Crust (see p. 112)

4 eggs, separated

1 tablespoon grated lemon peel

5 tablespoons fresh lemon juice

1½ cups sugar, divided

¼ cup plus 1 tablespoon cornstarch

⅛ teaspoon salt

1½ cups cold water

2 tablespoons butter

¼ teaspoon cream of tartar

½ teaspoon vanilla extract

1. To prebake piecrust: Preheat oven to 425°F. Prick crust with fork all over and bake for 8–10 minutes, until lightly browned. Remove from oven and allow to cool.
2. Lower oven temperature to 325°F.
3. To make the filling: Lightly beat the egg yolks to combine, and set aside.
4. Put the lemon peel and juice together in a bowl, and set aside.
5. Combine 1 tablespoon cornstarch with ⅓ cup water in a small saucepan and simmer, whisking constantly, until thick. Set aside and allow to cool until ready to prepare meringue.
6. Combine 1 cup sugar, ¼ cup of cornstarch, the salt, and 1½ cups cold water in a heavy-bottomed saucepan. Simmer over medium heat, whisking frequently. When the mixture starts to thicken and turn clear, whisk in the egg yolks, half at a time, whisking vigorously after each addition to prevent eggs from curdling. When the yolks are completely mixed in, add the butter and the lemon peel and juice. Reduce heat to a simmer, whisking constantly. After a minute or so, remove from heat and cover pan to prevent a skin from forming.
7. To make the meringue: Mix together the remaining ½ cup sugar and the cream of tartar in a bowl and set aside. Using an electric mixer on high speed, beat the egg whites and vanilla for a few seconds until they foam. Add the sugar mixture a large spoonful at a time, continuing

to beat. When the mixture forms soft peaks, add the cooled cornstarch and water, a large spoonful at a time, and beat until it forms stiff peaks.

8. If the filling has cooled significantly while making the meringue, reheat briefly, whisking constantly. Pour the filling into the prebaked pie shell. Top with the meringue, beginning at the outside edge and moving toward the center. Spread the meringue with a scraper or the back of a large spoon and create small peaks across the surface. Make sure the topping is attached to the edge of the pie crust to prevent it from pulling back when baked. Bake until the meringue is golden brown all over, about 20 minutes. Cool to room temperature. Serve the same day.

Yield: 1 9-inch pie, 6 to 8 servings

BOOK CLUB PROFILE

"Environmentalists have a reputation for being serious and pessimistic—you don't get a lot of funny books about the environment," says Kate Moffat, leader of the Sierra Club Book Group of Portland, Maine. Moffat chose Bill Bryson's *A Walk in the Woods* as the first selection in the group's Living In and Loving the Woods reading series, a subject especially appropriate for Maine, one of the most densely forested states in the nation and home of the northern terminus of the Appalachian Trail, Mt. Katahdin. A departure from more serious environmental works the group has read, Bryson's memoir was a huge hit. "We soaked up this book," says Moffat.

The Sierra Club Book Group discusses books about the environment over Mexican fare one Friday a month at Granny's Burritos in downtown Portland. "We like to start off by making sure everyone is fed," says Moffat. The Sierra Club's Maine chapter's mission is "to explore, enjoy, and protect the wild places of the earth." The book club is a terrific way to orient new members to environmental issues: "It has been a wonderful activity for new members if they don't want to go on an outing or write letters," says Moffat.

The group loved Bryson's version of "healthy" trail food: "The idea of packing Snickers and junk food had us roaring—that stuff won't last you a mile. That the food was an afterthought was hysterical! I would encourage anyone hiking the Appalachian Trail or going into the wilderness to read this book," says Moffat.

Members of the Sierra Club Book Group especially enjoyed Bryson's account of hiking the

Hundred Mile Wilderness, a section of the Appalachian Trail in Maine that many consider to be the most rugged and challenging part of the entire trail. Though they hail from Maine, most in the club "had never been to the Hundred Mile Wilderness and wanted to hear what it was like," says Moffat.

More Food for Thought

Bryson and Katz's food choices for the trip have given many book clubs quick ideas for meeting snacks. The South Florida PTA Book Club discussed *A Walk in the Woods* for their annual "couples night," when husbands are invited to a potluck and discussion. To bring them closer to the trail, the dinner menu featured venison stew, trail mix, and candy bars. Member Holly Evans set the mood for her guests, decorating the front porch of her home with a camping cook pot and a walking stick.

The Book Bags of New Prague, Minnesota, had a hobo dinner when they discussed *A Walk in the Woods*, with hamburgers, potatoes, and carrots cooked in the oven. They recorded their impressions in nature journals while they ate Snickers bars, gorp (a trail mix of dried fruit and nuts), and Little Debbie cakes, favorites of Bryson and Katz.

The Weight of Water

Anita Shreve

....

LITTLE, BROWN, *1997*

(available in paperback from Back Bay, 1998)

J EAN, the narrator of *The Weight of Water*, is a photographer assigned to shoot a photo essay at the site of an 1873 double ax-murder on Smuttynose Island, ten miles southeast of Portsmouth, New Hampshire (a historical event). In her background research for the assignment, Jean discovers a long-neglected translation of an account of the murders written twenty-five years after the event by survivor Maren Hontvedt. As Jean immerses herself in Maren's century-old story, she also personally struggles to cope with her increasing suspicions that her husband, Thomas, is having an affair.

In this emotionally gripping story, Anita Shreve tells a double tale, masterfully alternating between Jean's voice and that of Maren Hontvedt. In both the "then" and "now" scenes of the novel, we find a small group of people confined to small quarters in an atmosphere of intensified emotions—love, hate, jealousy—all ultimately leading to violence.

To help with her project, Jean's brother-in-law, Rich, invites her to sail to Smuttynose in his forty-one-foot sloop, docking there for the duration of Jean's project. Rich's new girlfriend, Adaline, joins the crew, along with Thomas, a celebrated poet and alcoholic, and Thomas and Jean's five-year-old daughter, Billie. The tension on the boat grows, as Jean finds herself attracted to Rich, threatened by Billie's reverence for Adaline, and suspicious that Thomas may be cheating on her.

Maren's accounts of events a century earlier, interspersed with scenes on the boat, form the text of the novel. Maren describes the desolate small house on barren Smuttynose Island where she and her husband, John, live after emigrating from Norway. After three years alone in America, Maren and John are joined by John's brother, Matthew, Maren's sister, Karen, and her brother, Evan, with his new wife, the lovely Anethe.

As the shocking story of murder on the island unfolds, the relationships on the boat also evolve painfully. The tone of *The Weight of Water* is tense and unsettling throughout, as old relationships founder on secrets newly revealed. "The weight of water," remarks Jean, "causes pressure to increase with depth." In this novel, the depth of feelings and the pressures within relationships build to untenable levels, with violent and sad consequences.

The food in *The Weight of Water* reflects the story's varied settings. Maren and John Hontvedt have recently emigrated from Norway. Maren attempts, through her cooking, to re-create tastes of her beloved Norweigan homeland in her New Hampshire island home. She offers Louis Wagner, a mate on John's boat, some home-baked *konfektkake,* or chocolate cake, which he eats steadily until it's gone. Upon hearing that her brother, Evan, will soon be arriving on the island, Maren jubilantly prepares delicacies that she "knew he loved in Norway and probably thought never to have again:" *rommegrot* (sour cream porridge), *krumkake* (a thin, crispy wafer), and *skillingsbolle* (cinnamon buns).

Many of the foods mentioned in *The Weight of Water* reflect the book's New England coastal setting. On Rich's boat, the group prepares a typical New England clambake, with lobsters, mussels, and corn, as well as salad and garlic bread. A century before, Maren also cooks with the harvests of the sea, serving dried salted cod and fish chowder, a soup she believes has "a wonderful aroma."

PAUL EHLEN'S SWEDISH PANCAKES

Like the seafood prepared by both Jean and Maren in *The Weight of Water,* pancakes transcend time and place. Thomas and Billie make pancakes—"kidney shaped, oil glistened, and piled high upon a white platter"—for breakfast on the boat, and Jean takes a series of photos after they eat that captures the essence of their relationship at that moment.

Pancakes, made by mixing ground grains with water or milk, have been around for thousands of years, and almost every culture has its own version of this classic. In tribute to the Scandinavian characters in *The Weight of Water,* we offer below a recipe for a simple and delicious Swedish pancake.

At www.wutheringbites.com, their website featuring book reviews and recipes, the Seattle-area Wuthering Bites book club suggests pairing this recipe for Swedish pancakes with *The Weight of Water.* "The characters would have enjoyed these tasty pancakes on a cold, bleak winter's morning," the website states.

Stephanie Koura, a former chef and longtime member of Wuthering Bites, posted the recipe, which came from her husband's half-Swedish, half-Norwegian great-grandmother. "She learned to cook on a farm in Minnesota, where she grew up, and is remembered fondly in the family for her kindness and wonderful cooking," says Koura.

The pancakes have an eggy texture, similar to a thick crêpe. Koura's husband, Paul Ehlen, makes them for breakfast or brunch and serves them dusted with powdered sugar and drizzled with lemon butter. For your book club meeting, try these pancakes spread with jelly or lingonberries, Swedish preserves similar to cranberry sauce (see Purchasing Information, p. 499), and rolled up.

3 eggs

1¼ cups milk

¾ cup sifted all-purpose flour

1 tablespoon sugar

½ teaspoon salt

1. Beat the eggs in a medium-size bowl. Whisk in the milk. Add the remaining ingredients and stir until mixture is just smooth.

2. Heat a griddle or skillet over medium heat. Grease lightly with butter or cooking spray. Ladle enough batter onto the warm griddle to make a thin pancake of desired size. Cook on both sides, turning once, until pancake is golden brown. Enjoy immediately with syrup, jam, or powdered sugar and lemon butter.

Yield: 10 to 12 pancakes

BOOK CLUB PROFILE

Everything about the Bookenders Book Club of Lee's Summit, Missouri, reflects the sixteen members' profound love of books. "When I close a book, I am closing a world of people I have been living with for days," says Kathy Hayes, a charter member of the group, which started in 1992. "At times, I miss them and wish to continue in their lives. Discussing a book with my book club gives me closure. I can get it out of my head and move on."

The structure of Bookenders' monthly meetings encourages meaningful dialogue about books. The hostess begins each meeting with information about the author's life and reviews of the book. "We have often recognized authors' personal life experiences in their books," says Hayes. "Knowing about the author's life gives us a better insight into the book." Members often come to meetings with notable passages marked. "Sometimes a member will have a question and another member will have marked it and will be able to respond," says Hayes.

A different hostess selects the book each month. Bookenders enjoy all genres except romance and mystery. "We have read a couple of good mysteries" like Stephen L. Carter's *The Emperor of Ocean Park* (see p. 120), says Hayes, "but for the most part mysteries are just a 'who done it.' We love all eras and a variety of authors. And nothing—I mean nothing— beats the classics." The group's vast reading list, along with ratings and reviews of each book, can be found on the group's website (www.bookenders.com), which Hayes maintains. Some of their favorites: John Irving's *A Prayer for Owen Meany* (see p. 363), Ursula Hegi's *Stones from the River* (see p. 416), Barbara Kingsolver's *The Poisonwood Bible* (see p. 353), and Harriet Beecher Stowe's *Uncle Tom's Cabin*.

The diverse backgrounds of the Bookenders add spice to their discussion of any book. Hayes calls the Kansas City area "a melting pot of the United States"; book club members come from New York, Boston, Chicago, Kansas, Michigan, and England. Their social and economic histories—some grew up in affluence, others on the other end of the spectrum—give "a credibility to their opinions and add interest to discussions," says Hayes.

At meetings, Bookenders sip drinks—wine, soda, tea, and other beverages—while they discuss the book, and eat dessert when the discussion ends. Sometimes members prepare desserts that match the theme of the book. "Eating thematic food helps place us in the era and setting of the book we're reading," says Hayes. Group members also share food in December during the club's annual Christmas party and book exchange.

The group's thirst for close reading and analysis of interesting texts was quenched with Anita Shreve's *The Weight of Water*, a book they highly recommend. Group discussion took place on the group's annual pontoon boat ride, when they usually discuss a water-related book.

The Bookenders especially liked the book's subtlety as it moved between two different time periods. "At times, the switching between the past and the present seemed confusing," says Hayes. "But then you discover that she switches from the past to the present because Jean, the photographer doing the story about the murders, is reading or thinking about the past, but is brought to the present by an interruption of her thoughts with present life. It's very skillfully done."

Members agreed that group discussion of the book greatly enhanced their appreciation for the complexity of the book's plot and characters. "The more we discussed the characters, relationships, and actions in *The Weight of Water*, the more we realized how subtle the author was in crafting these," says Hayes. "It was as if we were peeling away a layer at a time. There is much more to this book than meets the eye. That's why we felt it should be read more than once and discussed in order to be fully appreciated."

Group members enjoyed reading a fictionalized account of an actual event and left the meeting curious about the truth. "Reading this book made me want to research the actual documents myself," says Hayes. "No one will know the real truth, but I would like to believe that the author's version is the true source."

More Food for Thought

Chef Julia Shanks of Interactive Cuisine in Cambridge, Massachusetts, creates menus to match literary selections for book clubs in the Boston area. For *The Weight of Water*, she suggests a Norwegian menu: gravlax with mustard-dill sauce, spinach soup, Norwegian meatballs with spiced cream sauce, potato pancakes, and kringles (almond coffee cake) for dessert.

Wuthering Bites book club member and former chef Stephanie Koura of Seattle posts food ideas and recipes to pair with books on her group's website.

For *The Weight of Water*, she lists three recipes that, while not intended as a meal, provide culinary inspiration for book clubs: her husband Paul's Swedish pancakes; Scandinavian spice cookies, a recipe she found on a Norwegian genealogy recipe page; and Jansson's Temptation, a "classic Scandinavian side dish" of potatoes, onions, and anchovies. "Don't let the anchovies turn you off," Koura advises. "They meld wonderfully with the cream to give this dish a sea-tinged saltiness." See the group's website, www.wutheringbites.com, for more information and recipes.

Where the Heart Is

Billie Letts

....

WARNER, *1995*

(available in paperback from Warner, 1998)

W HEN NOVALEE NATION, seventeen years old and seven months pregnant, stops in a Sequoyah, Oklahoma, Wal-Mart to buy sandals, her boyfriend, Willy Jack Pickens, speeds away, stranding her. The novel *Where the Heart Is* tells the story of Novalee's abandonment, and the caring community that accepts and embraces her.

Far from her few friends in Tellico Plains, Tennessee, where she grew up in foster care, and with nothing but $7.77 in her pocket, Novalee draws on her own resources. She lives covertly in the Wal-Mart, eating canned peas and carrots, until the day she delivers her baby in the store. When reporters learn of her story, she becomes famous. Sam Walton, Wal-Mart's founder, visits Novalee in the hospital, thanks her for the publicity she has brought to his business, and offers her a job. Thus begins Novalee's new life in Sequoyah.

Over time, Novalee meets an eclectic mix of Sequoyah residents who embrace and nurture her. Sister Husband, an evangelist and dispenser of welcome kits to new residents, opens her trailer home to Novalee and her daughter, Americus. Moses Whitecotton, a photographer, helps Novalee purchase her first real camera. Young Benny Goodluck welcomes Novalee to town with a buckeye tree sapling, a promise of good luck. And an eccentric librarian, Forney Hull, feeds Novalee's thirst for books, and falls in love with her.

As Novalee negotiates new friendships and endures the pain of violence and loss that visits her community, she begins to understand a concept that has always eluded her—home. At its core, *Where the Heart Is* is a powerful testament to the redemptive powers of a loving community.

Providing food is one of the many ways that Novalee's new friends take care of her. Soon after Novalee is discovered in Sequoyah, Forney Hull prepares a birthday dinner for her. The meal of orange-almond bisque, tournedos Wellington, asparagus mousse, and wine stuns Novalee, moving her to declare the event "the most perfect night of my life." But Novalee is uncomfortable with fine dining and, ultimately, with the class differences that make her feel unworthy of Forney's attention. The dry wine tastes sour to her. She is embarrassed for Forney when she finds that the bisque, a soup she assumes should be hot, is cold.

Although Forney has a flair for gourmet cooking, the vast majority of food mentioned in *Where the Heart Is* smacks of down-home comfort. On her first visit to Sister Husband's trailer, Novalee gobbles cornbread and buttermilk. The foods that end up in picnic baskets or that neighbors bring one another include jelly sandwiches, cinnamon rolls (see p. 336), sugar cookies, peanut butter cookies, creamed chicken, squash soup, sweet-potato pie (see p. 423), and banana bread.

BANANA BREAD

Banana bread is a fitting accompaniment to a discussion of *Where the Heart Is.* For centuries, various cultures have cooked with bananas, although banana bread is a relatively recent phenomenon. In her book, *Bananas: An American History* (Smithsonian Institution Press, 2000), Virginia Scott Jenkins suggests that banana bread may have been invented by a Depression-era housewife looking for a way to make some extra money. Banana bread recipes started appearing in popular American cookbooks in the 1920s. It has remained a quintessential comfort food ever since.

The Refreshing Reading Book Club in Atlanta, Georgia, has read and discussed fiction for twenty-three years. At each year's first meeting, the group has come to expect charter member Linda Wener's dark, moist banana bread. "It's become a tradition that I host the opening meeting each year," says Wener, "and when I don't bake this banana bread, I hear about it!"

Wener first sampled this banana bread at the elegant Beaver Club in Montreal, Canada. After trying unsuccessfully to duplicate the sweet bread, she wrote to *Gourmet* magazine, which procured the recipe from the restaurant. "The recipe came to us in mammoth proportions," says Wener. "My mother-in-law and I translated the amounts for the home baker, and voilà!"

The long, slow cooking time gives this banana bread a deep, rich color and a wonderfully complex flavor. For a full banana flavor, it's important to use very ripe fruit, with dark skins. Wener serves her banana bread with fruit and small pastries. She suggests toasting leftovers for a special treat.

1 pound very ripe peeled bananas
   (about 4 to 5 large bananas)
2 cups sugar

7 teaspoons baking soda
¼ teaspoon salt
4 eggs

3 cups all-purpose flour	1 cup buttermilk
½ cup vegetable oil	

1. Adjust oven rack to center position and preheat to 275°F. Combine the bananas, sugar, baking soda, and salt in the bowl of an electric mixer. Beat on high speed for 1 minute. Add the eggs, 1 at a time, mixing in after each addition. Beat in the flour. Add the oil and buttermilk. Beat for 2 minutes until smooth and well blended.

2. Grease the bottom and sides of 2 8½x4½x2½-inch loaf pans with butter or cooking spray. Line the bottom of each pan with parchment and grease top of parchment. Pour batter into pans and bake for 2½ hours (yes, 2½ hours!).

BOOK CLUB PROFILE

"We are women with families, jobs, lives, loves, and daily struggles and problems. Our book club is a means to reconnect with who we are and what we want out of life," says Rhonda Haney, of the importance of Atlanta's We Just Wanna Have Fun Book Club.

Since its founding in 1997, the We Just Wanna Have Fun Book Club's many activities have helped forge a close bond among the eleven African-American members. Over the years, the women—all professionals, and sometimes stay-at-home moms, in their late thirties to early fifties—have shared outings to a winery, evening theater, salsa lessons, and Christmas parties. But books are the glue that hold the women together. The group reads primarily African-American authors, both classic and contemporary, and especially enjoyed Tananarive Due's *My Soul to Keep* (see p. 286), Eric Jerome Dickey's *Milk in My Coffee* (see p. 271), Sue Monk Kidd's *The Secret Life of Bees* (see p. 398), and Pearl Cleage's *I Wish I Had a Red Dress,* about a social worker recovering from the death of her husband.

The We Just Wanna Have Fun women always serve food at monthly meetings, and sometimes the food matches the theme of the book. "Food is part of the fun!" says Haney. They prepared Ethiopian fare for *My Soul to Keep* and New England clam chowder for Chris Bohjalian's *Midwives,* a novel about a New England midwife accused of murder. "Sometimes we do whatever is easiest for the hostess, or whatever strikes our fancy, like salads, appetizers, quiches, seafood, pasta. And always lots of wine," says Haney.

Everyone brings a favorite soul food dish for the group's annual Black History Month celebration, an event attended by family members. The women encourage their children to research a famous black person who has made an important contribution to building the black community. Haney's daughter has presented findings on Harriet Tubman, who led slaves to freedom before the Civil War, and Shaka Zulu, the famous eighteenth-century Zulu warrior. "Our hope is that our children are learning something about black history that they don't get in their schools," says Haney.

The group found support for its belief in strong community in a book they all loved, Billie Letts's *Where the Heart Is*. Group discussion focused mainly on the numerous interesting characters populating the book, and the way that this quirky but loving Oklahoma community embraced Novalee when she moved to town. "Novalee goes to live with the 'kook' in the community, but she was a good woman who helped Novalee get on her feet. The black photographer, the librarian, all those people helped to shape Novalee into a wonderful, well-rounded person," says Haney. The group also discussed the characters they deplored, like Novalee's boyfriend and her mother, who surfaced only after Novalee became famous.

The group saw themselves in the strong, supportive community that uplifted Novalee. "Novalee had an extended family, very much like the communities we as black women were raised in," says Haney. "In many ways our book club is an attempt to keep that sense of support alive." The benefits of strong community—to the book club and to Novalee—are tremendous. "Everyone in the book club is a transplant from some other part of the country, but when we're together it's like home," says Haney. "Novalee was able to experience the same sense of joy in knowing she had an extended family to help hold her up, nourish her and her daughter, Americus, and to be there for her like no one else in her life had been. Novalee could have become a bitter, angry person, but so many people supported her, she ultimately ended up growing into this wonderful person. It was almost like a redemption story."

More Food for Thought

Members of the We Just Wanna Have Fun Book Club served down-home Southern cooking for their discussion of *Where the Heart Is*. The menu included fried chicken, cornbread, macaroni and cheese, collard greens (see p. 150), and potato salad (see p. 187). "This was the kind of down-home cooking we'd expect from the characters in the book, with a soulful twist," says Haney, a member since 1999. "It's the kind of comfort food that you crave when you want to celebrate from the overwhelming joy of having come through hard times."

Wild Swans:
Three Daughters of China

Jung Chang

....

RANDOM HOUSE, *1991*

(available in paperback from Anchor, 1992)

I N *WILD SWANS*, Jung Chang tells the history of three generations of her extended family, spanning almost seventy-five years of recent Chinese experience. Chang captures the full sweep of the dramatic movements transforming China, while illuminating the large and small changes these political traumas and altered social expectations exacted on the lives of the Chinese middle class. Chang describes her family's daily lives, their fears and insecurities, and their close interdependence, even as they are breaking drastically, sometimes painfully, from long-held tradition.

Chang's grandmother, Yu-fang, is born in 1909 in Manchuria to a small-town police official. At a young age, her feet are broken and bound into "three-inch golden lilies" in the painful traditional manner. Without riches, Yu-fang's father knows that his beautiful and intelligent daughter is his most important asset. He soon finds a way to advance his career by agreeing to give Yu-fang as a concubine to General Xue, an older, wealthy general.

Chang compassionately describes Yu-fang's isolated life as a concubine, the birth of Chang's mother Bao Qin, Yu-fang's escape from General Xue's household, and her subsequent marriage to the kindly Dr. Xia. Dr. Xia looks favorably on his new wife despite her having been a concubine, and gives her a certain amount of freedom. He also treats Bao Qin as his daughter, giving her a new name, De-hong, a name made up of the characters for "wild swan" and "virtue."

De-hong grows up in Dr. Xia's household during the tumultuous Japanese occupation, the liberation by the Kuomintang under Chiang Kai-shek, and the severe backlash against the "rightist" Kuomintang by the Communist insurgents. Caught up in the wave of Communist idealism, she meets and marries a Communist rebel leader from distant Sichuan, Chang's father, Wang-yu. Gradually Chang's parents advance within the Communist bureaucracy. By the time Chang, the second of five children, is born, her parents are party members with certain privileges. She is given the name Er-hong, which means "second wild swan."

With the insight and perspective of an adult, Chang describes the sweeping changes in Chinese society, her embarrassment at living with considerable entitlements in China's ideologically classless society, the physical and psychological effects of the Cultural Revolution on her family, and her family's eventual internal exile.

Wild Swans vividly portrays the grand diversity within China. Even its myriad eating habits seem caught up in the country's political turmoil, as traditional ways yield to ideology, if not modernity. For Chang's grandmother, a specific food is considered appropriate "for every occasion and condition in China." Special foods are a way to celebrate traditional holidays like the Winter Festival and the Chinese New Year; "poached eggs in raw sugar juice with fermented glutinous rice" are proper for a woman who has just given birth, and Chang's grandmother shares snacks like soy-pickled vegetables with a Japanese woman who visits often, although she and the Japanese woman are not able to communicate well in the language of the other.

Chang's grandmother felt her young daughter had "rebellious bones," learning few traditional skills like cooking. But as De-hong travels from the harsh Manchurian climate, across broad expanses of China, up the Yangtze River to lush Sichuan, she finds an abundance she had never encountered. As Chang writes of her mother's experience: "For the first time in her life, my mother could eat rice and fresh vegetables every day." De-hong tastes the spicy foods of Sichuan, with exotic names like "tiger fights the dragon," "imperial concubine chicken," "hot saucy duck," and "suckling golden cock crows to the dawn."

Under the Communists, food, like every other aspect of life, is imbued with political overtones. During the economically misguided Great Leap Forward, a program so preoccupied with steel output that agriculture is neglected, famine is rampant. A farmer's act of keeping enough food from his labors for his own family, or a peasant eating more than his or her own share, becomes an act of subversion.

Despite Mao's failed economic policies, the Communist party still exhorts the people to greater efforts. The ancient Chinese proverb noted a seeming truism: "No matter how capable, a woman cannot make a meal without food." The Communists reversed this wisdom, announcing during a parade in Sichuan that "capable women can make a meal without food."

Jung Chang's Stir-Fried Carrots

Many of the dishes described in *Wild Swans* are simple, as the people are forced to make do with whatever foods happen to be available. Jung Chang provided us with the following simple recipe for stir-fried carrots. "I invented this recipe myself," says Chang. "Jon, my husband, loves it. It's his favorite dish."

For a complete Chinese meal, try pairing Jung Chang's carrots with our Scallion-Ginger Fried Rice (see p. 163) and Spicy Shrimp in Black Bean Sauce (see p. 469).

1 pound carrots, peeled or well-scrubbed

Vegetable oil for stir-frying

Salt

6 to 8 scallions, finely chopped

1. Slice carrots into thin strips, about 2 inches long and ¼ inch thick. You should have about 3 cups.
2. Pour oil into a large skillet to a depth of ½ inch and place over high heat. When the oil is hot add a large pinch of salt (use more or less according to taste). Add carrots and fry, stirring constantly, until carrots begin to wither. Pour off excess oil. Add the scallions and continue to stir-fry until they release their aroma, about 1 minute. Serve immediately.

Yield: 6 to 8 servings

BOOK CLUB PROFILE

"For many of us, this is only book we read each month that doesn't rhyme," says Kathy Barber of her South Florida Preschool PTA (SFPPTA) book club's reading selection. "We are stay-at-home moms, and the book club is a lifeline out of changing diapers, picking up toys."

The South Florida Preschool PTA, a nonprofit mother's support and child advocacy group in Miami, Florida, is dedicated to the health, safety, and well-being of children and youth. It provides social and educational programs for their membership's parents. One of those programs is a book club.

The idea for the book club's elaborate book-themed menus began with the first meeting in 1995. Jeanette McIntosh, who founded the book club with a few other mothers, recalls the original members enjoyed the cans of Campbell's Chicken Soup she handed them as parting gifts when they read Jack Canfield and Mark Victor Hansen's *Chicken Soup for the Soul*.

The concept of food inspired by books evolved into elaborate literary feasts as the group swelled from five members to twenty. "Our group is focused on books," says Barber, "but we express ourselves creatively through food."

The host prepares a menu related to the literary selection, decorates in the book's theme, and often invites members to dress as the book's characters. When they read Anita Diamant's *The Red Tent* (see p. 374), host Pat Gladieux served Middle Eastern food, including hummus, grape leaves, figs, olives, and dates, under a flowing red cloth she had draped from her living room ceiling to create an illusion of being in a tent. Similarly, member Helen Puche prepared a buffet feast of African foods for the group's discussion of Barbara Kingsolver's *The Poisonwood Bible* (see p. 353).

To ensure variety in their reading, the club selects an annual list of reading topics, including mystery or science fiction in October, a short or inspirational book in December, and a romance in February. For their annual Couples Night, they invite their husbands and select books geared to the men's interests, such as Sebastian Junger's *The Perfect Storm* (see p. 340) and Bill Bryson's *A Walk in the Woods: Rediscovering America on the Appalachian Trail* (see p. 473).

The group enjoys books about relationships between mothers and daughters, such as Janet Fitch's *White Oleander* and Elizabeth Strout's *Amy and Isabel*. Over pork fried rice, egg rolls, and moon cakes, a dessert served at Chinese festivals and special occasions, the group discussed Jung Chang's *Wild Swans*. The book provoked one of the group's most interesting discussions.

Several SFPPTA book club members have adopted daughters from China and the group discussed raising adopted Chinese children in America as well as Americans' awareness of Chinese customs and traditions. "Reading *Wild Swans* made these women realize the importance of learning about and passing on Chinese culture to their children," says Barber.

Donna Lyons, a Chinese member of the book club, says Chang's story showed how raising children in America can sometimes conflict with the Chinese customs and traditions she learned. "Chinese children are taught to be respectful of their elders and not to question authority," says Lyons. " In America, children have more freedom to express their thoughts and views and are actually encouraged to be assertive."

Barber invited her mother, Joyce Allgood, who had traveled to China, to participate in the discussion of *Wild Swans*. In college, Allgood had dated a Chinese student whose extended family in China had sacrificed to send him to America for a college education. At that time, Allgood learned the strength of Chinese family ties and values. In reading Chang's book, Allgood was again impressed by the importance of the extended family in Chinese culture.

Barber says most SFPPTA book club members, all in their thirties and forties, could not understand the oppression Chang describes in *Wild Swans*. "For example, the restriction on fashion imposed by Mao, where all women were required to wear a plain dark-colored Mao jacket," says Barber. "Chang's mother and a friend quietly rebelled by sewing pink lining on the inside cuffs, appearing to conform and be good Communist leaders, while inside their clothes they strived to maintain their feminine identities. The women in our group couldn't imagine a government restricting their choice of clothing."

Barber says the story of Chang's grandmother, whose parents bound her feet in accordance with the cultural norms of beauty, also resonated strongly with the group. "She could not work in the fields. She had no ability to do anything other than walk short distances behind the man who kept her," says Barber.

More Food for Thought

"Food gives more context for the book," says Suzanne Brust, "and is one way to immerse yourself in the culture about which you're reading." Based in St. Paul, Minnesota, Brust's book club is composed of four married couples who discuss literature in their homes after church on Sunday afternoons. When her group discussed *Wild Swans*, Brust served Chinese potstickers (dumplings steamed on one side and pan-fried on the other), chicken satay, and curry soup.

Lisa von Drehle hosted dinner for her Chicago book club's discussion of *Wild Swans*. "I made a trip to Chicago's Chinatown and purchased some ready-made barbecued pork dumplings." For the main course, von Drehle served oriental chicken salad, a favorite recipe from *The Silver Palate Good Times Cookbook*, by Julee Rosso and Sheila Lukins (Workman, 1985), and fortune cookies. "This was the perfect meal for a hot, midsummer discussion," she adds.

Winter Wheat

Mildred Walker

....

1944

(available in paperback from University of Nebraska Press, 2003)

Fᴵʀˢᴛ ᴘᴜʙʟᴵˢʜᴇᴅ ᴵɴ 1944, *Winter Wheat* is the story of eighteen-year-old Ellen Webb, whose family runs a wheat farm in north-central Montana. During a single year in the early 1940s, Ellen leaves home for college, falls in love, returns home, takes a position as a teacher, and experiences heartbreak and tragedy. From these events, which fall so swiftly one upon the other, emerge maturity, insight, and the beginning of wisdom.

Her parents' marriage is often puzzling to Ellen; there is love in their relationship and yet at times their contrasting temperaments create tension and strain. Ellen is more sympathetic to her father, Ben, than her mother, Anna. Ben is a transplanted New Englander who still suffers from shrapnel wounds inflicted during the First World War. Anna, Russian-born and stoic, met Ben in Russia and nursed him back to health after he was wounded.

When a good crop of winter wheat makes it possible for Ellen to attend college in Minnesota, she discovers that despite a life of outdoor work in the wheat fields, farm life has in fact been a cloistered, limited existence.

Problematic for Ellen is her love for Gil, whom she meets at the college. When Ellen brings Gil to visit her family in Montana, Gil, accustomed to the amenities of urban life and the comforts of a middle-class home, reacts strongly to the "emptiness" of farm life. His discomfort around Anna increases Ellen's ambivalence toward her life on the farm, her future, and her parents' marriage. The experience ultimately causes Gil to end the relationship. "We are too separated in background and interests and ways of looking at things to be happy together," writes Gil to Ellen. "I felt a sense of strangeness with you in that wild, desolate country." In time, Ellen's parents, by their own example, help her understand the true nature of their lasting marriage and of their deep attachment to each other, and in time, Ellen comes to understand better her relationship to Gil—and to know her own heart.

When a poor wheat crop keeps Ellen from returning to school, she takes a position as a country teacher in isolated Prairie Butte, a town eighty-five miles north of her parents' farm. Here, Ellen transforms her solitude into a sense of freedom and she finds the strength to confront professional and personal crises.

Walker draws sharp contrasts between rural life and urban culture and between the generations, each with its own hopes, disappointments, secrets, and sorrows. Revelation and renewal are powerful themes in *Winter Wheat*. The new crop appears after the hard winter, long buried family secrets come to light, life is altered by unexpected change, and love reawakens.

In *Winter Wheat*, the kitchen is Anna's domain. When she is not planting, harvesting, or feeding animals, the kitchen is filled "with the warm smell of good food." Ellen adores her mother's homemade butter and her bread freshly baked in round loaves. Anna makes homemade dandelion and raisin wines and dresses the turkeys she raises to sell during the holidays.

IRINA SHVED'S BORSCH (BEET SOUP)

Ripley Hugo, a poet and faculty member at the University of Montana, is Mildred Walker's daughter. Hugo's memoir about her mother, *Writing for Her Life* (University of Nebraska Press, 2003) makes an excellent companion to *Winter Wheat* and Walker's other novels, such as *If a Lion Could Talk*, about a New England missionary couple's attempt to bring Christianity to Native Americans, and *The Body of a Young Man*, exploring the longtime friendship between two couples.

Hugo told us that Anna's hearty cooking in the novel—chicken and dumplings, mashed potatoes, turkey, biscuits—is typical Montana prairie dinner fare. In the novel, Ben notes that Anna "could make all the dishes he'd had back in Vermont as well as though she were a New Englander herself, instead of a Russian." But it is borsch (also spelled borscht), the Russian red beet soup, that is Anna's specialty, says Hugo, and Anna simmers and dishes up borsch throughout *Winter Wheat*. It is part of the heritage she has brought to Montana. In Russia, Anna nursed Ben back to health with her borsch. Anna jokes, "Borsch is good. Even Ben'll stand the cabbage smell for it."

When Gil, Ellen's college boyfriend, visits the ranch, he is introduced to Anna's "famous Russian soup," which leaves the kitchen "fragrant and warm." When Ben and Anna visit Ellen in Prairie Butte, Anna brings borsch and Ellen serves her students the "hearty soup" whose fragrance fills the schoolroom. When the students are curious about the foreign "red" soup, Ellen explains that it's "beet soup they make where it's a lot colder than this."

Although the origin of borsch is debated, it is a distinctive feature of Russian cuisine, and many variations of the soup exist throughout regions of Eastern Europe. It is served hot or cold, thick or thin, and with or without meat. Hugo explained that her mother had carefully researched Russian culture while writing *Winter Wheat*, "even to the extent of finding descriptions of the kind of house Anna might have lived in." Many Russian immigrants in Montana became successful wheat farmers, and they brought their traditional cuisine, such as borsch, with them. Hugo enjoys the crocks of borsch her friend in Missoula, Irina Shved, frequently brings her. Shved, who was raised in Russia, shared with us the recipe for Russian borsch she learned from her mother.

Serve borsch with a loaf of freshly baked bread for your discussion of *Winter Wheat* and a taste of Montana.

1 pound chicken, beef, or pork
2–3 peeled uncooked beets (about 1 pound)
2–3 carrots, diced
1 large potato, diced
1 bay leaf
½ small head green cabbage, shredded

2 tablespoons vegetable oil
½ small onion, thinly sliced
1 6-ounce can tomato paste or 3 tablespoons
  ketchup
Salt and pepper

2 teaspoons finely chopped parsley
2 tablespoons finely chopped chives

½ cup sour cream

1. Fill a soup pot with 3 quarts of water and place over high heat. Add the chicken, beef or pork to the pot. Add the beets, carrots, potato, and bay leaf. Reduce heat and simmer 20 minutes. Remove soup from heat. Remove beets and place in a bowl to cool. Add the cabbage to the soup.

2. Shred the beets using a grater. Heat vegetable oil in a frying pan and sauté onions until golden. Add the shredded beets and sauté for 5 more minutes. Stir in the tomato paste and heat until bubbling. Add the mixture to the soup pot and simmer 30 minutes, or until meat is tender.

3. Remove the meat and cut into bite-sized pieces. Return to pot. Season to taste with salt and pepper. Serve garnished with parsley, chives, and sour cream.

Yield: 8 servings

The Mintz, Levin, Cohn, Ferris, Glovsky, and Popeo Literary Discussion Group had its genesis in 1988 as a Law and Literature discussion group for the Boston law firm's summer associates. The group read several short works and plays, such as Eugene O'Neill's autobiographical play *Long Day's Journey Into Night,* about a family shattered by lies and deception. A Brandeis University humanities professor facilitated a discussion of how themes in these works related to law firm life.

The successful discussions led the firm to expand the group to include both partners and associates, using volunteer lawyers as facilitators. "Through literary themes, our intent was to stimulate more open discussion on what were sensitive topics at the time," says Peter Biagetti, one of the firm's managing partners, "such as competitiveness or the balancing of work and home pressures." Biagetti recalls reading "The Enemy," a short story by Pearl Buck about enemies forced to deal with each other as fellow human beings, a theme he says was "a handy stepping-off point for lawyers."

In 1997, the book group was reconfigured at the firm's annual retreat for the partners and spouses from Mintz, Levin's offices across the country. Heidi Brown, whose husband, Rich Moche, is a partner in the firm's Boston office, saw the opportunity to create a book club focusing on literary fiction that didn't necessarily have a legal angle, so spouses could feel comfortable participating. "It certainly gave the group a less academic, more recreational purpose," says Brown, "and people who love to read could come together, talk, and get to know one another."

Brown became the group's discussion leader, a task she calls "a labor of love." Although Brown is not a professional facilitator, she is an avid reader, a former marketing director for a bookstore chain, and the former director of the Harvard Square Book Festival in Cambridge, Massachusetts. "The book group members do most of the work; they're serious readers and like to talk about what they read," says Brown. The group is successful, she adds, "because the fact that its members are lawyers, or are living with one, is left at the door when the discussion begins."

Brown finds it particularly challenging to select books for the group. She avoids books members are likely to have read already and looks for undiscovered literary gems. She also searches for titles that will appeal to men and women across generational lines, since the club's members range in age from thirty to ninety-six.

"Mildred Walker's *Winter Wheat* has a universal appeal and timeless quality that made the novel an excellent choice," says Brown. "*Winter Wheat* was not bound by contemporary scenes and issues, allowing the group to settle on broader themes of family, relationships, community, marriage, and separation. People latched on to the notion of community, or lack of one, and the physical and emotional consequences of rural living without benefit of close neighbors or regular communication."

The group explored the contrast between the romanticism of the farming life often portrayed by filmmakers and novelists and the reality of the harsh and lonely conditions depicted in *Winter Wheat*.

The group appreciated the appeal of the rural setting and the dramatic Montana backdrop, but recognized the grim reality of farm life under severe conditions. Although the dryland farmers were bound by a shared interest in weather and other farming concerns, the group thought the characters lacked the interdependence that might create stronger bonds among them. "We felt that the physical distance separating neighbors and the characters' stoicism kept them from forming solid ties as a community," says Brown.

Brown says her group will forgive most flaws in a novel if the writing is of high quality, and Walker's style, and the simplicity and lyricism of her language, appealed to all the members. Further, several of the members could relate personally to the setting or the time period, as several had come of age during the 1940s or had grown up in small rural villages. "Their impressions of the time, or their experiences growing up in the country, added richness to the discussion," says Brown.

More Food for Thought

Beth Boyson, a reference librarian at the Bozeman Public Library in Montana, facilitates the Friends of Bozeman Public Library Book Club, which she has nick-named "The World's Greatest Book Club." When the group read *Winter Wheat* as part of the One Book Montana program, which invites all Montanans to read the same book, Boyson served fresh warm wheat bread and wheat muffins with butter and honey, all donated by a local bakery. She also placed a few bags of wheat in the middle of the "campfire circle" for their book discussion. "The breads and wheat took us into the setting of the book," says Boyson. Some members had considerable knowledge of wheat farming, such as the various types of grain and grinding techniques, which also contributed to the discussion.

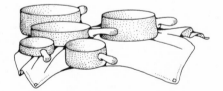

Recipe for a Book Club

I F YOU'RE THINKING about joining a book club or forming one of your own, we offer the following ideas to get you started:

1. Go to a local bookstore or library. Many bookstores sponsor book clubs or can refer you to one.

2. Let your current interests lead you to a book club. Your workplace, church, temple, or your professional, civic, or social organization might have a book club. If not, start one!

3. Go online. Websites such as Booksense (www.booksense.com), Reading Group Guides (www.readinggroupguides.com), Good Books Lately (www.goodbookslately.com), and Book Reporter (www.bookreporter.com) recommend books and provide discussion questions and background information. Depending on your reading interests, other websites such as www.mosaicbooks.com or www.greatbooks.org list local reading groups and selections. Visit the websites of the book clubs featured in this book for creative ideas to help your book club succeed.

4. Check out books on book clubs, such as *Good Books Lately: The One-Stop Resource for Book Groups and Other Greedy Readers* (March 2004) by Ellen Moore and Kira Stevens, the annual edition of *Reading Group Choices* (www.readinggroupchoices.com), and *The Book Group Book: A Thoughtful Guide to Forming and Enjoying a Stimulating Book Discussion Group* by Ellen Slezak (Editor) and Margaret Eleanor Atwood (Chicago Review Press, 2000); or try *Fiction & Friends*, a newsletter for book clubs (e-mail: nkemmitt@earthlink.net).

5. Let the individual personality of your group emerge. When starting, it is helpful to have members get to know one another and discuss group goals. Decide how many members you will have, how often and where you will meet, the types of books you will read and how they will be chosen, and who will provide food for your meetings. Take into account the time that

members have to devote to your book club. Bring discussion questions, articles, or other pertinent information to enhance the discussion. Rotate responsibility for running the meeting and providing food.

6. Keep a record of books read, books suggested by members, members' reactions to books, and foods served, to help you plan for future meetings. If you like, develop a rating system and share information on a group website or in a newsletter.

7. Contact authors who speak to book clubs over the phone. Many publishers' and authors' websites have contact information. This is a proven hit with book clubs and a great way to generate discussion.

8. Attend author readings and events, and take in film versions of books you've read.

9. Enjoy the luxury of talking about books and indulging in good eats. Have fun!

Purchasing Information

BEAN-THREAD NOODLES (SAIFUN)
Pages 55, 412

The Oriental Pantry
423 Great Road (2A)
Acton, MA 01720
Tel: 978-264-4576
www.orientalpantry.com

BERBERE PASTE
Page 287

Great American Spice Company
628 Leesburg Road
Fort Wayne, IN 46808
Tel: 1-888-502-8058
www.americanspice.com

BLACK BEAN SAUCE
Page 470

The Oriental Pantry
423 Great Road (2A)
Acton, MA 01720
Tel: 978-264-4576
www.orientalpantry.com
Selected Trader Joe's grocery stores.

For store locations, see www.traderjoes.com
Tel: 1-800-SHOPTJS (1-800-746-7857)

BROWN BEAN SAUCE (E.G., KOON CHUN BEAN SAUCE)
Page 53

The Oriental Pantry
423 Great Road (2A)
Acton, MA 01720
Tel: 1-978-264-4576
www.orientalpantry.com

CORIANDER SEED
Pages 140, 159

Penzeys Spices stores or by mail order
Tel: 1-800-741-7787
www.penzeys.com

DASHI, MIRIN, UDON NOODLES, NORI, WASABI
Page 388

The Oriental Pantry
423 Great Road (2A)
Acton, MA 01720
Tel: 978-264-4576

www.orientalpantry.com
Some ingredients also available from selected
Whole Foods Market stores.
For store locations, see
www.wholefoodsmarkets.com.
Tel: 1-888-746-7936

DURKEE FAMOUS SAUCE
Page 134

http://nicespices.com/
Selected grocery stores and Super Wal-Marts

GARAM MASALA
Page 139

Kalustyan's
123 Lexington Avenue
New York, NY 10016
Tel: 1-800- 352-3451
www.kalustyans.com

INDIVIDUALLY QUICK-FROZEN PEACHES
Selected Trader Joe's grocery stores.
For store locations, see www.traderjoes.com.
Tel: 1-800-SHOPTJS (1-800-746-7857)

JUNIOR'S CHEESECAKE
Page 280

Junior's
386 Flatbush Avenue at DeKalb Avenue
Brooklyn, NY 11201
Tel: 1-800-958-6467
www.juniorscheesecake.com

LINGONBERRIES
Page 296

Caviar Assouline
505 Vine Street
Philadelphia, PA 19106
Tel: 1-800-521-4491
www.caviarassouline.com
Gourmet Food store, www.amazon.com.

LUZIANNE COFFEE
Page 236

Reily Foods
Tel: 1-800-692-7895
www.luzianne.com

LYLE'S GOLDEN SYRUP
Page 177

www.ethnicgrocer.com.
Tel: 1-866-438-4642
Selected Whole Foods Market stores.
For store locations, see
www.wholefoodsmarket.com
Tel: 1-888-746-7936

MANGO PULP
Page 206

Kalustyan's
123 Lexington Avenue
New York, NY 10016
Tel: 1-800-352-3451
www.kalustyans.com

MIDDLE EASTERN PICKLES

Page 277

Ali Baba Mediterranean and Middle Eastern Grocery
110 Centre at Riverchase
Hoover, AL
Tel: 205-823-2222
www.alibabarst.com/form.htm

MINOR'S LOBSTER BASE

Page 101

Allserv
Tel: 1-800-827-8328
www.soupbase.com

MOLDS FOR CHOCOLATE FROGS

Page 179

www.chocolatevault.com/frogs.htm
Tel: 1-800-297-5467

MORELLO CHERRIES

Page 111

www.ethnicgrocer.com
Tel: 1-866-438-4642
Selected Trader Joe's grocery stores.
For store locations, see www.traderjoes.com.
Tel: 1-800-SHOPTJS (1-800-746-7857)

MUSTARD OIL

Page 205

Kalustyan's
123 Lexington Avenue
New York, NY 10016
Tel: 1-800-352-3451
www.kalustyans.com

PRALINES

Page 237

Aunt Sally's Praline Shops
810 Decatur Street
New Orleans, LA 70116
Tel: 1-800-642-7257
www.auntsallys.com

RED BUSH TEA (ROOIBOS)

Page 315

Kalahari Red Tea
www.kalahariusa.com

RED LENTILS, MANGO PICKLES, MAJOR GREY'S MANGO CHUTNEY

Pages 380, 381

Large grocery stores
www.ethnicgrocer.com
Tel: 1-866-438-4642

ROSEWATER

Page 370

www.ethnicgrocer.com
Tel: 1-866-438-4642
Selected Whole Foods Market stores.
For store locations, see
www.wholefoodsmarkets.com.
Tel: 1-888-746-7936

SHEBA TE'J HONEY WINE

Page 290

Brotherhood Winery
100 Brotherhood Plaza Drive
Washingtonville, NY

Tel: 845-496-3661
www.wines.com/brotherhood

SHORT-GRAIN RICE

Pages 230, 266

Kalustyan's
123 Lexington Avenue
New York, NY 10016
Tel: 1-800-352-3451
www.kalustyans.com
Selected Whole Foods Market stores.
For store locations, see
www.wholefoodsmarkets.com.
Tel: 1-888-746-7936

SICILIAN SUMAC

Page 231

Penzeys Spices
Purchase on-line, by phone, or from retail stores
(locations available at website).
Tel: 1-800-741-7787
www.penzeys.com

SLIVERED BLANCHED ALMONDS

Pages 370, 418

www.nuts4u.com
Tel: 1-800-NUTS4U2
Selected Whole Foods Market stores.
For store locations, see
www.wholefoodsmarkets.com.
Tel: 1-888-746-7936

SWEET SALAD CUBES

Page 188

Mount Olive Pickle Company
Corner of Cucumber and Vine
Mount Olive, NC 28365
Tel: 1-800-672-5041

UNSWEETENED COCONUT

Page 354

The Baker's Catalogue
Tel: 1-800-827-6836
www.bakerscatalogue.com.
Selected Trader Joe's grocery stores.
For store locations, see www.traderjoes.com.
Tel: 1-800-SHOPTJS (1-800-746-7857)

VANILLA SUGAR

Page 283

Penzeys Spices
Purchase on-line, by phone, or from retail stores
(locations available at website).
Tel: 1-800-741-7787
www.penzeys.com

WHITE CASTLE HAMBURGERS

Page 280

For locations of White Castle restaurants and
retailers selling White Castle hamburgers, see
www.whitecastle.com.

Acknowledgments

MANY PEOPLE BROUGHT *The Book Club Cookbook* to reality. Our agent, Marianne Merola, believed in *The Book Club Cookbook* from the beginning. She has given us her unwavering support and sage advice, providing perspective and good humor during an occasionally arduous process. Sara Carder, our editor at Tarcher/Penguin, guided us surely each step of the way. Her thoughtful insights helped shape and refine *The Book Club Cookbook* to its present form.

We are grateful to our publisher, Joel Fotinos, for enthusiastically supporting our initiative and for the assistance and support of the talented Penguin staff and associates who contributed to the project in many ways: our publicist Ken Siman, copy editor Laura Starrett, Amanda Dewey, who designed the interior, Kathy Kikkert, who designed the cover, Ashley Shelby and Wendy Hubbert. Travis Buchanan of Brandt and Hochman Literary Agents, Inc., provided able administrative assistance.

Peter Zheutlin carefully read every page. We are indebted to him for his insights and for the time and energy he devoted to critiquing the manuscript, providing feedback, and refining our prose. Peter Krupp and Doris Gelman also read large chunks of the book, which has benefited from their thoughtful ideas and suggestions.

We are grateful to the authors who contributed comments and/or recipes, or simply offered guidance and direction: Mitch Albom, Jung Chang, Tracy Chevalier, Donna Woolfolk Cross, Anita Diamant, Andre Dubus III, Tananarive Due, Leif Enger, Jim Fergus, Julia Glass, Khaled Hosseini, Sue Monk Kidd, Jhumpa Lahiri, Erik Larson, Jonathan Lethem, Naguib Mahfouz, Bernice Mc-Fadden, Gita Mehta, Azar Nafisi, Queen Noor, Ann Packer, Ann Patchett, Jewell Parker Rhodes, Lee Smith, Dava Sobel, Ron Suskind, Lalita Tademy, and Donna Tartt. The participation of Ripley Hugo, Cedric Jennings, and Joan Tademy Lothery greatly enriched *The Book Club Cookbook*.

Andrew Gelman, our recipe writer and primary developer, has been involved with our project since its inception. His culinary creativity and dogged pursuit of perfection ensured successful recipes, and we are grateful for his unwavering commitment. Mary Kate Dillon, Marji Marcus, and Jane Morse Rifkin also put their cooking and baking expertise to work for us, with spectacular results.

Many friends, family, and acquaintances donated time and ingredients to test our recipes. Their suggestions improved our book beyond measure. Our heartfelt appreciation goes to Cheryl Aglio-Girelli, Kay Allison, Steve Allison, Peter Alpert, Myra Anderson, Carole Arsenault, Joan Balaban, Don Berk, Susan Bonaiuto, Heidi Brown, Anna Burgess, Laurie Burgess, Molly Burgess, Lucia Gill Case, Karen Cheyney, Stella Chin, Michael Collatta, Sharon Conway, Beth Corkery, Donna Cullinan, Susan Daoust, Janice Davoren, Jennie DeLisi, Christine Demers, Patrick Dillon, Denise DiRocco, Anna Fassler, Michele Feldman, Doris Gelman, Sharon Gillespie, Ann Marie Gluck, Leslie Gordon, Kimberly Greenberg, Herb Haber, Lyn Hadden, Elizabeth Hefferon, Pat Hession, Nancy Holly, Laura Katz, Vicki Kaufman, Sue Kinel, Marie Krinsky, Connie Leonard, Becky Lingard, Julia Lipman, Susan McNeice, Melissa Meehan, Ceci Ogden, Eileen O'Keefe, Jackie Peck, Jayne Raphael, Steve Rockefeller, Debra Rostowsky, Judy Safian, Stan Sclaroff, Carla Sidell, Char Sidell, Donna Skinner, Susie Smart, Sara Smolover, Debbie Squires, Suzanne Wildman, Leslie Zheutlin, and Michael Zheutlin. Rebecca Drill, Kim Evans, and Lynn Hamlin hosted recipe-tasting parties, festive events that allowed us to test and receive feedback on many recipes simultaneously.

Julia Blatt, Suzanne Church, Sharon Conway, Suzanne Diamond, Eric Fassler, Kim Garden, Lois Gelman, Louis Hutchins, Fabienne Madsen, Barbara Matorin, Debbie Pryor, Larni Rosenlev, and Abby Schwartz went above and beyond the call of duty to help us perfect our recipes.

We are fortunate to be surrounded by talented friends, family, and community members who supported us in ways too numerous to mention in full. They directed us to book clubs, sent recipe ideas, relevant articles and contact information, and provided computer support and legal advice. Thanks to Marie Berliner, Lucia Gill Case, Karen Cheyney, Denise DiRocco, Jim Dillon, Rebecca Drill, Jody Feinberg, Audrey Forgeron, Janet Gelman, Kimberly Greenberg, Tracy Greenfield, Cally Haber, Nancy Haber, Charmin Hooper, Martha Hooper, Lyndy Johnson, Judy Bart Kancigor, Larry Krupp, Emily Lessner, Leslie Levy, David Minard, Lisa Newfield, Eileen O'Keefe, Carol Pankin, Jayne Raphael, Sarine Rodman, Richard Rosenlev, Sallie Sanford, Danny Seti, Nina Silber, Clara Silverstein, Wanda Spivey, Lisë Stern, Virginia Valentine, and Zhanna Volynskaya.

We extend our appreciation to the restaurants and chefs who generously contributed recipes: Vicki Lee Boyajian of Boston, Massachusetts; Britta's Café of Irvine, California; Greg Case of Somerville, Massachusetts; Fountain Court Restaurant of San Francisco, California; Masala Art of Needham, Massachusetts; Milwaukee School of Engineering of Milwaukee, Wisconsin; Northern Trust Bank of Miami, Florida; One Main Street Café of Salinas, California; Scott Peacock of Decatur, Georgia; Shaw's Crab House and Blue Crab Lounge of Chicago, Illinois; Taal Restaurant of Fullerton, California; and Zaytoon's of Brooklyn, New York.

Several chefs and culinary historians provided culinary guidance and historical information. We extend our appreciation to John T. Edge of the Southern Foodways Alliance at the University of Mississippi; John Folse of Chef John Folse Culinary Institute at Nicholls State University in Thibodaux, Louisiana; culinary historian Mary Gunderson; and Julia Shanks of Interactive Cuisine in Cambridge, Massachusetts.

The Book Club Cookbook would not have been possible without the generosity, creativity, and enthusiasm of hundreds of book club members across the United States. In surveys and interviews, these members shared their stories and, in some cases, their recipes and food ideas with us. They took the time to poll fellow members for reading preferences, update us on their book selections and menus, and send us group photographs and minutes of meetings. We are indebted to the book clubs featured in *The Book Club Cookbook* as well as the many wonderful book clubs we contacted but could not feature due to space limitations.

From Judy:

This book could not have been written without my husband, Peter Zheutlin. His contributions are countless: his unfailing confidence and encouragement, and his guidance, humor, childcare, and superb editing skills. I am grateful for his listening and love. My sons, Danny and Noah, provided love, support, patience, and inspiration; they tested and tasted (and Noah offered many recipes for crabby patties). They reminded me what really matters. I am indebted to my sister Lois, who tested recipes daily and listened patiently during marathon late-night phone calls, always giving sound advice and solving problems. And to Babe, for always being available with support and enthusiasm, I cannot express enough thanks.

From Vicki:

Thanks to my remarkable family, who made the writing of this book possible. My children, Aaron, Ben, and Joanna, each in their own way, supported the project, by drafting cover designs, critiquing recipes, or making their own lunches. The *Harry Potter* entry, in particular, benefited from their expertise. Their love energized me. Thanks to my father, Harvey Levy, and my father-in-law, Alan Krupp, who cheered me on, and provided childcare and Chinese food. My sister, Larni Rosenlev, put her busy life on hold to whip up everything from green salsa to eggrolls, with her characteristic sparkle. Finally, my husband, Peter, supported me lovingly as this project went from a whim, to an idea, to a consuming reality. After an exhausting day at the office, he often worked into the wee hours sharpening the prose between loads of laundry. To him, boundless thanks and love.

Index

About the Authors

Judy Gelman, a public relations consultant, and Vicki Levy Krupp, an educator, have participated in many book clubs. Both are avid readers and cooks. Seeking to combine their passion for books, food, and book clubs, they met over stacks of books, endless cups of coffee, and bagels at a local sandwich shop, where *The Book Club Cookbook* was born. They both live with their families in Needham, Massachusetts.

Please visit their website at www.bookclubcookbook.com.